Objectifying
Real-Time Systems

ADVANCES IN OBJECT TECHNOLOGY

Dr. Richard S. Wiener
Series Editor

Editor
Journal of Object-Oriented Programming
and
Report on Object Analysis and Design
SIGS Publications, Inc.
New York, New York

and

Department of Computer Science
University of Colorado
Colorado Springs, Colorado

Additional Volumes in Preparation

Objectifying
Real-Time Systems

John R. Ellis

Harris Corporation
Palm Bay, Florida

and

Florida Institute of Technology
Melbourne, Florida

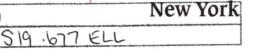

$SIGS$
BOOKS

New York

The material in this book and the examples on
diskette are intended for educational purposes only
and not for actual use in any system.

PUBLISHED BY
SIGS Books, Inc.
588 Broadway, Suite 604
New York, New York 10012

Library of Congress Catalog Card Number: 93-087467

SIGS Books ISBN 0-9627477-8-5
Prentice Hall ISBN 0-13-125550-9

This book is printed on acid-free paper.

Printed in United States of America
10 9 8 7 6 5 4 3 2 1
First Printing April 1994

To Mom and Dad —
You always tell me how proud you are of me;
but I don't tell you enough how thankful I am to you.

Series Introduction

The Advances in Object-Oriented Technology series seeks to present readers with books that provide incisive and timely information relating to object-oriented programming and programming languages, object-oriented requirements, object-oriented domain analysis, and object-oriented design. In addition, testing, metrics, formal methods and applications of object technology to areas including object-oriented databases, real-time systems, emergent computation, neural networks, and object-oriented distributed systems will be featured. The books are aimed at practicing software development professionals, programmers, educators, and students in computer-related disciplines.

Objectifying Real-Time Systems by John R. Ellis presents an important methodology for capturing the requirements of real-time software systems. The methodology is derived from Real-Time Structured Analysis (RTSA) techniques, and the notation is an adaptation of the Ward/Mellor version of RTSA. Software requirements analysis establishes the foundation upon which design and implementation

v

stand. The author presents these principles with great clarity and generously provides illustrations throughout the book with many examples derived from real systems implemented in Turbo Pascal. An accompanying diskette contains the source programs of the examples, thus enabling the reader to experiment and verify executions without keying in code.

The first part of the book introduces the basic principles associated with objects. The examples written in Turbo Pascal make it easy to understand the basic concepts without being distracted by the complexity typically associated with more powerful object-oriented languages.

The second part of the book focuses on developing and illustrating the process of Real-Time Object-Oriented Structured Analysis (RTOOSA). The reader learns how to create each of the six RTOOSA Requirements Model products and how these products interact to allow verification of a complete and consistent model. A comprehensive guide to objectifying real-time systems, I believe you will find this book interesting, educational, and informative.

Richard S. Wiener
Series Editor

Change is a measure of time and, in the autumn,
time seems speeded up. What was is not and
never again will be; what is is change.
— Edwin Way Teale

Preface

This is a very exciting time in the development of software engineering. Object-oriented techniques have drawn great attention from all quarters of the software development community, academia, industry, and the Government. New businesses are springing up and old ones are reorienting their markets to this new technology, supported by technical magazines, books devoted to methodologies, Computer-Aided Software Engineering (CASE) toolsets, compilers and implementation toolsets, training, and so forth. American and international standards committees are scurrying to try to bring order as the Ada 9X committee attempts to add object-oriented programming features to Ada, and other committees are working at standardizing a dialect of C++.

I am as enthused as anyone about this technology, especially its application to embedded real-time systems. I see object-oriented software development as a means to more reliable software in less time and for less cost. In an effort to spread my enthusiasm, I have developed courses in object-oriented software development and have presented them at several divisions of Harris Corporation's Electronic

Systems Sector and as graduate-level courses at Florida Institute of Technology. But with all the promise that object-oriented technology holds, we have not yet harnessed its potential.

Most of the highly respected experts and acknowledged authorities in software methodology definition have published articles and books trying to define a process by which engineers in the trenches developing real systems might apply object-oriented techniques to their daily projects. I have found that much good work has been done and that each effort has certain merits, but none has yet hit the mark. Some of my concerns with these current object-oriented methodologies include the following:

- Most tend to become entangled in what I consider design decisions, particularly during the critical analysis process. Specifically, the agents of dynamic behavior in a system are its *objects*. Premature emphasis of *classes* concentrates on static implementation artifacts.

- There is little (if any) concern about capturing functional and performance requirements or correlating functional and performance requirements to the products of the object/class analysis. A system that is decomposed to objects allocates elements of required system behavior to the behaviors of specific objects. It may be hard to recognize overall system functions when only the objects and their behaviors are available for review.

- The notations associated with these techniques are *revolutionary* in that they are completely different from anything used with the popular methodologies of the previous (non-object-oriented) generation. It will be a tedious process to educate all those who will need to understand the analysis products for review, test, and maintenance.

- The new object-oriented analysis notations fail to capitalize on the excellent products, providing critical requirements information, available from pre-OO methodologies.

This book presents a methodology for capturing the requirements of a real-time software system. This methodology is an *evolution* of popular Real-Time Structured Analysis (RTSA) techniques into the object-oriented development era. Although predominantly concerned with identifying objects and their behaviors, it adapts the notation of RTSA and capitalizes on some key RTSA products. Those who have learned RTSA notation (particularly the Ward/Mellor version) should be able to understand my adapted object-oriented notation with little or no additional training.

Software requirements analysis is but one phase of the development life cycle. However, it establishes the foundation on which design and implementation build. It is also the best place to begin an object-oriented view of the system, leading to an object-oriented design and an implementation based on objects. Not feeling that I could satisfactorily cover the full development process in a single book, I chose to concentrate on that foundation. Some attention to the remaining phases is given briefly in Chapter 17.

Through its contractors, the Government builds some of the most complex real-time software systems in the world. Various governmental agencies also have some of the most exacting standards for software development to ensure product quality. Lives depend on many of these software systems! Although this book is not just about developing Government software systems, I have chosen many examples from some projects with which I am familiar. Certainly the requirements for such high levels of system reliability carry over to many commercial products, including medical systems, microwave ovens, automobile cruise controls, and many others. Failures of such systems can become life-threatening or involve significant financial penalties. One common characteristic of all real-time systems is that they often tend to require high degrees of quality (reliability, safety, etc.). Therefore, as you consider the examples I provide, realize that the principles apply to any real-time software system.

The time will come when diligent research over long periods will bring to light things which now lie hidden. . . . And so this knowledge will be unfolded only through long successive ages. There will come a time when our descendants will be amazed that we did not know things that are so plain to them.
— Seneca, *Natural Questions*, Book 7, first century

Acknowledgments

Writing this book was an undertaking of great magnitude that would not have been possible without the support of a number of wonderful people. At the top of the list has to be my dear wife, Claire. She always has a "go-getter" attitude about difficult tasks, which has influenced me. I have invested over two years of my limited free time writing this book. Claire has been most understanding and has encouraged me at times when she would have preferred we were doing other things together. This book really could not have been completed without her support. Now I owe her.

I also owe my sincere appreciation to the managers and engineers at Harris Corporation, Government Aerospace Systems Division (GASD), for the opportunities I have had to develop and use the concepts presented in this book. Their confidence in me allowed me to venture into an unproven technology and demonstrate its value. Later, I was invited to present my work to numerous groups of engineers from several divisions which served as voluntary training classes. As a result, the interaction with these engineers has helped me refine the methodology. Each of these professionals has helped make this book possible.

I would also like to extend special thanks to four good friends and professional associates for their assistance in the preparation of this book. They contributed untold hours reviewing my drafts to challenge my assertions and polish the rough spots. Three of these friends—Brian Donahue, Steve Von Edwins, and Jim Clamons—are long-time colleagues at Harris GASD. We have worked together on various projects over the last sixteen years and their professional expertise has greatly influenced my thinking while I formalized the process defined in this book. Dr. Charles Engle, the remaining reviewer, is my good friend and mentor at Florida Institute of Technology. He has been a driving force in getting me involved in the academic community, including the writing and publication of this book and the creation of the graduate level course based on it that I am currently teaching. His review, in particular, has been helpful in getting a non-Harris-engineer's viewpoint. In some ways, I am "preaching to the choir" with my professional Harris associates, but Dr. Engle provided a less biased critique. I am truly indebted to each of these individuals.

Another special thanks to Erin O'Leary and the fine people at Blackbird International in Tempe, Arizona for permission to use their beautiful artwork at various points in this book. I have worked with the Blackbird team for quite some time in purchasing personalized T-shirts and sweatshirts for some of our development teams at Harris. Their aircraft artwork is exciting and serves to build team spirit for our engineers working on systems such as the RAH-66 Comanche, the F-22 Advanced Tactical Fighter, the F-117A Stealth Fighter, and the Space Station Freedom. I'm sure the excitement of such embedded real-time systems will be conveyed to the reader through the beautiful Blackbird action drawings (see Figures 3.4, 9.5, and B.1).

Contents

Part II Specifying a System the Object-Oriented Way

Appendices

If builders built buildings the way programmers
wrote programs, then the first woodpecker
that came along would destroy civilization.
— Weinberg's Second Law

Chapter *1*

Introduction

In a never-ending crusade to discover better (i.e., quicker and cheaper) ways to
develop quality software (i.e., software that reliably fulfills its user's needs), software gurus have come to the conclusion that state-of-the-art software developers
should use "object-oriented" development techniques: Object-Oriented Analysis
(OOA), Object-Oriented Design (OOD), and Object-Oriented Programming
(OOP). Being creative types by nature, software methodologists have had great fun
deriving new acronyms building on the double "O." Perhaps, in that vein, I should
have titled this book "SMOOT" (Still More Object-Oriented Techniques). Fortunately, I didn't.

What of this *new* technology? First, it's not so new! In the mid-1960s, Gerry
Sussman, then a young MIT student, apprenticed himself to the legendary hacker
Bill Gosper. As related in Steven Levy's book *HACKERS—Heroes of the Computer
Revolution*, the guru Gosper would sometimes relate his personal philosophy of
programming with offhand remarks like "Well, data is just a dumb kind of pro-
gramming." Sussman found that Gosper used this philosophy in his code. Sussman

Figure 1.1. Object-Oriented Software Development, An important new technology or a passing fad?

observed that "Gosper sort of imagined the world as being made out of all these little pieces [of data], each of which is a little machine which is a little independent local state. And [each state] would talk to its neighbors." [Levy, 1985]

About the same time, the driving concepts of modern object-oriented software development were being formalized with the creation of the SIMULA programming language. Simulation was a natural environment in which to introduce object-oriented concepts because "simulation" (i.e., modeling) programs dealt largely with interactions among models of real-world entities.

Then, by 1980, most of our current criteria for object-oriented languages were formalized in the Smalltalk language, developed by Xerox PARC (Palo Alto Research Center). But Smalltalk was interpretive and not considered useful for real world systems. So developers of the "accepted languages" did not pick up on object-oriented language features.

In addition, the out-of-the-mainstream development of object-oriented concepts far outpaced the evolution of methodologies to support them. If you are old enough to recall the accepted principles of "software engineering" at the dates mentioned above, you can understand that object-oriented concepts were far ahead of their time. It would have been akin to handing a caveman a sliderule (Figure 1.2), merely a curious artifact with little application.

When I reported to my first Air Force duty station in 1969, the ink still wet on my Master's diploma, the latest fad was to develop *modular programs*. The criteria for defining modules had not yet evolved. For example, David Parnas's "On the Criteria for Decomposing Programs into Modules" was published in the December, 1972 issue of *Communications of the ACM*. By the mid-1970s, modules had become synonymous with functionally decomposed subroutines developed in a "top-down, structured" manner (which was quickly adopted as the only "right" way to design and implement programs).

> There is no question that structured programming (whatever it is) is an "in" thing. It is currently advocated by many leading computer scientists at major North American and European universities, by the Federal Systems Division (FSD) of IBM, and by a growing number of commercial software companies. Anything such a diverse computing group can agree upon is worthy of attention. [McGowan/Kelly, 1975]

About this time, traditional data-processing flow charts were falling from favor. Alternate techniques of requirement and/or design representation, such as Warnier-Orr diagrams and IBM's HIPO (Hierarchical Input/Processing/Output) charts, appeared but never gained widespread acceptance. One concept that has endured is a structured textual description of process algorithms, which has been variously called structured English, pseudocode, and P-Specs (i.e., *process specifications*).

Figure 1.2. Are today's programmers ready to use object-oriented software development techniques?

The name that is generally applied to this presentation is "PDL" (for Program Design Language, Process Description Language, or variations thereof). The basic goal of all these representations was to force software engineers to apply structured design and programming techniques. Using traditional flow charts, such structure could be achieved only with strict self-discipline.

A significant contribution to requirements and design representations emerged in the late 1970s with the introduction of the Data Flow Diagram (DFD) from work done by Edward Yourdon and Tom DeMarco. The methodologies for analysis and design that encompass the creation of DFDs are respectively called *Structured Analysis* and *Structured Design* (SA/SD). SA, in particular, was designed to be a general systems specification process, but was more enthusiastically received by a majority of the software community. However, real-time system developers felt that SA/SD were unable to portray essential characteristics of real-time problems.

By the mid-1980s, Derek Hatley, Edward Yourdon, and the team of Paul Ward and Stephen Mellor had published extensions to the DFD approach that considered process timing and concurrency. The associated analysis and design techniques are called *Real-Time Structured Analysis* and *Real-Time Structured Design* (RTSA/RTSD).

Ward/Mellor attempted to differentiate their "event driven" decomposition heuristics from those of "functional decomposition" used with earlier SA-based methodologies, but their RTSA is still based on decomposing algorithms in a top-down manner based on functions. RTSD maps the RTSA "transformations" fairly directly into physical implementation entities (subroutines, procedures, or functions). The result: a distinct lack of accommodation for object-oriented principles.

Widespread interest in object-based programming was accompanied by (sometimes reluctant) acceptance of the Ada programming language. Early attempts

Figure 1.3.   Ada, the lady who unwitting-
ly spurred on significant interest in Object-
Oriented Programming.

to program in Ada often pointed out the difficulties of using traditional functional decomposition techniques for Ada program units. I was personally involved in one early Ada project in which the software engineers encountered problems when trying to code the interfaces of a functionally decomposed set of packages. The engineers were forced to return to the design phase to provide a greater object orientation. Ada certainly sparked an increased enthusiasm for object-oriented techniques. The widely touted *Ada mindset* is just a form of object-oriented thinking.

Then, in the late 1980s, interest in object-oriented programming took a strong upswing when object-oriented extensions were offered for many popular programming languages. A few of the better known languages included Object-Pascal, Turbo Pascal 5.5 (and later versions), and QuickPascal; Objective-C and C++; and CLOS (Common LISP Object System).

So we've reached the point where there is increasing interest in object-oriented software development. Whether this is only a fad or an enduring technology will depend largely on whether a methodology can be developed that efficiently leads to object-oriented programs. In this regard, there is no lack of effort from some well-known software engineering authorities. But more on this later.

THE "SOFTWARE CRISIS"

There has been an urgent problem in software development dating back to the mid-1960s. Some people projected the requirement for more software than all available engineers could possibly develop:

> Calculating the requirements for computer programmers for all new microcomputer products, we come up with a need for about one million programmers by 1990! When we look at the fact that U.S. electronics engineering schools produced only about 17,000 graduates in 1979, the

challenge looks even greater. It is clear that our success is leading to what we call the "software crisis." [Intel Microsystem 80 iAPX86 and iAPX88 Product Description, 1980]

Others have related the crisis to the qualifications of those who develop critical software:

The schedule and cost pressure created by the lack of qualified manpower have led project managers to abandon the good programming practices known at the time in attempts to find shortcuts and meet the project constraints. It is no wonder the record shows so many overruns and marginal products. [Jensen/Tonies, 1979]

Barry Boehm first published a graph showing a projected 20-year shift in software's project content in a well-known May 1973 *Datamation* article ("Software and Its Impact: A Quantitative Assessment"). I first saw this graph on the cover of the October 1975 issue of *Defense Management Journal* (Figure 1.4). Inside, Rita McCarthy used the graph in her article "Applying the Technique of Configuration Management to Software," suggesting that the software content of systems would grow from 20% to 80% between 1955 and 1985. This graph was republished many times during the late 1970s and the 1980s. For example, Gloria Swann used it in the introduction to her 1978 book, *Top-Down Structured Design Techniques.*

The message from all of these references is the same. Software was projected to become the overwhelming source of cost in new system developments. Have these predictions come true? General Bernard P. Randolph, then Commander of the Air Force Systems Command, speaking on "Software, Ada, and the Air Force" at the Tri-Ada 1989 conference in Pittsburgh, stated:

Figure 1.4. Projected hardware/software cost trends: Boehm's forecast was published on the cover of the October 1975 *Defense Management Journal.*

Just stop and think about the dramatic changes in software. Twenty-five years ago, the ratio of bucks between hardware and software was 80% hardware and 20% software. Today it is just the opposite: 20% hardware and 80% software. When we put the first F-4s into Vietnam, we didn't have any computers on those airplanes. The early F-16s in 1981 had seven computer systems and fifty digital processors, 135,000 lines of code. Right now, the F-16C has double the computer systems, six times the digital processors, and double the lines of code. And the ATF [Advanced Tactical Fighter, since renamed the F-22], and I'm not an expert, but we're talking about the number crunching power of a Cray computer on the ATF. Something like a million lines or more of code. And when you stop and think about the impact on the commercial world, now the third largest industry in the United States, behind automobiles and oil. The United States is going to be spending over 110 billion dollars on software this year. And the Department of Defense is going to spend over 30 billion dollars on software in fiscal 1990. That's ten percent of the entire budget! So we're talking about big, expensive, and frustrating. Because the fact is that we've got much publicized problems like the B-1, the B-1 defensive avionics, and lots of others that you all are directly familiar with. [Randolph, 1989]

What is important is that software cost/schedule performance is frequently regarded as one of the leading program risks. Congressman John Murtha, then Chairman of the House Appropriations Defense Subcommittee, in the keynote address at the same Tri-Ada 1989 conference, stated:

A couple of years ago they came to us and they delayed the C-17 [a new transport aircraft] substantially. It was a priority for the Army but the Air Force felt they needed these other systems and it just couldn't fit into the budget. And I understand how that works. But as they looked at the C-17, as they looked at the potential for even flying it, they told our committee, and I can remember sitting there listening to the witnesses, "It's just a software problem." Now this was just two or three years ago. This C-17 has been delayed at least a year. They had to fire the original contractor because he couldn't work it out. And the way we did it, the Air Force recognized they had a problem, we recognized they had a problem, we kept telling them they had a problem, and they kept telling the prime contractor. But under the contract, he was responsible for the development of the software and the Air Force could only go so far. So, consequently, that C-17 is still not flying because of the problems that developed. [Murtha, 1989]

Even if we can't agree what the crisis is, its symptoms are fairly obvious:

1. Actual software costs seldom come close to initial estimates and are often perceived as excessive.
2. Software is often late and frequently is delivered with less than the capabilities promised by the developers.
3. Building quality (reliability, maintainability, etc.) into software systems is more difficult than our intuition tells us it should be!
4. Software frequently fails to meet user expectations, or quickly becomes obsolete.

And the situation is exacerbated by factors such as the following:

1. Software engineers for embedded systems are often subservient to other engineering organizations, which fail to understand the life-cycle implications of software development.
2. Organizations often operate on inertia, retaining archaic programming languages and practices long past their usefulness.
3. Formal education does not adequately prepare engineers because students seldom face realistic problem environments in class projects.

The results of inadequate software can be more than an inconvenience, as reported in this Associated Press story in *Florida Today* (June 6, 1991):

> A computer problem in the Patriot air defense system that permitted an Iraqi Scud missile to destroy a U.S. barracks had been detected five days before the fatal attack.
>
> The computer in the Patriot battery whose radar had picked up the incoming Scud failed to track the missile as it roared toward Dhahran. Thus, no computer instructions were given to the Patriot missiles and none were launched, the Army said.
>
> The Patriot computer screen did not show an incoming Scud because the computer software could not calculate quickly enough the missile's path. [*Florida Today*, June 6, 1991]

Ultimately, the Patriot system problem was traced to the real-time clock. The system was specified to require maintenance every eight hours, so the clock needed to remain within tolerance for only that long. At the time of the Dhahran incident, the system that should have intercepted the Scud had been operating continuously for over a hundred hours. The timing problem was known and new software containing a fix was to be installed at the system's next maintenance!

The criticality of embedded software systems was again pointed out (even though it turned out not to be at fault) in *Aviation Week & Space Technology* (McGraw-Hill), Vol. 134, No. 24, June 17, 1991:

> The No. 5 [Bell Boeing V-22] Osprey crashed from an altitude of about 15 ft. at Boeing Helicopter's Wilmington, Del., Flight Test Center at about 6:10 P.M. EDT on June 11 after pilots lost control of the hovering aircraft just minutes after it began its maiden flight.
>
> Speculation immediately after the crash centered on software problems that had previously been discovered in the Osprey's automatic flight control system or AFCS. During tests of V-22 No. 2 at the Naval Air Test Center at Patuxent River, Md., on May 16, the aircraft experienced an uncommanded roll to the right while in hover. Subsequent investigation found that a software switch in the flight control system had allowed the uncommanded transient control input.
>
> Software corrections in the AFCS have been developed and validated in simulation and are ready to be validated in aircraft, Bell Boeing officials said. Despite the previous software problem, however, the issue is a moot point for the crash because the AFCS was not engaged at any time during the maiden flight of aircraft No. 5. [*Aviation Week & Space Technology*, June 17, 1991]

Again, the problem ended up not being attributed to faults in the software. In this case, technicians incorrectly installed two of three attitude gyroscopes in an inverted position. The software's fault-tolerant two-out-of-three voting logic accepted the two bad inputs over the one good one. The result was an inability to stabilize the aircraft.

Although neither of these instances was ultimately the result of faulty software, software in each case was in the path where it could have caused these corresponding failures. Perhaps one of the most publicized cases of a catastrophic software "bug" occurred in the medical industry. The following account is related in the May 15, 1987 issue of *Datamation*.

An Ottawa, Canada company, Atomic Energy of Canada Ltd. (AECL), built a linear accelator radiation machine commonly used for radiation treatment of cancers. The machine, called the Therac 25 ("25" refers to the 25 million electron volt power of the machine), was used at medical facilities across the United States and Canada. Its basic operation was described as follows:

The Therac administers two types of radiation therapy, X-ray and electron, for different cancers. In X-ray mode, a high-intensity electron beam strikes a tungsten target, which absorbs much of the beam's intensity and produces therapeutic X-rays. In electron mode, the Therac's computer, a PDP-11 manufactured by Digital Equipment Corp., retracts the metal target from the beam path and lowers the beam intensity by a factor of 100. [*Datamation*, May 15, 1987]

When several patients began suffering complications leading to death following treatments on the Therac 25, an investigation was launched. In each fatal case, a "Malfunction 54" code appeared on the console screen during treatment. Further analysis showed that this malfunction arose as the result of an unusual sequence involving use of the up-arrow key to edit certain parameters on the screen. The findings:

Hager [a radiological physicist who researched the problem] discovered that during the malfunction the Therac scrambled the two modes, retracting the target as it should for electron mode but leaving the beam intensity set on high for X-rays. The unobstructed high-intensity beam traveled through the accelerator guide, destroying any human tissue in its path. [*Datamation*, May 15, 1987]

The result was exposure to 25,000 rads in less than a second. This dose is 100 times higher than the average treatment of 200 rads! According to the article, "Doses of 1,000 rads can be fatal if delivered to the whole body." The problem was traced to the Therac's editor software! Who would have thought that an editor code bug could kill patients? By the way, the short-term fix was to pry the up-arrow keycap from the VT100 console keyboard!

REUSABLE SOFTWARE — ATTACKING THE CRISIS

I believe that, although many facets of the "software crisis" as previously perceived still exist, there is a major new element to it. In an era of reduced defense spending and increased competition for diminishing consumer dollars, it is extremely critical that companies reduce software costs to remain competitive and therefore viable. The nature of software development limits the manner in which its cost drivers can be reduced:

There is one outstanding difference between software engineering and all other branches of engineering. Engineers usually deal with material (visible and tangible) objects. From the beginning of time, engineers have designed wheels, bridges, chariots, steam engines, airplanes, and electronic hardware. Electrical engineering is the most abstract of the classical engineering fields since electricity is not a material, but, through the use of appropriate tools, electricity exhibits characteristics that are both visible and tangible. Software, however, is nonmaterial in every sense. Software is better visualized as a process. [Jensen/Tonies, 1979]

There are exactly two ways to reduce software cost. Either increase engineering productivity or develop less software. Of the two, I seriously doubt that we will see an order of magnitude improvement in productivity in the near future. So the better strategy is to adopt an engineering methodology built around software reuse. Here's something to think about:

The subcommittee found that many companies, primarily the large prime contractors, are in the process of establishing internal proprietary software reuse libraries. Further, those companies are drawing from those libraries whenever practical to use in the development of proposals and subsequently, the software development project. There is evidence that, in some of these cases, software reuse made the difference in winning the contract. ["The Business Issues Associated with Software Reuse," report of a study conducted by the National Security Industrial Association, Subcommittee on Software Reuse, September 13, 1990 draft]

Before the advent of structured programming, there was little benefit in attempting to reuse software. "Spaghetti code" only worked in its original application, if at all. With structured programming came the potential for ad hoc reuse. Sometimes, opportunities to reuse functionally decomposed modules were discovered, after which application-specific code was removed or modified. One unfortunate by-product of algorithmic decomposition is that application specifics tend to be spread across multiple modules. One goal of object-oriented design is the creation of reusable software parts (the equivalent of hardware-integrated circuit chips). Proper OOD removes application specifics from all lower-level object-based modules, allowing more direct reuse.

I believe that the single most important argument for using object-oriented techniques is their positive effect on software reusability. The benefits may be minimal for the first few applications. But in this critical stage, proper use of object-oriented techniques can lead to a library of reusable components. Thereafter, an analysis/design approach that draws from the reuse library can reap direct benefits in reduced cost and development schedule.

The term "software reuse" immediately conjures up the image of code reuse. If reuse were limited to code alone, the benefit would be minimal. The development process must structure the design documentation and test documentation and results to allow their direct reuse as well. These are far more costly than the code. If a modification must be made to the "reused" code, previous testing results are invalidated and retesting is required. As you learn more about object-oriented programming, you will see that extending library objects can be accomplished without invalidating the baselined documentation.

THE CASE FOR OBJECT-ORIENTED SOFTWARE DEVELOPMENT

Developing object-oriented software is merely a reflection of how one looks at the problem domain. Most software engineers currently involved in creating embedded, real-time systems either were introduced to top-down, structured techniques as their first (and until now, only) analysis and design mindset, or they have well over a decade of inertia in their use. Reluctance in adopting a new mindset is natural and stems from two primary sources.

First, software developers are under constant schedule pressure (Figure 1.5). The aggressive schedule to which projects are bid normally means that the first project documents (detailing the development requirements) become due shortly after personnel are assigned. When we are required to turn out something quickly, it is natural to fall back on our most comfortable tools. This conservative approach avoids spending time "climbing the learning curve" or wasting time correcting mistakes made while first applying new methods. So expediency dictates falling back on old "tried and true" methods.

Second, new techniques are seldom fully refined when first introduced. There may be flaws that will be corrected in time. So engineering managers frequently balk at accepting the risk associated with adopting a new methodology. They would like someone else to be first and establish the viability of the new approach. That is, there is a risk associated with changing from the comfortable to an unknown.

Even when the benefits of a new approach seem intuitively obvious, and eventual significant payback appears inevitable, and the new approach is sure to become a future standard, managers

Figure 1.5. There seldom seems to be enough time to introduce new tools and methodologies.

act as though their careers depend solely on their performance on the current project. (In many American companies this is true.) When software personnel are already trained in a methodology, probably supported by Computer-Aided Software Engineering (CASE) tools already in place, there is no training cost or learning curve inefficiency associated with staying with an old methodology.

For those who develop software under contract, the great paradox of adopting a new methodology, such as object-oriented analysis/design with an integrated reuse strategy, is this: If a manager can reap immediate benefits by reusing the efforts of a previous project, you (the software developer) are strongly encouraged to do so. However, you will be summarily prohibited from expending even minimal additional effort in making your current development more reusable for future projects. So, how can we ever get reusable components into a reuse library?

Not to make program managers appear short-sighted or self-centered, there are legal issues associated with expending contracted project resources for efforts not directly related to the products of that contract. The customer, who is paying for the development, is not interested in contributing to the developer's efficiency on future projects, some of which may be for that customer's competitors!

So a significant constraint is levied on our "new" methodology. Components that are more reusable than those developed under current methodologies must be a no-cost benefit. For those who develop software for their company's commercial products, this is not a real constraint, but a desirable feature.

If my earlier contention is true—that *developing object-oriented software is merely a reflection of how one looks at the problem domain*—then it should cost no more to develop more reusable object-oriented units. I assert that this is often true (to at least some useful extent)!

In addition, the integration of objects from the reuse library must be seamless. The analysis process must be problem oriented. That is, it must first determine what object behaviors are needed to satisfy the problem requirements and then consider object implementations from the library that can contribute to satisfying those requirements. If reuse is considered too early in the process, you may tend to add requirements that are by-products of the existing objects rather than based on the customer's needs. Another undesirable effect of going to the reuse library too early is attempting to force-fit an inappropriate object into the design because, intuitively, it seems like it should fit. I have observed students of my Object-Oriented Software Development course try to reuse objects from previous examples in homework assignments because the earlier objects were physically similar to what they needed. Unfortunately, the corresponding objects' behaviors were subtly different. In this case, the effort to reuse the previously developed objects was many times what was needed to merely develop a new object.

Understanding these constraints, it is possible to define a methodology that capitalizes on reuse, rather than being victimized by it.

Beyond supporting reuse, object-oriented development has positive benefits in testing and maintenance. By localizing behaviors in objects, it is frequently easier to isolate problems or install modifications.

WHAT IS REAL-TIME OBJECT-ORIENTED STRUCTURED ANALYSIS (RTOOSA)?

At least two documented attempts have been made to begin with RTSA products and map them into an object-oriented design [Gomaa, 1988; Ward, 1989]. These approaches begin the design process by regrouping the functionally decomposed elements of RTSA according to predefined guidelines into logical objects. The benefits of starting with the widely used RTSA methodology are obvious. To name a few: Analysts are already familiar with the methodology, having used it often in the past; CASE tools are usually already in place and familiar; and the notation is widely recognized and understood by engineers of many disciplines, a necessity for effective system-level reviews.

I endorse these benefits, but have three primary objections to this approach. First, it does not promote consideration of the problem from an object-oriented perspective. As such, it promulgates a functional decomposition mindset during the critical analysis phase. This can make the design process needlessly complex. Second, because the correlation between the lowest-level icons from the analysis diagrams and the icons of the design diagrams is complex, it is more difficult to trace back and forth between analysis and design. This is especially important when changes are required. Finally, it does not appear that integration with a reuse library is very straightforward.

As Ward/Mellor built on previous Structured Analysis concepts to provide Real-Time Structured Analysis, I have extended the Ward/Mellor RTSA by introducing object-oriented principles to the analysis process.

The Ward/Mellor RTSA methodology establishes a sequence of abstract models of the problem domain and thereby establishes the requirements for the solution domain [Ward/Mellor, 1985]. One of these models is called the *behavioral* model. This model consists of a hierarchical network of *transformation schema* (real-time extensions to the Yourdon-style DFDs). The top-level transformation schema identifies the critical *transformations* (i.e., "bubbles" that specify transformation of one or more inputs into one or more outputs). Each transformation from the top-level schema is expanded in a second-level schema. This decomposition continues until the logic of each primitive transformation is expressed in another form (e.g., with PDL, a truth table, etc.). The heuristics by which this hierarchical breakdown is accomplished are based on decomposing transformations into their constituent functional elements. During this process, "data stores" are identified on appropriate schema by a distinct icon.

The Ward/Mellor methodology is sound, except that, when an object-oriented approach is more appropriate, the decomposition heuristics lack an object orientation. This book introduces guidelines to decompose a system using objects. This prompted the need to identify a new icon to represent an *object* on the same level as a data transformation.

By defining new heuristics for decomposition, the products of analysis become objects and their constituent *fields* (stored data) and *methods* (the procedures and functions that act on the fields). These analysis objects define the required characteristics that can be matched to those of objects in the reuse library to determine suitable fits as the starting point for design. The mapping between analysis and design is direct and easily traceable. Elements (objects) in the design are also traceable back to the products of analysis, making it easier to maintain the requirements document during development and operational deployment.

Real-Time Object-Oriented Structured Analysis (RTOOSA) uses notation now familiar to engineers of other disciplines. The products are therefore reviewable with less risk of misunderstanding or investment in retraining the *rest of the world*. Because the notation is virtually identical to that of RTSA now supported by CASE tools, new tools are not necessary to support RTOOSA. This removes the cost and schedule risk associated with procuring and learning new CASE tools from the first projects that attempt to adopt an object-oriented strategy.

Finally, RTOOSA supports software development with integrated reuse. Applying RTOOSA to a problem builds a Requirements Model in which all required objects have been defined in terms of their fields and methods. Following RTOOSA, one of the first design activities is to match object requirements against the characteristics of objects in the reuse library. When all reusable objects have been identified, the next step is to generate the *class hierarchy* (*classes* define the essential characteristics for their instantiated objects, while the hierarchy specifies which characteristics are *inherited* from previous generations).

So, RTOOSA is not a radical departure from those tried and true techniques with which most software engineers are so comfortable. The major adjustment is to adopt an *object-oriented mindset*.

THE ORGANIZATION OF THIS BOOK

Before you can effectively employ RTOOSA, you must fully understand the nature of software objects! Much of the process of learning about objects involves acquiring a working knowledge of common object-oriented programming concepts. Once all implications of objects are understood, applying this mindset using the

Real-Time Object-Oriented Structured Analysis methodology becomes almost intuitively obvious.

This book has been written assuming you know neither Object-Oriented Programming nor Real-Time Structured Analysis. The book's two parts address these respective topics.

Part I introduces the essential characteristics of objects. Each of these characteristics is introduced through example programs written in Turbo Pascal®. This programming language was chosen for several reasons. Pascal is an English-like structured language with high "readability." Languages such as C++ have more extensive object-oriented programming capabilities, but the syntax of such languages is more cryptic and unintelligible to anyone who does not actively program in them. Turbo

Figure 1.6. Borland International has introduced object-oriented extensions to Turbo Pascal beginning with version 5.5.

Pascal 5.5 and later versions include a full set of object-oriented extensions that may be used to demonstrate all the essential characteristics of OOP. In addition, the Turbo integrated development environment (which Borland calls its IDE) provides a user-friendly way to step through the example programs (and the exercise projects that you are encouraged to develop) to examine the status of the program's objects. This book is not meant to be a reference for programming Turbo Pascal, or for doing OOP. I firmly believe that it is not possible to appreciate fully the implications of software objects unless you have first-hand contact with such objects. Without such appreciation, you are unlikely to adopt an object-oriented mindset.

Part II assumes you have developed the essential object-oriented mindset, either after working through Part I or from previous OOP experience. Part II develops RTOOSA, the definition of a system's requirements through abstract models of a specific problem's domain. The distinction between the Requirements Model and the Design Model is first emphasized. Then each of the elements of the Requirements Model is described in detail. The final chapter of Part II picks up the products of RTOOSA and suggests how they lead to the physical products of a

Turbo Pascal® is a registered trademark of Borland International.

Design Model. This chapter also addresses how the products of RTOOSA feed directly into planning for the integration and testing of the final product.

Throughout this book numerous examples are derived from realistic real-time embedded systems. No example is an exact implementation of any actual system. Usually the examples have been somewhat simplified and therefore do not represent a fully operational implementation. However, the examples are sufficiently similar to systems on which I have worked at Harris Corporation's Government Aerospace Systems Division and are sufficiently complete to demonstrate how the methodology should be applied.

The example Turbo Pascal programs were developed using Turbo Pascal Version 6.0 and tested on a PC-clone, 16 MHz 386SX. Source code for these programs is provided on the diskette accompanying this book. Most of the examples operate in the graphics screen mode. Although they have been developed using a VGA display, graphics use the Borland Graphics Interface (BGI) and therefore should be compatible with any color graphics adapter supported by an installed BGI driver. Hercules monochrome displays should work equally well with these examples if the specified colors in the programs are changed to reflect shades displayable with the Hercules card. Unit *GRAFINIT.PAS* in Chapter 3 is used throughout to initialize the graphics interface. This unit identifies the path to the BGI drivers' directory in a string variable called *BGIFilePath*. Change the string value to specify the directory for the system on which you will run these programs. Some example programs' performance is dependent on the throughput of its host processor. These programs behave reasonably on a 16-MHz 386SX, but appear somewhat "fast" on a 33-MHz 386. It may be necessary to adjust or insert *delay* statement parameters to get acceptable images on your system.

Everything You Need to Know about Objects

*National Security Chief Brent Scrowcroft once dodged a question in
a press briefing by saying: "That's a good question, and let me state the
problem more clearly without going too deeply into the answer."*
— Quoted by Christopher Conte in
The Wall Street Journal from *Reader's Digest,*
Vol. 138, No. 827, March 1991

Chapter *2*

The Object-Oriented Mindset

In Part I of this book, we develop an *object-oriented mindset*. In the simplest terms, this mindset reflects a pattern of thinking by which an engineer envisions a system as a set of interacting "objects." These *objects* represent both real and abstract entities. *Objects* have characteristics implicit in our mindset. Before defining an analysis methodology that relies on this mindset, we must first establish an initial familiarity with those characteristics.

OUR FIRST DEFINITION OF AN "OBJECT"

As the first step in becoming object-oriented, let's establish a preliminary definition of an object. Later, we will refine this definition by using specific terms that evoke the essential characteristics of objects. Full appreciation of objects will come as you develop a working knowledge of these terms through examples and exercises. For now, our first definition relies only on a typical programmer's common experiences:

> **Object** [a preliminary definition]: a logical programming entity, consisting of data (types and variables) and subprograms (functions and procedures) that in some manner represent a real or abstract entity and its behaviors.

It took a couple of decades to decide that modular programming meant designing systems by identifying "highly cohesive, loosely coupled" program/subprogram modules [e.g., Page-Jones, 1980]. Analysis began by identifying the major functions of the system. Then each function was decomposed into a series of subprograms, each of which implemented one aspect of the function. Each subprogram was supposed to implement fully a single function (i.e., *highly cohesive*) while minimizing dependencies on other program units (i.e., *loosely coupled*).

In our object-oriented mindset, we are still concerned about cohesion and coupling. High cohesion for objects results from concentrating all aspects of an object, its "value" and "behavior," in the programming entity we call the *object*. Loose coupling is achieved by permitting access to the object's value(s) through only predefined interface procedures and functions. No undeclared dependencies are permitted in or out of the object.

So our new mindset does not invalidate or violate our prior notion of good programming practices. Quite the opposite, object orientation provides a mechanism that directly enforces these desirable traits. The following characteristics of the two mindsets contrast the principle emphasis of each:

> **Structured Programming Mindset:** A program consists of a set of procedures and functions, the totality of which defines an algorithm that solves the problem at hand. The data being manipulated is of only secondary interest. The main program must be defined first so all else flows down from it.

> **Object-Oriented Programming Mindset:** Programs exist only to manipulate data, so analysis centers on the data and the limited, but well-defined, ways in which it may be manipulated. The main program is probably the least important aspect of the software and is often left as the last element to be defined.

In keeping with our concept of objects representing real-world entities, we will refer to the software that *uses* an object as a *client* of that object. Therefore, the following definition becomes useful as we examine the characteristics of objects:

> **Client:** any software (an object or otherwise) that invokes the services of an object is said to be a client of that object.

THE PRIMARY CHARACTERISTICS OF OBJECTS

Four primary characteristics underlie the principles of object-oriented programming. Although we will explore each of these more fully in the following chapters, the following definitions will get us started:

> **Encapsulation:** the mechanism of modularity by which the fields (data structures) and methods (procedures and functions that define the object's behavior) of an object are structured to allow only explicitly defined access to the object's structure and behavior while hiding implementation details from the object's clients.

> **Inheritance:** a relationship between objects wherein one object automatically acquires fields and methods from one or more other objects. Inheritance is illustrated by hierarchy diagrams that show ancestor/descendent relationships in the same manner as a family tree.

> **Polymorphism:** the property by which objects in a hierarchy can share a single method name, wherein each object implements the method in a manner dictated by its unique requirements.

> **Identity:** the nature of objects by which each instance exists as a unique entity with ownership of its fields and methods. The definition of an object's fields and methods are declared as a class, from which multiple unique instances may be declared.

Although there is no standard terminology for object-oriented programming elements, terms defined by Smalltalk are more widely used than others. For this book, I generally use the following commonly accepted terms:

> **Class:** the collection of fields and methods that are common to (potentially) multiple entities (objects). A class may be considered a mold from which objects are extracted.

Object: a member of a class. Objects have an individual identity, whereby they own their own copies of the fields and methods (although the compiler may actually allow method code to be shared) declared by their class.

Field: a data structure that retains the state or value of an object.

Method: a procedure or function that is invoked to implement some aspect of the object's behavior.

As we explore these characteristics with Turbo Pascal program examples, your examination of Borland's documentation will show that Turbo Pascal uses different terms for these concepts. To Turbo Pascal, a *class* is called an "object" and an *object* is called an "instance of an object." If you proceed into object-oriented programming with C++, you will find that *fields* are called "member variables" and *methods* are called "member functions." So, although terminology is not consistent across different languages, the basic concepts are.

How Objects Communicate

Objects are representations of real entities in the problem space (and later in the solution space). In our object paradigm, objects communicate by sending messages to one another. A message to an object requests that object to invoke one of its methods.

Let's draw an analogy to a real-world situation with which we are all familiar. Consider a class called "people." This designation is pretty abstract. Members of this class would have the general characteristics that are common to all elements of the class (i.e., to all people). This class wouldn't be very interesting because its members would have *only* those characteristics that are common to all people. Such people lacking individual personalities and capabilities are not interesting, unless you are looking for extras to make up a crowd scene in a motion picture.

Invoking our *inheritance* characteristic, we can identify descendent classes, each of which has unique and specialized *behavior* (e.g., skills)., For example, our experience can attribute skills to "engineers," "word-processing specialists," and other professional people.

Class: people

Descendent classes: engineers, word-processing specialists,
                         administrators, program managers

Remember that classes are merely molds from which objects are cast. Assume that an individual in Figure 2.1 (call him "Duane") is an object of the class *engineer*. Duane needs the services of another object, so he sends a *message*, via a phone call, to an instance of the class *word-processing specialist* (call her "Carolyn"). In this message, Duane is asking Carolyn to invoke her Document Update procedure to make a change to a Software Requirements Specification (SRS). There are several important points to be made from this example that carry over to our software object paradigm.

Figure 2.1. An "object" sending a "message."

1. The message must be sent to the correct individual, illustrating the importance of an object's *identity*. Another *word-processing specialist* may not have access to Duane's SRS, so it is important the message goes specifically to Carolyn. Also, Carolyn, as a word-processing specialist, has the skills necessary to change the document. A member of the class *program manager* would probably be unable to perform this function.

2. How Carolyn executes the function is unimportant to Duane. He doesn't care if Carolyn converts his document to another word processing format, copies the document file to a 3.5" floppy drive, carries it over to another computer to make the changes, uploads the resulting print file to a mainframe computer, and dumps it to a laser printer. All that is important to Duane is that he be given a document with the corrections properly included. This demonstrates a key characteristic of objects. Objects have interfaces to define those parts of their behaviors accessible to clients, while hiding the details of the implementation of these behaviors.

The way we read a line of code that requests an object to invoke one of its methods is quite different from invoking a procedure in a structured programming language, as illustrated on the next page.

Structured Programming:

ZipCode := MakeInt(InputString);

"Call the function MakeInt with the parameter InputString and store the returned value as ZipCode."

Object-Oriented Programming:

ZipCode := InputString.MakeInt;

"Send a message to the object InputString asking it to apply its method MakeInt; the returned value is stored as ZipCode."

From this example, recognize where the emphasis is placed. In structured programming, the reader's attention is immediately drawn to the function *MakeInt*. The data on which the function operates are passed as a parameter in the function call, making it incidental to the function itself. Contrast this with the object-oriented statement, where the primary emphasis is on the *InputString* object, which contains a string (or string pointer) as its data and *MakeInt* as one of its methods. The name of the object appears first, with the name of its method (i.e., the function *MakeInt*) appended to it. This reversal of reference clearly reflects the difference in mindset associated with the respective approaches.

In addition, this example again emphasizes object ownership of the methods defining its behavior. Although the prototypes of the procedures and functions that constitute an object's behavior-defining *methods* are declared in the class definitions, each member of a class has individual ownership of its methods. This is a subtle, but important concept.

DEFINING OBJECTS IN TURBO PASCAL

There are three stages to creating an object and making it available for use by a client, regardless of the implementation language. These are:

1. The class must be declared. The class declaration specifies the names and data types of each field and identifies each method of the class. The

class declaration also includes the level of *protection* for each field and method (i.e., specifies to which clients fields and methods are directly accessible).

2. The implementation of each method must be defined, specifying the associated object behaviors.

3. An object instance of the class must be declared such that the object is known to the client code.

Now the client can send messages to the object to access its state/value or invoke its behaviors.

Because this book's examples are programmed in Turbo Pascal 6.0, I will describe the Turbo Pascal 6.0 syntax associated with these elements. Don't worry if you are unfamiliar with the Pascal object-oriented extensions provided by Turbo Pascal. They are quite intuitive and not difficult to learn. For a complete definition of Turbo Pascal and its constructs, refer to the Borland documents.

Object classes are declared in the *type* declaration section of a Turbo Pascal program. Class declarations may be interspersed with other type declarations. The class name is specified where the class is declared. If the class is descended from another class, then its heritage (i.e., its ancestor's class name) is specified. Then, globally visible fields and methods are listed, followed by *private* fields and methods. Figure 2.2 summarizes the syntax of the Turbo Pascal object class declaration while excluding definitions for commonly understood elements (e.g., letter, digit, etc.).

The following example illustrates two object-class declarations:

```
type
   GeoPosition = object
      procedure Init( InitLat, InitLon : real );
      procedure SetPosition( NewLat, NewLon : real );
      function LatitudeIs  : real;
      function LongitudeIs : real;
   private
      Latitude  : real;   { -90 .. +90 degrees }
      Longitude : real;   { -180 .. +180 degrees }
   end;   { object = GeoPosition }

   AircraftPosition = object( GeoPosition )
      procedure Init( InitLat, InitLon : real;
                                  InitAlt : integer );
      procedure SetAltitude( NewAlt : integer );
      function AltitudeIs  : integer;
   private
      Altitude  : integer;   { altitude in feet }
   end;   { object = AircraftPosition }
```

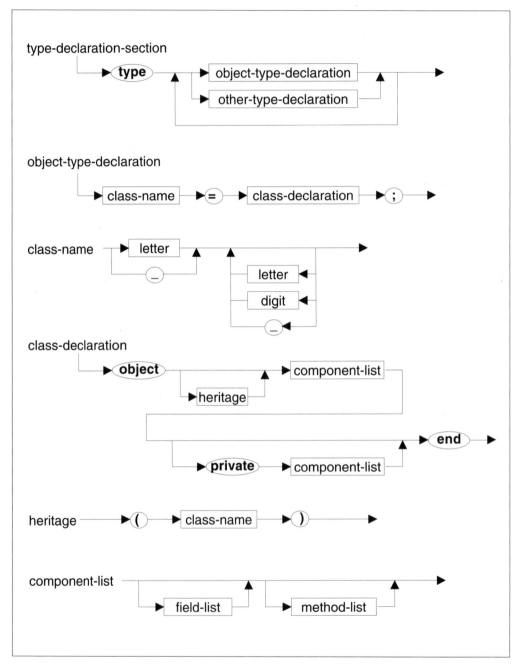

Figure 2.2. Declaring a Turbo Pascal object class defines a template for class members.

This example illustrates several of the characteristics of objects (which we will pursue more fully in later chapters).

The two Turbo Pascal "objects" (classes) are declared in an ancestor (*GeoPosition*) and descendent (*AircraftPosition*) relationship. In such a relationship, the descendent object inherits the fields and methods of the ancestor. Specifically, *AircraftPosition* inherits the fields *Latitude* and *Longitude* and the methods *SetPosition*, *LatitudeIs*, and *LongitudeIs* from *GeoPosition*. *Aircraft-Position* can use these fields and methods exactly as if they had been declared in *GeoPosition* and therefore does not need to declare them explicitly. On the other hand, the method *Init* must behave differently for each of these object classes. It is therefore redeclared for the descendent *AircraftPosition* class. To emphasize the need for a different method, notice that the descendent's *Init* method is declared with a different parameter list.

By declaring the fields of these classes *private*, clients are prohibited from directly reading or writing their values. For a client to access or manipulate these fields, it must ask an object of the class to invoke one of its *public* methods (i.e., those declared before the keyword *private*). This is the mechanism by which *encapsulation* is enforced. The value of this mechanism lies in the concept of information hiding, first introduced by David Parnas in an article published in the December 1972 issue of *Communications of the ACM*. Because the actual format of the data stored in the fields is hidden from client programs, those formats may be changed without affecting the clients so long as the access methods are modified to ensure that the formats of the returned values are not changed. This localizes the effects of many types of changes, enhancing the maintainability of software that uses good object-oriented programming practices.

The second stage of creating an object is to define the specific object behaviors associated with each class method. Continuing the example begun above, the methods of each of the two objects are individually specified.

```
{====== IMPLEMENTATION METHODS FOR GeoPosition ======}
procedure GeoPosition.SetPosition(
                    NewLat, NewLon : real );
    begin
       Latitude  := NewLat;   { set latitude }
       Longitude := NewLon;   { set longitude }
    end;   { GeoPosition.SetPosition }

procedure GeoPosition.Init( InitLat, InitLon : real );
    begin
       SetPosition( InitLat, InitLon );
    end;   { GeoPosition.Init }

function GeoPosition.LatitudeIs  : real;
    begin
       LatitudeIs := Latitude;
```

```
    end;    { GeoPosition.LatitudeIs }

function GeoPosition.LongitudeIs : real;
    begin
        LongitudeIs := Longitude;
    end;    { GeoPosition.LongitudeIs }

{=== IMPLEMENTATION METHODS FOR AirCraftPosition ====}
procedure AircraftPosition.Init(
                    InitLat, InitLon : real;
                                 InitAlt : integer );
    begin
        Latitude  := InitLat;    { set latitude }
        Longitude := InitLon;    { set longitude }
        Altitude  := InitAlt;    { set altitude }
    end;    { AircraftPosition.Init }

procedure AircraftPosition.SetAltitude(
                                    NewAlt : integer );
    begin
        Altitude := NewAlt;
    end;    { AircraftPosition.SetAltitude }

function AircraftPosition.AltitudeIs  : integer;
    begin
        AltitudeIs := Altitude;
    end;    { AircraftPosition.AltitudeIs }
```

Methods fall into three general categories: those that *get data*, those that *set data*, and those that generate some type of *side effects* (e.g., display a data value on the screen, send a parameter to a sensor, etc.). For this rather simplistic example, all the defined methods either get or set data. Most interesting classes have behaviors that go beyond merely reading and writing their fields. For example, each of these classes should probably have an *Update* method to communicate with such aircraft subsystems as its Inertial Navigation System and altimeter. There also might be methods that convert the location fields to a flat-earth model format (such as the UTM coordinate system) used by map makers.

The final stage in creating an object is to *instantiate* (i.e., create an instance of) the object instance using its class as a "mold." This creates a unique member of the class. This declaration may be accomplished several ways, but for this example, a static instance adequately demonstrates the concept. Other ways to instantiate objects will be addressed in later chapters. The following excerpt from a client program creates a single instance of the *AircraftPosition*.

```
    var
        MyPosition    : AircraftPosition;
    begin
        { initialize the object with default values }
        MyPosition.Init( { InitLat => } 0.0,
                         { InitLon => } 0.0,
```

```
                                { InitAlt => } 0          );
              . . . . . . . . . . .
        end.
```

As this declaration illustrates, creating an instance of an object may be as easy as declaring a variable in Pascal. Of course, the client normally needs to initialize the fields of the object before any other code tries to access them. In our example, the fields were given default values. In real systems, it might be better to use crew member inputs or initial values read from sensors to initialize the object.

Object encapsulation provides the facilities to enhance program "safety." A Boolean field, possibly called *Initialized*, can be provided for classes containing critical values on which the system relies. This field is initially set to *false* by the Init method. Then, when valid values are written into the object's fields, the *Initialized* field is set to *true*. Each class method that returns or uses the value of a field would only do so when the "Initialized" field is *true*. Such a strategy prevents clients from using invalid data, possibly causing the system to do something that could endanger the user.

As we examine objects more closely through program examples, you will find objects declared as described above. If you don't yet understand how an object is brought into existence, please go back and restudy this example now. If you still are confused, consult the Borland tutorial provided with your Turbo Pascal software.

A BETTER DEFINITION OF AN "OBJECT"

Now that we have touched on some essential characteristics of objects, and even had a first encounter with Turbo Pascal syntax, it is time to develop a more technically complete definition of an object.

Object: a logical programming entity that encapsulates state or value in data fields and predefined behavior in methods. Each object is an instance of a class, but has unique identity distinct from all other objects. Fields and methods may either be defined by the object's class or inherited from ancestor classes.

Class: a common structure and behavior shared by a set of objects. Classes have an interface segment, describing the visible characteristics of member objects, and an implementation segment, defining the hidden implementation secrets of its behavior.

There are two elements to an object's fields. Each field has an associated data type declaration to define the static aspect of the field. For each field, a "variable" is declared of the corresponding type to hold the current value associated with the field, (i.e., its dynamic aspect).

The ways that an object may change state or value are limited to those defined by the object's methods. These methods may only be invoked as the result of messages sent to the object requesting invocation of a particular method. Only methods that are defined as visible (i.e., are not *private*) may be requested via a message. Requests to invoke a private or undefined method are normally caught at compilation time and treated as compilation errors.

When we properly hide an object's fields by declaring them *private*, we emphasize the abstraction of the object while making its internal structure unavailable to its clients.

SUMMARY

In this chapter we have built a working definition of an object by briefly examining the essential characteristics that differentiate objects from other programming entities. We introduced the syntax of Turbo Pascal's object-oriented extensions in preparation for far more exhaustive investigations of our critical object characteristics through programmed examples.

The following chapters will individually address these critical object characteristics.

The greatest curse of the gods is
to survive your own children.
— Old Chinese Saying

Chapter *3*

Inheritance from the Family Tree

For many people, the word *inheritance* conjures up thoughts of genetics and an image of the family tree. Inheritance in the object-oriented paradigm is consistent with these intuitive notions. The object-oriented counterpart to the family tree is the class hierarchy tree. Each node of the *class hierarchy tree* represents an object class. It is connected to its immediate ancestor class (its "parent") above and, if any, one or more descendent classes (its "children") below. The implication of these relationships is that each class inherits the fields and methods from every ancestor class tracing upward on the diagram to the top (commonly called *base*) class.

The concept for such a hierarchical diagram is not new. The ancient Greeks Plato and Aristotle are generally credited with originating classification schemes for plants and animals. In a hierarchical classification tree, the upper levels define

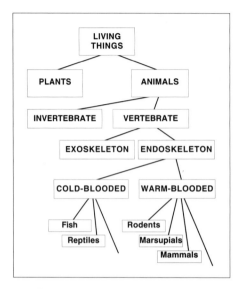

Figure 3.1. A biologist's typical classification of living things.

very general characteristics. Each succeeding level down the tree introduces additional specific characteristics, while retaining the characteristics of every node traced upward. Consider the biologist's classification hierarchy shown in Figure 3.1. In this example, *mammals* are *warm-blooded* creatures, and therefore have an *endoskeleton*, which makes them *vertebrate* and *animals*, which are *living things*. Not all warm-blooded animals have the same traits (mammals don't carry their young around in pouches), but all mammals, marsupials, rodents, and so forth are warm-blooded.

This concept of classification by common traits can be applied to any group of objects that have common traits. For the sake of discussion, consider a hierarchy of "vehicles." Before you can select categories for objects, it is necessary to determine which objects belong in the hierarchy domain and which do not. In this case, we need a definition that allows us to recognize objects as vehicles and reject all nonvehicle objects. For example, we can use the first definition from *The American Heritage Dictionary*:

Vehicle: a device for carrying passengers, goods, or equipment.

Vehicles include a wide variety of objects, including cars and trucks, ships and boats, spacecraft, and a wide variety of aircraft, as suggested by Figure 3.2.

The criteria for the structure of a hierarchy tree is highly problem domain specific. Figure 3.3 suggests a class hierarchy tree that addresses our vehicle objects. In this particular tree, first-level selection criteria are based on where each type of vehicle travels: *Space, Air, Aquatic,* and *Land*. Clearly, each of these categories implies certain characteristics for its members. For example, *Space Vehicles* are those that can travel beyond the earth's atmosphere. Each of these categories may be further defined with increasingly more specific characteristics. Space Vehicles might be divided into *Manned* and *Unmanned*.

In the example tree, the *Air Vehicle* category has been expanded further by identifying three categories: *Wingless, Fixed-Wing,* and *Rotary-Wing*. Again, each of these categories may be further refined. Next-level categorization of *Wingless*

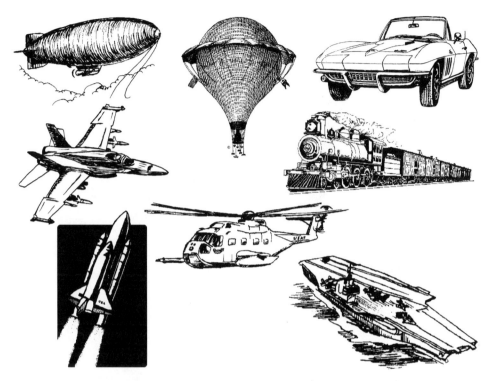

Figure 3.2. Some of the wide variety of objects that satisfy our definition of "vehicles."

Air Vehicles could be: *Blimps*, *Hot-Air Balloons*, and *Parasails*. Likewise, *Fixed-Wing Air Vehicles* could consist of: *Jet-Powered*, *Propeller-Powered*, and *Unpowered*.

Figure 3.3 shows expansion of the Rotary-Wing Air Vehicle category into *Civilian* and *Military* categories. This process continues until three specific military helicopter types have been specified.

Each node in the tree inherits all the essential characteristics of the node at every level above it in its path to the top level, *Vehicles*. Each level represents a different level of abstraction, ranging from very abstract *Vehicles* at the top to each of the specific helicopter types at the bottom of the tree. Each lowest level node gathers some of its characteristics from each of its ancestors. For example: tracing the full hierarchy of the *RAH-66 Comanche*, the following characteristics could possibly be inherited from the respective ancestors:

1. *Vehicles:* indicates a changing position (suggesting the need for navigation and speed measurement), the capacity to carry a crew and/or cargo.

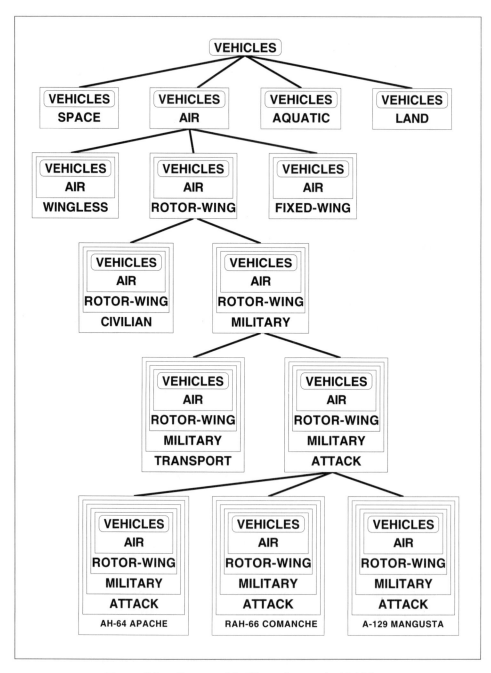

Figure 3.3.   One possible Hierarchy tree for Vehicles.

2. *Air:* position must be related in three-dimensional space, including the altitude component (navigation), and suggests the need for aviation-type communications systems.

3. *Rotary-Wing:* velocity computations must allow for lateral and rearward motion, driving navigation parameters. The flight controls for rotary-winged vehicles have unique characteristics, including a "collective" channel that permits vertical movement.

4. *Military:* provides for certain navigation (e.g., permitting use of military map-based coordinate systems) and communications (e.g., with data encryption capabilities) equipments.

5. *Attack:* provides for a weapon delivery capability and the need for Electronic Warfare Countermeasures.

6. *RAH-66 Comanche:* specifies a particular configuration of equipment, specific maintenance capabilities, and so forth.

Remember that, even at the lowest level, the tree nodes represent classes and not individual objects. For example, there may be many instances of the class *RAH-66 Comanche*.

To better illustrate this point, it is not possible to show a picture of a class, such as *RAH-66 Comanche*. Figure 3.4 shows (a drawing of) one instance of that class. Knowing that the object is a member of the specific class carries implicit knowledge that it exhibits all the characteristics of its class and the inherited characteristcs of each of its ancestor classes as well. This particular instance of the class *RAH-66 Comanche* is also known to be an *Attack Military Rotary-Winged Air Vehicle*.

A member of a sibling class, such as an instance of the class *AH-64 Apache* or of the class *A-129 Mangusta*, shares a common heritage suggesting many common characteristics. The lowest level classes typically dictate specific performance capabilities associated with each aircraft type. That is, all helicopters behave basically the same, but differ in such performance characteristics as maximum velocity, maximum rate-of-climb, maximum yaw rate, "pop-up" time, weapons payload, and so forth.

This hierarchical relationship seems to work pretty well. If a new class, in this example a new vehicle type, is needed, all that is necessary is to trace down the tree, deciding at each level which class best defines the characteristics of the new vehicle. Ultimately, the new class is added to the bottom of some branch to encompass the unique qualities not accumulated from the line of ancestors selected on the way down. At first examination, this all seems pretty simple.

Figure 3.4. One instance of the class *RAH-66 Comanche*.

ANOTHER KIND OF INHERITANCE?

It is sometimes difficult to choose a unique ancestry from a hierarchical tree because a class may exhibit strong traits from more than one class at some level of abstraction in the tree. Take for example, the *V-22 Osprey*, shown in Figure 3.5. It is sometimes referred to by the name of its unique technology, the *tilt-rotor*. The Osprey is clearly a *vehicle*, designed to transport fully loaded troops into combat zones. It is also obvious that this vehicle is an aircraft. But selecting a path at the next level of our vehicle classification tree is difficult. The Osprey is designed to take off and land vertically, like a helicopter. Once it is off the ground, the engines and rotors at the ends of the wings are rotated so the rotors act as propellers. So, although on the one hand the Osprey has characteristics of a *rotary-winged aircraft*, it can transform into a *fixed-wing aircraft*. This dual personality forces the analyst to select from between what may be two (or more) equally attractive alternatives. So, how does one choose?

To create a new class for *tilt-rotor* aircraft probably doesn't make much sense. That would lose any benefit that would be derived from selecting either existing class. The new class would have to duplicate characteristics from both. It would be better to select one and explicitly provide the needed characteristics from the other. Assuming both *rotary-winged* and *fixed-wing* classes have descendents for *civilian* and *military* applications, a new tilt-rotor class at this level would not have access to characteristics available at the next level for either of the available classes. Again, more work!

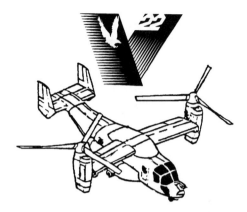

Figure 3.5. Objects may have characteristics that could be inherited from more than one sibling class, but linear inheritance limits ancestor selection to a single class!

If the new tilt-rotor class were to have enough members, then even all the extra work necessary to create a new class might be justified. However, this is unlikely for tilt-rotor aircraft.

So the logical conclusion in such situations is that one of the existing classes should be chosen. Either choice would be better than starting over. The best strategy is to select the class that contributes the most needed characteristics. For the Osprey, it would probably be best to capitalize on the V-22's helicopter-like capabilities. Later, when the special characteristics of the lowest-level class are defined, any fixed-wing characteristics that could not be inherited may be explicitly defined. Some of these characteristics may even cause us to "override" rotary-winged characteristics of the same name.

From this example we may generalize a strategy for selecting a class lineage from an existing hierarchy: Select a class at each level down the tree that provides for the maximum inheritance of applicable characteristics for the specific application.

But, why is this a problem at all?

What has been described with the hierarchical tree is called *linear inheritance*, whereby a class may inherit characteristics from only a single immediate ancestor. There are systems in which nonlinear (i.e., "multiple") inheritance permits attributes from two or more ancestors to be inherited. For example, C++ and CLOS, and to a limited extent Smalltalk, support multiple inheritance. Turbo Pascal supports only the linear inheritance model. How important is multiple inheritance?

The need for multiple inheritance in object oriented programming languages is still a topic of great debate. In our experience, we find multiple inheritance to be like a parachute: you don't always need it, but when you do, you're really happy to have it on hand. [Booch, 1991]

Although the structure of linear inheritance systems is simpler, it restricts the analyst to choosing from among multiple, possibly equally attractive, alternative classes. This requires the analyst explicitly to provide the characteristics needed but not available from the classes chosen, including those in the inheritance path. Fortunately, this is seldom a problem.

CLASS DEFINITIONS TO ENHANCE REUSE

As system developers, we frequently solve similar problems for different customers or for use in slightly different environments. Companies that develop aircraft display systems find that each system has certain similarities to every other display system they have ever made. This suggests that our greatest opportunities for reuse will probably come from specific problem domains. These problem domains are often easy to identify. Within Harris Corporation's Electronic Systems Sector, each division has specific *product lines* for which it is responsible. These product lines suggest problem domains in which software objects could likely be reused in future projects.

Within a problem domain, there is often a core of relatively stable classes that capture the domain's essential objects (interface objects, data base objects, etc.). An analyst should specify a system's objects in a manner that encourages future reuse. Before continuing on this track, consider the following definitions:

Abstract Class: a class whose definition is based on generalities that may be used by multiple descendent classes; an abstract class is declared with the expectation that it will have no direct instances.

Base Class: the first-level ancestor class in a class hierarchy tree; often an abstract class. A base class has no ancestor class.

When defining classes, one successful strategy that supports a high potential for reuse is to look at objects with an eye for extracting application specifics from a class and putting them into a descendent class while retaining the application-independent generalities in an abstract ancestor class. The abstract classes generated in this manner become excellent candidates for reuse. In sufficiently large systems, reuse may be immediately exercised in other segments of the same project.

Another approach that enhances reusability addresses objects that tend to need close coupling. When a "behavior" involves two (or more) objects, it is often best not to assign that behavior (i.e., method) to either object. Instead, create an encompassing object that ties the multiple lower-level objects together. The lower-level objects become more reusable because they do not carry potentially excess baggage with them.

Careful identification of base classes and abstract classes within a specific problem domain establishes the foundation on which reuse becomes practical and potentially profitable!

LOGICAL AND PHYSICAL MODULES

To this point, we have been describing objects as "logical" entities. This is contrasted with the physical elements of a specific programming language. For Turbo Pascal, the separately compilable entity is called a *unit* (the Ada equivalent is called a *package*).

When building a system around objects, the designer must allocate classes to units. In Chapter 17 we will go into greater detail regarding this process. For now, I will assert one overriding consideration concerning class allocation: *Restrict units to a small family of closely related classes that are likely to be used together. By all means, do not migrate "main program" logic into classes or their units.*

In the following examples, I will package classes in reasonable units. In each case, the object-based units will be followed by a main program that exercises objects instantiated from the classes. Each unit begins with the declaration of the unit's name. Clients may gain use of such classes by declaring the name of the desired units in a *uses* statement.

DEMONSTRATING INHERITANCE

The primary thrust of this book is learning to develop real-time embedded systems using an object-oriented approach. I leave discussion of the essential characteristics of this type of system until Part II. For now, whatever intuitive concept of real-time embedded systems you may have is probably sufficient. Based on that, you will probably agree that modern aircraft avionics systems are prime examples of real-time embedded systems. Therefore, as I introduce examples to demonstrate the primary characteristics of objects, most of them will draw from the avionics world.

Because we will use the PC to demonstrate avionics objects, the PC monitor will have to suffice as the medium by which we observe our object demonstrations. So we will begin by developing graphics objects. The accompanying program will illustrate how objects are declared, defined, and created. Then, these simple objects will demonstrate the principles of inheritance.

THE OBJECTS OF A GEOMETRIC OBJECTS UNIT

The Turbo Pascal unit GEO_OBJ1.PAS (Geometric Objects—1) illustrates how a reusable library unit might be created. In this physical unit, a small hierarchy of four object classes is defined. Figure 3.6 illustrates this hierarchy. As previously described, the first step in creating objects is to declare their classes in terms of their fields and methods.

The base class of a hierarchy is recognizable by the absence of a *heritage* field in its declaration. The base class of this hierarchy, called *Point*, establishes four fields: *X* and *Y*, the screen coordinates of the point, its *Color*, and a Boolean (*Visible*) that indicates whether the instance of this class is visible on the screen. In this case, *Point* is not an abstract class, as it would be perfectly reasonable to instantiate objects from it. Such objects, when displayed, would appear as single pixels on the screen.

For each class, it is customary to define an initialization method (call it *Init*) that is invoked to define an object before the client attempts to use it. This method normally sets the class's fields to default values or to values explicitly provided by the client as parameters. Later, we will give this method a unique identification and assign special attributes to it. For now, it will be a procedure indistinguishable from other methods, except for the naming convention.

Point's method *Draw* invokes a procedure (*PutPixel*) from Turbo Pascal's unit *Graph* to cause the image of the object, located at the values from the object's *X* and *Y* fields, to be drawn with the color specified by the value of the field *Color*. Once the image has been drawn to the screen, the value of the field *Visible* is set to "true." The method *Erase* performs the reciprocal function by redrawing the same point in the screen's background color (returned by the function *GetBkColor* from Turbo Pascal's *Graph* unit) and resets *Visible* to "false."

Point's method *Create* assigns values to each of the object's fields and then invokes the *Draw* method to make the newly created point appear on the screen. *Move* erases the object at its current location and redraws it at the coordinates passed as parameters. *SetNewColor* sets the object's *Color* field to the value passed as a parameter and then redraws the object in its new color. The functions *ColorIs*, *XCoordIs*, *YCoordIs*, and *IsVisible* return the respective field values.

This is a typical class and serves to illustrate two basic categories of methods:

Modifier Method: a method that causes a change of state or value for one or more of an object's fields, or otherwise operates on an object's fields.

Access Method: a method whose purpose is to make an object's fields available for reading or writing through the process specified in the method.

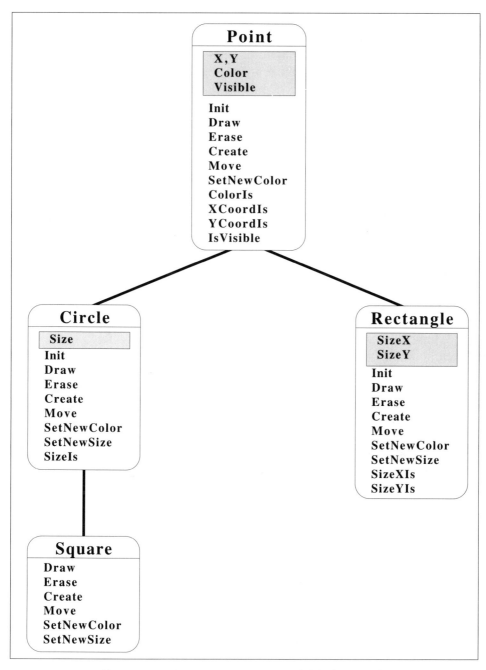

Figure 3.6.   Class hierarchy tree for GEO_OBJ1.PAS.

In Figure 3.7, the class *Circle* is declared as a descendent of *Point*. To define a circle requires but one more piece of information beyond what can be inherited from *Point*, namely the size (or radius) of the circle. Therefore, the descendent class declares but one field, *Size*. *Circle* must have methods to set and return the value of this additional field. In addition, *Circle* redefines methods that could have been inherited from its ancestor, *Point*. This is necessary because the commands for drawing a point are different from those for drawing a circle. These methods that override potentially inherited methods either invoke different graphics routines or invoke methods that use these image-specific routines. Therefore, they must be specified anew for *Circle*.

The class *Square* may appear to be declared incorrectly. Our intuition tells us that squares are not much like circles and, if anything, would be more closely related to rectangles. This is a case where analytic considerations must be favored over intuition.

Note that no additional information is required to define a *Square* over what is inherited from *Circle*. Therefore, no new fields are declared! As with the methods declared for *Circle*, those methods that either directly or indirectly relate to the differences between drawing circles and squares must be redefined. No other method declarations are needed.

A final class is declared for *Rectangle*. It is not obvious from which class *Rectangle* should be descended. A little analysis indicates that it actually makes little difference, so it has been assigned to be the descendent of *Point*.

The unit listing shows that the *interface* section ends after the declaration of the four classes. This is followed by an *implementation* statement that defines the beginning of the implementation section. All information in the implementation section is hidden from client programs.

This point marks the beginning of the second stage of object definition. Each of the methods that was declared in the *interface* section must be expanded in the *implementation* section to define its exact behavior.

In this unit, most logic in the methods is very straightforward. However, a few special instances bear further consideration.

Circle's method *Init* needs to initialize all the fields that its ancestor *Point* initialized plus the new field *Size* that *Circle* introduced. The code that accomplishes this appears as:

```
procedure Circle.Init;
  begin
    Point.Init;
    Size    := 0;
  end;    { Circle.Init }
```

```
unit Geo_Obj1;

{ Program:     Geometric Objects - Reusable geometric objects
  Filename:    Geo_Obj1.PAS
  Author:      John R. Ellis
  Last Update: 5 July 1991
  Copyright (c) 1991 by John R. Ellis

  Description: This unit provides basic low level geometric objects, from
               which more complex display objects may be built.

  Requirements: The "Draw" methods for each object require access to the
                Turbo Pascal Graph unit.
                                                                          }

interface

   type

      {==================================================================}
      {                      Object Declarations                         }
      {==================================================================}

      Point = object
               procedure Init;
               procedure Draw;
               procedure Erase;
               procedure Create( PtX, PtY, Colr : integer );
               procedure Move( PtX, PtY : integer );
               procedure SetNewColor( Colr : integer );
               function ColorIs    : integer;
               function XCoordIs    : integer;
               function YCoordIs    : integer;
               function IsVisible : boolean;
            private
               X,Y     : integer;     { screen coordinates of the point }
               Color   : integer;     { object display color }
               Visible : boolean;     { true when object is on-screen }
            end;      { object = Point }

      Circle = object( Point )
               procedure Init;
               procedure Draw;
               procedure Erase;
               procedure Create( PtX, PtY, Colr, Radius : integer );
               procedure Move( PtX, PtY : integer );
               procedure SetNewColor( Colr : integer );
               procedure SetNewSize( Radius : integer );
               function SizeIs : integer;
            private
               Size    : integer;
            end;       { object = Circle }
```

Figure 3.7.   Code listing: unit GEO_OBJ1.PAS.   *(continued)*

```
        Square = object( Circle )
                procedure Draw;
                procedure Erase;
                procedure Create( PtX, PtY, Colr, Radius : integer );
                procedure Move( PtX, PtY : integer );
                procedure SetNewColor( Colr : integer );
                procedure SetNewSize( Radius : integer );
            end;      { object = Square }

        Rectangle = object( Point )
                procedure Init;
                procedure Draw;
                procedure Erase;
                procedure Create(PtX, PtY, Colr, Width, Height : integer);
                procedure Move( PtX, PtY : integer );
                procedure SetNewColor( Colr : integer );
                procedure SetNewSize( Width, Height : integer );
                function SizeXIs : integer;
                function SizeYIs : integer;
              private
                SizeX, SizeY    : integer;
            end;      { object = Rectangle }

{——————————— end of interface section ———————————-}
implementation

  uses Graph;

{======================================================================}
{               Method Definitions for:   Point                        }
{======================================================================}
  procedure Point.Init;
    begin
      X        := 0;                  { Initialize to default position: 0,0 }
      Y        := 0;
      Color    := Graph.GetBkColor;  { Initialize to background color }
      Visible := false;
    end;    { Point.Init }

  procedure Point.Draw;
    begin
      Graph.PutPixel( X, Y, Color );
      Visible := true;
    end;    { Point.Draw }

  procedure Point.Erase;
    { Erase a pixel by redrawing it in the background color }
    begin
      Graph.PutPixel( X, Y, GetBkColor );
      Visible := false;
    end;    { Point.Erase }

  procedure Point.Create( PtX, PtY, Colr : integer );
```

```
    begin
      X      := PtX;
      Y      := PtY;
      Color := Colr;
      Draw;
    end;    { Point.Create }

  procedure Point.Move( PtX, PtY : integer );
    { To move a point, erase it at its present position and recreate
      it at the designated new position.    }
    begin
      Erase;
      Create( { PtX  => } PtX,
              { PtY  => } PtY,
              { Colr => } Color );
    end;    { Point.Move }

  procedure Point.SetNewColor( Colr : integer );
    { When setting a new color, redraw at its present position in the
      newly designated color.    }
    begin
      Create( { PtX  => } X,
              { PtY  => } Y,
              { Colr => } Colr );
    end;    { Point.SetNewColor }

  function Point.ColorIs   : integer;
    begin
      ColorIs  := Color;
    end;    { Point.ColorIs }

  function Point.XCoordIs   : integer;
    begin
      XCoordIs := X;
    end;    { Point.XCoordIs }

  function Point.YCoordIs   : integer;
    begin
      YCoordIs := Y;
    end;    { Point.YCoordIs }

  function Point.IsVisible : boolean;
    begin
      IsVisible := Visible;
    end;    { Point.IsVisible }

{==========================================================================}
{                  Method Definitions for:  Circle                         }
{==========================================================================}
  procedure Circle.Init;
    begin
      Point.Init;      { use ancestor's Init to set most defaults }
      Size   := 0;        { default Radius is 0 }
```

(continued)

```
   end;    { Circle.Init }
procedure Circle.Draw;
   begin
     Graph.SetColor( Color );    { set the active drawing color }
     Graph.Circle( X, Y, Size );
     Visible := true;
   end;    { Circle.Draw }

procedure Circle.Erase;
   { To erase a circle, redraw it in its current position but in the
     background color.  }
   var
     EntryColor   : integer;   { holds drawing color at entry }
   begin
     EntryColor := Graph.GetColor;    { remember drawing color at entry }
     Graph.SetColor( GetBkColor );
     Graph.Circle( X, Y, Size );
     Graph.SetColor( EntryColor ); { restore drawing color to entry val }
     Visible := false;
   end;    { Circle.Erase }

procedure Circle.Create( PtX, PtY, Colr, Radius : integer );
   begin
     X       := PtX;
     Y       := PtY;
     Color := Colr;
     Size   := Radius;
     Draw;
   end;    { Circle.Create }

procedure Circle.Move( PtX, PtY : integer );
   begin
     Erase;
     Create( { PtX     => } PtX,
             { PtY     => } PtY,
             { Colr    => } Color,
             { Radius => } Size     );
   end;    { Circle.Move }

procedure Circle.SetNewColor( Colr : integer );
   { Redraw circle over present position in new color. }
   begin
     Create( { PtX     => } X,
             { PtY     => } Y,
             { Colr    => } Colr,
             { Radius => } Size     );
   end;    { Circle.SetNewColor }

procedure Circle.SetNewSize( Radius : integer );
   begin
     Erase;
     Create( { PtX     => } X,
             { PtY     => } Y,
```

```
                    { Colr   => } Color,
                    { Radius => } Radius      );
      end;    { Circle.SetNewSize }

    function Circle.SizeIs : integer;
      begin
        SizeIs := Size;
      end;    { Circle.SizeIs }

{==========================================================================}
{                  Method Definitions for:  Square                         }
{==========================================================================}
    procedure Square.Draw;
      { Draw square centered at X,Y.   }
      var
        HalfSize  : integer;     { distance from center to sides of square }
      begin
        HalfSize := (Size div 2);
        Graph.SetColor( Color );   { set the active drawing color }
        Graph.Rectangle( { upper left corner  => } X-HalfSize, Y+HalfSize,
                         { lower right corner => } X+HalfSize, Y-HalfSize );
        Visible := true;
      end;    { Square.Draw }

    procedure Square.Erase;
      var
        EntryColor   : integer;   { holds drawing color at entry }
        HalfSize  : integer;      { distance from center to sides of square }
      begin
        EntryColor := Graph.GetColor;    { remember drawing color at entry }
        HalfSize := (Size div 2);
        Graph.SetColor( GetBkColor );   { set the active drawing color }
        Graph.Rectangle( { upper left corner  => } X-HalfSize, Y+HalfSize,
                         { lower right corner => } X+HalfSize, Y-HalfSize );
        Graph.SetColor( EntryColor ); { restore drawing color to entry val }
        Visible := false;
      end;    { Square.Erase }

    procedure Square.Create( PtX, PtY, Colr, Radius : integer );
      begin
        X      := PtX;
        Y      := PtY;
        Color := Colr;
        Size  := Radius;
        Draw;
      end;    { Square.Create }

    procedure Square.Move( PtX, PtY : integer );
      begin
        Erase;
        Create( { PtX    => } PtX,
                { PtY    => } PtY,
                { Colr   => } Color,
```

```
                   { Radius => } Size     );
         end;   { Square.Move }

     procedure Square.SetNewColor( Colr : integer );
        begin
           Create( { PtX     => } X,
                   { PtY     => } Y,
                   { Colr    => } Colr,
                   { Radius => } Size     );
        end;   { Square.SetNewColor }

     procedure Square.SetNewSize( Radius : integer );
        begin
           Erase;
           Create( { PtX     => } X,
                   { PtY     => } Y,
                   { Colr    => } Color,
                   { Radius => } Radius     );
        end;   { Square.SetNewSize }

{========================================================================}
{                Method Definitions for:  Rectangle                      }
{========================================================================}
     procedure Rectangle.Init;
        begin
           Point.Init;     { use ancestor's Init to set most defaults }
           SizeX   := 0;       { default X-width is 0 }
           SizeY   := 0;       { default Y-height is 0 }
        end;   { Rectangle.Init }

     procedure Rectangle.Draw;
        { Draw the Rectangle using X,Y as the upper left corner.  }
        begin
           Graph.SetColor( Color );   { set the active drawing color }
           Graph.Rectangle( { upper left corner  => } X, Y,
                            { lower right corner => } X+SizeX, Y+SizeY );
           Visible := true;
        end;   { Rectangle.Draw }

     procedure Rectangle.Erase;
        var
           EntryColor   : integer;   { holds drawing color at entry }
        begin
           EntryColor := Graph.GetColor;    { remember drawing color at entry }
           Graph.SetColor( GetBkColor );   { set the active drawing color }
           Graph.Rectangle( { upper left corner  => } X, Y,
                            { lower right corner => } X+SizeX, Y-SizeY );
           Graph.SetColor( EntryColor ); { restore drawing color to entry val }
           Visible := false;
        end;   { Rectangle.Erase }

     procedure Rectangle.Create( PtX, PtY, Colr, Width, Height : integer );
        begin
```

```
        X     := PtX;
        Y     := PtY;
        Color := Colr;
        SizeX := Width;
        SizeY := Height;
        Draw;
      end;   { Rectangle.Create }

  procedure Rectangle.Move( PtX, PtY : integer );
    begin
      Erase;
      Create( { PtX    => } PtX,
              { PtY    => } PtY,
              { Colr   => } Color,
              { Width  => } SizeX,
              { Height => } SizeY    );
    end;   { Rectangle.Move }

  procedure Rectangle.SetNewColor( Colr : integer );
    begin
      Create( { PtX    => } X,
              { PtY    => } Y,
              { Colr   => } Colr,
              { Width  => } SizeX,
              { Height => } SizeY    );
    end;   { Rectangle.SetNewColor }

  procedure Rectangle.SetNewSize( Width, Height : integer );
    begin
      Erase;
      Create( { PtX    => } X,
              { PtY    => } Y,
              { Colr   => } Color,
              { Width  => } Width,
              { Height => } Height   );
    end;   { Rectangle.SetNewSize }

  function Rectangle.SizeXIs : integer;
    begin
      SizeXIs := SizeX;
    end;   { Rectangle.SizeXIs }

  function Rectangle.SizeYIs : integer;
    begin
      SizeYIs := SizeY;
    end;   { Rectangle.SizeY }

{======================================================================}
{                        No Initialization Code                        }

end.
```

This code illustrates how a descendent class method can access its ancestor's methods by using "dot notation" to qualify the reference. In this example, *Circle*'s *Init* method invokes its ancestor's (i.e., *Point*'s) *Init* method with the statement "Point.Init;".

RELATIONSHIPS BETWEEN OBJECTS

You may now recognize the ancestor/descendent relationship between the *Point* and *Circle* classes introduced in the *GEO_OBJ1.PAS* unit because I led you down that path. However, if asked to describe a circle object, you might see a different relationship between *Point* and *Circle*. You might, for example, see a circle as an object that has a point at its center and a radius. That doesn't seem to fit into the model we have been building.

The inheritance relationship we have been considering is sometimes called the *derived-from* relationship (C++ actually calls the descendent class a "derived class") or the *kind-of* relationship. In Figure 3.7, we declared *Circle* as a descendent of the *Point* class. That derivation could be done by recognizing that the fields of *Circle* are a superset of those for *Point* and some of the method definitions are common between the two. Or, an analyst might say that a *Circle* is a special kind-of *Point*. That is, the *Circle* is a *Point* that is spread out by its *Radius*. This may not be the most obvious way of visualizing objects of these two classes. Fortunately, inheritance is not the only possible relationship between objects.

An alternative declaration for *Circle* illustrates a different point of view regarding the relationship between *Circle* and *Point*. This time, the analyst sees the (*Center*) *Point* as being a *part-of* the *Circle*. This representation of a circle might be expressed by the following class declaration:

```
Circle = object
        procedure Init;
        procedure Draw;
        procedure Erase;
        procedure Create ( CenterPt : Point;
                            Radius : integer );
        procedure Move ( PtX, PtY : integer );
        procedure SetNewColor ( Colr : integer );
        procedure SetNewSize ( Radius : integer );
        function ColorIs     : integer;
        function XCoordIs : integer;
        function YCoordIs : integer;
        function SizeIs      : integer;
        function IsVisible   : integer;
    private
        Center  : Point;
        Size    : integer;
    end;    { object = Circle }
```

Here, the *Center* (an instance of the class *Point*) of the circle is declared as a field of the class *Circle*. This represents the *Center* as a *part-of* the definition of the circle. Clearly this is a different view of the class *Circle* than that expressed in the unit *GEO_OBJ1.PAS*.

There are several implications of using the *part-of* relationship. For example, notice how the client must create an instance of the class *Point* to pass in as a parameter to *Create* an instance of the class *Circle*. Then, to change any of the fields of *Center*, a message must be passed to that object. Finally, the access methods that were inherited by *Circle* in *GEO_OBJ1.PAS* (namely *ColorIs, XCoordIs, YCoordIs*, and *IsVisible*) must be explicitly defined. The implementation of each of these will require explicitly sending a message to *Center* to invoke its access methods.

The *part-of* relationship may result in needing more code because nothing is inherited. However, it may more naturally reflect the analyst's view of the problem environment. Which is correct? Which is better? That will depend on the actual problem being considered. At this point, it is only important that you recognize that there is more than one relationship between objects, and although inheritance is a powerful characteristic of object-oriented programming, it is not the only relationship between two objects.

NOT EVERYTHING IN AN OBJECT-ORIENTED SYSTEM NEED BE AN OBJECT

It is an important concept of practical object-oriented programming that *not everything that is programmed needs to be an object*. In the next two program examples, two separate cases of nonobjects are introduced.

The first case of a nonobject entity is sometimes called a *free subprogram*.

> **Free Subprogram:** a procedure/function that provides a utility operation that is best not assigned as a method to a single class.

Free subprograms are useful in reducing the dependencies between classes. For example, numerous types of graphics objects could be defined. The *Geometric Objects* unit just examined must execute with the display in its graphics mode. A method could be added to the *Point* class to initialize the graphics mode. However, later we will have other graphics mode objects that will not be related to the *Geometric Objects*.

Another approach might be to define a *DisplayDevice* class for which the graphics mode initialization is assigned as a method. But, if there is no other basis for declaring a class (e.g., no state or value to be retained), then such a class serves no purpose other than to collect related procedures and functions.

Sometimes it is more flexible to isolate a utility operation from any single object. The *GrafInit* unit provided in Figure 3.8 suggests such a single function. When this function is invoked, it performs an automatic graphics adaptor mode detection and initialization and returns the status of this operation. The technique employed is specified by Borland in the Turbo Pascal 6.0 Programmer's Guide.

To use this unit, you will probably have to change the *BGIFilePath* constant to reflect the drive and path to the graphics driver routines in your installation.

```pascal
unit GrafInit;

{ Program:     Graphics Mode Initialization
  Author:      John R. Ellis
  Last Update: 20 June 1991
  Copyright (c) 1991 by John R. Ellis

  Description: This unit provides a utility routine to initialize the
               graphics mode.

  Requirements: Uses the standard Turbo Pascal Graph Unit.
                                                                      }

interface

  const
     { customize path to your *.BGI files for your Turbo installation }
     BGIFilePath = 'C:\Turbo\BGI';

  function GrafInitSuccess : integer; { returns error code; 0 = success }

{------------- end of interface section -------------}
implementation

  uses Crt,Graph;

  function GrafInitSuccess  : integer;
    var
      GDriver, GMode    : integer;
    begin
       { automatic graphics mode selection }
       DetectGraph( GDriver, GMode );
       InitGraph( GDriver, GMode, BGIFilePath );
       GrafInitSuccess := GraphResult;
    end;    { GrafInitSuccess }

{=====================================================================}
{                      No Initialization Code                         }

end.
```

Figure 3.8.   Code listing:unit GRAFINIT.PAS.

THE MAIN PROGRAM, THE MANIPULATOR OF OBJECTS

The second type of nonobject entity is the *main program*. While our analysis methodology will attempt to isolate application-specific concerns from our objects, the main program will necessarily reflect the personality of the particular problem being solved.

Our example, *Targets*, is no exception. This program simulates an aircraft weapons officer attempting to lock a missile system onto a target detected on the display. The program first generates a background of random pixels. Then it places a small square target indicator in the center of the display and a missile system sight, a white circle, near the bottom center of the display. The target then begins to wander around the screen, attempting to evade our attacks. By pressing the cursor arrow keys, the weapons officer can move the sight reticle. When the sight covers the target, its color changes to red, reflecting a "missile-lock" state. Missiles are fired by pressing the Enter key. A missile fired during missile lock will destroy the target; otherwise it will miss. After the target is destroyed, pressing any key will terminate the program. This logic is implemented in the program *TARGETS.PAS*.

In Turbo Pascal, the main program is identifiable by the keyword *program* followed by the program name. In the program listing in Figure 3.11 for the program *Targets*, the "uses" statement immediately follows the program name declaration. This statement makes our geometric objects available to *Targets*.

In the variable declaration section, instances of all objects used by *Targets* are declared. *APoint* is an object instantiated from the class *Point*, while *Target* is instantiated from *Square*, and *Sight* is instantiated from *Circle*. Finally, an array of class *Square* objects is instantiated as *Explosion*.

The program first initializes the graphics mode. This section of code will be the same for virtually any graphics mode program you may write.

Next the background pattern is drawn. Remember that only one instance of *Point* was declared. A short loop recreates the single instance of *APoint* 10,000 times. This is quite distinct from creating 10,000 instances of *Point*. When a message is sent to *APoint* to invoke its *Create* method while it is already *Visible*, a new pixel is drawn on the screen and the parameters of the new pixel are stored in *APoint*'s fields. The image based on the former values of *APoint* remains on the screen as a visible side effect of not erasing the image before all knowledge of its parameters was lost by the newly assigned field values.

The program then creates the *Target* and *Sight* reticle images (as shown in Figure 3.9) in their initial positions:

```
Target.Create( { PtX    => } TargetX,
               { PtY    => } TargetY,
               { Colr   => } Green,
               { Radius => } 8            );
```

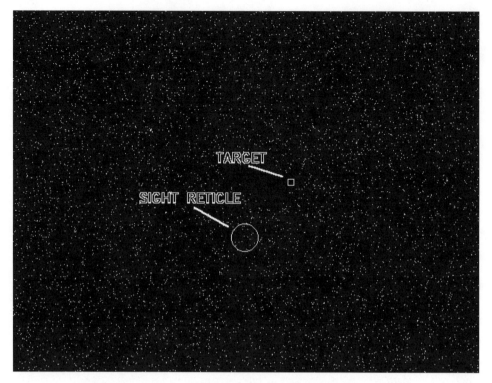

Figure 3.9. The screen Image for the TARGETS program.

```
Sight.Create(  { PtX     => } SightX,
               { PtY     => } SightY,
               { Colr    => } White,
               { Radius  => } 18              );
```

At this point, movement of the *Target* and the *Sight* is computed and the two object positions are compared. If the *Target* is within the coverage of the *Sight*, then the color of *Sight* is changed to red and the *LockedOn* Boolean is set to "true."

The "firing" logic is handled by the code:

```
if (CntrlChar = EnterKey) and LockedOn
  then
    begin                        { shot hit the target }
      Target.Erase;
      for i := 1 to 64 do
        Explosion[i].Create(
                { PtX     => } TargetX,
                { PtY     => } TargetY,
```

```
                  { Colr   => } (i mod MaxColor),
                  { Radius => } Target.SizeIs + i*6 );
       for i := 1 to 64 do
         Explosion[i].Erase;
       Sight.SetNewColor( { Colr => } white );
       Exit := true;
       repeat
         until KeyPressed;
   end
```

If the Enter key is pressed while *LockedOn* is "true," then a sequence of events occurs. First, a message is sent to *Target* to invoke its *Erase* method. Then, each of the 64 instances of the array object *Explosion* is individually created. This is contrasted with the 10,000 recreations of *APoint*, where the images remained on the screen as residual side effects. Here, each of the concentric squares in *Explosion* (see Figure 3.10) has individual identity. It is therefore possible to send a message to each, in turn, to invoke its *Erase* method. Finally, the *Sight* color is returned to white and exit from the loop is enabled.

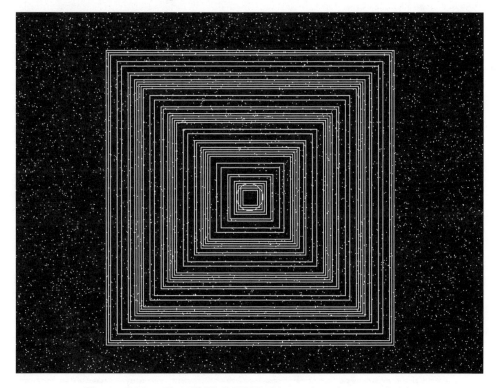

Figure 3.10. The "EXPLOSION" object, when the target is hit.

```
{ Program:      Targets: An Inheritance Demonstration Main Program
  Filename:     Targets.PAS
  Author:       John R. Ellis
  Last Update: 5 July 1991
  Copyright (c) 1991 by John R. Ellis

  Description:  This is a main line program which demonstrates object
                inheritance, using the Geometric Objects unit.

                This program instantiates a square "target" and a circle
                "sight" object.  The target moves randomly around the
                screen while the sight moves in response to the arrow
                keys.  When the sight is over the target, the sight
                changes color, simulating "target lock-on".  Pressing
                the Enter key during lock-on destroys the target.

  Requirements: Uses the standard Turbo Pascal Graph Unit.
                                                                          }

program Targets;

  uses Crt,Graph,GrafInit,Geo_Obj1;

const
  { the following constants define the control key codes }
  LeftArrow  = 75;
  RightArrow = 77;
  UpArrow    = 72;
  DownArrow  = 80;
  EnterKey   = 13;

    function CommandInputIs : integer;
      var
        Ch  : char;
      begin
        if KeyPressed
          then
            begin
              Ch := readkey;
              if ord(Ch) = EnterKey
                then CommandInputIs := EnterKey
                else if ord(Ch) = 0
                  then
                    begin
                      Ch := readkey;
                      CommandInputIs := ord(Ch);
                    end
                  else
                    CommandInputIs := 0;
            end;
      end;    { CommandInputIs }
```

Figure 3.11. Code listing: program TARGETS.PAS.

```
    var
          { object instance creation...... }
      APoint    : Point;      { from Geometric Objects unit }
      Target    : Square;     { from Geometric Objects unit }
      Sight     : Circle;     { from Geometric Objects unit }
      Explosion : array[1..64] of Square;
          { other variables used by the program...... }
      GError             : integer;
      MaxColor           : integer;   { greatest color value }
      MaxX               : integer;   { greatest X-axis value }
      MaxY               : integer;   { greatest Y-axis value }
      CntrlChar          : integer;   { keyboard input control character }
      SightX, SightY     : integer;   { coordinates of Sight on screen }
      TargetX, TargetY   : integer;   { coordinates of Target on screen }
      LockedOn           : boolean;   { true when sight over target }
      Exit               : boolean;   { controls main loop exit }
      i                  : integer;

begin
  Randomize;
      { Do the graphics mode set-up.............. }
  GError := GrafInitSuccess;
  if GError <> grOK
    then
      begin
        writeln('Graphics error:  ',GraphErrorMsg(GError) );
        writeln('Program aborted...');
        halt( 1 );
      end;
  MaxX     := GetMaxX;        { your graphics adaptor dependent... }
  MaxY     := GetMaxY;
  MaxColor := GetMaxColor;
  ClearDevice;
      { initialize the object instances.... }
  APoint.Init;
  Target.Init;
  Sight.Init;
  for i := 1 to 64 do
     Explosion[i].Init;
      { Draw the Target and Sight in their starting positions... }
  TargetX := MaxX div 2;   { start target at center of the screen }
  TargetY := MaxY div 2;
  SightX  := MaxX div 2;   { start sight centered near bottom of screen }
  SightY  := MaxY - 24;
      { Draw a background;  recreate the same instance over and over }
  for i := 1 to 10000 do
    APoint.Create( { PtX  => } random( MaxX ),
                   { PtY  => } random( MaxY ),
                   { Colr => } random( MaxColor ) );
  Target.Create( { PtX    => } TargetX,
                 { PtY    => } TargetY,
                 { Colr   => } Green,
                 { Radius => } 8          );
```

(continued)

```
Sight.Create(   { PtX    => } SightX,
                { PtY    => } SightY,
                { Colr   => } White,
                { Radius => } 18          );
LockedOn := false;
Exit := false;
while not Exit do
  begin
      { ......move the target randomly........ }
    TargetX := TargetX + round( 4.0 * (Random - 0.5) );
    if TargetX > MaxX
      then  TargetX := MaxX - 1
      else if TargetX < 0
             then TargetX := 0;
    TargetY := TargetY + round( 4.0 * (Random - 0.5) );
    if TargetY > MaxY
      then  TargetY := MaxY - 1
      else if TargetY < 0
             then TargetY := 0;
    Target.Move( { PtX => } TargetX,
                 { PtY => } TargetY );
      { ......move sight in response to user input....... }
    CntrlChar := CommandInputIs;
    if (CntrlChar = EnterKey) and LockedOn
      then
        begin             { shot hit the target }
          Target.Erase;
          for i := 1 to 64 do
            begin
              Explosion[i].Create( { PtX    => } TargetX,
                                   { PtY    => } TargetY,
                                   { Colr   => } (i mod MaxColor),
                                   { Radius => } Target.SizeIs + i*6 );
              sound( i * 100 )
            end;
          for i := 1 to 64 do
            begin
              Explosion[i].Erase;
              nosound
            end;
          Sight.SetNewColor( { Colr => } white );
          Exit := true;
          repeat
            until KeyPressed;
        end
      else
        case CntrlChar of
          UpArrow    : if SightY > 0
                          then
                            begin
                              SightY := SightY - 5;
                              Sight.Move( { PtX => } SightX,
                                          { PtY => } SightY );
```

```
                              end;
             DownArrow  : if SightY < MaxY
                             then
                                 begin
                                    SightY := SightY + 5;
                                    Sight.Move( { PtX => } SightX,
                                                { PtY => } SightY );
                                 end;
             RightArrow : if SightX < MaxX
                             then
                                 begin
                                    SightX := SightX + 5;
                                    Sight.Move( { PtX => } SightX,
                                                { PtY => } SightY );
                                 end;
             LeftArrow  : if SightX > 0
                             then
                                 begin
                                    SightX := SightX - 5;
                                    Sight.Move( { PtX => } SightX,
                                                { PtY => } SightY );
                                 end;
        end;   { case }
     if not LockedOn
        then            { ......check for Lock-On condition...... }
          begin
            if (abs(SightX - TargetX) < 11)and(abs(SightY - TargetY) < 11)
               then     { ......Lock-On conditions satisified...... }
                 begin
                    LockedOn := true;
                    Sight.SetNewColor( { Colr => } red );
                    sound( 220 );
                 end
          end
        else           { ......now Locked-On, check for loss of lock...... }
          if (abs(SightX - TargetX) > 15) or (abs(SightY - TargetY) > 15)
             then       { ......loss of Lock...... }
               begin
                  LockedOn := false;
                  Sight.SetNewColor( { Colr => } white );
                  nosound;
               end;
     end;   { loop }
       { final clean-up before exit....... }
     CloseGraph;
     ClearDevice;

end.
```

The final logic in the main loop determines when a target lock-on state is achieved, and conversely lost. Notice that the tolerances between achieving and losing "lock" are different. This provides a measure of *hysteresis* to reduce the sensitivity to minor fluctuations of position near the threshold point. This is a commonly used technique in embedded real-time systems.

SUMMARY

In this chapter, we introduced numerous essential concepts associated with object-oriented programming.

The central theme of this chapter is *inheritance*, based on *class hierarchy trees* that graphically illustrate the ancestor/descendent relationships among classes. We discussed the limitations of *linear inheritance* and how some object-oriented languages (but not Turbo Pascal) offer an alternative that permits characteristics to be inherited from multiple ancestors. *Abstract classes* were identified as key building blocks for a reuse library, which is most practically built around specific problem domains.

In the first full program example, a reusable unit of basic geometric objects was created. This unit included three generations of objects. The lowest descendent of this simple hierarchy (i.e., *Squares*), without declaring any fields of its own, demonstrated inheriting both of its ancestors' fields (screen coordinates and color form *Point* and size from *Circle*) when instances of *Square* were drawn on the display. These fields were accessed by *Square*'s methods as if they had been declared explicitly for *Square*.

This chapter also introduced a relationship between objects other than inheritance. The *part-of* relationship was illustrated by redefining the *Circle* class so that it was not descended from *Point*, but rather included a field that was an instance of *Point*. This made the instance of *Point* a *part-of* a circle rather than a descendent of its class.

Finally, two types of nonobjects were presented. The first, the *free subprogram*, represents a utility program not properly attached to any single object/class. The other is the main program, of which there must be at least one for each system.

PRACTICE

1. Write a program that declares four instances of the class *Square*. Arrange these objects on the display in the shape of the inverted "T," as are the cursor control keys on many PC keyboards. As each cursor key is pressed, change the color of the corresponding key on the display. When the key is released, redraw the corresponding square in its previous color. End the program when the Enter key is pressed.

2. Certain aircraft displays portray the aircraft altitude as a small triangular "bug" that moves up and down a scale proportional to the aircraft's altitude (see Figure 3.12). For this exercise, write a program with two objects. One will be a straight vertical line, representing the scale. The other implements the "bug." When the up arrow key is pressed, increase the aircraft altitude, causing the bug to move up the scale. Conversely, when the down arrow key is pressed, decrease the aircraft altitude, causing

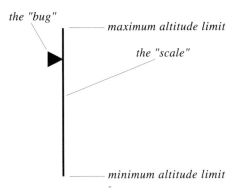

Figure 3.12. The objects in a very simple aircraft display.

the bug to move down the scale. Limit the movement of the bug so it can't move beyond the ends of the scale line. Use descendents of objects defined in the Geometric Objects unit, if it makes creation of these new objects easier.

3. Computer-generated aircraft displays usually include some type of heading indicator strip across the top of the screen, similar to the one shown in Figure 3.13. As the aircraft changes heading, the strip "slides" left or right so that the actual heading is at the center, over the fixed-position, inverted

Figure 3.13. Heading indicator object.

"V" marker. The solid *bug* might be used to show the computed bearing to a geographic point, such as a navigation waypoint or a mission target. Create the objects necessary to generate and update such a heading indicator strip. Test your object by responding to the left and right cursor key inputs to change your simulated aircraft heading.

*If you see in any given situation only what everybody
else can see, you can be said to be so much a
representative of your culture that you are a victim of it.*
— S.I. Hayakawa

Chapter **4**

Inheritance with Virtual Methods

The primary advantage of inheritance is that descendent classes need not duplicate the definition of fields and methods that are already available from an
ancestor class. Having said that, consider the object classes *Circle* and *Square*,
defined in the unit *Geo_Obj1* (Geometric Objects) in Chapter 3. In particular,
examine the definition of some of the methods from each of these classes:

```
procedure Circle.Create( PtX, PtY, Colr, Radius :
                         integer );
   begin
      X     := PtX;
      Y     := PtY;
      Color := Colr;
      Size  := Radius;
      Draw;
   end;   { Circle.Create }
```

```
procedure Square.Create( PtX, PtY, Colr, Radius :
                             integer );
  begin
    X     := PtX;
    Y     := PtY;
    Color := Colr;
    Size  := Radius;
    Draw;
  end;   { Square.Create }

procedure Circle.Move( PtX, PtY : integer );
  begin
    Erase;
    Create( { PtX    => } PtX,
            { PtY    => } PtY,
            { Colr   => } Color,
            { Radius => } Size          );
  end;   { Circle.Move }

procedure Square.Move( PtX, PtY : integer );
  begin
    Erase;
    Create( { PtX    => } PtX,
            { PtY    => } PtY,
            { Colr   => } Color,
            { Radius => } Size          );
  end;   { Square.Move }

procedure Circle.SetNewColor( Colr : integer );
  begin
    Create( { PtX    => } X,
            { PtY    => } Y,
            { Colr   => } Colr,
            { Radius => } Size          );
  end;   { Circle.SetNewColor }

procedure Square.SetNewColor( Colr : integer );
  begin
    Create( { PtX    => } X,
            { PtY    => } Y,
            { Colr   => } Colr,
            { Radius => } Size          );
  end;   { Square.SetNewColor }

procedure Circle.SetNewSize( Radius : integer );
  begin
    Erase;
    Create( { PtX    => } X,
            { PtY    => } Y,
            { Colr   => } Color,
            { Radius => } Radius    );
  end;   { Circle.SetNewSize }

procedure Square.SetNewSize( Radius : integer );
  begin
    Erase;
```

```
    Create( { PtX    => } X,
            { PtY    => } Y,
            { Colr   => } Color,
            { Radius => } Radius   );
  end;   { Square.SetNewSize }
```

Class *Circle*'s method definition code appears to be duplicated in the corresponding methods of descendent class *Square*. This seems to contradict my assertion that *the primary advantage of inheritance is that descendent classes need not duplicate the methods defined in the ancestor class!* If this example truly represents the extent of inheritance, then the usefulness of object-oriented programming would clearly be questionable. However, up to this point, we have been dealing with only one type of inheritance, called *static* inheritance. There is another type of inheritance that avoids this apparent contradiction to my nonduplication assertion.

STATIC VS. VIRTUAL METHODS

Before considering expanded inheritance capabilities, let's understand the mechanism that limits inheritance as we have used it so far. That mechanism concerns how linkages are established between the code that invokes an object's method and the method itself. The linkages used so far are static. That is, they are established during compilation as part of the executable code.

Returning to the respective *Circle* and *Square* class *Move* methods defined above, we find they are the equivalent of the following code using explicit method invocations:

```
    procedure Circle.Move( .... );
      begin
        Circle.Erase;
        Circle.Create( .... );
      end;   { Circle.Move }

    procedure Square.Move( .... );
      begin
        Square.Erase;
        Square.Create( .... );
      end;   { Square.Move }
```

The sequence in which the compiler seeks to satisfy nonexplicit method (or nonmethod procedure and function) invocations begins with the other methods of the current class and then considers the methods of each ancestor class in turn, until the reference can be satisfied. If the class *Square* were to inherit class *Circle*'s *Move* method, then it would not erase the square at the current position (although *Circle*'s *Erase* would clear a few of the square's pixels) but would create a circle at the new position.

The relationship of such static references is illustrated in Figure 4.1.

Our extended inheritance model is built around a new type of method called a *virtual method*.

> **Virtual Method:** a class method whose entry is achieved indirectly through a pointer stored in the class's Virtual Method Table.

> **Virtual Method Table:** a data structure, assigned to a class with declared or inherited virtual methods, which holds (among other things) pointers to the virtual method execution entry point. At runtime, control is passed to virtual methods through their pointers in the VMT.

All classes that contain virtual methods, either through explicit declaration or by inheritance from ancestor classes, are provided with a Virtual Method Table (VMT) during compilation. The VMT contains the entry address for each virtual method available to that class.

A virtual method is distinguished from static methods by having its linkage between the code that invokes the virtual method and the actual entry point not established until runtime. This requires an inherited method to "know" whether it is running in the context of the ancestor or descendent class and to link to methods defined for the proper context. This is a powerful concept that warrants additional elaboration. Contrast the compile-time structure of our *Circle* and *Square* classes illustrated in Figure 4.1, using all static methods, and that shown in Figure 4.2 with both static and virtual methods. Notice that Figure 4.2 does not contain *Create* or *Move* methods in the *Square* class. We want to inherit these methods from *Circle* and expect them correctly to invoke the *Square* class *Draw* and *Erase* methods as appropriate. Notice that the virtual methods contain the code that defines the behavior that differentiates one generation from the next. The general methods that invoke these methods frequently can be static, as with the *Create* or *Move* methods in this example.

In Figure 4.2, the control flow lines at the invocation of *Draw* and *Erase* in the methods *Create* and *Move* are shown to stop at the boundary of the enclosing procedures. This illustrates how the flow of control resulting from these procedure references will not be known until runtime. Control will pass through a VMT, but it could be the VMT belonging to either *Circle* or *Square*, as Figures 4.3 and 4.4 show.

Assume a client program that creates an instance of each class, *Circle* and *Square*, and then sends a message to each of those objects to invoke its respective *Move* method.

When the message is sent to the instance of *Circle*, the reference to the method

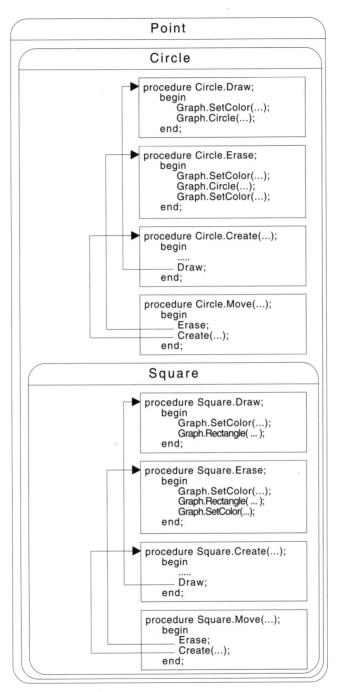

Figure 4.1.   Compile-time linkages for static methods.

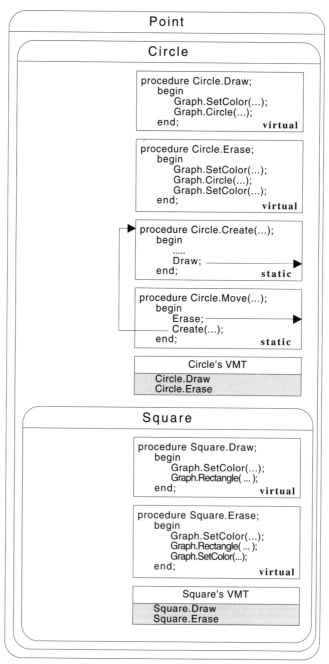

Figure 4.2.   Compile-time linkages for static/virtual methods.

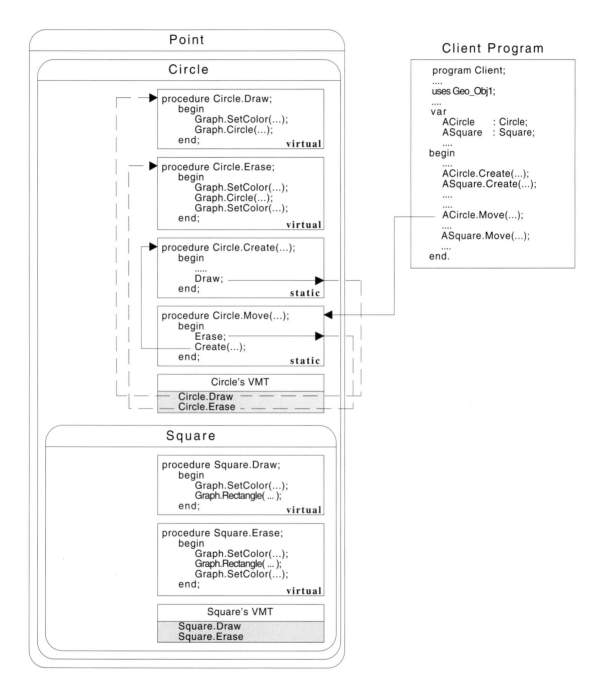

Figure 4.3. Runtime linkages in Circle's context.

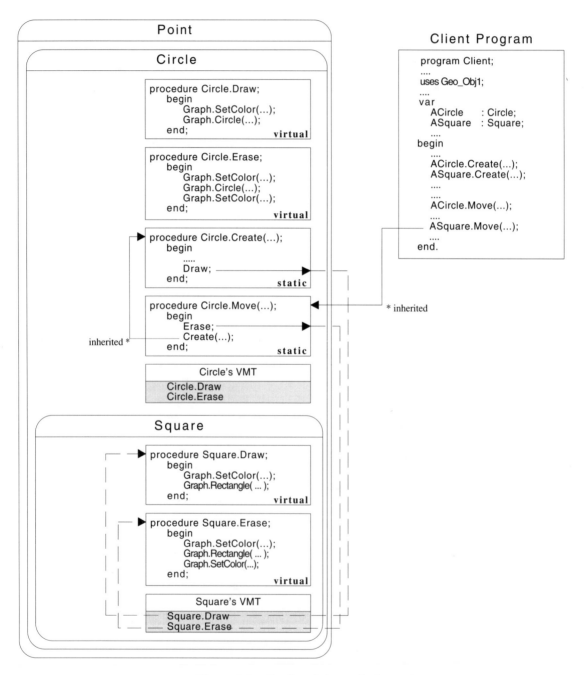

Figure 4.4.   Runtime linkages in Square's context.

Erase is passed through *Circle*'s VMT to enter *Circle.Erase*. When control is returned to *Move*, the reference to the method *Create* is resolved by its static linkage (i.e., determined at compile-time). However, inside *Create* is a reference to the method *Draw*. Because *Draw* is a virtual method, its entry also must be determined through *Circle*'s VMT to cause entry at *Circle.Draw*.

When later the client program sends the message to the instance of *Square*, a similar progression begins. Because there is no *Move* method declared for class *Square*, *Circle*'s *Move* method is inherited and control is passed directly to *Circle.Move*. This is a static linkage. When *Move* reaches the reference to the *Erase* method, it "knows" that it is now executing in the context of an instance of the class *Square* and uses *Square*'s VMT to determine where to enter the *Erase* method. This causes execution of *Square.Erase*. When control is returned to *Move*, reference to the method *Create* causes direct transfer by the static linkage to *Circle.Create*. Again, because *Square* did not specify a *Create* method, the one defined for *Circle* is inherited. And because *Circle.Create* is a static method, its linkage was established during compilation. When again in *Create*, the reference to the method *Draw* is recognized as invoking a virtual method. So control is passed through *Square*'s VMT to *Square.Draw*.

Consider two additional definitions:

Early Binding: establishing the linkage to a method at compilation time, as applies to static methods. The entry address is "hard coded" in-line. The transfer of control is direct.

Late Binding: establishing the linkage to a method at runtime, as applies to virtual methods. The entry address is stored in the Virtual Method Table. The transfer of control is indirect through the VMT entry.

The power of using virtual methods reflects back to the examples of duplicate code at the beginning of this chapter. No longer must the source code associated with ancestor and descendent methods be duplicated merely because they must link to different methods at runtime. Virtual methods allow the runtime environment to sort out the execution context and to select the appropriate methods.

However, this is not automatic. The programmer must take two steps to make this dynamic linkage mechanism work. First, the programmer must explicitly declare which of a class's methods will be virtual. Then, when the client instantiates an object of that class, the client must invoke a special type of method that establishes the link-up between the object and its class's Virtual Method Table.

DECLARING VIRTUAL METHODS

The syntax for declaring *virtual* methods is extremely easy. Merely add the keyword *virtual* to the end of the method declaration in the class definition. For example, our classes *Circle* and *Square* might be declared with virtual methods as follows:

```
Circle = object( Point )
      procedure Init;
      procedure Draw;  virtual;
      procedure Erase; virtual;
      procedure Create(PtX,PtY,Colr,Radius : integer);
      procedure Move( PtX, PtY : integer );
      procedure SetNewColor( Colr : integer );
      procedure SetNewSize( Radius : integer );
      function SizeIs : integer;
   private
      Size    : integer;
   end;       { object = Circle }

Square = object( Circle )
      procedure Draw;  virtual;
      procedure Erase; virtual;
   end;        { object = Square }
```

Note that the biggest difference between this declaration and that in the *Geo_Obj1* unit in Chapter 3, aside from the declaration of virtual methods, is that the class *Square* now only specifies two methods and no fields. Everything else will be inherited directly from *Circle*.

Intuitively, squares are not related to circles, and I've had engineers tell me that this example attacks their sensibilities. However, sometimes you must forgo intuitive notions and analyze the data. As this example illustrates, except for the mechanics of drawing the two shapes, these two forms have everything in common. To achieve the most from inheritance, analysis needs to center on the fields and methods required for various objects, and to classify them purely on the basis of common elements. Set aside the prejudices of prior experiences.

Although declaring virtual methods is straightforward, a few more rules must be followed:

1. Virtual methods may be inherited and therefore need not be declared for every descendent class.

2. Once a method is declared *virtual* in a class, it must be declared *virtual* in all descendent classes that explicitly redeclare it.

3. A descendent class may declare a method *virtual* when the method was nonvirtual (i.e., static) in its ancestor class(es). However, as stated in #2 above, further descendent classes that redeclare the method must declare it *virtual*.

4. Virtual methods within a hierarchy must have exactly the same parameter list in every class in which they are used.

Although this final point may seem restrictive, it is reasonable from an implementation point of view.

CONSTRUCTOR METHODS

To reemphasize a prior point, each *class* having one or more virtual methods is provided with a Virtual Method Table during compilation. The VMT contains pointers to virtual methods that apply for all objects instantiated from that class, so a single VMT is all that is required. However, not all objects are instantiated at compilation time (the use of dynamic objects is discussed in Chapter 6). Therefore, a special mechanism is required to make the linkage between an object and its class's VMT. That mechanism is called a "constructor."

> **Constructor:** a class method that contains implicit code to link an object to its class's Virtual Method Table. The constructor must be invoked before any of the object's virtual methods or the system will fail (possibly indeterminately).

Declaration of the constructor is the same as that of any other method except that the keyword "constructor" replaces "procedure." Our *Circle* and *Square* classes are finally declared correctly as:

```
Circle = object( Point )
    constructor Init;
    procedure Draw;  virtual;
    procedure Erase;  virtual;
    procedure Create(PtX,PtY,Colr,Radius : integer);
    procedure Move( PtX, PtY : integer );
    procedure SetNewColor( Colr : integer );
    procedure SetNewSize( Radius : integer );
    function SizeIs : integer;
  private
    Size    : integer;
  end;     { object = Circle }

Square = object( Circle )
    procedure Draw;  virtual;
    procedure Erase;  virtual;
  end;     { object = Square }
```

By convention, Turbo Pascal constructors are named "Init" although there is no requirement for this (C++ constructors always have the same name as the class). As with all other methods, naming is at the programmer's discretion. By adhering to the convention, the invocation of constructor methods in client programs is more easily recognized. Constructors are normally defined to initialize the fields of an object, either to default values or to values passed as parameters.

There are several rules regarding the use of constructors:

1. All classes that declare or inherit virtual methods must declare at least one constructor method.

2. Constructor methods may be inherited if the descendent class places no new requirements on them.

3. A class's constructor method must be invoked before any of the class's declared or inherited virtual methods. Failure to do so will result in an indeterminate system failure (it has locked up my machine so it wouldn't even respond to Ctrl/Alt/Del).

4. Because a virtual method cannot be invoked before the class constructor, constructor methods cannot themselves be virtual methods.

It is also possible to define multiple constructors, such as to initialize objects in different ways according to the current system operating mode or the information that is available at the time of instantiation. This practice is common in C++.

When to Use Virtual Methods

Thus far I have highlighted the power of using virtual methods. They enhance the reuse capabilities of object-oriented programming systems by making more of a class reusable in descendent classes. Virtual methods obviate the need to recompile ancestors' source code when extending functionality and eliminate duplicating ancestor method code in a descendent. An ancestor class can access methods from descendent classes that were not known at compilation time and, in fact, could be in a different unit that was written days, months, or even years later. The real value of this capability lies in the ability to package objects in documented and pretested modules. These modules can be reused and extended without the redevelopment expense associated with modifying non-object-based modules.

Although good things are almost never free, all of this power has only a minor cost associated with it.

When accessing a virtual method, the entry address is not "hard coded" into the program during compilation, so control will not be directly transferred to a virtual method at execution time. The method entry address is stored in a table, the VMT. There is a small storage penalty for the memory required to hold the VMT of each class using virtual methods. Then, there is a small execution time penalty for execution of the constructor code to link the object instance to its VMT. Finally, again at execution time, there is a minor penalty for the time required to transfer control indirectly through an entry in the VMT.

These penalties are small and normally acceptable when compared to the benefits. Static methods do use slightly less memory and execute slightly faster than virtual methods. In some embedded real-time systems, the difference may be sufficient to dictate avoiding use of virtual methods for specific cases.

As a general guideline in the creation of real-time systems, build for functionality first and later tune for performance. Most real-time systems spend 90% of their time in 10% or less of their code and 50% of their time in 5% of their code. Design and implementation time often is wasted worrying about code that is infrequently executed and does not drive the system performance at all. If there are development savings to be realized, permit minor performance penalties where their effects are inconsequential to overall system performance!

In this case, design your system to use virtual methods. Get the system up and running. Analyze the system performance. Then, if a performance problem exists in an area where virtual methods are used, go back and replace virtual methods with "duplicate code" static methods. It takes but a few keystrokes with modern editors to copy method code from an ancestor class to its descendent classes. However, seldom will replacing virtual methods with static methods solve a performance problem!

In general, you want to *specify virtual methods whenever, in your infinite foresight, you anticipate that an object may need to access one or more of a descendent object's methods.* Fortunately, these methods have two characteristics that aid in their identification. First, they are methods that are referenced by other methods (such as our *Erase* and *Draw* methods are referenced by methods such as *Create* and *Move*). Second, they define behavior that is conspicuous to a given generation and will likely be redefined for descendent classes (as each generation of geometric objects redefines the *Erase* and *Draw* methods).

The decision is moot if the ancestor class has already declared a method to be virtual. All descendent classes that override the ancestor definition by redeclaring the method must declare those methods virtual.

In general, the penalty for using virtual methods is extremely slight and far overshadowed by the benefits.

IMPROVING OUR GEOMETRIC OBJECTS UNIT

In the previous chapter, we introduced a unit containing general-purpose geometric objects to illustrate the basic concepts of inheritance. Then, our knowledge of inheritance was limited to *static inheritance*, and the unit therefore exhibited some undesirable duplications of code. In this chapter, an improved version of the geometric objects unit illustrates proper use of both static and virtual methods.

The first thing you see in our revised unit is that many of the methods that had been declared in the descendent classes *Circle*, *Square*, and *Rectangle* have disappeared. Thanks to making the *Draw* and *Erase* methods virtual in each generation, other methods may be inherited rather than redefined.

Also note that a new method, *SetNewPosition*, was defined for the base class *Point*. This method merely sets the fields *X* and *Y* with values passed as parameters. However, by using this (static) method in defining other methods, rather than invoking the generation unique *Create* method, more methods may be inherited by descendent classes.

In additon, this new method was declared *private*. Because this *SetNewPosition* can change the *point*'s location-designating fields without moving the *point* on the screen, its use by a client can create an inconsistency between a *point*'s current state and its visible representation. To prevent a client from creating such an inconsistency, the method *SetNewPostion* is hidden from clients. A client must use the visible *Move* method to change a point's position.

This minor modification to the original structure is typical of the type of decisions the analyst/designer must make in designing for reuse. The amount of time needed to make such a decision is inconsequential for the experienced object-oriented analyst, but greatly enhances the ability to reuse or extend for reuse an existing set of existing objects.

To verify the proper functionality of our modified unit, compile it and change the *uses* reference in *TARGETS.PAS* from *Geo_Obj1* to *Geo_Objs* (Figure 4.5).

SUMMARY

In this chapter, we highlighted the shortcomings of *static* methods and offered an alternative type of inheritance using *virtual methods*. Virtual methods allow inheriting methods that were unavailable with static linkages. *Early binding* prevents a class method from "knowing" a descendent's methods. On the other hand, virtual method entry data are stored in a *Virtual Method Table*. Entry to virtual methods is determined at runtime, using *late binding*. This is accomplished by an indirect transfer through the method pointer in the VMT.

Guidance was provided suggesting when to use virtual methods. Finally, our geometric objects unit was recreated using a combination of static and virtual methods to illustrate how reusability is enhanced.

```
unit Geo_Objs;

{ Program:     Geometric Objects - Reusable geometric objects
  Author:      John R. Ellis
  Last Update: 6 August 1992
  Copyright (c) 1992 by John R. Ellis

  Description:  This unit provides basic low level geometric objects, from
                which more complex display objects may be built.

  Requirements: The "Draw" methods for each object require access to the
                Turbo Pascal Graph unit.
                                                                       }

interface

   type

      {===================================================================}
      {                      Object Declarations                          }
      {===================================================================}

      Point = object
              constructor Init;
              procedure Draw;  virtual;
              procedure Erase; virtual;
              procedure Create( PtX, PtY, Colr : integer );
              procedure Move( PtX, PtY : integer );
              procedure SetNewColor( Colr : integer );
              function ColorIs    : integer;
              function XCoordIs    : integer;
              function YCoordIs    : integer;
              function IsVisible : boolean;
          private
              X,Y     : integer;      { screen coordinates of the point }
              Color   : integer;      { object display color }
              Visible : boolean;      { true when object is on-screen }
              procedure SetNewLocation( PtX, PtY : integer );
          end;      { object = Point }

      Circle = object( Point )
              constructor Init;
              procedure Draw;  virtual;
              procedure Erase; virtual;
              procedure Create( PtX, PtY, Colr, Radius : integer );
              procedure SetNewSize( Radius : integer );
              function SizeIs : integer;
           private
              Size    : integer;
          end;      { object = Circle }

      Square = object( Circle )
```

Figure 4.5. Code listing: unit GEO_OBJS.PAS.   *(continued)*

```
               procedure Draw;  virtual;
               procedure Erase; virtual;
          end;     { object = Square }

     Rectangle = object( Point )
               constructor Init;
               procedure Draw;  virtual;
               procedure Erase; virtual;
               procedure Create(PtX, PtY, Colr, Width, Height : integer);
               procedure SetNewSize( Width, Height : integer );
               function SizeXIs : integer;
               function SizeYIs : integer;
            private
               SizeX, SizeY   : integer;
          end;     { object = Rectangle }

{————————-- end of interface section ————————-}
implementation

  uses Graph;

{======================================================================}
{               Method Definitions for:  Point                         }
{======================================================================}
  constructor Point.Init;
    begin
      X        := 0;              { Initialize to default position: 0,0 }
      Y        := 0;
      Color    := Graph.GetBkColor;  { Initialize to background color }
      Visible := false;
    end;   { Point.Init }

  procedure Point.Draw;
    begin
      Graph.PutPixel( X, Y, Color );
      Visible := true;
    end;   { Point.Draw }

  procedure Point.Erase;
    { Erase a pixel by redrawing it in the background color }
    begin
      Graph.PutPixel( X, Y, GetBkColor );
      Visible := false;
    end;   { Point.Erase }

  procedure Point.SetNewLocation( PtX, PtY : integer );
    begin
      X      := PtX;
      Y      := PtY;
    end;   { Point.SetNewLocation }

  procedure Point.Create( PtX, PtY, Colr : integer );
    begin
```

```
      SetNewLocation( { PtX => } PtX,
                      { PtY => } PtY );
      SetNewColor(   { Colr => } Colr );    { this method draws point too }
    end;   { Point.Create }

  procedure Point.Move( PtX, PtY : integer );
    { To move a point, erase it at its present position and recreate
      it at the designated new position.    }
    begin
      Erase;
      SetNewLocation( { PtX => } PtX,
                      { PtY => } PtY );
      Draw;
    end;   { Point.Move }

  procedure Point.SetNewColor( Colr : integer );
    { When setting a new color, redraw at its present position in the
      newly designated color.    }
    begin
      Color := Colr;
      Draw;
    end;   { Point.SetNewColor }

  function Point.ColorIs   : integer;
    begin
      ColorIs   := Color;
    end;   { Point.ColorIs }

  function Point.XCoordIs   : integer;
    begin
      XCoordIs := X;
    end;   { Point.XCoordIs }

  function Point.YCoordIs   : integer;
    begin
      YCoordIs := Y;
    end;   { Point.YCoordIs }

  function Point.IsVisible : boolean;
    begin
      IsVisible := Visible;
    end;   { Point.IsVisible }

{========================================================================}
{               Method Definitions for:  Circle                          }
{========================================================================}
  constructor Circle.Init;
    begin
      Point.Init;     { use ancestor's Init to set most defaults }
      Size   := 0;        { default Radius is 0 }
    end;   { Circle.Init }

  procedure Circle.Draw;
```

```
   begin
     Graph.SetColor( Color );    { set the active drawing color }
     Graph.Circle( X, Y, Size );
     Visible := true;
   end;    { Circle.Draw }


 procedure Circle.Erase;
   { To erase a circle, redraw it in its current position but in the
     background color.  }
   var
     EntryColor   : integer;    { holds drawing color at entry }
   begin
     EntryColor := Graph.GetColor;    { remember drawing color at entry }
     Graph.SetColor( GetBkColor );
     Graph.Circle( X, Y, Size );
     Graph.SetColor( EntryColor );{ restore drawing color to entry val }
     Visible := false;
   end;    { Circle.Erase }

 procedure Circle.Create( PtX, PtY, Colr, Radius : integer );
   begin
     Size := Radius;
     Point.Create( { PtX  => } PtX,
                   { PtY  => } PtY,
                   { Colr => } Colr );
   end;    { Circle.Create }

 procedure Circle.SetNewSize( Radius : integer );
   { redraw circle in new size }
   begin
     Erase;
     Size := Radius;
     Draw;
   end;    { Circle.SetNewSize }

 function Circle.SizeIs : integer;
   begin
     SizeIs := Size;
   end;    { Circle.SizeIs }

{==========================================================================}
{                 Method Definitions for:  Square                          }
{==========================================================================}
 procedure Square.Draw;
   { Draw square centered at X,Y.  }
   var
     HalfSize  : integer;    { distance from center to sides of square }
   begin
     HalfSize := (Size div 2);
     Graph.SetColor( Color );   { set the active drawing color }
     Graph.Rectangle( { upper left corner  => } X-HalfSize, Y+HalfSize,
                      { lower right corner => } X+HalfSize, Y-HalfSize );
```

```
      Visible := true;
   end;    { Square.Draw }

 procedure Square.Erase;
    var
      EntryColor    : integer;    { holds drawing color at entry }
      HalfSize  : integer;     { distance from center to sides of square }
    begin
      EntryColor := Graph.GetColor;     { remember drawing color at entry }
      HalfSize := (Size div 2);
      Graph.SetColor( GetBkColor );    { set the active drawing color }
      Graph.Rectangle( { upper left corner  => } X-HalfSize, Y+HalfSize,
                       { lower right corner => } X+HalfSize, Y-HalfSize );
      Graph.SetColor( EntryColor );{ restore drawing color to entry val }
      Visible := false;
    end;    { Square.Erase }

{=======================================================================}
{                Method Definitions for:  Rectangle                     }
{=======================================================================}
 constructor Rectangle.Init;
    begin
      Point.Init;     { use ancestor's Init to set most defaults }
      SizeX    := 0;      { default X-width is 0 }
      SizeY    := 0;      { default Y-height is 0 }
    end;   { Rectangle.Init }

 procedure Rectangle.Draw;
    { Draw the Rectangle using X,Y as the upper left corner.  }
    begin
      Graph.SetColor( Color );    { set the active drawing color }
      Graph.Rectangle( { upper left corner  => } X, Y,
                       { lower right corner => } X+SizeX, Y+SizeY );
      Visible := true;
    end;    { Rectangle.Draw }

 procedure Rectangle.Erase;
    var
      EntryColor    : integer;    { holds drawing color at entry }
    begin
      EntryColor := Graph.GetColor;     { remember drawing color at entry }
      Graph.SetColor( GetBkColor );    { set the active drawing color }
      Graph.Rectangle( { upper left corner  => } X, Y,
                       { lower right corner => } X+SizeX, Y-SizeY );
      Graph.SetColor( EntryColor ); { restore drawing color to entry val }
      Visible := false;
    end;    { Rectangle.Erase }

 procedure Rectangle.Create( PtX, PtY, Colr, Width, Height : integer );
    begin
      SizeX := Width;
      SizeY := Height;
      Point.Create( { PtX  => } PtX,
```

(continued)

```
                        { PtY  => } PtY,
                        { Colr => } Colr );
      end;   { Rectangle.Create }

   procedure Rectangle.SetNewSize( Width, Height : integer );
      begin
        Erase;
        SizeX := Width;
        SizeY := Height;
        Draw;
      end;   { Rectangle.SetNewSize }

   function Rectangle.SizeXIs : integer;
      begin
        SizeXIs := SizeX;
      end;   { Rectangle.SizeXIs }

   function Rectangle.SizeYIs : integer;
      begin
        SizeYIs := SizeY;
      end;   { Rectangle.SizeY }

{========================================================================}
{                         No Initialization Code                         }

   end.
```

PRACTICE

1. Verify that the inverted "T" cursor exercise (#1) from Chapter 3 functions properly with the newly defined geometric objects unit.

2. Repeat Exercise 2 from Chapter 3. Define a class called *Bug* descended from the class *Circle* with no new data fields (i.e., let the size of the symbol be defined by a single size parameter). How few methods are required for the new class?

   Create a new class for linear scale objects. Implement the new class in two ways:

   a. Make an object of the class *Bug* a local variable hidden in the implementation section.

   b. Make the instance of *Bug* a field in the linear scale object.

   What are the advantages and disadvantages of each implementation?

3. Create an engine temperature gauge object, as shown in Figure 4.6. Use two instances of the Geometric Objects unit class *Circle* to make the bezel. Use the up and down cursor arrow keys to change the temperature readings, but don't permit the needle to go beyond the limits of the face of the instrument.

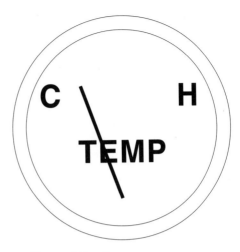

Figure 4.6.   Temperature gauge.

Chapter **5**

Encapsulation:
Walls around Objects

It is useful to think of objects as if they were protected by impenetrable castle walls, through which access is limited to a few well-placed and guarded gates. Nothing can disturb the well-encapsulated object except as authorized by the guards at the gates.

This analogy illustrates a concept that is strictly enforced by very few object-oriented programming languages. In fact, inflexible, unconditional enforcement of encapsulation is not always desirable for real-time systems. In most systems, the walls are not nearly as formidable as they appear. Objects are hidden behind "translucent walls" of client discipline. As long as users choose to abide by the rules and respect the sanctity of the object's encapsulation, it exists. But nothing precludes an undisciplined user from violating the thinly veiled protection of the object (e.g., by typecasting C++ object pointers).

In Chapter 3 we considered class declarations and the corresponding definitions of the methods declared for each class. At the very start of the program, you found the Turbo Pascal keyword *interface* preceding class declarations. Following object (and nonobject) declarations appears the Turbo Pascal keyword *implementation*, followed by the code that defines the behaviors of the class methods. These two sections of the unit, its *interface* and *implementation* sections (roughly corresponding to an Ada package *specification* and *body*), define what in the unit is visible and invisible, respectively, to clients. Theoretically, users of a unit need only see the *interface* section of a unit to use that unit. Whatever is placed in the *implementation* section is "hidden" from the client. Clients should rely only on the "contract" defined by the *interface* section, and assume nothing regarding how that contract is fulfilled in the *implementation* section.

In performance sensitive real-time systems, it may be necessary to make certain object fields globally visible to improve system throughput. This can be dangerous and impact the software's maintainability. However, at least in systems where the designer has the flexibility to determine the fields' visibilities, there is an option available to resolve certain types of performance problems. As a designer, do not consider this a license to avoid encapsulation. Global visibility should be the rare exception rather than the rule.

Depending on your choice of implementation language, up to three levels of protection are available:

Public: fields and/or methods that are globally visible and therefore are directly accessible by all clients. This level represents a lack of protection. The only level of encapsulation is that provided by the programmer's discipline.

Private: fields and/or methods that are known to the methods of the declaring class, but hidden from descendent objects and external clients.

Protected: fields and/or methods that are known to the methods of the declaring class and all its descendents, but hidden from all external clients.

Object-oriented languages such as Turbo Pascal 5.5 offer only public protection, which is to say, no enforced protection at all.

At the extreme, languages such as Smalltalk consider all fields *private*, such that their values may be manipulated or returned only through the provided methods.

C++ is the only popular language that provides all three categories of protection for both fields and methods.

The protection provided by the *private* declaration of Turbo Pascal 6.0 differs from the definition above. Fields and methods declared *private* in Turbo Pascal 6.0 are completely visible within the *unit* in which they are defined (which could include the main program unit), but are completely hidden in all other units. With the Turbo Pascal 6.0 definition, an object's fields are *not* protected from access by a client in the same unit. Conversely, the methods of descendent classes defined in another unit (or the main program) cannot access the *private* fields of its ancestor classes if they reside in a different unit.

There are several guidelines that, if followed, should strengthen a class's encapsulation. These guidelines can serve as a mechanism by which to develop Turbo Pascal 6.0 objects in the exercises at the end of the next few chapters:

1. Provide *public* methods to read and/or write any field(s) to which a descendent class or client may need access.

2. When writing methods for a class, try to restrict field access to that provided by the read/write methods. This restricts the number of places in the class code that directly read/write the fields of the class.

3. When writing methods for a descendent class, always try to access the ancestor's fields through its access methods. Even if the descendent class has direct visibility into the ancestor's fields, it should not allow widespread direct access to the ancestor's fields.

ENCAPSULATION AND COHESION

Several aspects of encapsulation are worth examining. First, an encapsulated object should exhibit a high degree of functional cohesion. A functionally cohesive "module" is bound by a single objective or goal. In object-oriented programming, that goal encompasses the behavior of the single object.

The *Clocks* unit described in this chapter (listing given in Figure 5.2) demonstrates encapsulation of the behavior of a class that implements a normal time-of-day clock. Its sole purpose is to maintain a display object that looks like the familiar analog clock face.

The *Clocks* unit actually embodies two object classes. The first is an abstract class that could be used to represent any two-hand clock-like dial instrument. The second class, derived from the first, provides the specific behavior of a time-of-day clock.

There are two ways that an analyst or programmer might come to the conclusion that two classes are desired.

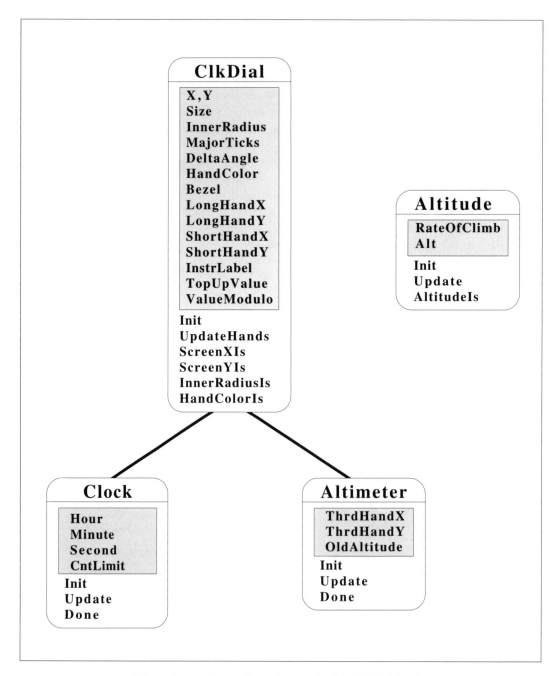

Figure 5.1.   Class Hierarchy tree for DASHPNL1.PAS.

If the immediate problem is to create a display of an aircraft instrument panel on which various standard gauges, dials, and other instruments are to be drawn and updated in real time, then the analyst can look at all the objects to identify common elements. Among these instruments, he discovers that more than one behaves like a clock, having multiple hands in which one moves an increment as the result of the other completing a revolution. Such common characteristics of that group of instruments could be gathered into an abstract class. Then descendent classes, which inherit the common behavior of the abstract ancestor class, add the specific behaviors for particular instruments. In the unit *Clocks*, the abstract class *ClkDial* and its descendent *Clock* are defined.

For a different problem set, you might arrive at the same hierarchy from a different sequence of decisions. Assume that your initial problem has nothing to do with flight instruments. Perhaps you are given a project to develop a desktop toolset, consisting of such objects as a clock, calendar, calculator, and memopad. In this domain, there is no obvious commonality between the clock and other entities of the problem space. Therefore, the analyst would probably define a single *Clock* class with all of the necessary characteristics. When the desktop project is completed, each of the developed classes is placed in a reuse library.

Now the flight instrument panel project arrives, perhaps as part of a flight simulator program. During requirements analysis, the systems analyst searches the reuse library for objects that have possible application to the flight instrument display on the new project. Out pops the *Clock* object class from the desktop toolset project. But this class is very specific, satisfying only the requirement for a time-of-day clock. Unfortunately, it is not adaptable for other instruments, such as the altimeter, which have similar characteristics. The analyst must now decide how to address these other instruments.

One option is simply to create a new *Altimeter* class that duplicates much of the code from the reused *Clock* class. The result would be two classes with no family relationship, only coincidental similarities in their implementing code. This option reflects the traditional approach to reuse. When another clock-like instrument comes along, the whole process is repeated and yet another similar, but unrelated, class is born. If a change is needed to the common characteristics, then it must be made in each class separately.

An object-oriented strategy drives a different thought process. The analyst must examine the *Clock* class to identify which characteristics (fields and methods) are generally applicable to all clock-like instruments and which are specific to a time-of-day clock. The common characteristics are extracted from the *Clock* class and placed in a new abstract ancestor class. The *Clock* class is redeclared as a descendent of the new abstract class. If this process is done properly, then client programs that have declared objects of the *Clock* class should not even notice the change! This strategy logically results in both the abstract ancestor class and the descendent *Clock* class being packaged in the same physical unit, as illustrated in the accompanying code example (Figure 5.2).

The example *Clocks* unit fully encapsulates the behavior of the *Clock* object class. In addition to drawing the image of a clock on the display, it contains the mechanisms by which the current time is maintained. For this example, a somewhat complex time update mechanism that uses one of the PC's interval timers is provided. This mechanism is hidden in the unit's *implementation* and therefore will not directly affect the client.

After declaring variables and constants needed in the *implementation* but not to be visible to the client, a procedure *ISR* (Interrupt Service Routine) is defined. This procedure is linked into the timer interrupt during *Clock.Init* by the statement:

```
SetIntVec( $1C, @ISR );
```

The *SetIntVec* procedure, from the Turbo Pascal *DOS* unit, sets the interrupt vector of the specified interrupt (in this case, 1C *hexadecimal*) to the entry address of the appropriate processing routine (i.e., @*ISR*). Once this vector is established, each time the timer interrupt is raised, control is passed to the procedure *ISR*.

During *Clock.Init*, the timer is programmed with the frequency at which it must raise the timer interrupt. This may range between approximately 18.2 times per second and about 1.19 million times per second. The example is set to raise the interrupt at 20 times per second. So, if the set-up is completed correctly, the procedure *ISR* will be executed automatically at 20 times per second.

In most real-time systems, it would be desirable to have the interrupt service routine determine when the display requires updating and then to update it. Interrupt service routines executing under DOS have a limitation in that they may not raise another interrupt. Because functions such as reading the DOS time-of-day require use of software interrupts, a DOS-based application must use a different mechanism.

So, the example *ISR* merely increments a local counter *cnt*. The method *Clock.Update* compares this counter to a programmed threshold (*CntLimit*, set with a client-provided value in *Clock.Init*). Whenever the counter exceeds the threshold, the current time is read from DOS (via *DOS.GetTime*) and the inherited method *UpdateHands* updates the image on the display. This mechanism provides two benefits. First it reduces the display flicker caused by erasing and redrawing the clock hands repeatedly. It also reduces the amount of processing time spent in the display update. This may not be a factor in the simple client program for this example, but as the number of functions in the system increases, system performance degrades. With this mechanism, the client may request an update as

```
unit Clocks;

{ Program:     Clocks — A library unit which displays a clock
  Author:      John R. Ellis
  Last Update: 17 July 1991
  Copyright (c) 1991 by John R. Ellis

  Description: This unit provides an abstract object class which displays
               two-handed clock like instruments and a descendent class
               which defines a time-of-day clock, including a real-time
               update mechanism.

  Requirements: The "Update" method requires access to the Turbo Pascal
               Graph unit.
                                                                     }
interface

  uses Geo_Objs;

  type

      {====================================================================}
      {                      Object Declarations                          }
      {====================================================================}

      ClkDial = object              { abstract class }
              constructor Init( XPos,YPos : integer; { screen position }
                                Diameter  : integer; { Bezel Diameter }
                                BzlColor  : integer; { Bezel Color }
                                HndColor  : integer; { Color for both }
                                MajorTics : integer; { # of long marks }
                                MinorTics : integer; { # of short marks }
                                InstrLabl : string;  { Label field }
                                BgHandAng : real;    { angle for big hand }
                                SmHandAng : real; { angle for little hand }
                                TopValue  : integer; { 12 o'clock value }
                                ValueMod  : integer );
              procedure UpdateHands( BgHandAng : real;
                                     SmHandAng : real );
              function ScreenXIs     : integer;
              function ScreenYIs     : integer;
              function InnerRadiusIs : integer;
              function HandColorIs   : integer;
            private
              X,Y         : integer;   { screen coords of center point }
              Size        : integer;   { Bezel Diameter }
              InnerRadius : integer;   { inner Bezel radius }
              MajorTicks  : integer;   { # of MajorTick marks }
              DeltaAngle  : real;      { Angle between MajorTick marks }
              HandColor   : integer;   { Hands Color }
              Bezel       : array[1..2] of Circle;
```

Figure 5.2.   Code listing: unit CLOCKS.PAS.   *(continued)*

```
                    LongHandX   : integer;   { end point of "long" hand }
                    LongHandY   : integer;
                    ShortHandX  : integer;   { end point of "short" hand }
                    ShortHandY  : integer;
                    InstrLabel  : string[18];
                    TopUpValue  : integer;
                    ValueModulo : integer;
                end;     { object = ClkDial }

        Clock = object( ClkDial )
                constructor Init( XPos,YPos : integer; { screen position }
                                 Diameter  : integer;   { Bezel Diameter }
                                 BzlColor  : integer;   { Bezel Color }
                                 HndColor  : integer;   { Color for both }
                                 Interval  : word       { 20 pps pulses } );
                procedure Update;
                destructor Done;
              private
                Hour,Minute,Second : word;   { current time of day }
                CntLimit           : word;   { counts update threshold }
                end;     { object = Clocks }
{———————— end of interface section ————————}
implementation

  uses Dos,Graph;

  var
    cnt       : word;       { Interrupt Service Routine tick counter }
    OldTimer  : pointer;    { holds original timer interrupt vector }
  const
    TimerCntrl = $43;       { control parameters for timer setup }
    Timer0     = $40;
    Mode3      = $36;

procedure ISR;  { clock Interrupt Service Routine }
    interrupt;
    begin
      cnt := cnt + 1;
    end;   { ISR }

{========================================================================}
{               Method Definitions for:  ClkDial                         }
{========================================================================}
constructor ClkDial.Init( XPos,YPos : integer; { screen position }
                         Diameter  : integer;   { Bezel Diameter }
                         BzlColor  : integer;   { Bezel Color }
                         HndColor  : integer;   { Color for both }
                         MajorTics : integer;   { # of long marks }
                         MinorTics : integer;   { # of short marks }
                         InstrLabl : string;    { Label field }
                         BgHandAng : real;      { angle for big hand }
                         SmHandAng : real; { angle for little hand }
```

```
                         TopValue   : integer; { 12 o'clock value }
                         ValueMod   : integer );
var
   i,j    : integer;        { iterators }
   Angle           : real;       { angle from vertical of major tick }
   SinAngle        : real;       { sin & cos of Angle }
   CosAngle        : real;
   DeltaMinorAngle : real;       { angle between minor ticks }
   MajorTickLength : integer;  { line length for major tick }
   MinorTickLength : integer;  { line length for minor tick }
   FarX,FarY       : integer;  { coords of far end of tick mark }
   NearX,NearY     : integer;  { coords of near end of tick mark }
begin
   X := XPos;
   Y := YPos;
   InstrLabel   := InstrLabl;
   TopUpValue   := TopValue;
   ValueModulo  := ValueMod;
   LongHandX := X;
   LongHandY := Y;
   ShortHandX := X;
   ShortHandY := Y;
   Size := Diameter;
   MajorTicks := MajorTics;
   HandColor  := HndColor;
   InnerRadius := Size - 3;
   Graph.SetLineStyle( { LineStyle => } SolidLn,
                       { Pattern   => } 0,
                       { Thickness => } NormWidth );
   Bezel[1].Init;         { create outer circle of bezel }
   Bezel[1].Create( { PtX    => } X,
                    { PtY    => } Y,
                    { Colr   => } BzlColor,
                    { Radius => } Size      );
   Bezel[2].Init;         { create inner circle of bezel }
   Bezel[2].Create( { PtX    => } X,
                    { PtY    => } Y,
                    { Colr   => } BzlColor,
                    { Radius => } InnerRadius   );
   MajorTickLength := (InnerRadius) div 7;
   MinorTickLength := (InnerRadius) div 15;
   DeltaAngle      := 2.0 * Pi / MajorTics;
   DeltaMinorAngle := DeltaAngle / (MinorTics+1);
   Angle  := Pi;    { vertical angle from X,Y upward }
     { set graphics parameters for tick marks..... }
   Graph.SetLineStyle( { LineStyle => } SolidLn,
                       { Pattern   => } 0,
                       { Thickness => } NormWidth );
   Graph.SetColor( { Color   => } BzlColor );
   for i := 1 to MajorTics do
     begin
       SinAngle := sin( Angle );
       CosAngle := cos( Angle );
```

(continued)

```
             FarX  := X + round( SinAngle * (InnerRadius) );
             FarY  := Y + round( CosAngle * (InnerRadius) );
             NearX := X + round( SinAngle * (InnerRadius-MajorTickLength) );
             NearY := Y + round( CosAngle * (InnerRadius-MajorTickLength) );
             Graph.Line( { X1 => } NearX,
                         { Y1 => } NearY,
                         { X2 => } FarX,
                         { Y2 => } FarY );     { Draw major tick mark }
             for j := 1 to MinorTics do
               begin
                 SinAngle := sin( Angle + j*DeltaMinorAngle );
                 CosAngle := cos( Angle + j*DeltaMinorAngle );
                 FarX  := X + round( SinAngle * (InnerRadius) );
                 FarY  := Y + round( CosAngle * (InnerRadius) );
                 NearX := X + round( SinAngle*(InnerRadius-MinorTickLength));
                 NearY := Y + round( CosAngle*(InnerRadius-MinorTickLength));
                 Graph.Line( { X1 => } NearX,
                             { Y1 => } NearY,
                             { X2 => } FarX,
                             { Y2 => } FarY );     { Draw minor tick mark }
               end;
             Angle := Angle + DeltaAngle;
           end;    { MajorTick loop }
         { Display the hands in their initial position..... }
       UpdateHands( { BgHandAng => } BgHandAng,
                    { SmHandAng => } SmHandAng );
     end;   { ClkDial.Init }

procedure ClkDial.UpdateHands( BgHandAng : real;
                               SmHandAng : real );

    var
      i             : integer;
      Angle         : real;
      SinAngle      : real;
      CosAngle      : real;
      DisVal        : integer;  { label for positions around dial }
      FarX, FarY    : integer;  { far end of hand's line }
      BgHandLength  : integer;
      SmHandLength  : integer;
      MultX,DivX    : word;

        function MakeStr( i : integer ) : string;
        var
          s : string;
        begin
          str( i,s );
          MakeStr := s;
        end;  { local subprogram: MakeStr }

    begin
        { Erase Old Hands first }
      Graph.SetColor( { Color => } Graph.GetBkColor );
```

```
Graph.SetLineStyle( { LineStyle => } SolidLn,
                     { Pattern    => } 0,
                     { Thickness  => } NormWidth );
Graph.Line( { X1 => } X,
            { Y1 => } Y,
            { X2 => } LongHandX,
            { Y2 => } LongHandY );
Graph.SetLineStyle( { LineStyle => } SolidLn,
                     { Pattern    => } 0,
                     { Thickness  => } ThickWidth );
Graph.Line( { X1 => } X,
            { Y1 => } Y,
            { X2 => } ShortHandX,
            { Y2 => } ShortHandY );
   { Rewrite the Label field..... }
Graph.SetColor( { Color   => } White );
Graph.SetTextStyle( { Font      => } SansSerifFont,
                     { Direction => } HorizDir,
                     { CharSize  => } 4 );
MultX := InnerRadius;
DivX := 120;
SetUserCharSize( { MultX => } MultX,
                 { DivX  => } DivX,
                 { MultY => } MultX,
                 { DivY  => } DivX   );
Graph.SetTextJustify( { Horiz => } CenterText,
                       { Vert  => } CenterText );
Graph.OutTextXY( { X          => } X,
                 { Y          => } Y - (InnerRadius div 3),
                 { TextString => } InstrLabel );
   { Rewrite the numbers...... }
DivX := 150;
SetUserCharSize( { MultX => } MultX,
                 { DivX  => } DivX,
                 { MultY => } MultX,
                 { DivY  => } DivX   );
DisVal := TopUpValue;
Angle  := 0.0;     { vertical angle from X,Y upward }
for i := 1 to MajorTicks do
  begin
    SinAngle := sin( Angle );
    CosAngle := cos( Angle );
    Graph.OutTextXY(
        { X          => } X+round(SinAngle*3.0*InnerRadius/4.0),
        { Y          => } Y-round(CosAngle*3.0*InnerRadius/4.0),
        { TextString => } MakeStr(DisVal) );
    DisVal := (DisVal + 1) mod ValueModulo;
    if DisVal = 0
      then DisVal := 1;
    Angle := Angle + DeltaAngle;
  end;    { MajorTick loop }
  { Draw Big Hand first...... }
```

(continued)

```
          LongHandX   := X + round( (sin( BgHandAng ) * (InnerRadius)) * 0.8 );
          LongHandY   := Y + round( (cos( BgHandAng ) * (InnerRadius)) * 0.8 );
          Graph.SetLineStyle( { LineStyle => } SolidLn,
                              { Pattern   => } 0,
                              { Thickness => } NormWidth );
          Graph.SetColor( { Color   => } HandColor );
          Graph.Line( { X1 => } X,
                      { Y1 => } Y,
                      { X2 => } LongHandX,
                      { Y2 => } LongHandY  );
            { Then draw the Little Hand..... }
          ShortHandX  := X + round( (sin( SmHandAng )*(InnerRadius)) * 0.6 );
          ShortHandY  := Y + round( (cos( SmHandAng )*(InnerRadius)) * 0.6 );
          Graph.SetLineStyle( { LineStyle => } SolidLn,
                              { Pattern   => } 0,
                              { Thickness => } ThickWidth );
          Graph.Line( { X1 => } X,
                      { Y1 => } Y,
                      { X2 => } ShortHandX,
                      { Y2 => } ShortHandY  );
        end;   { ClkDial.UpdateHands }

   function ClkDial.ScreenXIs  : integer;
     begin
       ScreenXIs := X;
     end;    { ClkDial.ScreenXIs }

   function ClkDial.ScreenYIs  : integer;
     begin
       ScreenYIs := Y;
     end;    { ClkDial.ScreenYIs }

   function ClkDial.InnerRadiusIs : integer;
     begin
       InnerRadiusIs := InnerRadius;
     end;    { ClkDial.InnerRadiusIs }

   function ClkDial.HandColorIs : integer;
     begin
       HandColorIs := HandColor;
     end;    { ClkDial.HandColorIs }

{==========================================================================}
{                 Method Definitions for: Clocks                           }
{==========================================================================}
 constructor Clock.Init( XPos,YPos : integer; { screen position }
                         Diameter  : integer; { Bezel Diameter }
                         BzlColor  : integer; { Bezel Color }
                         HndColor  : integer; { Color for both }
                         Interval  : word    { 20 pps pulses }  );
      const
        lsb_cnt   = $F4;   { lsb = 0.838408484 usec }
        msb_cnt   = $E8;   { $E8F4 => 50.0 msec; or 20 cnts/sec }
```

```
      var
        Sec100             : word;
        HourHandAng        : real;
        MinuteHandAng      : real;
      begin
        CntLimit := Interval;
        cnt := CntLimit + 1;     { force update on first call }
        Dos.GetTime( Hour, Minute, Second, Sec100 );
        MinuteHandAng :=Pi - (Pi * ( Minute * 60.0 + Second ) / 1800.0);
        if Hour > 11
          then Hour := Hour - 12;
        HourHandAng := Pi - (Pi * ( Hour * 60.0 + Minute ) / 360.0);
        ClkDial.Init( { XPos      => } XPos,
                      { YPos      => } YPos,
                      { Diameter  => } Diameter,
                      { BzlColor  => } BzlColor,
                      { HndColor  => } HndColor,
                      { MajorTics => } 12,
                      { MinorTics => } 4,
                      { InstrLabl => } 'CLOCK',
                      { BgHandAng => } MinuteHandAng,
                      { SmHandAng => } HourHandAng,
                      { TopValue  => } 12,
                      { ValueMod  => } 13      );
            { set up the hardware interval timer.... }
        port[TimerCntrl] := Mode3;
        port[Timer0] := lsb_cnt;   { initialize timer interval }
        port[Timer0] := msb_cnt;
            { set up the timer interrupt vector.... }
        GetIntVec($1C,OldTimer);   { save the old timer pointer }
        SetIntVec($1C,@ISR);
      end;    { Clock.Init }

  procedure Clock.Update;
      var
        Sec100  : word;
        HourHandAng        : real;
        MinuteHandAng      : real;
      begin
        if cnt > CntLimit
          then
            begin
              Dos.GetTime( Hour, Minute, Second, Sec100 );
              MinuteHandAng :=Pi - (Pi*( Minute * 60.0 + Second ) / 1800.0);
              if Hour > 11
                then Hour := Hour - 12;
              HourHandAng := Pi - (Pi * ( Hour * 60.0 + Minute ) / 360.0);
              UpdateHands( { BgHandAng => } MinuteHandAng,
                           { SmHandAng => } HourHandAng );
              cnt := 0;
            end;
      end;    { Clock.Update }
```

(continued)

```
destructor Clock.Done;
   begin
        { restore the hardware interval timer.... }
      port[TimerCntrl] := Mode3;
      port[Timer0] := 0;
      port[Timer0] := 0;
        { restore the timer interrupt vector.... }
      SetIntVec($1C,OldTimer);
   end;    { Clock.Done }


{=========================================================================}
{                         No Initialization Code                          }

end.
```

frequently as is convenient without worrying about degrading the system performance or the display image.

The importance of this example is that all the complexity of this mechanism, including the control of the processor timer and the time-of-day being read from the DOS timer, is encapsulated with the *Clock* object class and hidden from the client. The full functionality of an object of the *Clock* class is defined in this one unit. This is an excellent example of high functional cohesion.

The astute reader will notice that one of *Clock*'s methods is declared with the keyword *destructor* rather than *procedure*. For now, it is sufficient that *destructor* methods, like *constructor* methods, are procedures that have special properties. In this example, those special properties have no effect. We will delve more deeply into *destructor* methods when we examine dynamic objects in the next chapter. The use of a *destructor* is included here so the *Clock* class may be used, without change, when we later understand the significance of *destructor* methods.

A typical aircraft analog altimeter (an instrument that displays the aircraft's altitude) has an appearance similar to that of a clock. It has only ten digits around its dial, as opposed to twelve for a clock. The altimeter "minute hand" shows 100 feet for each digit on the dial. The "hour hand" indicates thousands of feet, moving one digit (i.e., 1,000 ft.) each time the "minute hand" completes a revolution. Because it is not unusual for an aircraft to exceed 10,000 feet (one revolution of the "hour hand"), an additional hand is needed to represent tens of thousands of feet ($n \times 10{,}000$ ft.). With this additional hand, the behavior of the altimeter differs from the abstract class *ClkDial*.

The amount of code that may be inherited from *ClkDial* is significant, suggesting we declare the class *Altimeter* as a descendent of *ClkDial*.

The *Altmeter* unit (listing provided in Figure 5.4) illustrates another analyst decision, namely determining the boundaries between objects. In the previous *Clocks* unit, all interface with the abstract concept of "time" is included in the *Clock* object class.

It would be easy to embed the mechanism that determines changes in altitude within the *Altimeter.Update* method. In the driving demonstration program, the operator uses the up and down cursor arrow keys to change the "aircraft" rate-of-climb (somewhat simulating the effect of pulling back or pushing forward on an aircraft stick or steering yoke). But is it reasonable to tie the implementation of the altimeter to how the altitude is computed?

In this case, the relationship between an altimeter and the altitude it displays is a one-way dependency. The altimeter depends on the abstract concept of altitude, whose value it represents graphically. But the numeric value of an aircraft's altitude may be used by numerous functions (such as flight controls, navigation, weapons delivery, communications, etc.) without ever providing an altimeter to display it. In this context, it seems unreasonable to place the *Altitude* update mechanism in the *Altmeter* unit.

As a further justification for not embedding altitude update in the *Altmeter* unit, the implementation I have provided for changing altitude is based on a simple interpretation of two keyboard keys. As our model becomes more complex, we may choose to compute the rate-of-climb based on the aircraft's pitch (angle that the nose points up or down) and roll (angle that the wings are rotated from horizontal) attitude. Such a change to how the system determines altitude has no bearing on how the altimeter displays altitude. It is therefore better to separate the altimeter from the abstract notion of altitude. When the altitude model changes, the code for the altimeter is not changed and therefore does not require regression testing to verify that no undesired side effects have crept in due to the change.

So, for several reasons, we will create a separate object (and unit) to represent the abstract notion of "altitude." But, we have stated that the altimeter has a dependency on altitude. How should we best relate that dependency?

One way to specify such a dependency is to declare an object of the class *ACAltitude* in the interface section of the unit *Altmeter*. This ensures that an altimeter cannot exist without an altitude object. By declaring the object in the interface section, it becomes available to all system "altimeter" users (they must include the unit *Altmeter* in their context by including it in a *uses* statement). This takes the responsibility from the main program for ensuring that an altitude object is declared and permits the altimeter to access its value without requiring that a formal parameter be passed.

Because the *Altmeter* unit assumes responsibility for declaring the altitude object, it also must be responsible for initializing that object. This is done in the unit initialization code (the last few lines of the unit). Unit initialization code is executed only once during system start-up. In this case, the initialization code sends a message to the object *AirCraftAlt* to have it invoke its *Init* method.

With this relationship to altitude established, the *Altimeter.Update* method may interrogate the altitude object (i.e., *AirCraftAlt*) to return its current value:

```
Alt := AirCraftAlt.AltitudeIs;
```

The method then checks to see if the value has changed since the last update of the display. If it has not, then the display update operation is bypassed to prevent an unwanted flicker as the hands are erased and redrawn. If there has been a change, then the position of the altimeter hands is updated on the displayed instrument.

The altimeter's *Update* method illustrates how an object may be extended to add functionality. The hundreds and thousands of feet hands on the altimeter are mapped to the minute and hour hands of the inherited *ClkDial* class. All processing for these two hands will be provided by the inherited *UpdateHands* method from *ClkDial*. This descendent's *Update* method must implement the added hand to represent tens of thousands of feet. It does this in four steps:

1. Erase the 10,000 foot hand at its previous location (this function forces including fields in the descendent class to remember where this hand was last drawn).

2. Compute the angle for each of the three hands.

3. Invoke the inherited *UpdateHands* method to update the hundreds and thousands of feet hands.

4. Draw the 10,000 foot hand.

This technique fully exploits the common behavior of the abstract ancestor class by only adding processing that represents unique requirements of the descendent class and invoking inherited ancestor (i.e., common processing) methods where possible.

The *Altitude* unit (listing provided in Figure 5.5) defines a very simple object *ACAltitude*. This unit illustrates how a prototype system may be quickly constructed using a combination of reused objects (perhaps the *Clocks* unit classes), new objects (such as from the *Altmeter* unit), and simple prototype objects (such as the keyboard-driven implementation in the *Altitude* unit). In our example flight instrument panel system, it would reduce our project risk to have our "customer's" concurrence on our instruments' representations without worrying about how the displayed values are computed. Early customer buy-in to such concerns can reduce project cost and increase customer confidence as the system matures and future decisions are based on the completed work.

For this example, the main program *DashPanel* becomes an almost trivial exercise. Because the behavior of the system is predominantly defined in its objects, the main line simply exercises those objects. Figure 5.3 shows the image generated by this program.

The system initialization processing requires initializing the graphics interface, drawing a line across the screen to represent the top of the flight instrument panel (above this line is reserved for an "out-the-window" view), and sending messages to each of the instruments to initialize themselves at specific locations on the screen.

When initialization is complete, the program enters a simple loop. When the operator presses the *Enter* key, the program exits the loop. Otherwise, a message is sent to the *AirCraftAlt* object to "update" its value, followed by messages to each of the instrument objects to update their displays.

Once out of the loop, a little clean-up processing is done (e.g., having the clock object restore the timer interrupt vector) and the program terminates.

For each object defined in this example, the design includes as much of the

Figure 5.3. The screen image of the DashPnl1 program.

```
unit Altmeter;

{ Program:     Altimeter — A library unit which displays an altimeter
                           gauge
  Author:      John R. Ellis
  Last Update: 17 July 1991
  Copyright (c) 1991 by John R. Ellis

  Description: This unit provides a object class, descended from the
               abstract clock-dial class, which displays a typical
               aircraft altimeter instrument.

  Requirements: The "Draw" methods for each object require access to the
                Turbo Pascal Graph unit.
                                                                          }
interface

  uses Clocks,Altitude;

  var
       { object instance creation...... }
    AirCraftAlt : ACAltitude;     { Altimeter must know of altitude }

   type

      {===================================================================}
      {                         Object Declarations                       }
      {===================================================================}

      Altimeter = object( ClkDial )
              constructor Init( XPos,YPos : integer; { screen position }
                                Diameter  : integer; { Bezel Diameter }
                                BzlColor  : integer; { Bezel Color }
                                HndColor  : integer  { Color for both } );
              procedure Update;
              destructor Done;
            private
              ThrdHandX    : integer;    { 10,000 ft hand screen coords }
              ThrdHandY    : integer;
              OldAltitude  : word;       { current altitude }
            end;      { object = Altimeter }

  {———————— end of interface section ——————-}
  implementation

    uses Dos,Graph;

  {===================================================================}
  {                Method Definitions for: Altimeter                  }
  {===================================================================}
   constructor Altimeter.Init( XPos,YPos : integer; { screen position }
                               Diameter  : integer; { Bezel Diameter }
```

Figure 5.4.   Code listing: unit ALTMETER.PAS.

```
                        BzlColor  : integer; { Bezel Color }
                        HndColor  : integer  { Color for both } );
  var
    HourHandAng       : real;
    MinuteHandAng     : real;
  begin
    ClkDial.Init( { XPos      => } XPos,
                  { YPos      => } YPos,
                  { Diameter  => } Diameter,
                  { BzlColor  => } BzlColor,
                  { HndColor  => } HndColor,
                  { MajorTics => } 10,
                  { MinorTics => } 4,
                  { InstrLabl => } 'ALT',
                  { BgHandAng => } Pi,
                  { SmHandAng => } Pi,
                  { TopValue  => } 0,
                  { ValueMod  => } 10    );
    ThrdHandX := ScreenXIs;
    ThrdHandY := ScreenYIs;
  end;    { Altimeter.Init }

procedure Altimeter.Update;
  var
    Alt               : word;     { current altitude }
    HourHandAng       : real;     { ft x 100 per unit }
    MinuteHandAng     : real;     { ft x 1,000 per unit }
    ThirdHandAng      : real;     { ft x 10,000 per unit }
  begin
    Alt := AirCraftAlt.AltitudeIs;
    if Alt <> OldAltitude
      then
        begin
            { erase 10,000 ft hand first.... }
          Graph.SetColor( { Color => } Graph.GetBkColor );
          Graph.SetLineStyle( { LineStyle => } SolidLn,
                              { Pattern   => } 0,
                              { Thickness => } NormWidth );
          Graph.Line( { X1 => } ScreenXIs,
                      { Y1 => } ScreenYIs,
                      { X2 => } ThrdHandX,
                      { Y2 => } ThrdHandY  );
            { compute angles for the three hands..... }
          MinuteHandAng := Pi - (Pi * ( Alt mod 1000 ) / 500.0);
          HourHandAng   := Pi - (Pi * Alt / 5000.0);
          ThirdHandAng  := Pi - (Pi * Alt / 50000.0);
            { use ancestor method to update normal two hands.... }
          UpdateHands( { BgHandAng => } MinuteHandAng,
                       { SmHandAng => } HourHandAng );
            { and add the third hand for 10,000 ft reading.... }
          ThrdHandX := ScreenXIs +
                        round((sin(ThirdHandAng)*(InnerRadiusIs))*0.5);
          ThrdHandY := ScreenYIs +
```

(continued)

```
                         round((cos(ThirdHandAng)*(InnerRadiusIs))*0.5);
             Graph.SetLineStyle( { LineStyle => } SolidLn,
                                 { Pattern    => } 0,
                                 { Thickness  => } NormWidth );
             Graph.SetColor( { Color   => } HandColorIs );
             Graph.Line( { X1 => } ScreenXIs,
                         { Y1 => } ScreenYIs,
                         { X2 => } ThrdHandX,
                         { Y2 => } ThrdHandY  );
             OldAltitude := Alt;
           end;
    end;    { Altimeter.Update }

 destructor Altimeter.Done;
    begin
    end;    { Altimeter.Done }

{=======================================================================}
{                          Initialization Code                          }

begin
  AirCraftAlt.Init;      { Initialize the altitude object }
end.
```

(end)

```
unit Altitude;

{ Program:     Altitude — A unit which manages the aircraft altitude
  Author:      John R. Ellis
  Last Update: 17 July 1991
  Copyright (c) 1991 by John R. Ellis

  Description: This unit provides a simulated aircraft altitude object.
               This version interrogates the up and down cursor arrow
               keys to increase/decrease the rate of climb, and
               therefrom, the alitude.

  Requirements: none.
                                                                       }
interface

  type

     {=================================================================}
     {                     Object Declarations                         }
     {=================================================================}

     ACAltitude = object
```

Figure 5.5.   Code listing: unit ALTITUDE.PAS.

```
                    constructor Init;
                    procedure Update( ControlKey : integer );
                    function AltitudeIs : word;
                 private
                    RateOfClimb  : integer;
                    Alt          : word;              { 0 .. 65535 }
                 end;       { object = ACAltitude }

{——————— end of interface section ——————-}
implementation

{=======================================================================}
{               Method Definitions for: Altitude                        }
{=======================================================================}
 constructor ACAltitude.Init;
    begin
      RateOfClimb := 0;
      Alt := 250;
    end;     { ACAltitude.Init }

 procedure ACAltitude.Update( ControlKey : integer );
    const
      UpArrow     = 72;
      DownArrow   = 80;
    begin
      case ControlKey of
         UpArrow    : RateOfClimb := RateOfClimb + 10;
         DownArrow  : RateOfClimb := RateOfClimb - 10;
      end;    { case }
      Alt := Alt + RateOfClimb;
    end;      { ACAltitude.Update }

 function ACAltitude.AltitudeIs : word;
    begin
      AltitudeIs := Alt;
    end;      { ACAltitude.AltitudeIs }

{=======================================================================}
{                          No Initialization Code                       }

 end.
```

(end)

```
{ Program:    Aircraft Dash Panel simulator
  Author:     John R. Ellis
  Last Update: 17 July 1991
  Copyright (c) 1991 by John R. Ellis
```

Figure 5.6.   Code listing: program DASHPNL1.PAS.   *(continued)*

```
   Description:   This is a main line program which demonstrates object
                  encapsulation.
                  This program "draws" two flight instruments: a standard
                  clock and an altimeter.  The clock displays standard
                  system time, while the altimeter responds to the up and
                  down cursor keys.

   Requirements: Uses the standard Turbo Pascal Graph Unit.
                                                                          }

program DashPanel;
   uses Crt,Graph,GrafInit,Clocks,Altmeter;

const
   { the following constants define the control key codes }
   LeftArrow  = 75;
   RightArrow = 77;
   UpArrow    = 72;
   DownArrow  = 80;
   EnterKey   = 13;

      function CommandInputIs : integer;
         var
            Ch  : char;
         begin
           if KeyPressed
             then
               begin
                 Ch := readkey;
                 if ord(Ch) = EnterKey
                   then CommandInputIs := EnterKey
                   else if ord(Ch) = 0
                     then
                       begin
                         Ch := readkey;
                         CommandInputIs := ord(Ch);
                       end
                     else
                       CommandInputIs := 0;
               end;
         end;   { CommandInputIs }

   var
         { object instance creation...... }
      TheClock     : Clock;
      TheAlt       : Altimeter;
         { other variables used by the program...... }
      GError       : integer;
      MaxColor     : integer;     { greatest color value }
      MaxX         : integer;     { greatest X-axis value }
      MaxY         : integer;     { greatest Y-axis value }
      CntrlChar    : integer;     { keyboard input control character }
      Exit         : boolean;     { controls main loop exit }
```

```
begin
      { Do the graphics mode set-up.............. }
  GError := GrafInitSuccess;
  if GError <> grOK
    then
      begin
        writeln('Graphics error:  ',GraphErrorMsg(GError) );
        writeln('Program aborted...');
        halt( 1 );
      end;
  MaxX      := GetMaxX;         { your graphics adaptor dependent... }
  MaxY      := GetMaxY;
  ClearDevice;
    { draw horizontal line representing top of dash panel.... }
  Graph.SetLineStyle( { LineStyle => } SolidLn,
                      { Pattern   => } 0,
                      { Thickness => } ThickWidth );
  Graph.SetColor( { Color   => } white );
  Graph.Line( { X1 => } 0,
              { Y1 => } MaxY div 2,
              { X2 => } MaxX,
              { Y2 => } MaxY div 2  );
    { initialize the object instances.... }
  TheClock.Init( { XPos     => } MaxX div 4,
                 { YPos     => } 3 * MaxY div 4,
                 { Diameter => } MaxY div 8,
                 { BzlColor => } White,
                 { HndColor => } Green,
                 { Interval => } 100 { 5 seconds }   );
  TheAlt.Init(   { XPos     => } 3 * MaxX div 4,
                 { YPos     => } 3 * MaxY div 4,
                 { Diameter => } MaxY div 8,
                 { BzlColor => } White,
                 { HndColor => } White   );
  Exit := false;
    { Set up is complete;  main loop for normal processing.... }
  while not Exit do
    begin
      CntrlChar := CommandInputIs;
      if CntrlChar = EnterKey
        then
          Exit := true
        else
          AirCraftAlt.Update( { ControlKey => } CntrlChar );
      TheClock.Update;
      TheAlt.Update;
      delay( 100 );
    end;   { loop }

    TheClock.Done;   { cleans up ISR vector }
    CloseGraph;

end.
```

behavior of the object as possible. Where dependencies exist between objects, the design must assign responsibility for such dependencies in a logical and consistent manner.

ENCAPSULATION AND INFORMATION HIDING

In addition to using encapsulation to establish object cohesion, fully defining the behaviors associated with an object, encapsulation implements the concept of information hiding.

David Parnas was one of the first to extol the virtues of information hiding in software design. This philosophy has gained acceptance as more systems are developed using Ada. It increases in importance as systems increase in size and complexity and becomes a critical element in designing reusable software components.

Objects provide two types of information hiding. First, by using available protection features of a particular programming language, the implementation data structure of an object's fields may be hidden from the client. This prevents the client from relying on a structure that may change during the life of the system using the object. The second type of information hiding addresses method definitions, along with support utilities and local data, as included in the *implementation* section of the unit. A client should not rely on a particular implementation.

The underlying concept of information hiding is based on establishing a "contract" between an object and its clients. That contract, determined in the *public* parts of the class declaration, establishes exactly which object behaviors the client may invoke. The client "agrees" to use the object only according to the terms of the contract. If the client contains code that violates the terms of the contract by attempting to capitalize on information that is supposed to be hidden, then the long-term maintainability of the system is at risk. Although the client may initially work correctly, its long-term behavior will be indeterminate due to possible side effects associated with changes to the hidden implementations. This is considered poor programming practice. Software quality evaluations should attempt to ferret out such programming practices each time the design and code are reviewed.

One common misconception that I've encountered among my colleagues is that "hidden" data must be unknown to the analyst or programmer who is attempting to use an object or module. The purpose of information hiding is to restrict a client program's access and reliance on the implementation of the hidden information. Object-oriented programming languages provide the means to enforce information hiding principles. Specifically, they limit "visibility" to that declared in the interface section of a unit (or Ada package specification, etc.) and, even there, permit protection of fields and methods in object class declarations. However, it is usually necessary for an analyst to understand the hidden information.

When developing embedded real-time systems, the characteristics of which will be considered in Part II of this book, processing time and memory are frequently critical resources. Any requirements analysis or implementation design must be done within the limitations of these resources. Because data structures and implementation algorithms are normally specified in the hidden parts of an object or module, the analyst must be able to factor the effects that the implementation has on these resources. A similar concern often exists regarding the effect of a particular algorithm on the accuracy or precision of a particular computation. Without a detailed understanding of such hidden information, the analyst cannot determine whether a proposed object or module will meet specific solution constraints or user requirements.

Implementation details may include object or module dependencies on other hardware or software entities that likewise could impact system performance. For example, a module that implements a user interface to a standard mouse object could be implemented in many ways. On a PC-based system, perhaps the easiest approach is to have the *Mouse* class merely provide a wrapper around the underlying DOS mouse support. The included unit *MOUSE.PAS* illustrates how this can be accomplished.

From the user viewpoint, the *Mouse* unit encapsulates the behavior of a standard mouse. This unit's two-level hierarchy is illustrated in Figure 5.7. The top level is an abstract class called *AnyMouse* that provides common fields and methods needed by the two second-level classes, *GraphicMouse* and *TextMouse*. These descendent classes provide objects that operate in the two screen modes, graphics and text, respectively.

In addition to declaring these three classes, the interface segment of this unit defines data structures and symbolic constant definitions to which clients need access. For example, when *Mouse* methods return the "button status," the client can use the provided symbolic values to determine which buttons were pressed. Specifically, the client program might have a "case construct" to check for "PrNone" (no buttons pressed), "PrL" (left button pressed), "PrR" (right button pressed), and so forth. By including such data in the unit interface, the user may more easily use the object and write more readable code. Because all users can use common symbolic values, reviewers will more easily understand the meaning of the code as well.

On the other hand, consider the constant declarations in the implementation section. The Mouse Interrupt Commands assign symbolic names to the interrupt command values passed to the DOS Mouse Interrupt Service Routine, ISR (i.e., interrupt 33 *hexadecimal*). There is no reason a client program would ever need to use these symbolic values because how the methods use the DOS Mouse support to implement the object methods is considered hidden information. Not making such data known to a client discourages the client from attempting to capitalize on knowledge regarding the implementation, such as writing an equivalent routine rather than using one that has been provided.

If the user writes such low-level routines to interface directly with the DOS Mouse ISR and later the DOS interfaces change, then adapting to the new DOS release would be significantly more difficult. Not only would changes have to be made in the *Mouse* unit, as expected, but changes could be required in many units of the client program. What would happen if one of these changes were missed when performing updates?

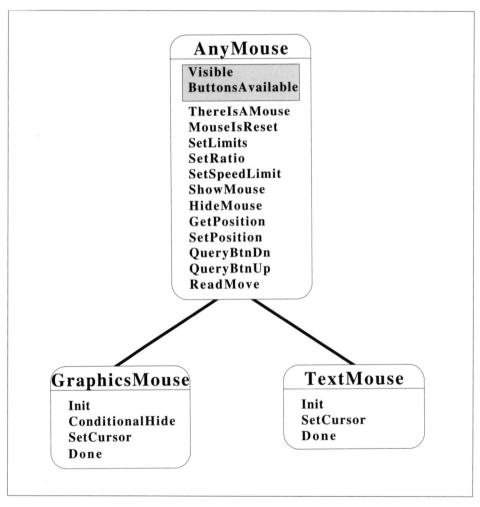

Figure 5.7.   Class hierarchy tree of the unit MOUSE.PAS.

```
unit Mouse;

{ Program:     Mouse — A library unit which provides mouse support
  Author:      John R. Ellis
  Last Update: 18 July 1991
  Copyright (c) 1991 by John R. Ellis

  Description: This unit provides a toolbox of low level mouse routines
               for use in Turbo Pascal programs.  It supports both
               graphics and text mouse constructs.

  Requirements: Use of this unit requires installation of mouse hardware
               and software.  These routines should work with both serial
               mice and bus mice, so long as they are 100% Microsoft
               Mousecompatible.  These include the 2-button Microsoft
               mouse, the 3-button Logitech mouse, and the 3-button PC
               -Mouse mouse.

               The mouse system file (normally MOUSE.COM or MOUSE.SYS)
               must be installed before these routines may be used.

  Reference:   DOS mouse operations are based on data from:
                         The Programmer's PC Sourcebook
                         by Thom Hogan
                         Microsoft Press; 1988
                                                                       }
interface

   type

      { The following record type mimics the format of the status data
        returned after certain mouse functions are invoked.     }
      MouseStatus = record
         Status : integer;  { Button Status: see Button Press Defintions }
         Count  : integer;  { Cnt of button presses, set to 0 after call }
         XPos   : integer;   { Horizontal Position at last press }
         YPos   : integer;   { Vertical Position at last press  }
      end;    { MouseStatus type }

      { The following record type defines the structure of a screen/cursor
        mask used to define a graphics cursor block.  A graphics cursor is
        a 16 x 16 bit array...with the screen and cursor masks working
        interacting as follows:
              Screen Mask Bit        Cursor Mask Bit            Effect
              ———————--         ————————   ————————

                   0.                     0                    0
                   0                      1                    1
                   1                      0                 Unchanged
                   1                      1                 Inverted     }
      GraphicCursor  = record
         ScreenMask : array [0..15] of word;
```

Figure 5.8.   Code listing: unit MOUSE.PAS.   *(continued)*

```
        CursorMask : array [0..15] of word;
        HotX      : integer;        { HotX, HotY is the pixel whose }
        HotY      : integer;        { position is returned for the cursor }
    end;   { GraphicCursor type }

const

    { Mouse interrupts are handled by DOS Interrupt 33h }
        MouseIntr = $33;

    { Button Definitions }
        ButtonLeft   = 0;
        ButtonRight  = 1;
        ButtonMiddle = 2;

    { Button Press Definitions...these values may be used to interpret
      Button Status values (e.g., Status or BtnStatus) to identify
      which buttons have been pressed.      }
        PrNone = 0;    { no button pressed }
        PrL    = 1;    { Left Button pressed }
        PrR    = 2;    { Right Button pressed }
        PrLR   = 3;    { Left & Right Buttons pressed }
        PrM    = 4;    { Middle Button pressed }
        PrLM   = 5;    { Left & Middle Buttons pressed }
        PrMR   = 6;    { Middle & Right Buttons pressed }
        PrAll  = 7;    { All 3 Buttons are pressed }

    { Cursor Type Definitions }
        Software   = 0;
        Hardware   = 1;

    {===================================================================}
    {  The following cursor is provided as a default.  The user may     }
    {  define other cursor shapes using this one as a model.            }
    {===================================================================}
    Default : GraphicCursor =          {+-+-+-+-+-+-+-+-+-+-+-+-+-+-+-+}
       (ScreenMask : ( $3FFF, $1FFF,   {|   . . . . . . . . . . . .|}
                       $0FFF, $07FF,   {|  H   . . . . . . . . . . .|}
                       $03FF, $01FF,   {|  * *   . . . . . . . . . .|}
                       $00FF, $007F,   {|  * * *   . . . . . . . . .|}
                       $003F, $003F,   {|  * * * *   . . . . . . . .|}
                       $01FF, $00FF,   {|  * * * * *   . . . . . . .|}
                       $F0FF, $F87F,   {|  * * * * * *   . . . . . .|}
                       $F87F, $F87F ); {|  * * * * * * *   . . . . .|}
        CursorMask : ( $0000, $4000,   {|  * * * * * * * *   . . . .|}
                       $6000, $7000,   {|  * * * * *         . . . .|}
                       $7800, $7C00,   {|  *      *  *     . . . . .|}
                       $7E00, $7F00,   {|          * *    . . . . .|}
                       $7F80, $7C00,   {|. . . .   * *   . . . . . .|}
                       $4C00, $0600,   {|. . . .     * *   . . . . .|}
                       $0600, $0300,   {|. . . . .   * *   . . . . .|}
                       $0300, $0000 ); {|. . . . .       . . . . . .|}
        HotX : $0001;  HotY : $0001 ); {+-+-+-+-+-+-+-+-+-+-+-+-+-+-+-+}
```

```
    {===================================================================}
    {                      Object Declarations                          }
    {===================================================================}
type

   AnyMouse = object              { abstract class }
              function  ThereIsAMouse  : boolean;
              function  MouseIsReset   : boolean;
              procedure SetLimits( XMin, YMin,
                                   XMax, YMax  : integer );
              procedure SetRatio( HorMickeys, VerMickeys : integer   );
              procedure SetSpeedLimit( Threshold : integer );
              procedure ShowMouse;
              procedure HideMouse;
              procedure GetPosition( var BtnStatus,
                                         XPos, YPos : integer );
              procedure SetPosition( XPos, YPos  : integer   );
              procedure QueryBtnDn(    Button   : integer;
                                   var Mouse    : MouseStatus  );
              procedure QueryBtnUp(    Button   : integer;
                                   var Mouse    : MouseStatus  );
              procedure ReadMove(   var XMove, YMove : integer );
            private
              Visible          : boolean;
              ButtonsAvailable : integer;
            end;    { object: AnyMouse }

   GraphicMouse = object( AnyMouse )
              constructor Init;
              procedure ConditionalHide( Left, Top,
                                         Right, Bottom : integer );
              procedure SetCursor( Cursor : GraphicCursor );
              destructor Done;
            end;    { object: GraphicMouse }

   TextMouse = object( AnyMouse )
              constructor Init;
              procedure SetCursor( CursorType, C1, C2 : word );
              destructor Done;
            end;    { object: TextMouse }

{------------ end of interface section ------------}
implementation

  uses Crt, Graph, Dos;

  const

    { Mouse Interrupt Commands }
       ResetMouseCmd              = $00;
       ShowMouseCmd               = $01;
       HideMouseCmd               = $02;
       GetStatusCmd               = $03;
```

(continued)

```
         SetPositionCmd                = $04;
         QueryBtnDownCmd               = $05;
         QueryBtnUpCmd                 = $06;
         SetMouseHorizontalLimitsCmd   = $07;
         SetMouseVerticalLimitsCmd     = $08;
         SetGraphicsCursorCmd          = $09;
         SetTextCursorCmd              = $0A;
         MouseReadMoveCmd              = $0B;
         SetAspectRatioCmd             = $0F;
         ConditionalHideCmd            = $10;
         SetSpeedLimitCmd              = $13;

  var

     Regs : registers;          { used for low level DOS interface }

     {================================================================}
     {              IMPLEMENTATION METHODS FOR AnyMouse               }
     {================================================================}

    function AnyMouse.ThereIsAMouse  : boolean;
       { This function determines whether or not a mouse is installed.
         First, it checks to see if an address for the mouse interrupt
         service routine is stored in the DOS interrupt service table.
         The address for the mouse ISR is stored at segment 0, offset
         CCh-CFh.  If every value stored in the interrupt table for
         interrupt 33h is 0, then the mouse software has not been
         successfully installed.  If there is an address at the location,
         then it checks to make sure the contents at that address is not
         IRET (207).  If the interrupt 33h entry points to something
         other than IRET, then it is probably a valid instruction for
         the mouse ISR and therefore we assume the mouse software is
         installed correctly.                                          }

       const
         IRET = 207;       { op code for IRET (Interrupt Return) }
       var
         MouseSegment    : word ABSOLUTE $0000:$00CE;
         MouseOffset     : word ABSOLUTE $0000:$00CC;
       begin
         if (MouseSegment = 0) and (MouseOffset = 0)
           then
             ThereIsAMouse := false
           else
             ThereIsAMouse := MEM[MouseSegment:MouseOffset] <> IRET;
       end;    { AnyMouse.ThereIsAMouse }

    function AnyMouse.MouseIsReset : boolean;
       { This function resets the mouse interface to its default
         parameters and returns whether or not the operation was
         successful.  This function also sets the BtnCount field
         indicating the number of buttons found. }
       begin
```

```
       Regs.AX := ResetMouseCmd;
       intr( MouseIntr, Regs );
          { returns (in AX) -1 if mouse is present, 0 if not    }
          {          (in BX) number of buttons available, 2 or 3 }
       MouseIsReset := Regs.AX <> 0;
       ButtonsAvailable := Regs.BX;
     end;     { AnyMouse.MouseIsReset }

   procedure AnyMouse.SetLimits( XMin, YMin,
                                 XMax, YMax  : integer );
     { This procedure sets the screen limits (in pixels) for mouse
       movement.  If this unit is used with higher resolution graphics,
       parts of the screen will not be accessible unless this procedure
       is invoked to set the actual limits.  }
     var
       LesserValue, GreaterValue : integer;
     begin
       if XMin < XMax
         then
           begin
             LesserValue := XMin;
             GreaterValue := XMax;
           end
         else
           begin
             LesserValue := XMax;
             GreaterValue := XMin;
           end;
       Regs.AX := SetMouseHorizontalLimitsCmd;
       Regs.CX := LesserValue;
       Regs.DX := GreaterValue;
       intr( MouseIntr, Regs );
       if YMin < YMax
         then
           begin
             LesserValue := YMin;
             GreaterValue := YMax;
           end
         else
           begin
             LesserValue := YMax;
             GreaterValue := YMin;
           end;
       Regs.AX := SetMouseVerticalLimitsCmd;
       Regs.CX := LesserValue;
       Regs.DX := GreaterValue;
       intr( MouseIntr, Regs );
     end;      { AnyMouse.SetLimits }

   procedure AnyMouse.SetRatio( HorMickeys, VerMickeys : integer   );
     { This procedure controls the ratio of physical mouse movement to
       screen cursor movement with the x- and y-axis arguments (Hor
       Mickeys and VerMickeys) expressed in the number of mickeys (units
```

(continued)

```
      of mouse motion) required to cover eight pixels on the screen.
        Allowable values are 1 to 32767 mickeys, but the appropriate
      values are dependent on the number of mickeys per inch reported
      by the physical mouse: values which may be 100, 200, or 320 mic
      keys per inch, depending on mouse hardware.  Default values are
      8 mickeys/8 pixels horizontal and 16 mickeys/8 pixels vertical.
      For a mouse reporting 200 mickeys/inch, this takes 3.2 inches
      horizontal and 2.0 inches vertically to cover a 640x200 pixel
      screen.    }
    begin
      Regs.AX := SetAspectRatioCmd;
      Regs.CX := HorMickeys;     { Horizontal mickeys/8 pixels }
      Regs.DX := VerMickeys;     { Vertical mickeys/8 pixles }
      intr( MouseIntr, Regs );
    end;      { AnyMouse.SetRatio }

  procedure AnyMouse.SetSpeedLimit( Threshold : integer );
    { This procedure sets a threshold speed (in physical mouse
      velocity units, mickeys/second) above which the mouse driver
      adds an acceleration component, allowing fast movements with the
      mouse to move the cursor further than slow movements.  The
      actual acceleration component is determined by the mouse driver
      that is installed, some of which are constants (e.g., x2) while
      others are variable.   }
    begin
      Regs.AX := SetSpeedLimitCmd;
      Regs.DX := Threshold;
      intr( MouseIntr, Regs );
    end;      { AnyMouse.SetSpeedLimit }

  procedure AnyMouse.ShowMouse;
    { This procedure turns the mouse cursor on.  Note that the DOS
      ShowMouse and HideMouse functions increment and decrement a
      counter, respectively.  If the counter is zero or negative,
      the cursor is hidden; if one or greater, the cursor is visible.
      Therefore, successive "hide" operations must be countermanded
      by a corresponding number of "show" operations to make the
      cursor visible.      }
    begin
      if not Visible
        then
          begin
            Regs.AX := ShowMouseCmd;
            intr( MouseIntr, Regs );
            Visible := true;
          end;
    end;      { AnyMouse.ShowMouse }

  procedure AnyMouse.HideMouse;
    { This procedure turns the mouse cursor off.  See the note for the
      ShowMouse procedure.    }
    begin
      if Visible
```

```
          then
            begin
              Regs.AX := HideMouseCmd;
              intr( MouseIntr, Regs );
              Visible := false;
            end;
     end;        { AnyMouse.HideMouse }

  procedure AnyMouse.GetPosition( var BtnStatus,
                                    XPos, YPos : integer );
    { This procedure returns the mouse cursor position (XPos,YPos)
      and the status of the mouse buttons.  Position coordinates
      are in pixels.  BtnStatus is an integer value with the three
      least significant bits indicating the current status of the
      left, right, and (if present) middle buttons.  The corresponding
      bits in BtnStatus (starting with bit 0) will be set if the
      button is down, or clear if the button is up.     }
    begin
      Regs.AX := GetStatusCmd;
      intr( MouseIntr, Regs );
      BtnStatus := Regs.BX;
      XPos      := Regs.CX;
      YPos      := Regs.DX;
    end;       { AnyMouse.GetPosition }

  procedure AnyMouse.SetPosition( XPos, YPos  : integer    );
    { This procedure moves the mouse cursor to the specified absolute
      screen coordinates (XPos,YPos) in pixels on the screen.  In
      text mode, pixel coordinates are still used, but are rounded off
      to position the cursor to the nearest character cell (e.g., with
      an 8x8 test display, XPos/YPos of 80,25 would correspond to
      column 11 and row 4 of the screen.    }
    begin
      Regs.AX := SetPositionCmd;
      Regs.CX := XPos;
      Regs.DX := YPos;
      intr( MouseIntr, Regs );
    end;        { AnyMouse.SetPosition }

  procedure AnyMouse.QueryBtnDn(     Button   : integer;
                                 var Mouse    : MouseStatus );
    { This procedure reports the current status of all of the buttons,
      a count of the number of times the requested button has been
      pressed since the last call to QueryBtnDn for this button, and
      the mouse coordinates when the requested button was pressed.  }
    begin
      Regs.AX := QueryBtnDownCmd;
      Regs.BX := Button;    { use symbolic: ButtonLeft, ButtonRight,
                                            or ButtonMiddle }
      intr( MouseIntr, Regs );
      Mouse.Status   := Regs.AX;
      Mouse.Count    := Regs.BX;
      Mouse.XPos     := Regs.CX;
```

(continued)

```
        Mouse.YPos      := Regs.DX;
    end;        { AnyMouse.QueryBtnDn }

procedure AnyMouse.QueryBtnUp(      Button    : integer;
                                var Mouse     : MouseStatus  );
    { This procedure is a counterpart for QueryBtnDn except it reports
      the number of times the requested button has been released.   }
    begin
    Regs.AX := QueryBtnUpCmd;
    Regs.BX := Button;      { use symbolic: ButtonLeft, ButtonRight,
                                           or ButtonMiddle }
    intr( MouseIntr, Regs );
    Mouse.Status    := Regs.AX;
    Mouse.Count     := Regs.BX;
    Mouse.XPos      := Regs.CX;
    Mouse.YPos      := Regs.DX;
    end;        { AnyMouse.QueryBtnUp }

procedure AnyMouse.ReadMove( var XMove, YMove : integer );
    { This procedure returns a total horizontal and vertical step
      count (XMove,YMove) since the last call to the ReadMove
      procedure.  For a "normal" mouse, the step count varies from
      a low of 1/100 inch increments (100 mickeys/inch) for older
      mice to 1/200 inch for more modern mice and 1/320 inch
      increments (320 mickeys/inch) for a HiRes mouse.  Movement
      step counts range from -32768..+32767, with positive values
      indicating rightward (horizontal) and downward (vertical;
      assuming mouse cable is pointed away from the user).  Both
      counts reset to zero after this call.   }
    begin
    Regs.AX := MouseReadMoveCmd;
    intr( MouseIntr, Regs );
    XMove := Regs.CX;
    YMove := Regs.DX;
    end;        { AnyMouse.ReadMove }

{====================================================================}
{              IMPLEMENTATION METHODS FOR GraphicsMouse              }
{====================================================================}

  procedure GraphicMouse.SetCursor( Cursor : GraphicCursor );
    { This procedure loads a new graphic cursor and screen mask,
      making it the active graphics mouse pointer.  Predefined
      cursors are provided with this unit for use here.      }
    begin
    Regs.AX := SetGraphicsCursorCmd;
    Regs.BX := Cursor.HotX;
    Regs.CX := Cursor.HotY;
    Regs.DX := ofs( Cursor.ScreenMask );
    Regs.ES := seg( Cursor.ScreenMask );
    intr( MouseIntr, Regs );
    end;        { GraphicMouse.SetCursor }
```

```
   procedure GraphicMouse.ConditionalHide( Left, Top,
                                            Right, Bottom : integer );
      { This procedure designates a rectangular section of the screen
        where the mouse cursor will automatically be hidden.  It is
        used primarily to guard an area of the screen that will be
        repainted.  The cursor is automatically hidden if it is in or
        moves into the area designated.  The area set by calling this
        procedure will be cleared and the mouse cursor enabled over
        the entire screen by calling ShowMouse.  }
      begin
        Regs.AX := ConditionalHideCmd;
        Regs.CX := Left;
        Regs.DX := Top;
        Regs.SI := Right;
        Regs.DI := Bottom;
        intr( MouseIntr, Regs );
      end;      { GraphicMouse.ConditionalHide }

   constructor GraphicMouse.Init;
      { This procedure provides a mechanism to initialize the graphics
        mouse by performing the following functions:  1. enable the
        mouse to cover the entire graphics screen, 2. setting the
        default mouse cursor, 3. centering the cursor on the screen, and
        4. making the cursor visible.   }
      var
        Temp  : boolean;
      begin
        Visible := false;
        if Lastmode = Mono    { fix for Hercules bug }
          then
            begin
              mem[$40:$49] := 6;
              Temp := MouseIsReset;
            end;
        SetLimits( 0, 0, GetMaxX, GetMaxY );
        SetCursor( Default );          { default graphics cursor }
        SetPosition( GetMaxX div 2, GetMaxY div 2 );
        ShowMouse;
      end;      { GraphicMouse.Initialize }

  destructor GraphicMouse.Done;
    begin
    end;     { GraphicMouse.Done }

{===================================================================}
{              IMPLEMENTATION METHODS FOR TextMouse                 }
{===================================================================}

  procedure TextMouse.SetCursor( CursorType, C1, C2 : word );
     { This procedure is used to select between a hardware or software
       cursor.

       The hardware cursor uses the video controller to create
```

(continued)

the cursor with the arguments (C1 and C2) identifying the start
and stop scan lines for the cursor. The number of scan lines
in a character cell is determined by the hardware video
controller and monitor, but as a general rule, for monochrome
systems, the range is 0..7 and for CGA is 0..14, top to bottom.
C1=6 and C2=7generally produces an underline cursor. C1=2 and
C2=5 or 6 produces a block cursor that works well even on high
resolution VGA system.

For software cursors, the C1 parameter (screen mask) is AND'd
with the existing screen character and attributes at the mouse
cursor location, determining which elements are preserved.
Next, the C2 parameter (cursor mask) is XORed with the results
of the previous operation to determine which characteristics
are changed. Generally, the least significant 8-bits of C1
should be $..00 or $..FF (normally $..00). For C2: bits 0..7
specify the ASCII character to be used as a cursor; bits 8..10
define the foreground color; bit 11 specifies intensity
(1=high);bits 12..14 specify background color; and bit 15
specifies blink(1=blink). For example, C1=$7F00 preserves
color attributes;and C2=$8018 would produce a blinking up
-arrow cursor or $0018 would produce a non-blinking up-arrow.   }
```
    begin
      Regs.AX := SetTextCursorCmd;
      Regs.BX := CursorType;      { use symbolic: software or hardware }
      Regs.CX := C1;              { screen mask or scan start line }
      Regs.DX := C2;              { cursor mask or scan stop line }
      intr( MouseIntr, Regs );
    end;        { TextMouse.SetCursor }

  constructor TextMouse.Init;
    { This procedure provides a mechanism to initialize the text
      mouse.It sets the mouse limits by retrieving (from the CRT
      unit) the minimum and maximum window settings and converting
      them from character coordinates to pixel coordinates.  The
      cursor is set to the hardware underline cursor and the cursor
      is made visible.  }
    begin
      Visible := false;
      SetLimits( lo( WindMin ) * 8,  hi( WindMin ) * 8,
                 lo( WindMax ) * 8,  hi( WindMax ) * 8  );
      SetCursor( Hardware, 2, 6 );    { default to block cursor }
      SetPosition( 0, 0 );
      ShowMouse;
    end;        { TextMouse.Initialize }

  destructor TextMouse.Done;
    begin
    end;      { TextMouse.Done }

{=================================================================}
                { no initialization code }
end.
```

The effects of hiding such support data, and similar support or utility procedures/functions, may not seem significant. After all, a client could duplicate the data or support routines. But the subtle message to a user is that this information is hidden in the implementation section to make it more difficult to violate the implied contract. Hopefully, this subtlety will be sufficient.

The *Mouse* unit methods use the standard Turbo Pascal interface to DOS interrupt services. The DOS unit defines a record type called *registers* with fields corresponding to the Intel 80X86 hardware registers. Also hidden in the implementation segment is the declaration of a variable, *Regs*, of the type *registers*. A Turbo Pascal routine that wishes to raise a DOS interrupt first satisfies any ISR input register requirements by loading the corresponding fields of the *Regs* variable. Then the software interrupt is invoked by the *intr* procedure, passing a code specifying which interrupt is to be raised and the variable holding the input register values (i.e., *Regs*). When control is returned from the ISR, the *Regs* variable holds the output register values.

Generally, DOS software ISRs are entered with an interrupt command in the AX register. The assignment of commands and other input/output register values may be determined from any good DOS book that describes the low-level functions. For this unit, I used Thom Hogan's *The Programmer's PC Sourcebook*. It should be intuitively clear how the technique described here for the mouse could be applied to other low-level DOS functions.

SUMMARY

Encapsulation is an important characteristic of object-oriented programs. It establishes cohesive modules. Such modules are much easier to maintain because they isolate all behaviors of an object in one place, limiting the search for code affected by many types of changes. Encapsulation is also closely related to the concept of information hiding.

The public information in a unit's interface section specifies a type of contract between client programs and an object of a given class. As long as clients abide by the contract, they can be isolated from the details of a selected implementation. Such isolation is an important element of easy maintenance. As long as the class does not change its public information, changes in implementation will normally be transparent to its clients. Should internal structures change, access methods may likewise change to maintain a constant interface to the object.

Although information hiding is an important aspect of object encapsulation, it does not imply that a user cannot be aware of the hidden information. In fact, there are almost always good reasons why the user should know implementation details.

PRACTICE

1. Expand the inverted "T" cursor exercise (#1) from Chapter 4 by interfacing the *Mouse* unit defined in this chapter. When the left mouse button is pressed while the cursor is over one of the four squares, change the color of the corresponding square. When the button is released or the cursor moves from over the button, return the square to its previous color.

2. Use the *ClkDial* class as the foundation of a navigation compass. Use the short hand to represent the desired heading and the long hand to represent the actual heading. Write a "Dash Panel" program that demonstrates an instance of the new compass class. Use the left arrow key to turn more to the left and the right arrow key to turn more to the right.

3. Create a digital stopwatch consisting of two buttons and a digital minutes and seconds readout. Label one button "START/ STOP". Selecting the left mouse button while the cursor is over this button should alternately start and stop the update of the readout counter. Label the other button "RESET". Selecting the left mouse button while the cursor is over this button should stop the readout update if it is running and reset the readout to "00:00". Figure 5.9 shows the objects associated with the stopwatch object.

Figure 5.9. Objects.

4. Aircraft "Head Up Displays" (HUD) often include an altitude indicator strip along one vertical edge of the display. The five-sided, fixed-position pointer provides a digital readout of altitude while the vertical strip "slides" up and down to reflect changes in the aircraft altitude. Create an altitude indicator strip similar to that shown in Figure 5.10. Use the up and down arrow cursor control keys to command changes of your simulated aircraft altitude.

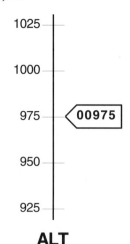

Figure 5.10. Altitude indicator strip.

Chapter **6**

Dynamic Objects: Runtime Instances

All objects discussed to this point are considered *static* objects. They are instantiated from their classes in a *var* declaration. The memory required for the object is allocated at compilation time from the program's data segment or stack space. This memory is immediately available at the beginning of program execution and remains allocated to the corresponding objects until execution terminates. The advantage of instantiating static objects is its simplicity.

The alternative is to create *dynamic* objects that are instantiated during execution, so that the memory required to hold them is not allocated until the objects are needed. Then, when these objects are no longer required, they may be destroyed and their memory reclaimed.

Although static objects are simple, they are also inflexible. Even if a system has multiple modes with mutually exclusive data structure requirements, an implementation based on static objects must provide sufficient memory to hold all data structures simultaneously. The system could make more effective use of its memory if memory were allocated for the objects associated with each operating mode as that mode was activated and then relinquished when the mode was deactivated. Then the relinquished memory could be reused for the objects of the next mode. In embedded real-time systems, this strategy can mean that less memory needs to be installed. Less memory can mean smaller hardware, using less power, generating less heat, and so forth.

As we will demonstrate shortly, dynamic objects also readily support another relationship among objects, the *uses* relationship. In this relationship, an object may be passed to the methods of another object as parameters. With the passed object comes all of its methods. Such passed objects may actually be from one of several generations in a class hierarchy, even further increasing the flexibility of this mechanism. The power of this capability will be examined in Chapter 7 under the name of *polymorphism*.

TRACKING DYNAMIC OBJECTS THROUGH POINTERS

Dynamic objects are instantiated at runtime. That is, after program execution has begun, explicit statements in the client program command the creation of the new object instance. This process includes a request to allocate the memory to hold the object. With most object-oriented programming systems, this memory is taken from a memory storage area called the *heap*. The client knows of the newly created object instance by a variable that holds a *pointer* to its allocated memory on the heap. So, to use dynamic objects, you must understand the use of pointers.

Before a dynamic object instance can be created, a variable to hold a pointer to the object will usually be declared. One way to do this is to declare a static variable of a type that points to a specific object class. For example, if the client program wanted to create a dynamic instance of a circle (as defined in our *Geometric Objects* unit), it could do so with a statement such as:

```
var
    ACircle   : ^Circle;
```

This statement allocates a static variable to hold a pointer to the dynamic object (for DOS systems, a pointer consists of two words that hold the *segment* and *offset* of a memory address). Now the client can instantiate the object by requesting that memory be allocated for it:

```
begin
    . . . . . . . . .
    new( ACircle );
```

Actually, this statement allocates the memory to hold the new object instance, but the object itself has not yet been created. The creation of a circle, as defined by the methods declared for the class *Circle*, requires that two messages be sent to the object. The notation for sending a message to a dynamic object is only slightly different from that of a static object:

```
. . . . . . . . . .
ACircle^.Init;
ACircle^.Create( { PtX    => } X,
                 { PtY    => } Y,
                 { Colr   => } BzlColor,
                 { Radius => } Size  );
. . . . . . . . . .
```

The notation difference consists of the addition of the caret ($\wedge$) reference symbol to the pointer name. This notation identifies the associated name as a pointer to an object and not the object itself. This same notation may now be used to send messages to the dynamic object requesting invocation of other class methods. For example:

```
. . . . . . . . . .
ACircle^.SetNewSize( { Radius => }
                          ACircle^.SizeIs + 10 );
ACircle^.Move( { PtX  => } ACircle^.GetX - 5,
               { PtY  => } ACircle^.GetY + 5  );
. . . . . . . . . .
```

As with static objects, a context block may be used to avoid having to explicitly declare the object for each message passed. For example:

```
. . . . . . . . . .
with ACircle^ do
  begin
    SetNewSize( { Radius => } SizeIs + 10 );
    Move( { PtX  => } GetX - 5,
          { PtY  => } GetY + 5  );
  end;    { with ACircle^ }
. . . . . . . . . .
```

Although these code segments are not part of a program, they would work if they were. Remember that we knew nothing of dynamic objects when we wrote the *Geometric Objects* unit. This shows how nothing special need be done in class definitions for them to be used for dynamic object instances. Method invocations within the object method definitions (e.g., *Circle*'s *Move* method invokes the *Erase*, *SetNewLocation*, and *Draw* methods) do not require the pointer referent ($\wedge$).

CONSTRUCTORS AND DYNAMIC OBJECT INITIALIZATION

We just allocated memory for a dynamic object by invoking the runtime memory manager's *new* procedure. Then the object was initialized in a separate step by sending a message to the new object (through its pointer) to have it invoke its initialization method. If that initialization method is declared as a *constructor*, then a shortcut initialization can be used.

Some object-oriented programming languages, such as C++, automatically invoke the object's constructor when the memory manager's *new* procedure is invoked. Turbo Pascal takes a slightly different approach.

The object-oriented extensions to Turbo Pascal permit passing the constructor to the memory manager's *new* procedure. This shortcut approximates how C++-like languages operate. In practice, this is coded as:

```
begin
    . . . . . . . . . .
    new( ACircle, Init );
    . . . . . . . . . .
```

This construct is valid only if *Init* is declared as a *constructor* in its class declaration. Turbo Pascal permits multiple constructors to be declared. At execution, however, only one constructor may be invoked.

If the constructor requires that actual parameters be passed, as in the following example from the demonstration program of this chapter, they are included in the statement as well:

```
begin
    . . . . . . . . . .
    new( Weapons, Init(
            { NumberOfTubes => } 19,
            { PanelX        => } (5 * MaxX) div 16,
            { PanelY        => } (5 * MaxY) div 8 ));
    . . . . . . . . . .
```

Turbo Pascal has an alternate form in which *new* may be treated as a function that returns a pointer value. This could be invoked as:

```
type
   PCircle  = ^Circle;
var
   ACircle  : PCircle;
begin
   . . . . . . . . . .
   ACircle := new( PCircle );
   . . . . . . . . . .
```

Finally, these two extensions can be combined:

```
var
  Weapons    : PRktSubsystem;
begin
  . . . . . . . . .
  Weapons := new( PRktSubsystem, Init(
          { NumberOfTubes => } 17,
          { PanelX        => } (5 * MaxX) div 16,
          { PanelY        => } (5 * MaxY) div 8 ));
  . . . . . . . . .
```

This illustrates a second significance of the constructor method. Recall that it was necessary for classes using virtual methods to invoke their *constructor* method to establish the linkage between an object instance and its class virtual method table.

DESTRUCTORS — GETTING RID OF DYNAMIC OBJECTS

As previously stated, dynamic objects are instantiated at runtime. They may also be disposed of at runtime, freeing their memory for other use. The deallocation of heap memory is achieved by invoking the memory manager's *dispose* procedure (the counterpart of *new*).

Before disposing of an object, it is frequently necessary to do certain object-specific clean-up processing. For example, an object may have opened a disk file or allocated memory for other dynamic objects. Object-oriented programming languages normally include a special method type called a *destructor*:

Destructor: a class method that, when used with the extended syntax of the dispose memory management procedure, allows for object clean-up and memory deallocation in a single step.

Turbo Pascal permits invoking an object's destructor when the memory manager's *dispose* procedure is called, in the same way the constructor may be tied to memory allocation with the *new* procedure.

Recalling the *Clock* class defined in the previous chapter, we defined a *destructor* that restored the interrupt vector for the hardware interval timer. If we were to create a dynamic instance of *Clock*, then its creation, use, and destruction might look like:

```
var
  TheClock    : ^Clock;
begin
  . . . . . . . . .
```

```
new( TheClock, Init(
              { XPos     => } MaxX div 4,
              { YPos     => } 3 * MaxY div 4,
              { Diameter => } MaxY div 8,
              { BzlColor => } White,
              { HndColor => } Green,
              { Interval => } 100 { 5 seconds } );
    . . . . . . . . .
      TheClock^.Update;  { inside of some loop }
    . . . . . . . . .
  dispose( TheClock, Done );
end.
```

The constructor *Init* set up the timer interrupt vector to point to the clock's new interrupt service routine. When use of *TheClock* is complete, the interrupt vector must be restored before the object *TheClock*'s memory is deallocated. In the dispose statement, *Done* is the name of *TheClock*'s destructor method. When used this way, the destructor is executed before the object's memory is deallocated.

Notice that the allocation and disposal of memory is requested by the client program and not by the object's methods themselves.

Although there are certain similarities between constructors and destructors, there are some distinct differences as well. Constructors cannot be virtual methods (remember that virtual methods are entered through the class Virtual Method Table, but the linkage between an object and its class VMT is established by invoking the object constructor). However, destructors may be either static or virtual methods. In fact, because you should assume that every object class will require unique clean-up processing, you should routinely declare destructors as virtual methods. This will ensure that the correct shutdown processing is always invoked.

Remember that constructors do nothing to allocate memory and destructors do nothing to deallocate it.

The above example of a dynamic instance of the object class *Clock* will work exactly as intended, even though we did not know about dynamic objects when we defined the class. As long as the class is declared with an appropriate constructor and destructor, both static and dynamic objects may be instantiated. With static object instances, the special characteristics of the keyword *destructor* are not required. However, as we demonstrated in the Chapter 5, no undesirable side effects are associated with invoking a static object's *destructor* method. It is simply treated as a procedure.

Therefore, by declaring classes with both constructors and destructors, the maximum flexibility is achieved because both static and dynamic objects may be instantiated from such classes.

A DYNAMIC OBJECT ROCKET CONTROL SYSTEM

This chapter's example program is fairly elaborate. In it, we create a complete rocket delivery subsystem for a hypothetical 3.0" Air-Launched Rocket (ALR) system. Rockets of this type have various uses, depending on the type of warhead and fuze mechanism installed. For example, a flare-like warhead, fuzed to detonate while still well above the ground, can be used to illuminate a battlefield during night combat. Or a high-explosive warhead, fuzed to "activate" at first impact but not detonate until nearly at a stop, can penetrate a bunker and explode inside. Our program includes an object class that may be configured with warheads and fuzes to support a variety of missions.

Such unguided rockets are typically launched from underwing multitube launcher assemblies, as illustrated in Figure 6.1. Our 3.0" ALRs are launched from seven- or 19-tube launchers. Each launcher has multiple zones: central (tubes 1 to 3), middle (tubes 4 to 7), and outer (tubes 8 to 19, for 19-tube launchers only), shown in Figure 6.1. The tube numbering order also specifies the firing sequence in each zone.

The rocket subsystem consists of two launchers, one on the port (left) and the other on the starboard (right) side of the aircraft (Figure 6.2), and a control panel (illustrated in Figure 6.3). Each zone may be loaded with only one rocket type (i.e., warhead/fuze pair), and both launchers must hold the same rocket type in their corresponding zones. Rocket firings must follow the tube number order in the

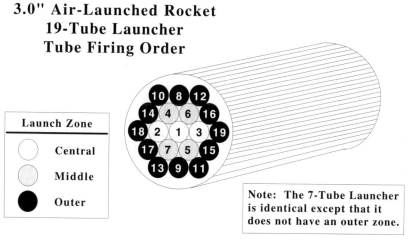

Figure 6.1. The "real world" model of our rocket launcher.

Figure 6.2. Our model has a pair of 19-tube rocket launchers.

selected zone, alternating from side to side in each zone.

Crew interface to the rocket subsystem is provided by a small control panel, generated on-screen by our example program. The panel has three horizontal lines, corresponding to the three launcher zones. The leftmost element of each line is an ARM button. When an ARM button is "pressed" (by pressing the left mouse button while the cursor is over it), the corresponding launcher zone is activated. The type of warhead mounted on the rockets in each zone is listed, along with the zone's available inventory. When a zone has been ARMed, "pressing" the FIRE button at the bottom of the panel "fires" one rocket from that zone. The available inventory is updated after each firing. The zone is *deactivated* automatically when the last rocket has been fired from that zone.

The object classes that implement this subsystem are illustrated in its class hierarchy diagram (Figure 6.4). Notice that two types of relationships are shown on this diagram. The *inheritance* relationship, used on previous hierarchy diagrams, is shown with a heavy solid line. The diagram shows that the class *TextBoxes* is descended from *Point* (from our *Geometric Objects* unit) and in turn is the ancestor of the class *Button*.

New on this diagram is the *part-of* relationship between classes. This relationship is different from inheritance but still identifies a strong dependency. For example, in this case the *RktSubsystem* class contains fields that are two objects of the *ALauncher* class and another that is an object of the *RktSubsysPanel* class. The *ALauncher* class has a field that contains 19 object instances of the ALRocket class. The broken lines run from the fields that specify the dependency to the class on which they are dependent. Where a single field specifies multiple instances of another class, the dependency path is labeled with its cardinality (number of instances). In this example, the number of such multiple instances is constant. If this were

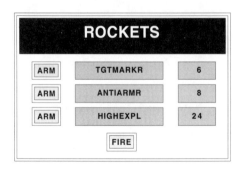

Figure 6.3. The rocket subsystem control panel.

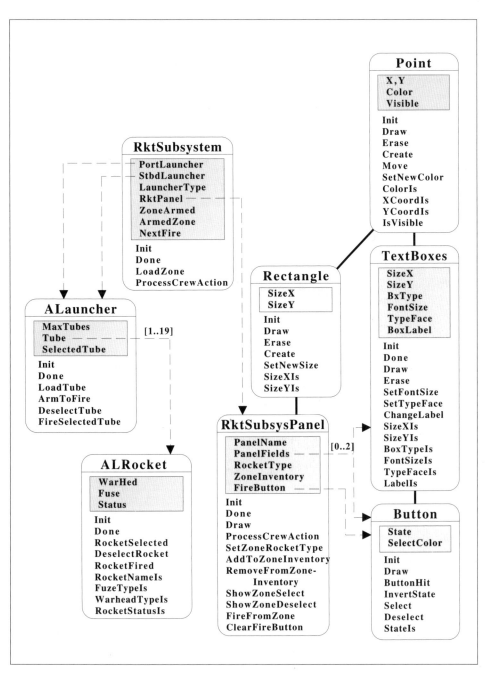

Figure 6.4.   Class hierarchy tree for the rockets subsystem.

not the case, then the label might read "[1..n]" to show an unspecified number of instances.

The following sections highlight the individual units and objects that make up this subsystem.

Text Boxes and Buttons, General Purpose Graphics

When programming for reuse, isolate objects that need not be tied to a single application (or even to an application domain, if possible). In our rockets subsystem, the primitive elements of the control panel are general-purpose graphics objects that could be used for any application requiring graphics mode control mechanisms.

The class *TextBoxes* provides a rectangle (a box) into which a text string is written. Text boxes serve as labels in the graphics mode displays. Such labels may be constant, as with the *ROCKETS* panel identification, or changed during execution, as with the zone inventory values.

The class *TextBoxes* extends the class *Point* from our Geometric Objects unit (see Chapter 4). *Point*'s virtual methods *Draw* and *Erase* must be redefined for each of its descendents. In addition, a destructor method named *Done* (the conventional name for destructors) is defined so text boxes may be instantiated as dynamic objects. The behavior of this class is self-explanatory.

Notice one additional new convention. In addition to declaring the object class *TextBoxes*, there is a type declared for pointers to that class. By convention, the names of these class pointer types will begin with the letter "P" followed by the name of the object class to which they point. In this case, the pointer type is named *PTextBoxes*. By always declaring a pointer type for each class, use of dynamic objects is made easier. For example, dynamic objects may be passed as parameters to procedures and functions. To accomplish this, the pointer type must be declared so it can be used in the formal parameter declaration.

The class *Button* extends *TextBoxes* by adding an active element. *Button* objects are used with the *GraphicMouse* class defined in Chapter 5. The active feature is embodied by the *State*, allowing the button to be *Selected* or *NotSelected*. The method that adds the new active behavior is *ButtonHit*, which, when given a set of screen coordinates (presumably the location of the mouse), tells whether those coordinates are over the button. Again, unique behavior for this descendent is defined by the *Init* and *Draw* methods. Notice that the destructor *Done* is inherited from *TextBoxes* (i.e., it is not formally declared in *Button*). The remaining newly declared methods define the behavior of the newly declared field *State*.

Objects instantiated from the class *Button* are intended for use with an object instantiated from *GraphicMouse*. To emphasize this intended dependency, the unit *Buttons* includes a static instantiation of *GraphicMouse*. This ensures that users of *Buttons* always have access to *GMouse*, the *GraphicMouse* instance.

```
unit TextBox;

{ Program:      Text-Box — a box with a text label in it..
  Author:       John R. Ellis
  Last Update:  27 July 1991
  Copyright (c) 1991 by John R. Ellis

  Description:  This unit provides an object class which represents
                a screen image which represents a box with a text
                label.

  Requirements: This unit assumes use of the Turbo Pascal Graph unit.
                                                                        }
interface

   uses Graph,Geo_Objs;

   type

       ARectangle = array[1..5] of Graph.PointType;

       LabelString = string[20];      { type for button label }

       BoxType  = ( Single, Double );        { box outline shapes }

       {===================================================================}
       {                       Object Declarations                         }
       {===================================================================}

       PTextBoxes = ^TextBoxes;
       TextBoxes = object ( Geo_Objs.Point )
                 constructor Init( PtX, PtY      : integer;
                                   Width, Height : integer;
                                   BoxOutline    : BoxType;
                                   FieldColor    : integer;
                                   LabelText     : LabelString );
                 destructor Done; virtual;
                 procedure Draw; virtual;
                 procedure Erase; virtual;
                 procedure SetFontSize( NewFontSize : integer );
                 procedure SetTypeFace( NewTextFont : integer );
                 procedure ChangeLabel( LabelText : LabelString ); {redraws}
                 function SizeXIs    : integer;
                 function SizeYIs    : integer;
                 function BoxTypeIs  : BoxType;
                 function FontSizeIs : integer;
                 function TypeFaceIs : integer;
                 function LabelIs    : LabelString;
               private
                 SizeX          : integer;   { horizontal box field size }
                 SizeY          : integer;   { vertical box field size }
```

Figure 6.5. Code listing: unit TEXTBOX.PAS. *(continued)*

```
              BxType        : BoxType;
              FontSize      : integer;
              TypeFace      : integer;
              BoxLabel      : LabelString;
         end;     { object = TextBoxes }


  {=================================================================}
  {                  Utility Procedure Declarations                 }
  {=================================================================}

    procedure MakeRectangle(     X1, Y1, X2, Y2   : integer;
                           var RectangleArray   : ARectangle );

  {------------- end of interface section ------------}
  implementation

  {=================================================================}
  {                    Free Utility Definition                      }
  {=================================================================}
   procedure MakeRectangle(     X1, Y1, X2, Y2   : integer;
                           var RectangleArray   : ARectangle );
      begin
        RectangleArray[1].X := X1;       { Set upper left corner }
          RectangleArray[1].Y := Y1;
        RectangleArray[2].X := X2;       { Set upper right corner }
          RectangleArray[2].Y := Y1;
        RectangleArray[3].X := X2;       { Set lower right corner }
          RectangleArray[3].Y := Y2;
        RectangleArray[4].X := X1;       { Set lower left corner }
          RectangleArray[4].Y := Y2;
        RectangleArray[5].X := X1;       { Return to upper left corner }
          RectangleArray[5].Y := Y1;
      end;   { Free Utility: MakeRectangle }


  {=================================================================}
  {           Method Definitions for:   TextBoxes                   }
  {=================================================================}
   constructor TextBoxes.Init( PtX, PtY      : integer;
                              Width, Height : integer;
                              BoxOutline    : BoxType;
                              FieldColor    : integer;
                              LabelText     : LabelString );
      begin
        SetFontSize( 10 );            { default FontSize }
        SetTypeFace( SmallFont );     { default TypeFace }
        BxType := BoxOutline;
        SetNewLocation( { PtX => } PtX,
                  { PtY => } PtY  );
          { ensure minimum dimensions }
        if Width < 20
          then SizeX := 20
          else SizeX := Width;
        if Height < 20
```

```
        then SizeY := 20
        else SizeY := Height;
      BoxLabel := LabelText;
      SetNewColor( FieldColor );   { draws new text box in this method }
   end;     { TextBoxes.Init }

destructor TextBoxes.Done;     { note: ancestor does not have destructor }
   begin
   end;     { TextBoxes.Done }

procedure TextBoxes.Draw;
   var
      BxWidth, BxHeight    : integer;  { working dimensions of button }
      BxRect               : ARectangle;
      TSize                : integer;  { font size computation var }
   begin
       { set a viewport for the button being drawn..... }
      SetViewPort( { UpperLeft  => } XCoordIs, YCoordIs,
                   { LowerRight => } XCoordIs+SizeX, YCoordIs+SizeY,
                   { Clipping   => } ClipOn );
      Graph.SetColor( ColorIs );
      Graph.SetFillStyle( SolidFill, ColorIs );
      case BxType of
          Single : begin
                     MakeRectangle( { UpperLeft     => } 0, 0,
                                    { LowerRight     => } SizeX, SizeY,
                                    { RectangleArray => } BxRect   );
                     Graph.FillPoly( { NumbPoints => } 5,
                                     { PolyPoints => } BxRect   );
                     BxWidth := SizeX - 10;
                     BxHeight := SizeY - 10;
                   end;
          Double : begin
                     Graph.Rectangle( { UpperLeft  => } 0, 0,
                                      { LowerRight => } SizeX,SizeY );
                     MakeRectangle( { UpperLeft      => } 3, 3,
                                    { LowerRight     => } SizeX-3,SizeY-3,
                                    { RectangleArray => } BxRect   );
                     Graph.FillPoly( { NumbPoints => } 5,
                                     { PolyPoints => } BxRect   );
                     BxWidth := SizeX - 12;
                     BxHeight := SizeY - 12;
                   end;
       end;    { case }
         { adjust fonts and string to fit in button }
      Graph.SetTextStyle( { Font      => } TypeFace,
                          { Direction => } HorizDir,
                          { CharSize  => } FontSize );
      for TSize := FontSize downto 1 do
        if ( Graph.TextWidth( BoxLabel ) > BxWidth )
          then
            Graph.SetTextStyle( { Font      => } TypeFace,
                                { Direction => } HorizDir,
                                { CharSize  => } TSize )
```

(continued)

```
                else
                  if ( Graph.TextHeight( BoxLabel ) > BxHeight )
                    then
                      Graph.SetTextStyle( { Font       => } TypeFace,
                                          { Direction => } HorizDir,
                                          { CharSize  => } TSize );
                { write the label into the box..... }
             Graph.SetColor( { Color => } Graph.GetBkColor );
             Graph.SetTextJustify( { Horiz => } CenterText,
                                   { Vert  => } CenterText   );
             Graph.OutTextXY( { X          => } SizeX div 2,
                              { Y          => } SizeY div 2,
                              { TextString => } BoxLabel        );
                { restore viewport to entire screen for return }
             SetViewPort( { UpperLeft   => } 0, 0,
                          { LowerRight => } GetMaxX, GetMaxY,
                          { Clipping   => } ClipOn );
         end;    { TextBoxes.Draw }

      procedure TextBoxes.Erase;
         begin
             SetViewPort( { UpperLeft   => } XCoordIs, YCoordIs,
                          { LowerRight => } XCoordIs+SizeX, YCoordIs+SizeY,
                          { Clipping   => } ClipOn );
             ClearViewPort;
         end;    { TextBoxes.Erase }

      procedure TextBoxes.SetFontSize( NewFontSize : integer );
         begin
             FontSize := NewFontSize;
         end;    { TextBoxes.SetFontSize }

      procedure TextBoxes.SetTypeFace( NewTextFont : integer );
         { NOTE:  The unit Graph defines the following candidate symbolic
                  input parameters for this method:
                      DefaultFont    = 0
                      TriplexFont    = 1
                      SmallFont      = 2
                      SansSerifFont = 3
                      GothicFont     = 4                          }
         begin
             TypeFace := NewTextFont;
         end;    { TextBoxes.SetTypeFace }

      procedure TextBoxes.ChangeLabel( LabelText : LabelString );
         begin
             BoxLabel := LabelText;
             Draw;                      { Redraws with new text }
         end;    { TextBoxes.ChangeLabel }

      function TextBoxes.SizeXIs : integer;
         begin
             SizeXIs := SizeX;
```

```
      end;    { TextBoxes.SizeXIs }

  function TextBoxes.SizeYIs : integer;
     begin
       SizeYIs := SizeY;
     end;    { TextBoxes.SizeYIs }

  function TextBoxes.BoxTypeIs  : BoxType;
     begin
       BoxTypeIs := BxType;
     end;    { TextBoxes.BoxTypeIs }

  function TextBoxes.FontSizeIs : integer;
     begin
       FontSizeIs := FontSize;
     end;    { TextBoxes.FontSizeIs }

  function TextBoxes.TypeFaceIs : integer;
     begin
       TypeFaceIs := TypeFace;
     end;    { TextBoxes.TypeFaceIs }

  function TextBoxes.LabelIs    : LabelString;
     begin
       LabelIs := BoxLabel;
     end;    { TextBoxes.LabelIs }

{=======================================================================}
{                       No Initialization Code                          }

  end.
```

(end)

```
unit Buttons;

{ Program:     Buttons — a display "Button" library unit
  Author:      John R. Ellis
  Last Update: 27 July 1991
  Copyright (c) 1991 by John R. Ellis

  Description: This unit provides an object class which represents
               a screen image which represents a "button," or push-
               to-activate switch.  Typically, clicking the mouse on
               the button activates a client-defined function.

  Requirements: This unit assumes use of the Turbo Pascal Graph unit.
                                                                        }
```

Figure 6.6.   Code listing: unit BUTTONS.PAS.   *(continued)*

```
interface

   uses Graph,Geo_Objs,TextBox,Mouse;

   type

      ButtonStates = ( NotSelected, Selected );

      {==================================================================}
      {                      Object Declarations                         }
      {==================================================================}

      PButton = ^Button;
      Button = object ( TextBox.TextBoxes )
               constructor Init( PtX, PtY       : integer;
                                 Width, Height : integer;
                                 ButnType      : TextBox.BoxType;
                                 NormColor     : integer;
                                 SelColor      : integer;
                                 LabelText     : LabelString );
               procedure Draw; virtual;
               function ButtonHit( ScrnX, ScrnY : integer ) : boolean;
               procedure InvertState;  { inverts state & redraws button }
               procedure Select;
               procedure Deselect;
               function StateIs : ButtonStates;
             private
               State         : ButtonStates;
               SelectColor   : integer;   { color when selected }
             end;     { object = Button }

   var
     GMouse   : GraphicMouse;

{————————- end of interface section ————————-}
implementation

{=======================================================================}
{                 Method Definitions for:  Button                       }
{=======================================================================}
 constructor Button.Init( PtX, PtY       : integer;
                          Width, Height : integer;
                          ButnType      : TextBox.BoxType;
                          NormColor     : integer;
                          SelColor      : integer;
                          LabelText     : LabelString );
     begin
       State := NotSelected;          { initial state    }
       SelectColor := SelColor;
       TextBoxes.Init( { PtX, PtY       => } PtX, PtY,
                       { Width, Height => } Width, Height,
                       { BoxOutline    => } ButnType,
                       { FieldColor    => } NormColor,
```

```
                         { LabelText      => } LabelText    );
    end;    { Button.Init }

procedure Button.Draw;
    var
       BtnWidth, BtnHeight : integer;  { working dimensions of button }
       BtnRect             : TextBox.ARectangle;
       TSize               : integer;  { font size computation var }
    begin
       { set a viewport for the button being drawn..... }
       SetViewPort( { UpperLeft  => } XCoordIs, YCoordIs,
                    { LowerRight => } XCoordIs+SizeXIs, YCoordIs+SizeYIs,
                    { Clipping   => } ClipOn );
       if State = Selected
         then
           begin
             Graph.SetColor( SelectColor );
             Graph.SetFillStyle( SolidFill, SelectColor );
           end
         else
           begin
             Graph.SetColor( ColorIs );  { normal color if not selected }
             Graph.SetFillStyle( WideDotFill, ColorIs );
           end;
       case BoxTypeIs of
          Single : begin
                     MakeRectangle( { UpperLeft    => } 0, 0,
                                    { LowerRight   => } SizeXIs,SizeYIs,
                                    { RectangleArray => } BtnRect );
                     Graph.FillPoly( { NumbPoints => } 5,
                            .           { PolyPoints => } BtnRect );
                     BtnWidth := SizeXIs - 10;
                     BtnHeight := SizeYIs - 10;
                   end;
          Double : begin
                     MakeRectangle( { UpperLeft  => } 3, 3,
                                    { LowerRight => } SizeXIs-3,SizeYIs-3,
                                    { RectangleArray => } BtnRect );
                     Graph.FillPoly( { NumbPoints => } 5,
                                     { PolyPoints => } BtnRect );
                       { always draw the outer rect in normal color }
                     Graph.SetColor( ColorIs );
                     Graph.Rectangle( { UpperLeft  => } 0, 0,
                                      { LowerRight => } SizeXIs,SizeYIs );
                     BtnWidth := SizeXIs - 12;
                     BtnHeight := SizeYIs - 12;
                   end;
       end;   { case }
          { adjust fonts and string to fit in button }
       Graph.SetTextStyle( { Font      => } TypeFaceIs,
                           { Direction => } HorizDir,
                           { CharSize  => } FontSizeIs );
       for TSize := FontSizeIs downto 1 do
```

(continued)

```
        if ( Graph.TextWidth( LabelIs ) > BtnWidth )
          then
            Graph.SetTextStyle( { Font      => } TypeFaceIs,
                                { Direction => } HorizDir,
                                { CharSize  => } TSize )
          else
            if ( Graph.TextHeight( LabelIs ) > BtnHeight )
              then
                Graph.SetTextStyle( { Font      => } TypeFaceIs,
                                    { Direction => } HorizDir,
                                    { CharSize  => } TSize );
          { write the label onto the button..... }
      if State = Selected
        then Graph.SetColor( { Color => } Graph.GetBkColor );
      Graph.SetTextJustify( { Horiz => } CenterText,
                            { Vert  => } CenterText   );
      Graph.OutTextXY( { X         => } SizeXIs div 2,
                       { Y         => } SizeYIs div 2,
                       { TextString => } LabelIs      );
          { restore viewport to entire screen for return }
      SetViewPort( { UpperLeft  => } 0, 0,
                   { LowerRight => } GetMaxX, GetMaxY,
                   { Clipping   => } ClipOn );
      end;    { Button.Draw }

function Button.ButtonHit( ScrnX, ScrnY : integer ) : boolean;
   begin
      if ( ScrnX >= XCoordIs ) and ( ScrnX <= XCoordIs+SizeXIs )
                                and
         ( ScrnY >= YCoordIs ) and ( ScrnY <= YCoordIs+SizeYIs )
         then
           begin
             InvertState;
             ButtonHit := true;
           end
         else
           ButtonHit := false;
      end;    { Button.ButtonHit }

procedure Button.InvertState;
   begin
      if State = NotSelected
        then State := Selected
        else State := NotSelected;
      Draw;                { redraw in new state }
      end;    { Button.InvertState }

procedure Button.Select;
   begin
      if State = NotSelected
        then InvertState;
      end;    { Button.Select }
```

```
procedure Button.Deselect;
   begin
     if State = Selected
       then InvertState;
   end;    { Button.Deselect }

function Button.StateIs : ButtonStates;
   begin
     StateIs := State;
   end;    { Button.StateIs }
{========================================================================}
{                      No Initialization Code                            }
end.
```

Rockets, Launchers, Control Panels

The physical entities of our rockets subsystem are comprised of three objects: the rockets, the launchers, and the control panel. In Part II of this book, we will develop a methodology that assists in identifying objects in the problem space. However, these objects fall out simply from reading a problem description.

The most primitive object of our subsystem is the rocket itself, defined in the class *ALRocket*. The class fields define the rocket configuration by its warhead and fuze types. These fields are relatively static because once the rocket has been initialized, these fields will not change. The final field specifies the current status of a rocket instance (*Null, Ready, Selected, Fire*).

This class uses function methods to perform an action and then return the status of the operation. The method *RocketSelected* attempts to change the rocket state to *Selected*. If it is successful, then *Successful* is returned as the function value. Similarly, the method *RocketFired* attempts to launch a rocket. If the rocket was not previously selected, then it cannot be fired, so *Failed* is returned as the function value. In a real rocket system, this method would contain the protocol needed to issue fire commands to the rocket and then confirm the launch.

The rocket subsystem consists primarily of three object instances: the two launchers and a control panel.

The launcher object (*ALauncher* class) contains a field that represents an array of 19 *Tube*s. Each *Tube* can "hold" a rocket, in the form of a pointer to an instance of the *ALRocket* class.

One of the major methods of the *ALauncher* class is *LoadTube*. Notice that this method is passed a rocket (a pointer to a dynamic object instance) and a tube into which the rocket is to be loaded. The result of this operation is returned in the

Results parameter. This example illustrates another relationship between objects, the *uses* relationship. The code that defines the behavior of the *LoadTube* method stores the pointer to the rocket, which it *uses*, in the designated element of the *Tube* array. This pointer may then be used to send messages to specific rockets to "select" and "fire" them.

Because the only copies of the pointers to the rocket instances are held in the *Tube* array field, to dispose of a launcher object without relinquishing the memory held by the individual rockets will "orphan" those objects. That is, they will continue to exist in heap memory, but there will be no way to send messages to them because there will no longer be pointers to them. The necessary clean-up is provided in the destructor:

```
destructor ALauncher.Done;
   var
    i      : integer;
   begin
    for i := 1 to MaxTubes do
      if Tube[i] <> nil
        then
           dispose( Tube[i],Done );
    end;      { ALauncher.Done }
```

For the sake of ensuring that the rocket has an opportunity to do its necessary clean-up, the *dispose* statement includes the optional extension to invoke the object destructor *Done*. This memory deallocation and rocket destructor invocation is repeated for each *Tube*. *ALauncher*'s destructor will be invoked when the subsystem object is ready to dispose of the launcher object.

The rocket control panel, described by class *RktSubsysPanel*, implements the panel illustrated in Figure 6.2. First, an instance of the class *TextBoxes* is used for the panel label "ROCKETS". A record type (*DisplayRecord*) defines the three graphics objects (one *Button* and two *TextBoxes*) required for each launcher zone. *RktSubsysPanel* has a field (*PanelFields*) that holds an array of three *DisplayRecords*, one for each zone. The final element of the panel is another *Button* instance, the "FIRE" button.

The primary function of the control panel object is to respond to the user's mouse inputs. The method that provides this behavior (*ProcessCrewAction*) interprets client-provided "Mouse" screen coordinates by determining whether any of the active *Buttons* has been selected. If one has, a corresponding action code is returned to the client.

Notice how all of the elements described above, making up the control panel itself, are implemented as dynamic objects. The class constructor *Init* instantiates each of these dynamic objects, drawing the individual entities on the display with default values (rocket types are "UNDEFINED" and each zone has an inventory of zero). The class destructor then disposes of each of these dynamic objects.

Putting It All Together

The objects discussed thus far represent real, physical entities (with the "control panel" being implemented as a screen image). The final object in this example is an abstraction. The rockets subsystem (class *RktSubsystem*) is a collection of previously described objects that interact in response to user commands.

At this point in our developing understanding of object-oriented systems, this may seem like a small point because of how we have built this model from the bottom up. However, in Part II of this book we examine a methodology for identifying the objects needed to satisfy a specific system's requirements. For large or complex systems, with potentially hundreds or thousands of discrete objects, the methodology must be able to combine groups of objects into higher-level "objects" that consist primarily of other objects. If these higher-level entities are themselves objects (as our control panel is a collection of *Buttons* and *TextBoxes*), then it is convenient to refer to the collection as a "mechanism." However, these higher-level objects often have no single physical counterpart and therefore must be defined as a higher abstraction, such as a "subsystem." For the purpose of describing complex, composite objects, the following definitions may be applied:

Mechanism: a complex object, consisting largely of other objects interacting in some well-defined manner to represent an entity in the real world.

Subsystem: a complex abstract object, consisting largely of other objects that have a logical relationship. A subsystem may be thought of as a collection of objects that relate to a common function. Avionics subsystems traditionally include: navigation, communications, flight controls, fire control, hydraulics, and so forth.

The *RktSubsystem* class has three of its fields holding instances of dynamic objects. Two of these correspond to the port (*PortLauncher*) and starboard (*StbdLauncher*) launchers. The other field (*RktPanel*) is the dynamic instance of the control panel.

The other fields support these objects. For example, the field *NextFire* remembers (for each of the three zones) which launcher, port or starboard, will be the one from which the next rocket should be launched. This field is necessary to satisfy the requirement that rocket firing in each zone alternate from side to side. The Boolean field *ZoneArmed* reflects whether or not the user has armed a zone, and if a zone has been armed, *ArmedZone* specifies which one. Finally, *LauncherType* indicates how many tubes each launcher has.

Other than the constructor and destructor, this class has two methods. The first loads all tubes of the specified zone, for both launchers, with the designated

```
unit Rockets;

{ Program:      Rockets — A Rocket system support unit
  Author:       John R. Ellis
  Last Update:  31 July 1991
  Copyright (c) 1991 by John R. Ellis

  Description:  This unit provides an object class which represents
                3.0" Air-Launched Rocket (ALR) objects.

  Requirements: Objects of the Rocket class should be used with the
                objects of the Launcher class.
                                                                        }
interface

   type
      { types needed to describe rocket configuration }
      WarheadType = ( Practice,      { flash/smoke marker for training }
                      Illumination,  { flare descending by parachute }
                      SmokeScreen,   { area coverage smoke canister }
                      TargetMarker,  { colored smoke stream }
                      AntiPersonnel, { airburst shrapnel }
                      AntiArmor,     { penetration & high explosive }
                      HighExplosive  { general purpose—big bang } );
      FuzeType    = ( Impact,        { quickfire at first impact }
                      Penetration,   { arms @ impact; fires at stop }
                      BurnoutSense   { fires at end of acceleration } );
      { rocket states ...... }
      RktStatus   = ( Null,          { undefined or already fired }
                      Ready,         { loaded and ready for use }
                      Selected,      { ready to be fired }
                      Fire           { igniter activated } );
      SuccessState = ( Successful, Failed );


      {===================================================================}
      {                        Object Declarations                        }
      {===================================================================}
      PALRocket = ^ALRocket;
      ALRocket = object
               constructor Init( WarHead : WarheadType;
                                 Fuze    : FuzeType );
               destructor Done; virtual;
               function RocketSelected : SuccessState;
               procedure DeselectRocket;
               function RocketFired   : SuccessState;
               function RocketNameIs   : String;
               function FuzeTypeIs     : FuzeType;
               function WarheadTypeIs   : WarheadType;
               function RocketStatusIs : RktStatus;
            private
               Warhed      : WarheadType;
               Fuse        : FuzeType;
```

Figure 6.7.   Code listing: unit ROCKETS.PAS.

```
              Status      : RktStatus;
           end;      { object = ALRocket }

{——————— end of interface section ————————-}
implementation

  uses CRT;

{=========================================================================}
{              Method Definitions for:  ALRocket                          }
{=========================================================================}
 constructor ALRocket.Init( WarHead : WarheadType;
                            Fuze    : FuzeType );
    begin
      Warhed := WarHead;
      Fuze   := Fuze;
      Status := Ready;
    end;      { ALRocket.Init }

 destructor ALRocket.Done;
    begin
    end;      { ALRocket.Done }

 function ALRocket.FuzeTypeIs    : FuzeType;
    begin
      FuzeTypeIs := Fuze;
    end;      { ALRocket.FuzeTypeIs }

 function ALRocket.WarheadTypeIs  : WarheadType;
    begin
      WarheadTypeIs := Warhed;
    end;      { ALRocket.WarheadTypeIs }

 function ALRocket.RocketNameIs    : string;
    begin
      case Warhed of
          Practice     : RocketNameIs := 'PRACTICE';
          Illumination : RocketNameIs := 'ILLUMIN ';
          SmokeScreen  : RocketNameIs := 'SMOKSCRN';
          TargetMarker : RocketNameIs := 'TGTMARKR';
          AntiPersonnel : RocketNameIs := 'ANTIPERS';
          AntiArmor    : RocketNameIs := 'ANTIARMR';
          HighExplosive : RocketNameIs := 'HIGHEXPL';
        else
          RocketNameIs := '*UNKNOWN';
        end;     { case }
    end;      { ALRocket.RocketNameIs }

 function ALRocket.RocketStatusIs  : RktStatus;
    begin
      RocketStatusIs := Status;
    end;      { ALRocket.RocketStatusIs }

 function ALRocket.RocketSelected : SuccessState;
```

(continued)

```
    var
      TempState   : SuccessState;
    begin
      TempState := Failed;
      if RocketStatusIs = Ready
        then
          begin
            Status := Selected;
            TempState := Successful;
          end;
      RocketSelected := TempState;
    end;    { ALRocket.RocketSelected }

 procedure ALRocket.DeselectRocket;
    begin
      Status := Ready;
    end;    { ALRocket.DeselectRocket }
 function ALRocket.RocketFired   : SuccessState;
    var
      TempState   : SuccessState;
    begin
      TempState := Failed;
      if RocketStatusIs = Selected
        then
          begin
            Status := Fire;
            CRT.Delay( 100 );
            { check to see if fire was successful, assume it was }
            Status := Null;
            TempState := Successful;
          end;
      RocketFired := TempState;
    end;    { ALRocket.RocketFired }


{==========================================================================}
{                        No Initialization Code                            }

end.
```

(end)

```
unit Launcher;

{ Program:     Launcher — A Rocket Launcher system support unit
  Author:      John R. Ellis
  Last Update: 31 July 1991
  Copyright (c) 1991 by John R. Ellis
```

Figure 6.8.   Code listing: unit LAUNCHER.PAS.

```
  Description:  This unit provides an object class which represents
                the two Launchers for 3.0" Air-Launched Rocket (ALR)
                objects.

  Requirements: This unit uses objects from the Rockets unit.
                                                                    }
interface

  uses Rockets;

  type
        { launcher firing zones.......... }
      ZoneType = ( Central,     { tubes 1..3 }
                   Middle,      { tubes 4..7 }
                   Outer        { tubes 8..19 } );

      SuccessState = ( Successful, Failed );

      {================================================================}
      {                      Object Declarations                       }
      {================================================================}

      PALauncher = ^ALauncher;
      ALauncher = object
              constructor Init( NumberOfTubes : integer );
              destructor Done; virtual;
              procedure LoadTube( TubeNumber : integer;
                                  Rocket     : Rockets.PALRocket;
                              var Results    : SuccessState );
              procedure ArmToFire( Zone      : ZoneType );
              procedure DeselectTube;
              function FireSelectedTube : SuccessState;
            private
              MaxTubes     : integer;       { number of tubes }
              Tube         : array[1..19] of Rockets.PALRocket;
              SelectedTube : integer;       { next tube to fire }
            end;      { object = ALauncher }

{------------- end of interface section -------------}
implementation

{==========================================================================}
{              Method Definitions for:  ALauncher                          }
{==========================================================================}
 constructor ALauncher.Init( NumberOfTubes  : integer );
    var
      i    : integer;
    begin
      MaxTubes := NumberOfTubes;
      for i := 1 to MaxTubes do
          Tube[i] := nil;        { empty tube has no rocket to point to }
    end;      { ALauncher.Init }
```

(continued)

```
destructor ALauncher.Done;
    var
      i    : integer;
    begin
      for i := 1 to MaxTubes do
        if Tube[i] <> nil      { deallocate memory for remaining rockets }
          then
            dispose( Tube[i],Done );
    end;    { ALauncher.Done }

procedure ALauncher.LoadTube( TubeNumber : integer;
                              Rocket     : Rockets.PALRocket;
                          var Results    : SuccessState );
    begin
      Results := Successful;
      if ( TubeNumber > 0 ) and ( TubeNumber <= MaxTubes )
        then
          if Tube[TubeNumber] = nil
            then
              Tube[TubeNumber] := Rocket
            else
              { attempt to load a rocket in a tube that's already loaded }
              Results := Failed
        else
          { attempt to load a rocket in a nonexistent tube }
          Results := Failed;
    end;    { ALauncher.LoadTube }

procedure ALauncher.ArmToFire( Zone     : ZoneType  );
    var
      MinTubeNo, MaxTubeNo   : integer;
      i                      : integer;
      Exit                   : boolean;
    begin
      case Zone of
        Central : begin
                    MinTubeNo := 1;
                    MaxTubeNo := 3;
                  end;
        Middle  : begin
                    MinTubeNo := 4;
                    MaxTubeNo := 7;
                  end;
        Outer   : begin
                    MinTubeNo := 8;
                    MaxTubeNo := 19;
                  end;
        end;      { case }
      SelectedTube := 0;
      Exit := false;
      i := MinTubeNo;
      while ( i <= MaxTubeNo ) and not Exit do
        begin
```

```
            if Tube[i]^.RocketSelected = Rockets.Successful
              then
                begin
                  SelectedTube := i;
                  Exit := true;
                end
              else
                i := i + 1;
         end;    { while...do }
    end;       { ALauncher.ArmToFire }

  procedure ALauncher.DeselectTube;
    begin
      Tube[SelectedTube]^.DeselectRocket;
      SelectedTube := 0;
    end;       { ALauncher.DeselectTube }

  function ALauncher.FireSelectedTube : SuccessState;
    begin
      FireSelectedTube := SuccessState( Tube[SelectedTube]^.RocketFired );
    end;       { ALauncher.FireSelectedTube }

{=======================================================================}
{                        No Initialization Code                         }

end.
```

(end)

```
unit RktSubsy;

{ Program:      Rockets Subsystem unit
  Author:       John R. Ellis
  Last Update:  31 July 1991
  Copyright (c) 1991 by John R. Ellis

  Description:  This unit provides an object class which represents
                an aircraft's rocket delivery subsystem.  The subsystem
                may have two launchers for 3.0" Air Launched Rockets.

  Requirements: Objects of this class reference launcher class objects
                from the Launcher unit, which in turn work with
                elements of the Rocket class.
                                                                       }
interface

   uses Geo_Objs,TextBox,Buttons,Rockets,Launcher;
```

Figure 6.9. Code listing: unit RKTSUBSY.PAS. *(continued)*

```
type
    ActionStatus = ( None,              { handled locally.... }
                     ZoneSelected,      { activated zone select button }
                     ZoneDeselected,  { deactivated zone select button }
                     RocketFired );   { fire button activated }

    ActiveLauncher = ( Port, Starboard );

    DisplayRecord = record
        SelectButton  : Buttons.PButton;
        ZoneSelected  : boolean;
        RktTypeField  : TextBox.PTextBoxes;
        RocketCount   : TextBox.PTextBoxes;
    end;    { record: DisplayRecord }

    {===================================================================}
    {                      Object Declarations                          }
    {===================================================================}

    PRktSubsysPanel = ^RktSubsysPanel;
    RktSubsysPanel = object ( Geo_Objs.Rectangle )
            constructor Init( PtX, PtY : integer );
            destructor Done; virtual;
            procedure Draw; virtual;
            procedure ProcessCrewAction( MouseX : integer;
                                         MouseY : integer;
                                     var Action : ActionStatus;
                                     var Zone   : Launcher.ZoneType );
            procedure SetZoneRocketType( Zone   : Launcher.ZoneType;
                                         RocketTypeName : String   );
            procedure AddToZoneInventory( Zone : Launcher.ZoneType );
            procedure RemoveFromZoneInventory(Zone :Launcher.ZoneType);
            procedure ShowZoneSelect( Zone : Launcher.ZoneType );
            procedure ShowZoneDeselect( Zone : Launcher.ZoneType );
            procedure FireFromZone( Zone        : Launcher.ZoneType;
                                var ZoneEmpty : boolean          );
            procedure ClearFireButton;
        private
            PanelName     : TextBox.PTextBoxes;
            PanelFields   : array[Launcher.ZoneType] of DisplayRecord;
            RocketType    : array[Launcher.ZoneType] of String;
            ZoneInventory : array[Launcher.ZoneType] of integer;
            FireButton    : Buttons.PButton;
        end;    { object = RktSubsysPanel }

    PRktSubsystem = ^RktSubsystem;
    RktSubsystem = object
            constructor Init( NumberOfTubes  : integer;
                              PanelX, PanelY : integer );
            destructor Done; virtual;
            procedure LoadZone( Zone     : Launcher.ZoneType;
                                WarHead  : Rockets.WarheadType;
                                Fuze     : Rockets.FuzeType   );
```

```
              procedure ProcessCrewAction( MouseX, MouseY : integer );
          private
              PortLauncher    : Launcher.PALauncher;
              StbdLauncher    : Launcher.PALauncher;
              LauncherType    : integer;        { number of tubes }
                  { the rocket control panel }
              RktPanel        : PRktSubsysPanel;
              ZoneArmed       : boolean;
              ArmedZone       : Launcher.ZoneType;
              NextFire        : array[Launcher.ZoneType] of ActiveLauncher;
          end;      { object = RktSubsystem }

{------------- end of interface section -------------}
implementation

  uses Graph,CRT;

{=====================================================================}
{                   Local Free Subprogram Definition                  }
{=====================================================================}
 function MakeStr( Intgr : integer ) : string;
    var
      Strng   : string;
    begin
      str( Intgr:2, Strng );
      MakeStr := Strng;
    end;   { local free subprogram: MakeStr }

{=====================================================================}
{              Method Definitions for:  RktSubsystem                   }
{=====================================================================}
 constructor RktSubsystem.Init( NumberOfTubes   : integer;
                                PanelX, PanelY : integer );
    var
      i                 : Launcher.ZoneType;
    begin
      ZoneArmed := false;
      for i := Launcher.Central to Launcher.Outer do
        NextFire[i] := Port;
      LauncherType := NumberOfTubes;
      new( PortLauncher, Init( { NumberOfTubes => } NumberOfTubes ));
      new( StbdLauncher, Init( { NumberOfTubes => } NumberOfTubes ));
          { initialize the rocket control panel...... }
      new( RktPanel, Init( { PtX => } PanelX,
                           { PtY => } PanelY ));
    end;     { RktSubsystem.Init }

 destructor RktSubsystem.Done;
    begin
      dispose( PortLauncher, Done );
      dispose( StbdLauncher, Done );
      dispose( RktPanel, Done );
    end;     { RktSubsystem.Done }
```

(continued)

```
procedure RktSubsystem.LoadZone( Zone      : Launcher.ZoneType;
                                 WarHead   : Rockets.WarheadType;
                                 Fuze      : Rockets.FuzeType  );
   { assumptions: 1. only one rocket type per zone
                  2. same rocket type in both launchers    }
   var
     NewRocket              : Rockets.PALRocket;
     LoadStatus             : Launcher.SuccessState;
     MinTubeNo, MaxTubeNo   : integer;
     i                      : integer;
   begin
     case Zone of
       Launcher.Central : begin
                            MinTubeNo := 1;
                            MaxTubeNo := 3;
                          end;
       Launcher.Middle  : begin
                            MinTubeNo := 4;
                            MaxTubeNo := 7;
                          end;
       Launcher.Outer   : begin
                            MinTubeNo := 8;
                            MaxTubeNo := 19;
                          end;
     end;      { case }
     for i := MinTubeNo to MaxTubeNo do
       begin
         new( NewRocket, Init( { WarHead => } WarHead,
                               { Fuze    => } Fuze     ));
         if NewRocket <> nil
           then
             begin
               PortLauncher^.LoadTube( { TubeNumber => } i,
                                       { Rocket     => } NewRocket,
                                       { Results    => } LoadStatus );
               if LoadStatus = Launcher.Successful
                 then RktPanel^.AddToZoneInventory( { Zone => } Zone );
             end;
         new( NewRocket, Init( { WarHead => } WarHead,
                               { Fuze    => } Fuze     ));
         if NewRocket <> nil
           then
             begin
               StbdLauncher^.LoadTube( { TubeNumber => } i,
                                       { Rocket     => } NewRocket,
                                       { Results    => } LoadStatus );
               if LoadStatus = Launcher.Successful
                 then RktPanel^.AddToZoneInventory( { Zone => } Zone );
             end;
       end;    { for loop }
     RktPanel^.SetZoneRocketType(
                       { Zone           => } Zone,
```

```
                             { RocketTypeName => } NewRocket^.RocketNameIs);
      end;      { RktSubsystem.LoadZone }

procedure RktSubsystem.ProcessCrewAction( MouseX, MouseY : integer );
      var
         ActionStat    : ActionStatus;
         Zone          : Launcher.ZoneType;
         ZoneGoneEmpty : boolean;

            procedure DisarmArmedZone;
                { disarm the "ArmedZone" on the active launcher.... }
               begin
                 if NextFire[ArmedZone] = Port
                   then PortLauncher^.DeselectTube
                   else StbdLauncher^.DeselectTube;
                 ZoneArmed := false;
               end;   { local subprogram: DisarmZone }

            procedure ArmZone( Zone  : Launcher.ZoneType );
                { arm the "Zone" on the active launcher for that zone }
               begin
                 if NextFire[Zone] = Port
                   then PortLauncher^.ArmToFire( { Zone => } Zone )
                   else StbdLauncher^.ArmToFire( { Zone => } Zone );
                 ZoneArmed := true;
                 ArmedZone := Zone;
               end;    { local subprogram: ArmZone }

            procedure FireFromArmedZone;
               begin
                 if NextFire[ArmedZone] = Port
                   then
                      if PortLauncher^.FireSelectedTube = Launcher.Successful
                        then
                           begin
                             NextFire[ArmedZone] := Starboard;
                             StbdLauncher^.ArmToFire( { Zone => } ArmedZone );
                           end
                        else
                   else
                      if StbdLauncher^.FireSelectedTube = Launcher.Successful
                        then
                           begin
                             NextFire[ArmedZone] := Port;
                             PortLauncher^.ArmToFire( { Zone => } ArmedZone );
                           end;
               end;    { local subprogram: FireFromArmedZone }

      begin
        RktPanel^.ProcessCrewAction( { MouseX => } MouseX,
                                     { MouseY => } MouseY,
                                     { Action => } ActionStat,
                                     { Zone   => } Zone );
```

(continued)

```
        case ActionStat of
            ZoneSelected    : begin
                                if ZoneArmed
                                  then
                                    DisarmArmedZone;
                                ArmZone( { Zone => } Zone );
                                RktPanel^.ShowZoneSelect( { Zone => } Zone );
                              end;
            ZoneDeselected : begin
                                DisArmArmedZone;
                                RktPanel^.ShowZoneDeselect({ Zone =>} Zone );
                              end;
            RocketFired     : if ZoneArmed
                                then
                                  begin
                                    FireFromArmedZone;
                                    RktPanel^.FireFromZone(
                                            { Zone       => } ArmedZone,
                                            { ZoneEmpty => } ZoneGoneEmpty );
                                    if ZoneGoneEmpty
                                      then
                                         DisarmArmedZone;
                                  end
                                else { nothing to fire, clear button... }
                                  RktPanel^.ClearFireButton;
        end;    { case }
    end;    { RktSubsystem.ProcessCrewAction }

{============================================================================}
{            Method Definitions for:  RktSubsysPanel                         }
{============================================================================}
constructor RktSubsysPanel.Init( PtX, PtY : integer );
    var
      Width, Height    : integer;
      i                : Launcher.ZoneType;
    begin
      for i := Launcher.Central to Launcher.Outer do
        begin
          PanelFields[i].ZoneSelected := false;
          RocketType[i] := 'UNDEFINED';
          ZoneInventory[i] := 0;
        end;
      Geo_Objs.Rectangle.Init;
      Width := ( GetMaxX * 5 ) div 16;
      Height := ( GetMaxY * 3 ) div 8;
      Geo_Objs.Rectangle.Create( { PtX, PtY   => } PtX, PtY,
                                 { Colr      => } white,
                                 { Width     => } Width,
                                 { Height    => } Height    );
      new( PanelName, Init( { PtX      => } XCoordIs+6,
                            { PtY      => } YCoordIs+6,
                            { Width    => } SizeXIs-12,
                            { Height   => } (SizeYIs div 6)-3,
```

```
                              { BoxOutline => } TextBox.Single,
                              { FieldColor => } LightBlue,
                              { LabelText  => } 'ROCKETS'    ));
        for i := Launcher.Central to Launcher.Outer do
          begin
            new( PanelFields[i].SelectButton,
                       Init({ PtX => } (XCoordIs+SizeXIs div 2)
                                               - (27*SizeXIs div 64),
                            { PtY => } YCoordIs+18
                                    + ((integer(i)+1)*SizeYIs div 6) -3,
                            { Width  => } SizeXIs div 6,
                            { Height => } (SizeYIs div 6)-8,
                            { ButnType => } TextBox.Double,
                            { NormColor => } LightGreen,
                            { SelColor  => } Cyan,
                            { LabelText => } 'ARM'    ));
            new( PanelFields[i].RktTypeField,
                       Init({ PtX => } (XCoordIs+SizeXIs div 2)
                                               - (3*SizeXIs div 16),
                            { PtY => } YCoordIs+18
                                    + ((integer(i)+1)*SizeYIs div 6) -3,
                            { Width  => } (4*SizeXIs div 10),
                            { Height => } (SizeYIs div 6)-8,
                            { BoxOutline => } TextBox.Single,
                            { FieldColor => } LightGray,
                            { LabelText  => } RocketType[i]  ));
            new( PanelFields[i].RocketCount,
                       Init({ PtX => } (XCoordIs+SizeXIs div 2)
                                               + (4*SizeXIs div 16),
                            { PtY => } YCoordIs+18
                                    + ((integer(i)+1)*SizeYIs div 6) -3,
                            { Width  => } (2*SizeXIs div 10),
                            { Height => } (SizeYIs div 6)-8,
                            { BoxOutline => } TextBox.Single,
                            { FieldColor => } LightGray,
                            { LabelText  => } MakeStr(ZoneInventory[i]) ));
          end;    { launch zone based for loop }
        new( FireButton, Init({ PtX       => } (XCoordIs+SizeXIs div 2)
                                               - (SizeXIs div 12),
                              { PtY       => } YCoordIs
                                               + (5*SizeYIs div 6),
                              { Width     => } SizeXIs div 6,
                              { Height    => } (SizeYIs div 6)-8,
                              { ButnType  => } TextBox.Double,
                              { NormColor => } LightRed,
                              { SelColor  => } Red,
                              { LabelText => } 'FIRE'    ));
    end;    { RktSubsysPanel.Init }

destructor RktSubsysPanel.Done;
    var
      i                 : Launcher.ZoneType;
    begin
```

(continued)

```pascal
      dispose( PanelName, Done );
      for i := Launcher.Central to Launcher.Outer do
        begin
          dispose( PanelFields[i].SelectButton, Done );
          dispose( PanelFields[i].RktTypeField, Done );
          dispose( PanelFields[i].RocketCount, Done );
        end;
      dispose( FireButton, Done );
    end;     { RktSubsysPanel.Done }

procedure RktSubsysPanel.Draw;
    var
      i          : Launcher.ZoneType;
    begin
      Geo_Objs.Rectangle.Draw;         { draws outer outline }
      Graph.Rectangle( { upper left  => } XCoordIs+3, YCoordIs+3,
                       { lower right => } XCoordIs+SizeXIs-3,
                                          YCoordIs+SizeYIs-3 );
    end;     { RktSubsysPanel.Draw }

procedure RktSubsysPanel.ProcessCrewAction( MouseX : integer;
                                            MouseY : integer;
                                        var Action : ActionStatus;
                                        var Zone   : Launcher.ZoneType );
    var
      i,j          : Launcher.ZoneType;
    begin
      for i := Launcher.Central to Launcher.Outer do
        begin
          if PanelFields[i].SelectButton^.ButtonHit(
                                        { ScrnX => } MouseX,
                                        { ScrnY => } MouseY )
            then
              if PanelFields[i].ZoneSelected
                then
                  begin
                    Action := ZoneDeselected;
                    Zone := i;
                  end
                else
                  begin
                    { arm the selected rocket.....}
                    if ZoneInventory[i] <> 0
                      then
                        begin
                          Action := ZoneSelected;
                          Zone := i;
                        end
                      else
                        begin
                          PanelFields[i].SelectButton^.Deselect;
                          Action := None;
                        end;
```

```
                        for j := Launcher.Central to Launcher.Outer do
                        if PanelFields[j].ZoneSelected and ( i <> j )
                            then
                                begin
                                  { deselect the armed rocket.....}
                                  ShowZoneDeselect( { Zone => } j );
                                end;
                  end;
            end;
       if FireButton^.ButtonHit( { ScrnX => } MouseX,
                                 { ScrnY => } MouseY )
          then
              Action := RocketFired;
       end;    { RktSubsysPanel.ProcessCrewAction }

procedure RktSubsysPanel.SetZoneRocketType( Zone   : Launcher.ZoneType;
                                            RocketTypeName : String   );
   begin
     RocketType[Zone] := RocketTypeName;
     PanelFields[Zone].RktTypeField^.ChangeLabel(
                        { LabelText => } RocketTypeName );
   end;    { RktSubsysPanel.SetZoneRocketType }
procedure RktSubsysPanel.AddToZoneInventory( Zone : Launcher.ZoneType );
   begin
     ZoneInventory[Zone] := ZoneInventory[Zone] + 1;
     PanelFields[Zone].RocketCount^.ChangeLabel(
                        { LabelText  =>} MakeStr(ZoneInventory[Zone]) );
   end;    { RktSubsysPanel.AddToZoneInventory }

procedure RktSubsysPanel.RemoveFromZoneInventory(
                                    Zone : Launcher.ZoneType);
   begin
     ZoneInventory[Zone] := ZoneInventory[Zone] - 1;
     PanelFields[Zone].RocketCount^.ChangeLabel(
                        { LabelText  =>} MakeStr(ZoneInventory[Zone]) );
     if ZoneInventory[Zone] = 0
       then
          begin    { zone now empty, deselect it.... }
            PanelFields[Zone].SelectButton^.Deselect;
            PanelFields[Zone].ZoneSelected := false;
          end;
   end;    { RktSubsysPanel.RemoveFromZoneInventory }

procedure RktSubsysPanel.ShowZoneSelect( Zone : Launcher.ZoneType );
   begin
     PanelFields[Zone].SelectButton^.Select;
     PanelFields[Zone].ZoneSelected := true;
     sound( 440 ); delay( 100 );
     nosound; delay( 100 );
     sound( 220 ); delay( 100 );
     nosound;
   end;    { RktSubsysPanel.ShowZoneSelect }
```

(continued)

```
procedure RktSubsysPanel.ShowZoneDeselect( Zone : Launcher.ZoneType );
   begin
     PanelFields[Zone].SelectButton^.Deselect;
     PanelFields[Zone].ZoneSelected := false;
   end;    { RktSubsysPanel.ShowZoneDeselect }

procedure RktSubsysPanel.FireFromZone( Zone      : Launcher.ZoneType;
                                  var ZoneEmpty : boolean          );
   var
     TimerCnt      : integer;
   begin
     RemoveFromZoneInventory( { Zone => } Zone );
     for TimerCnt := 1 to 5 do
       begin
         sound( 1760 ); delay( 100 );
         nosound; delay( 100 );
       end;
     FireButton^.Deselect;
     if ZoneInventory[Zone] = 0
       then ZoneEmpty := true
       else ZoneEmpty := false;
   end;    { RktSubsysPanel.FireFromZone }

 procedure RktSubsysPanel.ClearFireButton;
   begin
     FireButton^.Deselect;
   end;    { RktSubsysPanel.ClearFireButton }

{==========================================================================}
{                         No Initialization Code                           }

end.
```

rocket type. The other, *ProcessCrewAction*, interacts with the control panel object to respond to user commands to arm/disarm zones and fire rockets from the armed zone.

The *RktSubsystem* class constructor instantiates the dynamic objects for the two launchers and the control panel. In addition, it initializes the other class fields.

The *RktSubsystem* class destructor must dispose of its three dynamic objects (the two launchers and the control panel). When each of these objects is disposed of, its corresponding destructor is invoked to do the required clean-up. For the launchers, recall that the *ALauncher* destructor must dispose of all *ALRocket* dynamic objects that it holds in its *Tubes*. This is an example of good object disposal technique. *When objects have such dependencies, each object must assume responsibility for disposing of the objects it may have created.* This disposal is normally done in its destructor, and it invokes the dynamic objects' destructors, which continue the process until simple objects requiring no special clean-up are reached. Failure to perform such clean-up would result in objects continuing to consume space on the heap, but with no remaining pointers to them. These *orphaned* objects would uselessly hold memory until the system is finally shut down and all heap space is reclaimed.

In good object-oriented systems, most system behavior is defined in its objects. This tends to make the main program trivial. The main program *DASHPNL2.PAS* (Dash Panel, version 2) illustrates this point. *DASHPNL2.PAS* instantiates one object, *Weapons*, an instance of the class *RktSubsystem*. All other objects (launchers, rockets, control panel, etc.) are the responsibility of the *Weapons* object. So even the object interface at the main program level is kept simple.

The main program begins with initialization code that sets up the graphics mode, verifies that the mouse driver is installed, and resets and initializes the mouse (using the default arrow cursor). Then several lines are drawn to form a heavy horizontal line across the screen, representing the top of the dash panel itself

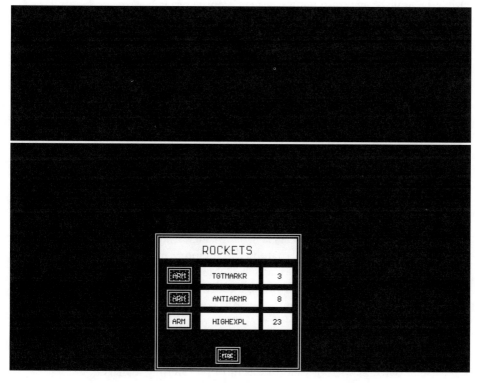

Figure 6.10.   Screen image of rocket subsystem control panel.

(the area above is reserved to represent the "out the cockpit window" view). Figure 6.10 shows the display screen generated by this program.

These preliminaries out of the way, the program instantiates the dynamic *Weapons* object and loads each of the three zones with a different rocket type.

Finally, the main program goes into its operational loop, which the user may exit by pressing the mouse's right button. Within the loop, the mouse is interrogated for its button status and screen position. When the left mouse button is pressed, the mouse screen coordinates are passed in a message to the *Weapons* object, requesting that its *ProcessCrewAction* method provide the proper reaction to the user mouse action at that screen position. This main loop controls the entire rockets subsystem in fewer than a dozen lines of code (counting statement semicolons, as now is commonly applied to Ada programs).

POWER, BUT NOT WITHOUT A PRICE

Wise men have often said that you can't get anything for nothing in this world. Using dynamic objects also has a price, a potential hazard, associated with it.

Operating system/runtime environments normally provide a memory manager that dynamically allocates and deallocates blocks of memory from an area called the heap. A typical heap manager services requests for memory by sequentially parceling out the requested blocks from the bottom (i.e., starting at the lowest physical address) of the heap. When blocks are relinquished, holes of unused memory become interspersed with the allocated memory. When the allocator reaches the top of the heap, it has to consider previously used memory to service the next request. Memory managers employ several approaches at this point. Most will attempt to find a contiguous block of deallocated memory that is large enough to satisfy the next request. Even with this approach, the memory may become sufficiently fragmented that it will not have a contiguous block big enough. The memory manager may then pack the allocated memory blocks to contiguous memory at the bottom of the heap and collect all of the unallocated memory above the top of the allocated memory. This process is usually called *heap compaction* or, more commonly, *garbage collection*. Alternately, the memory manager may return status reporting that insufficient memory was available to service the request.

There are two problems with garbage collection in real-time systems. First, you cannot predict when it will occur. Second, you cannot predict how long it will take. However, in general, it will happen when you can least afford interrupting the system processing, and it will take far longer than you can afford to be off-line. Because real-time systems cannot afford to have indeterminate behaviors of this type, use of dynamic memory allocations must be carefully managed.

If the memory manager simply reports when it cannot service a request for

```
{ Program:     Aircraft Dash Panel simulator
  Author:      John R. Ellis
  Last Update: 28 July 1991
  Copyright (c) 1991 by John R. Ellis

  Description: This is a main line program which demonstrates object
               encapsulation.

               This program "draws" a rockets subsystem control panel
               and provides interaction with the rocket selection
               and firing logic.

  Requirements: Uses graphics mode.
                                                                     }

program DashPanel;

  uses Crt,Graph,GrafInit,Mouse,Buttons,RktSubsy;

  var
        { object instance creation...... }
    Weapons        : PRktSubsystem;
        { other variables used by the program...... }
    GError         : integer;
    MaxColor       : integer;   { greatest color value }
    MaxX           : integer;   { greatest X-axis value }
    MaxY           : integer;   { greatest Y-axis value }
    MouseButtons   : integer;   { Mouse button codes }
    MouseX, MouseY : integer;   { Mouse X,Y coordinates }
    Exit           : boolean;   { controls main loop exit }
begin
      { Do the graphics mode set-up.............. }
  GError := GrafInitSuccess;
  if GError <> grOK
    then
      begin
        writeln('Graphics error:  ',GraphErrorMsg(GError) );
        writeln('Program aborted...');
        halt( 1 );
      end;
  MaxX   := GetMaxX;          { your graphics adaptor dependent... }
  MaxY   := GetMaxY;
  ClearDevice;
  if not GMouse.ThereIsAMouse
    then
      begin
        OutTextXY( { X,Y        => } 10, 10,
                   { TextString => } 'Mouse Driver Not Installed' );
        Delay( 5000 );
        Halt (2);
      end
    else
```

Figure 6.11.   Code listing: program DASHPNL2.PAS.   *(continued)*

```
     if not GMouse.MouseIsReset
       then
         begin
           OutTextXY( { X,Y        => } 10, 10,
                      { TextString => } 'Mouse Did Not Reset' );
           Delay( 5000 );
           Halt (3);
         end;
GMouse.Init;
  { draw horizontal line representing top of dash panel.... }
Graph.SetLineStyle( { LineStyle => } SolidLn,
                    { Pattern   => } 0,
                    { Thickness => } ThickWidth );
Graph.SetColor( { Color  => } white );
Graph.Line( { X1 => } 0,
            { Y1 => } 3*MaxY div 8,
            { X2 => } MaxX,
            { Y2 => } 3*MaxY div 8  );
Graph.SetLineStyle( { LineStyle => } SolidLn,
                    { Pattern   => } 0,
                    { Thickness => } NormWidth );
  { initialize the object instances.... }
new( Weapons, Init( { NumberOfTubes => } 19,
                    { PanelX        => } (5 * MaxX) div 16,
                    { PanelY        => } (5 * MaxY) div 8 ));
Weapons^.LoadZone(  { Zone     => } Launcher.Central,
                    { WarHead  => } Rockets.TargetMarker,
                    { Fuze     => } Rockets.Impact  );
Weapons^.LoadZone(  { Zone     => } Launcher.Middle,
                    { WarHead  => } Rockets.AntiArmor,
                    { Fuze     => } Rockets.Penetration  );
Weapons^.LoadZone(  { Zone     => } Launcher.Outer,
                    { WarHead  => } Rockets.HighExplosive,
                    { Fuze     => } Rockets.Impact  );
MouseButtons := Mouse.PrNone;        { no buttons pressed... }
GMouse.ShowMouse;
Exit := false;
  { Set up is complete;  main loop for normal processing.... }
while ( MouseButtons <> Mouse.PrR ) and not Exit do
  begin
    GMouse.GetPosition( { BtnStatus => } MouseButtons,
                        { XPos      => } MouseX,
                        { YPos      => } MouseY  );
    if MouseButtons = Mouse.PrL    { left button is action button }
      then
        begin
          GMouse.HideMouse;
          Weapons^.ProcessCrewAction( { MouseX => } MouseX,
                                      { MouseY => } MouseY  );
          GMouse.ShowMouse;
          repeat
            GMouse.GetPosition( { BtnStatus => } MouseButtons,
                                { XPos      => } MouseX,
```

```
                                { YPos       => } MouseY  );
                until MouseButtons = PrNone;
            end;
    end;   { loop }
  dispose( Weapons, Done );
  ClrScr;
  CloseGraph;

end.
```

memory, the real-time application must know what to do in such cases. This could range from mode changes that could free more memory to doing a total system reset. Neither of these is very nice.

Actually, the Turbo Pascal memory manager is pretty good. As memory is deallocated, it is either rejoined to the top of available heap memory (if it was the topmost block on the heap) or placed on a *free* list. Subsequent requests for memory are first run through the free list to see if a block of adequate size is available. (Consult the Turbo Pascal 6.0 Programmer's Guide for a more detailed description of this memory management algorithm.) This approach significantly delays the memory-critical situation, but does not guarantee that it won't happen if the system runs long enough.

It is always safe to use dynamic objects if they are treated as static objects, that is, if sufficient memory is available for all objects that will be instantiated dynamically. Then, do not attempt to dispose of dynamic objects until the system is ready to shut down. Because the heap is big enough to hold all dynamic objects, the garbage collector is never invoked.

Alternatively, when there is not sufficient heap space to hold all possible dynamic objects at one time, designate groups of dynamic objects that must be in memory at one time. These frequently will be tied to an operating mode that limits the total operations of the system at that time. In such cases, the disposal of dynamic objects from one mode and the allocation of memory for dynamic objects required by the new mode can often be made to happen at the time of the mode change. The timing requirements for the mode change should include enough time to accommodate the infrequent need to do garbage collection during any heap memory reallocations.

Another possible approach to controlling garbage collection is to rewrite the garbage collector (if necessary) to execute as a low-priority background process. Because real-time systems usually have a certain amount of processing reserve designed in, this "excess" time is often used to execute a continuous built-in-test (BIT) program. An *intelligent garbage collector* could share this excess time to clean up the heap, a little at a time. Then, unless allocation/deallocation activity becomes exceptionally heavy and/or the amount of excess time becomes too short, the chances of "big bang" garbage collection may be reduced to near zero. With sufficient loading analysis, this may be adequate for many real-time systems.

If these or similar approaches are not used, the system will proceed with the risk of unexpected garbage collection! Off-line analysis, coupled with detailed knowledge of the operations of a specific memory manager, can be used to predict how long the system is likely to run before it is susceptible to garbage collection. The danger is that the system may be run beyond its specified limits (remember how the Patriot missile systems were specified to be shut down for maintenance every eight hours, but ended up running well over a hundred hours; the resulting system timing failure permitted an Iraqi Scud missile to destroy a U.S. Barracks in Saudi Arabia during the Gulf War).

However memory management is handled for a given real-time system, it is important that the software analysts and designers understand that free use of dynamic objects may result in system failures if they do not allow for the undesirable side effects of heap usage.

SUMMARY

This chapter introduced dynamic objects, which are instantiated at runtime, as contrasted with static objects, which are instantiated at compilation time. The mechanisms for creating, destroying, and accessing dynamic objects were discussed at length.

While building a sample "subsystem" to demonstrate dynamic objects, we considered dependencies among objects other than the inheritance relationship. We suggested that complex objects, *mechanisms* and *subsystems*, collect objects that work together for a common purpose.

Finally, we examined how the memory manager allocates and deallocates heap memory to accommodate the creation and disposal of dynamic objects. Associated with these processes is the danger of heap compaction, or *garbage collection* striking without warning and interrupting normal system operations.

PRACTICE

1. Create a *subsystem* that simulates the control mechanism for a common automotive cruise control. Include *buttons* that permit functions (1) speed select, (2) increase speed, (3) decrease speed, (4) pause/resume, and (5) disengage.

2. Create a *subsystem* that simulates the operation of a push-button automobile radio. The radio control panel must include at least five "push buttons," where-

in the selection of one deselects the previously selected button. The frequency associated with the selected button must be displayed on the front panel. "Rocker controls" adjust the volume and manually change the frequency. A "program" button programs the currently displayed frequency to the selected push button.

3. Create a two-state push button with positive indication of the active state, as shown in Figure 6.12. Selecting the left cursor button anywhere over the push button will cause the state to toggle, changing the indicated status of both the old state, to its inactive color, and the new state, to its active color. Consider whether this new object would better be specified as a descendent of the Button class (from the unit Buttons) or as a new object class with two fields, each an instance of Button. Justify your chosen approach.

Figure 6.12.   The two-state push button objects.

*If a man does not keep pace with his companion, perhaps
it is because he hears a different drummer. Let him step to
the music which he hears, however measured or far away.*
— Henry David Thoreau

Chapter **7**

Polymorphic Objects

Rounding out the primary characteristics of objects is *polymorphism*. From the Greek word meaning "many shapes," *polymorphism* describes how objects within a hierarchy can share a method name while each method behaves according to the individual requirements of the corresponding class.

Those familiar with Ada (or C++ or several other languages) may conclude that this sounds like the *overloading* feature of these languages. Although there are superficial similarities, *polymorphism* is a more powerful mechanism than overloading. All overloading of a procedure or function name must be resolvable during compilation. Each instance of an overloaded procedure or function must have a unique set of parameters (i.e., differing in order, number, and/or types) so that the compiler can compare the actual parameters (where the procedure or function is invoked) against the formal parameter lists (where the procedures and functions are declared) for an exact match in order, number, and type. The programmer who invokes the overloaded procedure must know exactly which instance of the procedure or function is being invoked.

With *polymorphism*, nothing is settled at compilation time. In Chapter 4 we encountered one facet of *polymorphism* when we examined the late binding of virtual methods. The linkage to a virtual method is not resolved until a message is actually sent to an object requesting that the method be invoked. Only then can that object determine which procedure/function it actually needs. It does this by locating the method's entry in its Virtual Method Table. The programmer may not know exactly which procedure or function will execute when writing the code that invokes it.

So a key characteristic of *polymorphism* is its *late binding*. This feature distinguishes it from static *overloading*, such as that in Ada and C++.

OBJECT TYPE COMPATIBILITY

When discussing inheritance in Chapter 3, we only described a descendent's inheritance of fields and methods from its ancestors. In addition, a descendent class inherits *type compatibility* from its ancestors. This allows objects of a descendent class to be used anywhere objects of an ancestor's class may be used. This is particularly interesting when passing objects as parameters.

Consider the following procedure:

```
type
  PPoint    = ^GeoObjs.Point;
  PCircle   = ^GeoObjs.Circle;
  PSquare   = ^GeoObjs.Square;
..........
procedure DrawAnObject( PAnObject : PPoint );
  begin
    PAnObject^.Draw;
  end;
```

In this simple case, *DrawAnObject* may be passed a dynamic object instance of the class *Point* (by its pointer), as the formal parameter declares. However, because *Circle* and *Square* are descendent classes of *Point*, pointers to dynamic objects of these classes may likewise be passed to *DrawAnObject* as actual parameters.

Obviously, the linkage to a particular object class's *Draw* method can't be determined except at runtime. The programmer does not know exactly which procedure *Draw* (i.e., *Point*'s, *Circle*'s, *Square*'s, or a future descendent's not yet defined) will actually be invoked. In fact, the programmer doesn't care, trusting that whoever defines the relevant objects has properly provided the necessary behavior.

The power of *polymorphism* is illustrated by this chapter's example program. Before addressing the main program, we'll consider a general purpose data structure (a linked list) that can take advantage of *polymorphism* in several ways.

A GENERIC LINKED LIST OBJECT

To start this chapter's example, I'll introduce a general-purpose (reusable) linked list unit. I call this structure "general purpose" because it may be used to build lists of any data type, including complex objects with heterogeneous fields. This makes it a natural way to structure information read in from a data base.

The unit *LinkList* defines two classes: one an abstract class that represents the individual elements being listed and the other an abstract class to represent the list itself. Figure 7.1 illustrates this structure.

I have chosen to implement the list with double links. This type of architecture, wherein each node maintains a pointer (i.e., a "link") to both its preceding and following neighbors, allows far greater flexibility for certain list operations. For example, we will shortly consider a method to sort the list. The algorithm provided moves both forward and backward through the list. Such an algorithm is not very practical with singly linked lists.

Each node in our list is a record consisting of three pointers. Two of the pointers are the backward and forward links, pointing to the previous and next nodes, respectively. The third pointer points to a dynamic instance of the abstract class *NodeDataObj*. Our unit declares the node record as follows:

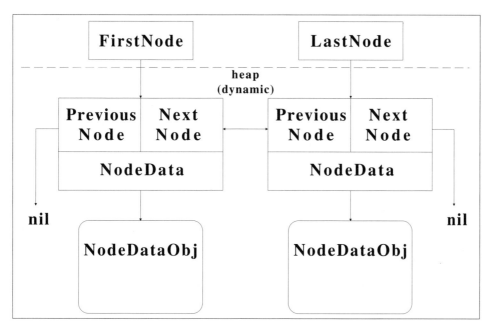

Figure 7.1. The data structures used by LINKLIST.PAS.

```
type
        NodePtr              = ^Node;
        Node    = record
                  PreviousNode    : NodePtr;
                  NextNode        : NodePtr;
                  NodeData        : NodeDataPtr;
             end;      { record: Node }
```

Because we want this list to handle virtually any data structure as its "node data," very little will be known about the object class *NodeDataObj*. This is exactly what an abstract class does. So we define our *NodeDataObj* class as:

```
        NodeDataPtr  = ^NodeDataObj;
        NodeDataObj  = object      { abstract class }
             constructor Init;
             destructor Done;  virtual;
          end;      { object: NodeDataObj }
```

This class has no fields, and when you examine the method definitions for the constructor and destructor, you will find that each is a null procedure consisting of only a *begin* and *end* statement. A class couldn't be more abstract (and seemingly useless) than *NodeDataObj*. It will obviously never have object instances.

When an application dictates a particular data structure of which lists are to be generated, a new class may be defined as a descendent of *NodeDataObj* to define the fields and methods of that class. However, thanks to extended type compatibility, the *Node* record will not need to be redefined for each descendent data object. The list's class depends on this node structure as well. If the node record structure had to be changed for each type of data to be listed, the implementation and use of a "general purpose" linked list would be much more bothersome.

If the data structure to be put into the list already exists as a class, so that it cannot be declared as a descendent of *NodeDataObj*, then the descendent class must be declared so that an instance of the existing class becomes a field in it:

```
        Images  = object ( NodeDataObj )
             GeoObject   : GeoObj.Point;
          end;      { object: Images }
```

With this new descendent class, *GeoObject* will support *polymorphism* because this field also may hold an instance of *Circle* or *Square*, or any other descendent of *GeoObj*'s *Point* class. With this class, we can create a list of geometric objects, where each is, in turn, sent a message to draw itself on the screen. Thanks to *polymorphism*, it is not necessary to know beforehand exactly what objects are put into the list. Everything resolves itself at runtime, and the proper objects appear on the screen.

The other class of this unit implements the list itself. It is defined as:

```
NodeListPtr  = ^NodeList;
NodeList     = object              { abstract object }
   constructor Init;
   destructor Done; virtual;
   procedure AddANode( NewData : NodeDataPtr );
   procedure DeleteANode( var Ptr : NodePtr );
   procedure SortList;
   function NodeBelongsBefore(Ptr_1,Ptr_2 : NodePtr)
                                  : boolean; virtual;
   procedure SwapNodes( Ptr_1,Ptr_2 : NodePtr );
       { iterator methods }
   function FirstNodeIs   : NodePtr;
   function LastNodeIs    : NodePtr;
   procedure GoToNextNode(  var Ptr : NodePtr );
   procedure GoToPreviousNode( var Ptr : NodePtr );
   function AtEndOfList( Ptr : NodePtr ) : boolean;
private
   FirstNode    : NodePtr;
   LastNode     : NodePtr;
end;   { object: NodeList }
```

The only permanent data regarding the linked list are represented by the fields pointing to the first and last nodes in the list. If these fields are the unique value *nil*, then the list is empty. Obviously, one of these fields being *nil* means that the other must be *nil* as well. All other data structures associated with the list are dynamic and are maintained in its nodes. The object representing the class may be either static or dynamic, but the list nodes and the corresponding data elements being listed must be dynamic. The power of the *NodeList* class lies in its methods, which define the behavior of the class.

Three groups of methods are associated with the behavior of our linked list. The first group contains the methods that maintain the list. This group supports the creation of a new (empty) list (with the constructor *Init*), adding and deleting list nodes, sorting the list (with supporting methods to determine whether two nodes are in the proper order and to swap nodes when they are not), and disposing of the list when it is no longer needed (with the destructor *Done*).

The second group of methods are called *iterator* methods. These methods allow a client to navigate the list. They permit a client to find the first and last nodes in the list, move forward and backward from a given node, and determine when one or the other end of the list has been reached.

The following code segment illustrates how a client might iterate through the nodes of the list:

```
type
   NewListType  = object ( NodeList )
       end;       { object: NewListType }
```

```
var
  TheList    : NewListType;
  Iterator   : NodePtr;
begin
  ..... { code that creates and fills the list }
  Iterator := TheList.FirstNodeIs;
  while not TheList.AtEndOfList( Iterator ) do
    begin
      ..... { uses the current node data }
      TheList.GoToNextNode( Iterator );
    end;
  ..... { rest of program }
end.
```

Methods that relate to the contents of the node's data object are usually required to make the list usable for a specific application. Such methods constitute the third group of list methods, those that are application specific. For example, based on a node pointer (such as the *Iterator* in the segment above), reading and/or writing the fields of the object at that node is often necessary. Typically, these methods will send messages for the node object's own methods and then perform related processing (such as displaying node data). These methods must be provided by the decendents to *NodeList*.

The method *NodeBelongsBefore* needs further explanation. The method *SortList* can order any descendent class of *NodeList* but it cannot know the criteria by which one node belongs before another in the ordered list. The class needs a method to compare the data at two nodes and report whether the two nodes are already ordered properly. This method I've called *NodeBelongsBefore*. However, this method doesn't know what data will ultimately be placed in the list, so it cannot be defined in this class. Instead, it is defined as:

```
function NodeList.NodeBelongsBefore( Ptr_1,Ptr_2 :
                                NodePtr ); boolean;
  begin
    halt(2);  { forces descendent to define method }
  end;      { NodeList.NodeBelongsBefore }
```

This method was defined as a virtual method because *SortList* will need to access the descendent's version of *NodeBelongsBefore*. To ensure that a descendent's method is used, this method will cause the program to quit if invoked. Therefore, the descendent class will have to redefine this method to use *SortList*. This is one way the designer of a reusable component can enforce design constraints on a future user. Note that C++ provides a mechanism called a *pure virtual member* to achieve the same effect.

Although *NodeList* is an abstract class (it lacks the application-specific behavior to make it useful), as was *NodeDataObj*, descendents of this class are unlikely to

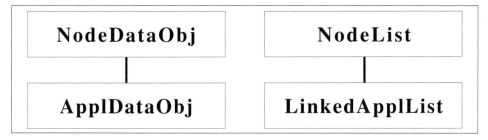

Figure 7.2.   Use of the LinkList unit requires definition of descendent classes for the defined abstract classes.

add fields. Also unlike *NodeDataObj*, a significant amount of a linked list's behavior is defined by the abstract class's methods defined in *NodeList*.

So, although the *LinkList* abstract classes provide differing levels of definition, each requires a descendent class to define the specifics of an application. This relationship is illustrated in Figure 7.2.

NodeDataObj needs a descendent class to define the data elements to be listed and, at a minimum, methods to set and retrieve its fields. A descendent of *NodeList* must define node-ordering criteria and any processing associated with the individual nodes, as well as any other operation on the whole list (e.g., *PrintTheList*).

Building on this reusable unit, we'll construct a sample application.

```
unit LinkList;

{ Program:     Linked List - A generic linked list library unit
  Author:      John R. Ellis
  Last Update: 19 August 1991
  Copyright (c) 1991 by John R. Ellis

  Description:  This unit provides the abstract objects necessary to
                create and manipulate a doubly linked list data structure.
                The data objects for the list may be any number of
                descendents of the provided NodeDataObj abstract object.

  Requirements:  No special requirements.
                                                                  }

interface

   type
```

Figure 7.3.   Code listing: unit LINKLIST.PAS.   *(continued)*

```
    {===================================================================}
    {                    Object Declarations                            }
    {===================================================================}

    NodeDataPtr  = ^NodeDataObj;
    NodeDataObj  = object                        { abstract class }
                     constructor Init;
                     destructor Done; virtual;
                 end;   { object: NodeDataObj }

    NodePtr      = ^Node;
    Node         = record
                     PreviousNode    : NodePtr;      { backwards link }
                     NextNode        : NodePtr;      { forward link }
                     NodeData        : NodeDataPtr; { data object pointer }
                 end;   { record: Node }

    NodeListPtr  = ^NodeList;
    NodeList     = object                        { abstract class }
                     constructor Init;           { allocates an empty list }
                     destructor Done; virtual;
                     procedure AddANode( NewData : NodeDataPtr );
                     procedure DeleteANode( var Ptr : NodePtr );
                     procedure SortList;
                     function NodeBelongsBefore( Ptr_1, Ptr_2 : NodePtr )
                                                 : boolean; virtual;
                     procedure SwapNodes( Ptr_1, Ptr_2 : NodePtr );
                         { iterator methods }
                     function  FirstNodeIs  : NodePtr;
                     function  LastNodeIs   : NodePtr;
                     procedure GoToNextNode( var Ptr : NodePtr );
                     procedure GoToPreviousNode( var Ptr : NodePtr );
                     function  AtEndOfList( Ptr : NodePtr ) : boolean;
                 private
                     FirstNode       : NodePtr;      { points to first node }
                     LastNode        : NodePtr;      { points to last node }
                 end;   { object: NodeList }
    {------------- end of interface section -------------}
    implementation

    {===================================================================}
    {          IMPLEMENTATION METHODS FOR NodeDataObj                   }
    {===================================================================}

    constructor NodeDataObj.Init;
       begin
       end;      { NodeDataObj.Init }

    destructor NodeDataObj.Done;
       begin
       end;      { NodeDataObj.Done }
```

```
{====================================================================}
{                 IMPLEMENTATION METHODS FOR NodeList                }
{====================================================================}

constructor NodeList.Init;
    begin
       FirstNode := nil;
       LastNode  := nil;
    end;    { NodeList.Init }

destructor NodeList.Done;
    begin
      while FirstNode <> nil do
        DeleteANode( { Ptr => } FirstNode );
    end;    { NodeList.Done }

procedure NodeList.AddANode( NewData : NodeDataPtr );
    { This method adds a new data record to the end of the linked list. }
    var
       NewNode   : NodePtr;
    begin
      new( NewNode );              { create new node in the heap }
      NewNode^.PreviousNode := LastNode;
      NewNode^.NextNode      := nil;
      NewNode^.NodeData      := NewData;
      if LastNode = nil
        then                       { new node will be first node in list }
           FirstNode := NewNode
        else                       { previous entries in list }
           LastNode^.NextNode := NewNode;
      LastNode := NewNode;
    end;    { NodeList.AddANode }

procedure NodeList.DeleteANode( var Ptr : NodePtr );
    begin
      if Ptr <> nil              { quit if no node to delete }
        then
          begin
            if Ptr^.PreviousNode = nil
              then
                FirstNode := Ptr^.NextNode
              else
                Ptr^.PreviousNode^.NextNode := Ptr^.NextNode;
            if Ptr^.NextNode = nil
              then
                LastNode := Ptr^.PreviousNode
              else
                Ptr^.NextNode^.PreviousNode := Ptr^.PreviousNode;
            if Ptr^.NodeData <> nil
              then dispose( Ptr^.NodeData, Done ); { get rid of data }
            dispose( Ptr );
            Ptr := nil;
          end;     { if }
```

(continued)

```
      end;   { NodeList.DeleteANode }

procedure NodeList.SortList;
   var
     Ptr_C : NodePtr;  { iterator walks through list from front }
     Ptr_B : NodePtr;  { node trying to find proper place in list }
     Ptr_A : NodePtr;  { next node to compare new node to }
     Exit  : boolean;  { loop exit control }
   begin
     Exit := false;
     Ptr_C := FirstNode;    { initialize iterator }
     if Ptr_C <> nil        { done if list is empty }
       then
         while not Exit do
           begin
             Ptr_A := Ptr_C;    { top of currently sorted list }
             GoToNextNode( { Ptr => } Ptr_C );  { on to next node }
             Ptr_B := Ptr_C;
             if Ptr_C = nil
               then Exit := true
               else
                 if not NodeBelongsBefore( { Ptr_1 => } Ptr_A,
                                           { Ptr_2 => } Ptr_B )
                   then
                     repeat
                       SwapNodes( { Ptr_1 => } Ptr_A,
                                  { Ptr_2 => } Ptr_B );
                       Ptr_B := Ptr_A;      { new node has moved }
                       GoToPreviousNode( { Ptr => } Ptr_A );
                     until ( Ptr_A = nil ) or
                           NodeBelongsBefore( { Ptr_1 => } Ptr_A,
                                              { Ptr_2 => } Ptr_B );
           end;  { while loop }
   end;   { NodeList.SortList }

function NodeList.NodeBelongsBefore(Ptr_1,Ptr_2 : NodePtr) : boolean;
   { This virtual method must be defined by descendent classes
     to compare the appropriate node values and return true if the
     node at Ptr_1 belongs before the node at Ptr_2; otherwise false
     must be returned. }
   begin
     halt(2);   { forces descendent to define this method }
   end;   { NodeList.NodeBelongsBefore }

procedure NodeList.SwapNodes( Ptr_1, Ptr_2 : NodePtr );
   var
     TempDataPtr   : NodeDataPtr;   { swap data pointer }
   begin
     TempDataPtr      := Ptr_1^.NodeData;
     Ptr_1^.NodeData := Ptr_2^.NodeData;
     Ptr_2^.NodeData := TempDataPtr;
   end;   { NodeList.SwapNodes }
```

```
function NodeList.FirstNodeIs  : NodePtr;
   begin
     FirstNodeIs := FirstNode;
   end;   { NodeList.FirstNodeIs }

function NodeList.LastNodeIs   : NodePtr;
   begin
     LastNodeIs := LastNode;
   end;   { NodeList.LastNodeIs }

procedure NodeList.GoToNextNode( var Ptr : NodePtr );
   begin
     if Ptr <> nil
       then Ptr := Ptr^.NextNode;
   end;   { NodeList.GoToNextNode }

procedure NodeList.GoToPreviousNode( var Ptr : NodePtr );
   begin
     if Ptr <> nil
       then Ptr := Ptr^.PreviousNode;
   end;   { NodeList.GoToPreviousNode }

function NodeList.AtEndOfList( Ptr : NodePtr ) : boolean;
   { Note that this function works for both forward searches
     (detects passing the last node) and backward searches
     (detects passing the first node).       }
   begin
     AtEndOfList := ( Ptr = nil );
   end;   { NodeList.AtEndOfList }
{====================================================================}
                    { no initialization code }
   end.
```

A MOVING MAP SYSTEM

In this chapter, a simple moving map display system will illustrate the two flavors of *polymorphism* described above. A fully operational digital moving map system normally displays three types of geographic features: area, linear, and point. Area features are represented by a color-coded background that suggests the visual appearance of the corresponding region of the earth's surface. For example, wooded areas might be represented by dark green, meadows and pastures by light green, bare ground by brown, and water by blue. Linear features depict roads, railroads, rivers and streams, power lines, and other features having such linear characteristics. Point features are discrete objects, such as buildings, airports, and bridges, or mission-related points, such as navigation waypoints and checkpoints, destinations, and targets. Point features are represented by symbols that suggest the nature of the feature.

Operational digital moving map systems on modern aircraft, such as those developed by the Harris Corporation's Government Aerospace Systems Division for the F-117A Stealth Fighter and the RAH-66 Comanche "Light Helicopter," use special hardware *map generators* to paint the area and linear features from Defense Mapping Agency data bases as the display background. A microprocessor-based "symbol generator" maps the geographic location of the point features to screen coordinates that correspond to the geographic coordinates on the background terrain image and then "draws" the proper symbol there. These are called *geographically registered* symbols, and the performance requirements generally dictate that the symbol be located within one pixel of its corresponding location on the underlying terrain image.

This chapter's example program develops a simple moving map symbol generator. In this system, the aircraft's location (used as the map reference location) is set to the center of the map display area and is marked by a crude stick-symbol

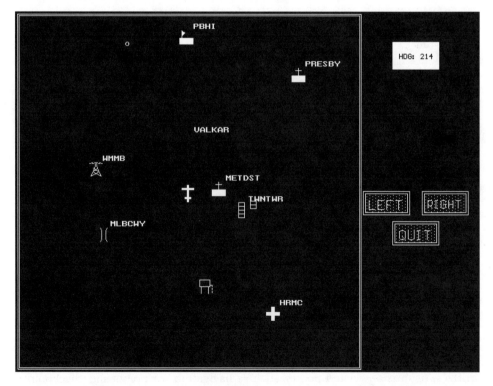

Figure 7.4.   The point feature generator screen display.

representing the aircraft. Nearby point feature symbols are drawn at the correct relative, properly scaled locations on the screen. The centered aircraft symbol remains stationary as the simulated aircraft "moves" over the terrain, while nearby point features appear and move on the map display. An example of the images generated by our system is seen in Figure 7.4.

The map maintains a "heading up" orientation, meaning that the top center of the display represents the direction directly in front of the aircraft. This orientation is popular because it presents the pilot with information that is easy to correlate to the view outside the cockpit window. For example, a symbol above and to the left of the aircraft symbol on the display represents a reference point ahead and to the left of the aircraft.

POINT FEATURE OBJECTS

The unit *PtFeatur* defines an abstract class *PtFeature* that declares all of the common characteristics of point features. This includes all of the fields and all of the behaviors (methods) except the object's ability to display itself. Each specific type of point feature (e.g., school, church, hospital, etc.) is introduced through a descendent class of the abstract *PtFeature* class. Each of these descendent classes inherits its entire definition except its explicitly defined ability to draw itself on the screen with its unique virtual *Display* method. The displayed shape of each of the descendent class symbols is shown in Figure 7.5.

PtFeature class fields include the corresponding point feature's important characteristics: its geographic location, a label that provides specific identity data about the point feature instance, and the symbol and text display color. Such information is usually static and is developed off-line by a Mission Planning System. In an operational system, the mission planning data are loaded into some type of avionics data base (reprogrammable read-only memory, disk, or tape) that the flight avionics computer reads in small increments as needed.

Additional fields are used to "remember" where the point feature symbol was last drawn on the screen [i.e., when *Visible* is "true" then (*ScrnX, ScrnY*)] specifies the screen coordinates where the symbol was last drawn). These data are used when erasing the symbol from its previous location before redrawing it to a new location relative to the aircraft (map reference) location when the aircraft has "moved."

Unlike globes, maps are rendered as flat representations of the earth's curved surface. Navigation systems normally provide position data as spherical latitude and longitude coordinates. The map subsystem must then translate latitude/longitude coordinates into east/west (or "easting") and north/south (or "northing") flat earth coordinates. There are several algorithms, such as Transverse Mercator and

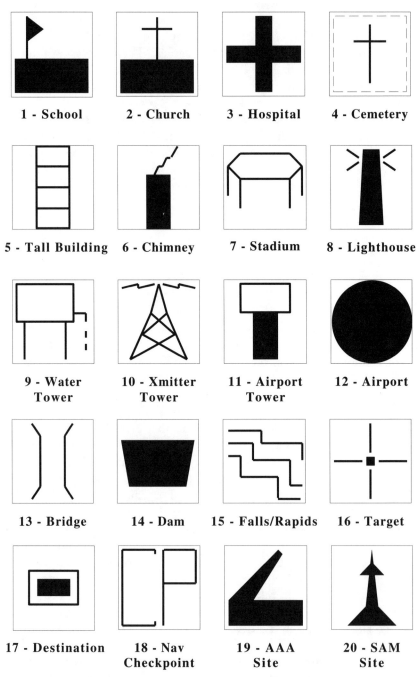

Figure 7.5. Some typical point feature symbols.

Lambert Conformal, to do this type of transformation. I have not provided these somewhat complex algorithms for our simple map system. Instead, all geographic references are assumed already to be in a flat earth *northing* (vertical or Y-axis) and *easting* (horizontal or X-axis) coordinate system. The northing and easting coordinates represent the distance in meters from some arbitrary reference point. To provide a reasonable map coverage area, geographic position coordinates are declared as long integers.

By now, the reader should find the code for most of *PtFeature*'s methods self-explanatory. A few of the methods, however, are worth discussing in greater detail.

The most interesting of *PtFeature*'s methods is *Show*. This method is invoked with the aircraft reference location and the display parameters necessary to draw a point feature on the screen. First the point feature symbol must be erased from its last displayed position (if it was drawn on the screen). The aircraft location is used as the map display reference position (*XRef*, *YRef*) and is mapped to the center of the display. *Show* uses these coordinates to determine how many pixels west/east (*XPos*) and north/south (*YPos*) of the reference screen position the point feature symbol should be displayed. Remember that the point feature's location is stored in its class fields *Easting* and *Northing*.

```
XPos := (Easting - XRef) div DScale;
YPos := (YRef - Northing) div DScale;
```

To achieve the proper screen position, the "North-up" referenced *XPos, YPos* must pass through a simple rotational coordinate transformation to determine the *heading-up* orientation. This transformation provides coordinates in pixels left/right and above/below the centered screen position. Adding the screen coordinates of the screen reference position (i.e., the map display center) to the rotated point feature coordinates provides the actual screen coordinates at which the point feature symbol should be displayed:

```
ScrnX := ScrnXCenter
   + round( (XPos * COrient) + (YPos * SOrient) );
ScrnY := ScrnYCenter
   - round( (XPos * SOrient) - (YPos * COrient) );
```

Notice that *Show* is provided with the sine (*SOrient*) and cosine (*COrient*) of the orientation angle (i.e., the aircraft heading angle, where zero degrees corresponds to north, 90 degrees to east, etc.). This assumes that the client program will sequence through several point features when generating a map display. Computer computations of the sine and cosine functions of an angle are relatively time-consuming operations. Because the client program must send the same *Show* message to multiple point features, it makes sense for the client to compute these function values once and provide them to each point feature object rather than sending the heading angle and having each point feature independently compute the same sine and cosine values of that angle. System development experience recognizes a program's performance sensitivity to such design decisions.

Once *Show* has determined where the point feature symbol should be drawn, it must determine whether those screen coordinates are within the defined range of the map display. If they are not, then the symbol cannot be displayed and processing is done.

If the symbol can be displayed within the defined bounds of the map, then a message is sent to have the point feature draw itself with its *Draw* method. However, the definition of *PtFeature.Display* is:

```
procedure PtFeature.Display;
  begin
    halt(2);
  end;    { PtFeature.Display }
```

PtFeature is an abstract class representing no specific point feature symbol and therefore is incapable of displaying itself. Asking an object of this class to display itself is therefore erroneous. This code prevents a client from attempting to send a message to an instance of the abstract class to *Show* itself by causing the system to abort. This programming style will catch the programmer's attention during testing and force correction before execution may be resumed. If several such safety checks exist in the system, using a unique error code and perhaps a diagnostic message will help the test engineer identify the source of the problem.

For the *Show* method to work, a descendent class must exist with a virtual *Display* method that knows how to draw the specific symbol assigned to that descendent class's point feature. For example, the symbol for an airport point feature is a filled circle. *PtFeature*'s descendent is declared as:

```
PAirPort  = ^AirPort;
AirPort  = object( PtFeature )
          procedure Display; virtual;
       end;    { object = AirPort }
```

And an airport's *Display* method is:

```
procedure AirPort.Display;
  begin
    Graph.SetFillStyle( { Pattern => } SolidFill,
                        { Color   => } PFColor   );
    Graph.FillEllipse(  { X       => } ScrnX,
                        { Y       => } ScrnY,
                        { XRadius => } 10,
                        { YRadius => } 10 );
  end;    { AirPort.Display }
```

Because *AirPort*'s Display method is a virtual method, as are the *Display* methods of all descendent classes of *PtFeature*, its ancestor's *Show* method can demonstrate its polymorphic ability to transfer control to the proper descendent's *Display* method. This is a good example of how to use virtual methods, as introduced in Chapter 4.

So, after determining that the symbol is within the display area, *PtFeature*'s *Show* method displays the symbol for the proper descendent's point feature and then adds the text label above and to the right of the symbol:

```
begin
  Visible := true;
  Graph.SetColor( PFColor );
  Display;   { show the point feature symbol }
      { show text label...... }
  SetTextStyle( DefaultFont, HorizDir, { Size => } 1 );
  SetTextJustify( LeftText, BottomText );
  OutTextXY( ScrnX+10, ScrnY-10, LabelTag );
end
```

If the current viewport is set by the client program to clip at the bounds of the map display, this code will display as many characters of the label as will fit within the map display area.

All listed point features' symbols have been defined in the context of a 21-pixel by 21-pixel square, centered at the "draw" screen coordinates. Labels are defined by a fixed area above and to the right of the symbol. *PtFeature*'s *Erase* method capitalizes on this commonality among point features. It "erases" a point feature symbol and its text by defining viewports around these areas and then clearing the viewports. *Erase* will work for all descendent classes defined in the unit *PtFeatur*. If a future descendent of *PtFeature* draws a symbol that falls outside these boundaries, that class will also have to define its own *Erase* method. Because this new descendent's *Erase* method will be invoked from *PtFeature* methods, *PtFeature* has declared *Erase* a virtual method. This will force descendents to redefine *Erase* as a virtual method and ensure accessibility from their ancestor.

I defined these classes assuming that point features could be added to and deleted from the data base in real-time. This suggests that the client program (in our example, the Map Display object defined below) will use dynamic instances of the descendent classes of the class *PtFeature*. When a dynamic instance of a visible point feature has been disposed, its *Show* method will never again be invoked. It is therefore important that its destructor *Done* remove the residual image of the point feature symbol from the display. Otherwise, it would remain at a static screen position (not moving like the other point feature symbols) until other point features passing over it nibble away on its image when they update themselves. All objects must take responsibility for their own clean-up in their destructors.

```
unit PtFeatur;

{ Program:     PointFeature - A Map Pt Feature Object unit
  Author:      John R. Ellis
  Last Update: 6 September 1991
  Copyright (c) 1991 by John R. Ellis

  Description: This unit provides classes which may be instantiated
               to create objects which represent geographic points
               to be displayed on a plan-view map display.

  Requirements: The "Display" method requires access to the Turbo
                Pascal Graph unit.
                                                                    }
interface

  type

      PFLabel   = string[6];
      PFType = ( SchoolPF,   ChurchPF,    HospitalPF, CemeteryPF,
                 TallBldgPF, ChimneyPF,   StadiumPF,  LitHousePF,
                 H2OTowerPF, XmtTowerPF,  AptTowerPF, AirPortPF,
                 BridgePF,   DamPF,       RapidsPF,   TargetPF,
                 DestnPF,    NavCPntPF,   AAASitePF,  SAMSitePF  );


      {====================================================================}
      {                      Object Declarations                           }
      {====================================================================}


      PPtFeature = ^PtFeature;
      PtFeature = object              { abstract class }
              constructor Init( XPos  : longint; { meters east of ref. }
                                YPos  : longint; { meters north of ref.}
                                Tag   : PFLabel; { text tag for symbol }
                                Color : word     { symbol/tag color } );
              destructor Done;   virtual;
              procedure Show( XRef   : longint; { "aircraft" easting }
                              YRef   : longint; { "aircraft" northing }
                              SOrient : real; { sin( "a/c" heading ) }
                              COrient : real; { cos( "a/c" heading ) }
                              DScale  : integer { meters per pixel } );
              procedure Display; virtual;
              procedure Erase; virtual;
              procedure Move( XPos, YPos    : longint );
              procedure ChangeLabel( NewTag : PFLabel );
              procedure ChangeColor( Color  : word );
              procedure PtFeatureIsAt( var XPos, YPos : longint );
              function PtFeatureLabelIs  : PFLabel;
              function PtFeatureColorIs  : word;
           private
              Easting    : longint;   { meters east of map ref. }
              Northing   : longint;   { meters north of map ref. }
```

Figure 7.6. Code listing: unit PTFEATUR.PAS.

```
            ScrnX       : integer;    { X-position of last display }
            ScrnY       : integer;    { Y-position of last display }
            Visible     : boolean;    { if PF is on display }
            LabelTag    : PFLabel;    { text display label }
            PFColor     : word;       { symbol/tag color }
        end;      { object = PtFeature }

PSchool   = ^School;
School    = object( PtFeature )       { (1) School }
        procedure Display; virtual;
        end;      { object = School }

PChurch   = ^Church;
Church    = object( PtFeature )       { (2) Church }
        procedure Display; virtual;
        end;      { object = Church }

PHospital = ^Hospital;
Hospital = object( PtFeature )        { (3) Hospital }
        procedure Display; virtual;
        end;      { object = Hospital }

PCemetery = ^Cemetery;
Cemetery = object( PtFeature )        { (4) Cemetery }
        procedure Display; virtual;
        end;      { object = Cemetery }

PTallBldg = ^TallBldg;
TallBldg = object( PtFeature )        { (5) Tall Building }
        procedure Display; virtual;
        end;      { object = TallBldg }

PChimney  = ^Chimney;
Chimney   = object( PtFeature )       { (6) Chimney }
        procedure Display; virtual;
        end;      { object = Chimney }

PStadium  = ^Stadium;
Stadium   = object( PtFeature )       { (7) Stadium }
        procedure Display; virtual;
        end;      { object = Stadium }

PLitHouse = ^LitHouse;
LitHouse = object( PtFeature )        { (8) Lighthouse }
        procedure Display; virtual;
        end;      { object = LitHouse }

PH2OTower = ^H2OTower;
H2OTower = object( PtFeature )        { (9) WaterTower }
        procedure Display; virtual;
        end;      { object = H2OTower }

PXmtTower = ^XmtTower;
```

(continued)

```
        XmtTower = object( PtFeature )           { (10) Transmitting Tower }
              procedure Display; virtual;
            end;      { object = XmtTower }

        PAptTower = ^AptTower;
        AptTower = object( PtFeature )           { (11) Airport Tower }
              procedure Display; virtual;
            end;      { object = AptTower }

        PAirPort = ^AirPort;
        AirPort  = object( PtFeature )           { (12) AirPort }
              procedure Display; virtual;
            end;      { object = AirPort }

        PBridge  = ^Bridge;
        Bridge   = object( PtFeature )           { (13) Bridge }
              procedure Display; virtual;
            end;      { object = Bridge }

        PDam     = ^Dam;
        Dam      = object( PtFeature )           { (14) Dam }
              procedure Display; virtual;
            end;      { object = Dam }

        PRapids  = ^Rapids;
        Rapids   = object( PtFeature )           { (15) Falls/Rapids }
              procedure Display; virtual;
            end;      { object = Rapids }

        PTarget  = ^Target;
        Target   = object( PtFeature )           { (16) Target }
              procedure Display; virtual;
            end;      { object = Target }

        PDestn   = ^Destn;
        Destn    = object( PtFeature )           { (17) Destination }
              procedure Display; virtual;
            end;      { object = Destn }

        PNavCPnt = ^NavCPnt;
        NavCPnt  = object( PtFeature )           { (18) Nav CheckPoint }
              procedure Display; virtual;
            end;      { object = NavCPnt }

        PAAASite = ^AAASite;
        AAASite  = object( PtFeature )           { (19) Anti-Aircraft Artil. }
              procedure Display; virtual;
            end;      { object = AAASite }

        PSAMSite = ^SAMSite;
        SAMSite  = object( PtFeature )           { (20) Surface/Air Missile }
              procedure Display; virtual;
            end;      { object = SAMSite }
```

```
   { free subprogram to set the screen coordinate limits for the
     map display...only display Pt Features within these limits. }
   procedure SetCoordLimits( MinX, MaxX, MinY, MaxY : integer );

{——————— end of interface section ———————}
implementation

  uses Graph;

  var
    ScrnXMin, ScrnXMax       : integer;
    ScrnYMin, ScrnYMax       : integer;
    ScrnXCenter, ScrnYCenter : integer;

{=======================================================================}
{                     Free Subprogram Definitions                       }
{=======================================================================}

   procedure SetCoordLimits( MinX, MaxX, MinY, MaxY : integer );
     { adjust for size of Pt Feature: 21 x 21 pixels }
     begin
       ScrnXMin := MinX + 21;
       ScrnXMax := MaxX - 21;
       ScrnYMin := MinY + 21;
       ScrnYMax := MaxY - 21;
       ScrnXCenter := (MinX + MaxX) div 2;
       ScrnYCenter := (MinY + MaxY) div 2;
     end;    { free subprogram: SetCoordLimits }

   procedure DrawRectangle( X1, Y1, X2, Y2 : integer;
                            Filled         : boolean;
                            SymbolColor    : word     );
     var
       Rect : array[1..4] of PointType;
     begin
       if Filled
         then        { solid rectangle }
           begin
             Rect[1].X := X1;    Rect[1].Y := Y1;   { upper left }
             Rect[2].X := X2;    Rect[2].Y := Y1;   { upper right }
             Rect[3].X := X2;    Rect[3].Y := Y2;   { lower right }
             Rect[4].X := X1;    Rect[4].Y := Y2;   { lower left }
             Graph.SetFillStyle( { Pattern => } SolidFill,
                                 { Color   => } SymbolColor   );
             Graph.FillPoly(SizeOf(Rect) div SizeOf(PointType), Rect);
           end
         else        { hollow rectangle }
           Graph.Rectangle( { upper left corner  => } X1, Y1,
                            { lower right corner => } X2, Y2  );
     end;    { free subprogram: DrawRectangle }

   procedure DrawTriangle( X1, Y1, X2, Y2, X3, Y3 : integer;
```

(continued)

```
                         SymbolColor          : word    );
        var
          Tri  : array[1..4] of PointType;
        begin
          Tri[1].X := X1;     Tri[1].Y := Y1;   { Point 1 }
          Tri[2].X := X2;     Tri[2].Y := Y2;   { Point 2 }
          Tri[3].X := X3;     Tri[3].Y := Y3;   { Point 3 }
          Tri[4].X := X1;     Tri[4].Y := Y1;   { back to Pt 1 }
          Graph.SetFillStyle( { Pattern => } SolidFill,
                            { Color   => } SymbolColor    );
          Graph.FillPoly( SizeOf(Tri) div SizeOf(PointType), Tri );
        end;    { free subprogram: DrawTriangle }

     procedure DrawPolygon( X1,Y1, X2,Y2, X3,Y3, X4,Y4 : integer;
                         SymbolColor  : word );
        var
          PolyG  : array[1..5] of PointType;
        begin
          PolyG[1].X := X1;    PolyG[1].Y := Y1;   { upper left }
          PolyG[2].X := X2;    PolyG[2].Y := Y2;   { upper right }
          PolyG[3].X := X3;    PolyG[3].Y := Y3;   { lower right }
          PolyG[4].X := X4;    PolyG[4].Y := Y4;   { lower left }
          PolyG[5] := PolyG[1];                    { close up polygon }
          Graph.SetFillStyle( { Pattern => } SolidFill,
                            { Color   => } SymbolColor    );
          Graph.FillPoly(SizeOf(PolyG) div SizeOf(PointType), PolyG);
        end;    { free subprogram: DrawPolygon }

{========================================================================}
{              Method Definitions for:  PtFeature classes               }
{========================================================================}
 constructor PtFeature.Init( XPos  : longint; { meters east of ref. }
                             YPos  : longint; { meters north of ref.}
                             Tag   : PFLabel; { text tag for symbol }
                             Color : word    { symbol/tag color } );
    begin
       Easting   := XPos;
       Northing  := YPos;
       LabelTag  := Tag;
       PFColor   := Color;
       Visible   := false;
       Graph.SetLineStyle( { LineStyle => } SolidLn,
                         { Pattern   => } 0,
                         { Thickness => } NormWidth );
    end;    { PtFeature.Init }

 destructor PtFeature.Done;
    begin
       if Visible
         then Erase;
    end;    { PtFeature.Done }

 procedure PtFeature.Show( XRef    : longint; { "aircraft" easting }
```

```
                        YRef    : longint; { "aircraft" northing }
                        SOrient : real;    { sin( "a/c" heading ) }
                        COrient : real;    { cos( "a/c" heading ) }
                        DScale  : integer  { meters per pixel } );
   var
     XPos, YPos : longint;
   begin
     if Visible
       then Erase;
     XPos := (Easting - XRef) div DScale;
     YPos := (YRef - Northing) div DScale;
     ScrnX := ScrnXCenter + round( (XPos * COrient) + (YPos * SOrient) );
     ScrnY := ScrnYCenter - round( (XPos * SOrient) - (YPos * COrient) );
     if (ScrnX >= ScrnXMin) and (ScrnX <= ScrnXMax) and
          (ScrnY >= ScrnYMin) and (ScrnY <= ScrnYMax)
       then
         begin
           Visible := true;
           Graph.SetColor( PFColor );
           Display;          { show the point feature symbol }
              { show text label...... }
           SetTextStyle( DefaultFont, HorizDir, { Size => } 1 );
           SetTextJustify( LeftText, BottomText );
           OutTextXY( ScrnX+10, ScrnY-10, LabelTag );
         end
       else
         Visible := false;
   end;    { PtFeature.Show }

procedure PtFeature.Display;
   begin
     halt(2);
   end;    { PtFeature.Display }

procedure PtFeature.Erase;
   var
     OldVP  : ViewPortType;
     TMaxX  : integer;
   begin
     GetViewSettings( { ViewPort => } OldVP );
     SetViewPort( { X1 => } OldVP.X1 + ScrnX - 10,
                  { Y1 => } OldVP.Y1 + ScrnY - 10,
                  { X2 => } OldVP.X1 + ScrnX + 10,
                  { Y2 => } OldVP.Y1 + ScrnY + 10,
                  { Clip => } true );
     ClearViewPort;
       { erase the label here }
     TMaxX := OldVP.X1 + ScrnX + 10 + 8*Length( LabelTag );
     if TMaxX >= OldVP.X2
       then TMaxX := OldVP.X2-1;
     SetViewPort( { X1 => } OldVP.X1 +ScrnX + 10,
                  { Y1 => } OldVP.Y1 +ScrnY - 18,
                  { X2 => } TMaxX,
```

(continued)

```
                      { Y2 => } OldVP.Y1 +ScrnY - 10,
                      { Clip => } true );
        ClearViewPort;
        SetViewPort( { X1 => } OldVP.X1,  { Y1 => } OldVP.Y1,
                      { X2 => } OldVP.X2,  { Y2 => } OldVP.Y2,
                      { Clip => } OldVP.Clip );
     end;    { PtFeature.Erase }

   procedure PtFeature.Move( XPos, YPos   : longint );
      begin
        Easting  := XPos;
        Northing := YPos;
      end;    { PtFeature.Move }

   procedure PtFeature.ChangeLabel( NewTag   : PFLabel );
      begin
        LabelTag := NewTag;
      end;    { PtFeature.ChangeLabel }

   procedure PtFeature.ChangeColor( Color : word );
      begin
        PFColor := Color;
      end;    { PtFeature.ChangeColor }

   procedure PtFeature.PtFeatureIsAt( var XPos, YPos : longint );
      begin
        XPos := Easting;
        YPos := Northing;
      end;    { PtFeature.PtFeatureIsAt }

   function PtFeature.PtFeatureLabelIs  : PFLabel;
      begin
        PtFeatureLabelIs := LabelTag;
      end;    { PtFeature.PtFeatureLabelIs }

   function PtFeature.PtFeatureColorIs  : word;
      begin
        PtFeatureColorIs := PFColor;
      end;    { PtFeature.PtFeatureColorIs }

   procedure School.Display;                  { 1 }
      begin
        DrawRectangle(ScrnX-9,ScrnY+1,ScrnX+9,ScrnY+9, true, PFColor);
        DrawTriangle(ScrnX-6,ScrnY-9,ScrnX-2,ScrnY-6,ScrnX-6,ScrnY-2,PFColor);
        Graph.Line( ScrnX-6, ScrnY-9, ScrnX-6, ScrnY+1 );
      end;    { School.Display }

   procedure Church.Display;                  { 2 }
      begin
        DrawRectangle(ScrnX-9,ScrnY+1,ScrnX+9,ScrnY+9, true, PFColor);
        Graph.Line(ScrnX,ScrnY-9,ScrnX,ScrnY+1);
        Graph.Line(ScrnX-4,ScrnY-6,ScrnX+4,ScrnY-6);
      end;    { Church.Display }
```

```
procedure Hospital.Display;              { 3 }
   begin
      DrawRectangle(ScrnX-2,ScrnY-9,ScrnX+2,ScrnY+9, true, PFColor);
      DrawRectangle(ScrnX-9,ScrnY-2,ScrnX+9,ScrnY+2, true, PFColor);
   end;     { Hospital.Display }

procedure Cemetery.Display;              { 4 }
   begin
      Graph.SetLineStyle( { LineStyle => } DashedLn,
                          { Pattern   => } 0,
                          { Thickness => } NormWidth );
      DrawRectangle(ScrnX-9,ScrnY-9,ScrnX+9,ScrnY+9, false, PFColor);
      Graph.SetLineStyle( { LineStyle => } SolidLn,
                          { Pattern   => } 0,
                          { Thickness => } NormWidth );
      Graph.Line(ScrnX,ScrnY-7,ScrnX,ScrnY+7);
      Graph.Line(ScrnX-4,ScrnY-3,ScrnX+4,ScrnY-3);
   end;     { Cemetery.Display }

procedure TallBldg.Display;              { 5 }
   begin
      DrawRectangle(ScrnX-4,ScrnY-10,ScrnX+4,ScrnY+10, false, PFColor);
      Graph.Line(ScrnX-4,ScrnY-5,ScrnX+4,ScrnY-5);
      Graph.Line(ScrnX-4,ScrnY,ScrnX+4,ScrnY);
      Graph.Line(ScrnX-4,ScrnY+5,ScrnX+4,ScrnY+5);
   end;     { TallBldg.Display }

procedure Chimney.Display;               { 6 }
   begin
      DrawRectangle(ScrnX-3,ScrnY-3,ScrnX+3,ScrnY+10, true, PFColor);
      Graph.Line(ScrnX-1,ScrnY-3,ScrnX,ScrnY-5);
      Graph.Line(ScrnX,ScrnY-5,ScrnX+1,ScrnY-5);
      Graph.Line(ScrnX+1,ScrnY-5,ScrnX+2,ScrnY-7);
      Graph.Line(ScrnX+2,ScrnY-7,ScrnX+3,ScrnY-7);
      Graph.Line(ScrnX+3,ScrnY-7,ScrnX+5,ScrnY-10);
   end;     { Chimney.Display }

procedure Stadium.Display;               { 7 }
   begin
      Graph.Line(ScrnX-6,ScrnY-8,ScrnX+6,ScrnY-8);
      Graph.Line(ScrnX-6,ScrnY-2,ScrnX+6,ScrnY-2);
      Graph.Line(ScrnX-6,ScrnY-8,ScrnX-9,ScrnY-5);
      Graph.Line(ScrnX-9,ScrnY-5,ScrnX-6,ScrnY-2);
      Graph.Line(ScrnX+6,ScrnY-8,ScrnX+9,ScrnY-5);
      Graph.Line(ScrnX+9,ScrnY-5,ScrnX+6,ScrnY-2);
      Graph.Line(ScrnX-9,ScrnY-5,ScrnX-9,ScrnY+2);
      Graph.Line(ScrnX-6,ScrnY-2,ScrnX-6,ScrnY+5);
      Graph.Line(ScrnX+6,ScrnY-2,ScrnX+6,ScrnY+5);
      Graph.Line(ScrnX+9,ScrnY-5,ScrnX+9,ScrnY+2);
   end;     { Stadium.Display }

procedure LitHouse.Display;              { 8 }
```

(continued)

```
      begin
        DrawPolygon( { X1,Y1 => } ScrnX-2, ScrnY-9,
                     { X2,Y2 => } ScrnX+2, ScrnY-9,
                     { X3,Y3 => } ScrnX+3, ScrnY+9,
                     { X4,Y4 => } ScrnX-3, ScrnY+9,
                     { SymbolColor => } PFColor );
        Graph.Line(ScrnX+3,ScrnY-7,ScrnX+6,ScrnY-9);
        Graph.Line(ScrnX+3,ScrnY-6,ScrnX+6,ScrnY-4);
        Graph.Line(ScrnX-3,ScrnY-7,ScrnX-6,ScrnY-9);
        Graph.Line(ScrnX-3,ScrnY-6,ScrnX-6,ScrnY-4);
      end;    { LitHouse.Display }

  procedure H2OTower.Display;                { 9 }
      begin
        DrawRectangle(ScrnX-9,ScrnY-9,ScrnX+5,ScrnY, false, PFColor);
        Graph.Line(ScrnX-7,ScrnY,ScrnX-7,ScrnY+9);
        Graph.Line(ScrnX+3,ScrnY,ScrnX+3,ScrnY+9);
        Graph.Line(ScrnX+5,ScrnY-2,ScrnX+8,ScrnY-2);
        Graph.Line(ScrnX+8,ScrnY-2,ScrnX+8,ScrnY);
        Graph.Line(ScrnX+8,ScrnY+2,ScrnX+8,ScrnY+4);
        Graph.Line(ScrnX+8,ScrnY+6,ScrnX+8,ScrnY+8);
      end;    { H2OTower.Display }

  procedure XmtTower.Display;                { 10 }
      begin
        Graph.Line(ScrnX,ScrnY-9,ScrnX+2,ScrnY-2);
        Graph.Line(ScrnX,ScrnY-9,ScrnX-2,ScrnY-2);
        Graph.Line(ScrnX+2,ScrnY-2,ScrnX+7,ScrnY+9);
        Graph.Line(ScrnX-2,ScrnY-2,ScrnX-7,ScrnY+9);
        Graph.Line(ScrnX+7,ScrnY+9,ScrnX-4,ScrnY+3);
        Graph.Line(ScrnX-7,ScrnY+9,ScrnX+4,ScrnY+3);
        Graph.Line(ScrnX-4,ScrnY+3,ScrnX+2,ScrnY-2);
        Graph.Line(ScrnX+4,ScrnY+3,ScrnX-4,ScrnY-2);
        Graph.Line(ScrnX+1,ScrnY-9,ScrnX+5,ScrnY-8);
        Graph.Line(ScrnX+5,ScrnY-8,ScrnX+5,ScrnY-9);
        Graph.Line(ScrnX+5,ScrnY-9,ScrnX+9,ScrnY-8);
        Graph.Line(ScrnX-1,ScrnY-9,ScrnX-5,ScrnY-8);
        Graph.Line(ScrnX-5,ScrnY-8,ScrnX-5,ScrnY-9);
        Graph.Line(ScrnX-5,ScrnY-9,ScrnX-9,ScrnY-8);
      end;    { XmtTower.Display }

  procedure AptTower.Display;                { 11 }
      begin
        DrawRectangle(ScrnX-6,ScrnY-9,ScrnX+6,ScrnY-2, false, PFColor);
        DrawRectangle(ScrnX-3,ScrnY-2,ScrnX+3,ScrnY+9, true,  PFColor);
      end;    { AptTower.Display }

  procedure AirPort.Display;                 { 12 }
      begin
        Graph.SetFillStyle( { Pattern => } SolidFill,
                            { Color   => } PFColor   );
        Graph.FillEllipse( { X       => } ScrnX, { Y       => } ScrnY,
                           { XRadius => } 10,    { YRadius => } 10      );
```

```
      end;    { AirPort.Display }

   procedure Bridge.Display;                { 13 }
      begin
        Graph.Line(ScrnX-5,ScrnY-9,ScrnX-3,ScrnY-6);
        Graph.Line(ScrnX-3,ScrnY-6,ScrnX-3,ScrnY+6);
        Graph.Line(ScrnX-3,ScrnY+6,ScrnX-5,ScrnY+9);
        Graph.Line(ScrnX+5,ScrnY-9,ScrnX+3,ScrnY-6);
        Graph.Line(ScrnX+3,ScrnY-6,ScrnX+3,ScrnY+6);
        Graph.Line(ScrnX+3,ScrnY+6,ScrnX+5,ScrnY+9);
      end;    { Bridge.Display }
   procedure Dam.Display;                   { 14 }
      begin
        DrawPolygon( { X1,Y1 => } ScrnX-9, ScrnY-5,
                     { X2,Y2 => } ScrnX+9, ScrnY-5,
                     { X3,Y3 => } ScrnX+7, ScrnY+6,
                     { X4,Y4 => } ScrnX-7, ScrnY+6,
                     { SymbolColor => } PFColor );
      end;    { Dam.Display }

   procedure Rapids.Display;                { 15 }
      begin
        Graph.Line(ScrnX-9,ScrnY-7,ScrnX-1,ScrnY-7);
        Graph.Line(ScrnX-1,ScrnY-7,ScrnX-1,ScrnY-4);
        Graph.Line(ScrnX-1,ScrnY-4,ScrnX+9,ScrnY-4);
        Graph.Line(ScrnX+9,ScrnY-4,ScrnX+9,ScrnY);
        Graph.Line(ScrnX-9,ScrnY-4,ScrnX-3,ScrnY-4);
        Graph.Line(ScrnX-3,ScrnY-4,ScrnX-3,ScrnY);
        Graph.Line(ScrnX-3,ScrnY,ScrnX+6,ScrnY);
        Graph.Line(ScrnX+6,ScrnY,ScrnX+6,ScrnY+6);
        Graph.Line(ScrnX+6,ScrnY+6,ScrnX+9,ScrnY+6);
        Graph.Line(ScrnX-9,ScrnY-1,ScrnX-6,ScrnY-1);
        Graph.Line(ScrnX-6,ScrnY-1,ScrnX-6,ScrnY+4);
        Graph.Line(ScrnX-6,ScrnY+4,ScrnX+3,ScrnY+4);
        Graph.Line(ScrnX+3,ScrnY+4,ScrnX+3,ScrnY+9);
        Graph.Line(ScrnX+3,ScrnY+9,ScrnX+9,ScrnY+9);
      end;    { Rapids.Display }

   procedure Target.Display;                { 16 }
      begin
        DrawRectangle(ScrnX-1,ScrnY-1,ScrnX+1,ScrnY+1, true,  PFColor);
        Graph.Line(ScrnX,ScrnY-9,ScrnX,ScrnY-2);
        Graph.Line(ScrnX,ScrnY+2,ScrnX,ScrnY+9);
        Graph.Line(ScrnX-9,ScrnY,ScrnX-2,ScrnY);
        Graph.Line(ScrnX+2,ScrnY,ScrnX+9,ScrnY);
      end;    { Target.Display }

   procedure Destn.Display;                 { 17 }
      begin
        DrawRectangle(ScrnX-4,ScrnY-2,ScrnX+4,ScrnY+2, true,  PFColor);
        DrawRectangle(ScrnX-6,ScrnY-4,ScrnX+6,ScrnY+4, false,  PFColor);
      end;    { Destn.Display }
```

(continued)

```
   procedure NavCPnt.Display;                 { 18 }
      begin
        Graph.Line(ScrnX-1,ScrnY-8,ScrnX-1,ScrnY-9);
        Graph.Line(ScrnX-1,ScrnY-9,ScrnX-9,ScrnY-9);
        Graph.Line(ScrnX-9,ScrnY-9,ScrnX-9,ScrnY+9);
        Graph.Line(ScrnX-9,ScrnY+9,ScrnX-1,ScrnY+9);
        Graph.Line(ScrnX-1,ScrnY+9,ScrnX-1,ScrnY+8);
        Graph.Line(ScrnX+1,ScrnY+9,ScrnX+1,ScrnY-9);
        Graph.Line(ScrnX+1,ScrnY-9,ScrnX+9,ScrnY-9);
        Graph.Line(ScrnX+9,ScrnY-9,ScrnX+9,ScrnY-1);
        Graph.Line(ScrnX+9,ScrnY-1,ScrnX+1,ScrnY-1);
      end;    { NavCPnt.Display }

   procedure AAASite.Display;                 { 19 }
      begin
        DrawRectangle(ScrnX-9,ScrnY+3,ScrnX+9,ScrnY+9, true, PFColor);
        DrawPolygon( { X1,Y1 => } ScrnX-9, ScrnY+3,
                     { X2,Y2 => } ScrnX+3, ScrnY-9,
                     { X3,Y3 => } ScrnX+4, ScrnY-8,
                     { X4,Y4 => } ScrnX-3, ScrnY+3,
                     { SymbolColor => } PFColor );
      end;    { AAASite.Display }

   procedure SAMSite.Display;                 { 20 }
      begin
        DrawTriangle(ScrnX,ScrnY-9,ScrnX+2,ScrnY+9,ScrnX-2,ScrnY+9,PFColor);
        DrawTriangle(ScrnX,ScrnY+3,ScrnX+6,ScrnY+9,ScrnX-6,ScrnY+9,PFColor);
        DrawTriangle(ScrnX,ScrnY-6,ScrnX+3,ScrnY-3,ScrnX-3,ScrnY-3,PFColor);
      end;    { SAMSite.Display }

{==========================================================================}
{                        No Initialization Code                            }

   end.
```

A Map Display Subsystem Object

The *MapDsply* unit ties together the various previously defined objects to create a somewhat complex object class called *MapDisplay*. This object embodies the abstract notion of a *subsystem* as we defined the term in Chapter 6. However, before delving too deeply into this complex class, let's first define some descendent classes that allow use of the generic linked list object described earlier in this chapter.

Recall that *NodeList*, an abstract object class that defines a generic linked list, and *NodeDataObj*, an abstract object class representing the data being listed, require application-specific descendents to give them enough substance to be useful. For our map display, *PtFeatList* and *PFListNode* are their respective application-specific descendents. *PtFeatList* defines a class to represent a list of point features that the map display will use to generate its moving map. *PFListNode* is a class whose instances hold point feature definitions.

Consider first *PtFeatList*, declared as follows:

```
PtFeatList = object( NodeList )
       end;      { object = PtFeatList }
```

The astute reader will wonder why this class is declared at all. It adds nothing, neither field nor method, to its ancestor's definition! In fact, it fails to define the application-specific method *NodeBelongsBefore*, meaning that an attempt to sort the point feature list will cause the system to abort (i.e., Halt). So clients may not even use the full functionality of the ancestor.

The answer lies in attempting to anticipate future growth of requirements for this type of list. For the current use in the map display, this simple declaration is sufficient. Our point feature list is not an ordered list, so there is no need for an operator to evaluate the ordering of two nodes. This does not preclude that a future instance—such as designating a flight plan of point features ordered by the sequence in which they become destinations or a list of enemy threats ordered by the priority of the danger that they pose—won't arise. It might become useful to provide a method that returns a pointer to the closest *AirPort* point feature. (See Exercise 1 at the end of this chapter.) So the trivial inclusion of a descendent declaration at this point can ease the growth of this class to add future functionality.

The nodes of our list are to point-to-point features. One easy way to satisfy this requirement is to have defined the *PtFeature* class as a descendent of *NodeDataObj*. Although that is not how it was defined, there is nothing to preclude going back and doing it now. When considering future reuse of our point feature classes, there is nothing to tie point features intrinsically to linked lists. It is not hard to imagine point features in environments devoid of such data structures. So, to avoid establishing an unnecessary binding that applies to only one type of application, we'll allow *PtFeature* to stand as a base class and bind it to the list node in a different way:

```
PFListNode = object( NodeDataObj )
     constructor Init( NewPF : PtFeatur.PPtFeature );
     destructor Done;     virtual;
   private
     PtFeat      : PPtFeature;
     end;     { object = PFListNode }
```

This defines the object class that holds the listed data. Its only field is a pointer to an object of the class *PtFeature* or, more usefully, to any object of a descendent class of *PtFeature* (e.g., *School*, *Church*, *Hospital*, etc.) through the facilities of extended type compatibility. This means that the point feature list that we build can actually contain any combination of objects derived from the class hierarchy having *PtFeature* as its base class. From the framework of Pascal's strong typing, this is a very heterogeneous list!

With the classes for the list of point features defined, now consider the class that defines the subsystem itself, *MapDisplay*.

First, *MapDisplay* is defined as a descendent class of *Rectangle* from the *Geo_Objs* (Geometric Objects) unit. The ancestor's characteristics will be used to establish the outer border of the map area on the screen and to hold the coordinates of the display area in its fields.

```
MapDisplay = object( Geo_Objs.Rectangle )
   constructor Init;
   destructor Done;   virtual;
   procedure AddPFToList( WhatType  : PtFeatur.PFType;
                          PFEast,PFNorth : longint;
                          PFTag     : PtFeatur.PFLabel;
                          PFColor : word  );
   procedure Update( var Abort : boolean );
private
   PFList       : PtFeatList;  { list of Pt Features }
   ACEasting    : longint;   { aircraft ref. easting }
   ACNorthing   : longint;   { aircraft ref. northing }
   ACHeading    : integer;   { aircraft heading }
   DisplayScale : integer;   { meters per pixel }
   RateOfTurn   : integer;   { heading change rate }
   HeadingField : TextBox.PTextBoxes;         { heading }
   LTurnButton  : Buttons.PButton;
   RTurnButton  : Buttons.PButton;
   QuitButton   : Buttons.PButton;
   end;      { object = MapDisplay }
```

The first field of this class creates a static instance of the point feature list, called *PFList*. This binds a list of point features to the subsystem that must display them. The next four fields contain the parameters that define the current position (*ACEasting*, *ACNorthing*), orientation (*ACHeading*), and scale (*DisplayScale*) of the map itself. The position parameters specify the geographic coordinates that map to the screen position at the exact center of the map. At that screen position will be a stick model of an airplane facing toward the top of the screen, illustrating the direction in which the aircraft is facing. This corresponds to the "up" direction on the map (the *heading-up* orientation). All visible symbols must be rotated around the map center so they are correctly oriented relative to the aircraft heading. The *DisplayScale* parameter specifies the number of meters of real-world distance that are mapped to each pixel on the display, allowing proper positioning of point feature symbols relative to one another.

The next class field, *RateOfTurn*, is a necessary element of the specific motion simulator implemented for this model. The *HeadingField* field holds a pointer to a dynamic instance of a text box. This text box, off to the side of the map, displays the current aircraft heading in integer degrees. This allows the "pilot" to correlate the up direction on the map to a compass heading.

The final three fields create dynamic instances of *Buttons* that the "pilot" may use to interact with the map and its motion.

A pair of *Buttons* (*LTurnButton* and *RTurnButton*) allow the system to simulate turns to the left and right. Each time one of these buttons is selected, the *RateOfTurn* field is decremented (turning more to the left) or incremented (turning more to the right), simulating momentary movement of the pilot's stick to the left or right and then back to center. Notice that *RateOfTurn* is rate limited, simulating the natural limitation of an aircraft's rate-of-turn. This model is somewhat accurate in that pushing the stick to the left and returning it to center will cause an aircraft to establish and maintain a continuous turn. To stop the aircraft from turning, the stick must be moved an equal distance to the right and returned to center.

Finally, the *QuitButton* field holds a pointer to a dynamic instance of *Button* that causes the subsystem to clean itself up, clearing all visible points from the display and deallocating all memory used to hold dynamic object instances, and shut down the subsystem.

Several important points are illustrated by the method definitions for the *MapDisplay* class.

Because this subsystem has been allocated the entire screen on which to create its display, its constructor, *Init*, becomes responsible for setting up the graphics mode and initializing the mouse. The borders of the map display are drawn on the screen by executing the *Create* method inherited from the ancestor class *Rectangle*. Actually, the object is "created" twice to draw a double line. The outer border, drawn first, becomes a residual image when the second *Create* is executed to create the inner border. No knowledge remains of the location, size, or color of the outer border. However, inherited methods *XCoordIs*, *YCoordIs*, *SizeXIs*, and *SizeYIs* will provide data regarding the map display area defined by the inner border.

The display parameters must be initialized and *Init* also must create and initialize the object instances identified by its fields (i.e., the point feature list, the heading display field, and the three control buttons).

MapDisplay's destructor *Done* must clean up the display and deallocate memory allocated for dynamic objects. The destructor code is:

```
destructor MapDisplay.Done;
   begin
      PFList.Done;   { dispose of the Pt Feature List }
      dispose( LTurnButton, Done );
      dispose( RTurnButton, Done );
      dispose( QuitButton, Done );
```

```
ClrScr;
CloseGraph;
end;    { MapDisplay.Done }
```

Because *PFList* was created as a static object, it does not itself require any memory deallocation. However, it does contain dynamic objects. So, it must clean up after itself. Tracking how this is accomplished provides a good illustration of how well-behaved objects manage themselves.

PFList is an object of the class *PtFeatList*. Because *PtFeatList* does not have an explicitly declared destructor *Done*, *PFList* inherits *Done* from its ancestor class *NodeList*. Recall the code from *NodeList.Done*:

```
destructor NodeList.Done;
  begin
    while FirstNode <> nil do
      DeleteANode( { Ptr => } FirstNode );
    end;    { NodeList.Done }
```

This repeatedly deletes the first node of the list until there are no "first nodes" left (i.e., the pointer to the first node becomes *nil*) and the list becomes empty. *NodeList*'s method to *DeleteANode* was defined as:

```
procedure NodeList.DeleteANode( var Ptr : NodePtr );
  begin
    if Ptr <> nil      { quit if no node to delete }
      then
        .... clean up node pointers so nothing
             points to the node being deleted ....
                (see its listing for details )
        if Ptr^.NodeData <> nil
          then dispose( Ptr^.NodeData, Done );
        dispose( Ptr );
        Ptr := nil;
      end;    { if }
    end;    { NodeList.DeleteANode }
```

The node's record field *NodeData* is a pointer (*NodeDataPtr*) to an object of the class *NodeDataObj*. However, when we added a node to the list (in *MapDisplay.AddPFToList*), we passed *NewPFNode* as the pointer to the new node's data. *NewPFNode* is declared as of type *PPFListNode*, a pointer to *PFListNode* and not a pointer to *NodeDataObj*. This works because *PFListNode* is a descendent class of *NodeDataObj* and, by extended type compatibility rules, is type compatible with its ancestor.

The distinction becomes important when *DeleteANode* invokes the data object's destructor.

```
then dispose( Ptr^.NodeData, Done );
```

Were it not for *polymorphism, NodeDataObj.Done* would be invoked and defined as a null procedure (only "begin" and "end"). However, because we declared *NodeDataObj.Done* a virtual method, *PFListNode*'s *Done* will actually be called. (This explains why we defined the null virtual destructor for *NodeDataObj* and illustrates why this type of declaration is good programming practice.)

```
destructor PFListNode.Done;
   begin
      dispose( PtFeat, Done );
   end;      { PFListNode.Done }
```

The list node has been asked to clean up after itself and it has a field *PtFeat* that is a pointer to an object of class *PtFeature*. But recall a few pages back how we decided that this field would only hold pointers to objects of descendent classes of *PtFeature* (such as *School, Church, Hospital*, etc.). Therefore, when disposing of objects of these descendent classes, it will be their destructors that execute. However, because we did not explicitly define destructors for these descendent classes, it will be the inherited *PtFeature.Done* that gets called upon:

```
destructor PtFeature.Done;
   begin
      if Visible
         then Erase;
   end;      { PtFeature.Done }
```

And the symbol, if it is visible on the display, is erased.

As the final destructor in the chain completes its execution, the software backs up this chain and deallocates the heap memory at each dispose command. First, because there can be no residual image of the point feature symbol, the memory holding the point feature is deallocated. Then, the list node that held the pointer to the point feature can be deallocated. Finally, the record that held the pointer to the node can be deallocated.

Thus every object in this complex structure neatly understands how to clean up after itself and is careful to offer the opportunity to any objects it has created. The importance of using a single destructor name (by convention *Done*) should be apparent from this example, as is the need to declare virtual destructors when their need may not be obvious when they are declared.

MapDisplay's *AddPFToList* has some interesting implications too. This method is passed an enumerated value that specifies the type of point feature to be added to the list, along with the parameters that define the point feature. The case statement based on the enumerated point feature type value selects a corresponding statement of the form:

```
SchoolPF   :   new( NewPFNode, Init( { NewPF => }
      new(PSchool,Init(PFEast,PFNorth,PFTag,PFColor))));
```

The second line of this statement is an example of the "function" extension of the memory manager procedure *new*, returning a pointer to the new point feature (in this case, to an object of the *School* descendent class of *PtFeature*). This pointer is passed to the constructor *Init* as a new dynamic instance of PFListNode is allocated. So, this somewhat powerful statement allocates memory for both the point feature and the list node that holds the point feature, invoking the constructors for both of those dynamic objects!

Notice in the code listing that *NewPFNode* is declared as a pointer to a dynamic object of the class *PtFeature* but is always set to a pointer to a dynamic object of a class descended from *PtFeature* (in the statement above, to a dynamic object of the class *School*).

This pointer to a descendent class object is passed in a message to *PFList* requesting that a node be added to the list (with the *AddPFToList* method). This mechanism builds a list with a variety of objects, all descended from *PtFeature*. This is how such a heterogeneous list can be constructed.

MapDisplay's *Update* method provides the dynamic operations of the moving map subsystem. First, it interrogates the three user control buttons to determine whether or not one has been selected. If one of the turn control buttons was selected, the *RateOfTurn* field is adjusted accordingly. Then the new aircraft heading is computed by adding the current *RateOfTurn* to the previous heading and the heading text box display is updated to display the new heading. Finally, it is time to redraw the point features on the map display:

```
Iterator := PFList.FirstNodeIs;
while not PFList.AtEndOfList( Iterator ) do
  begin
    PPFListNode(Iterator^.NodeData)^.PtFeat^.Show(
                  { XRef    => } ACEasting,
                  { YRef    => } ACNorthing,
                  { SOrient => } SinHeading,
                  { COrient => } CosHeading,
                  { DScale  => } DisplayScale );
    PFList.GoToNextNode( Iterator );
  end;    { iterator loop }
```

This code iterates through the list, starting at the first node. At each node, a message is sent to the point feature at that node to have it show itself using the current map reference parameters. Notice that this code does not know to what type

```
unit MapDsply;

{ Program:    MapDisplay - A Map Symbology Object Unit
  Author:     John R. Ellis
  Last Update: 6 September 1991
  Copyright (c) 1991 by John R. Ellis

  Description:  This unit provides a class which defines a map display
                showing point features representing specific objects
                in geographic space.

  Requirements: This unit uses the Turbo Pascal Graph unit for graphics
                display.
                                                                      }
interface

   uses LinkList,PtFeatur,Geo_Objs,TextBox,Buttons;

   type

      {================================================================}
      {                    Object Declarations                        }
      {================================================================}

      PPtFeatList = ^PtFeatList;
      PtFeatList = object( NodeList )
            end;      { object = PtFeatList }

      PPFListNode = ^PFListNode;
      PFListNode = object( NodeDataObj )
            constructor Init( NewPF : PtFeatur.PPtFeature );
            destructor Done;   virtual;
         private
            PtFeat      : PPtFeature;
            end;     { object = PFListNode }

      PMapDisplay = ^MapDisplay;
      MapDisplay = object( Geo_Objs.Rectangle )
            constructor Init;
            destructor Done;   virtual;
            procedure AddPFToList( WhatType  : PtFeatur.PFType;
                                   PFEast,PFNorth : longint;
                                   PFTag     : PtFeatur.PFLabel;
                                   PFColor : word );
            procedure Update( var Abort : boolean );
         private
            PFList       : PtFeatList;  { list of Pt Features }
            ACEasting    : longint;   { aircraft/map ref. easting }
            ACNorthing   : longint;   { aircraft/map ref. northing }
            ACHeading    : integer;   { aircraft heading }
            DisplayScale : integer;   { meters per pixel }
```

Figure 7.7.   Code listing: unit MAPDSPLY.PAS.   *(continued)*

```
                    RateOfTurn   : integer;   { heading change / iteration }
                    HeadingField : TextBox.PTextBoxes;   { display heading }
                    LTurnButton  : Buttons.PButton;
                    RTurnButton  : Buttons.PButton;
                    QuitButton   : Buttons.PButton;
                 end;      { object = MapDisplay }

  {—————————— end of interface section ——————————}
  implementation

    uses CRT,Graph,GrafInit,Mouse;

  {=======================================================================}
  {                     Local Free Subprogram Definition                  }
  {=======================================================================}
  function MakeStr( Intgr : integer ) : string;
     var
       Strng   : string;
     begin
       str( Intgr:3, Strng );
       MakeStr := Strng;
     end;   { local free subprogram: MakeStr }

  {=======================================================================}
  {               Method Definitions for:  PFListNode                     }
  {=======================================================================}
  constructor PFListNode.Init( NewPF : PtFeatur.PPtFeature );
     begin
       PtFeat := NewPF;
     end;     { PFListNode.Init }

  destructor PFListNode.Done;
     begin
       dispose( PtFeat, Done );
     end;    { PFListNode.Done }

  {=======================================================================}
  {               Method Definitions for:  MapDisplay                     }
  {=======================================================================}
  constructor MapDisplay.Init;
     var
       GError          : integer;
     begin
          { Do the graphics mode set-up.............. }
       GError := GrafInitSuccess;
       if GError <> grOK
         then
           begin
             writeln('Graphics error:  ',GraphErrorMsg(GError) );
             writeln('Program aborted...');
             halt( 1 );
           end;
       ClearDevice;
```

```
          { set up the mouse........... }
if not GMouse.ThereIsAMouse
  then
    begin
      OutTextXY( { X,Y          => } 10, 10,
                 { TextString => } 'Mouse Driver Not Installed' );
      Delay( 5000 );
      Halt (2);
    end
  else
    if not GMouse.MouseIsReset
         then
        begin
          OutTextXY( { X,Y         => } 10, 10,
                     { TextString => } 'Mouse Did Not Reset' );
          Delay( 5000 );
          Halt (3);
        end;
GMouse.Init;
GMouse.ShowMouse;
    { Initialize the list of point features......... }
PFList.Init;          { create an empty Pt Feature list }
Create( { PtX    => } 3,
        { PtY    => } 3,
        { Colr   => } LightBlue,
        { Width  => } GetMaxY-6,
        { Height => } GetMaxY-6 );
Create( { PtX    => } 5,
        { PtY    => } 5,
        { Colr   => } LightBlue,
        { Width  => } GetMaxY-10,
        { Height => } GetMaxY-10 );
SetCoordLimits( { MinX => } XCoordIs,
                { MaxX => } XCoordIs+SizeXIs,
                { MinY => } YCoordIs,
                { MaxY => } YCoordIs+SizeYIs );
ACEasting := 100000;   { initial aircraft location, meters east }
ACNorthing := 100000; { initial aircraft location, meters north }
ACHeading := 0;       { start out going due north }
RateOfTurn := 0;
DisplayScale := 24000 div ( GetMaxY-10 );   { 24 Km range }
new( HeadingField, Init(
              { PtX        => } (13*GetMaxX) Div 16,
              { PtY        => } 40,
              { Width      => } GetMaxX Div 10,
              { Height     => } GetMaxY Div 13,
              { BoxOutline => } TextBox.Single,
              { FieldColor => } LightBlue,
              { LabelText  => } 'HDG: '+MakeStr(ACHeading)));
new( LTurnButton, Init(
              { PtX        => } (12*GetMaxX) Div 16,
              { PtY        => } GetMaxY Div 2,
              { Width      => } GetMaxX Div 10,
```

(continued)

```
                          { Height     => } GetMaxY Div 15,
                          { ButnType   => } TextBox.Double,
                          { NormColor  => } LightGray,
                          { SelColor   => } LightGray,
                          { LabelText  => } 'LEFT' ));
        new( RTurnButton, Init(
                          { PtX        => } (14*GetMaxX) Div 16,
                          { PtY        => } GetMaxY Div 2,
                          { Width      => } GetMaxX Div 10,
                          { Height     => } GetMaxY Div 15,
                          { ButnType   => } TextBox.Double,
                          { NormColor  => } LightGray,
                          { SelColor   => } LightGray,
                          { LabelText  => } 'RIGHT' ));
        new( QuitButton, Init(
                          { PtX        => } (13*GetMaxX) Div 16,
                          { PtY        => } (GetMaxY Div 2) + 40,
                          { Width      => } GetMaxX Div 10,
                          { Height     => } GetMaxY Div 15,
                          { ButnType   => } TextBox.Double,
                          { NormColor  => } Cyan,
                          { SelColor   => } Cyan,
                          { LabelText  => } 'QUIT' ));
     end;    { MapDisplay.Init }

destructor MapDisplay.Done;
   begin
     PFList.Done;  { dispose of the Pt Feature List }
     dispose( LTurnButton, Done );
     dispose( RTurnButton, Done );
     dispose( QuitButton, Done );
     ClrScr;
     CloseGraph;
   end;    { MapDisplay.Done }

procedure MapDisplay.AddPFToList( WhatType   : PtFeatur.PFType;
                                  PFEast,PFNorth : longint;
                                  PFTag    : PtFeatur.PFLabel;
                                  PFColor : word );
   var
     NewPFNode : PPFListNode;
   begin
     case WhatType of
        SchoolPF   :   new( NewPFNode, Init( { NewPF => }
                new( PSchool,Init( PFEast,PFNorth,PFTag,PFColor ))));
        ChurchPF   :   new( NewPFNode, Init( { NewPF => }
                new( PChurch,Init( PFEast,PFNorth,PFTag,PFColor ))));
        HospitalPF :   new( NewPFNode, Init( { NewPF => }
                new( PHospital,Init( PFEast,PFNorth,PFTag,PFColor ))));
        CemeteryPF :   new( NewPFNode, Init( { NewPF => }
                new( PCemetery,Init( PFEast,PFNorth,PFTag,PFColor ))));
        TallBldgPF :   new( NewPFNode, Init( { NewPF => }
                new( PTallBldg,Init( PFEast,PFNorth,PFTag,PFColor ))));
```

```
        ChimneyPF  :   new( NewPFNode, Init( { NewPF => }
                 new( PChimney,Init( PFEast,PFNorth,PFTag,PFColor ))));
        StadiumPF  :   new( NewPFNode, Init( { NewPF => }
                 new( PStadium,Init( PFEast,PFNorth,PFTag,PFColor ))));
        LitHousePF :   new( NewPFNode, Init( { NewPF => }
                 new( PLitHouse,Init( PFEast,PFNorth,PFTag,PFColor ))));
        H2OTowerPF :   new( NewPFNode, Init( { NewPF => }
                 new( PH2OTower,Init( PFEast,PFNorth,PFTag,PFColor ))));
        XmtTowerPF :   new( NewPFNode, Init( { NewPF => }
                 new( PXmtTower,Init( PFEast,PFNorth,PFTag,PFColor ))));
        AptTowerPF :   new( NewPFNode, Init( { NewPF => }
                 new( PAptTower,Init( PFEast,PFNorth,PFTag,PFColor ))));
        AirPortPF  :   new( NewPFNode, Init( { NewPF => }
                 new( PAirPort,Init( PFEast,PFNorth,PFTag,PFColor ))));
        BridgePF   :   new( NewPFNode, Init( { NewPF => }
                 new( PBridge,Init( PFEast,PFNorth,PFTag,PFColor ))));
        DamPF      :   new( NewPFNode, Init( { NewPF => }
                 new( PDam,Init( PFEast,PFNorth,PFTag,PFColor ))));
        RapidsPF   :   new( NewPFNode, Init( { NewPF => }
                 new( PRapids,Init( PFEast,PFNorth,PFTag,PFColor ))));
        TargetPF   :   new( NewPFNode, Init( { NewPF => }
                 new( PTarget,Init( PFEast,PFNorth,PFTag,PFColor ))));
        DestnPF    :   new( NewPFNode, Init( { NewPF => }
                 new( PDestn,Init( PFEast,PFNorth,PFTag,PFColor ))));
        NavCPntPF  :   new( NewPFNode, Init( { NewPF => }
                 new( PNavCPnt,Init( PFEast,PFNorth,PFTag,PFColor ))));
        AAASitePF  :   new( NewPFNode, Init( { NewPF => }
                 new( PAAASite,Init( PFEast,PFNorth,PFTag,PFColor ))));
        SAMSitePF  :   new( NewPFNode, Init( { NewPF => }
                 new( PSAMSite,Init( PFEast,PFNorth,PFTag,PFColor ))));
      end;   { case }
    PFList.AddANode( { NewData => } NewPFNode );
  end;    { MapDisplay.AddPFToList }

procedure MapDisplay.Update( var Abort : boolean );
  var
    OldVP            : ViewPortType;
    Iterator         : NodePtr;
    RealHeading      : real;
    SinHeading       : real;
    CosHeading       : real;
    MouseButtons     : integer;    { Mouse button codes }
    MouseX, MouseY   : integer;    { Mouse X,Y coordinates }
    XCenter, YCenter : integer;
  begin
    Abort := false;
        { update the aircraft heading and location..... }
    GMouse.GetPosition( { BtnStatus => } MouseButtons,
                        { XPos      => } MouseX,
                        { YPos      => } MouseY   );
    if MouseButtons = Mouse.PrL    { left button is action button }
      then
        begin
```

(continued)

```
            GMouse.HideMouse;
            if LTurnButton^.ButtonHit( { ScrnX => } MouseX,
                                       { ScrnY => } MouseY )
              then
                begin
                  RateOfTurn := RateOfTurn - 1;
                  if RateOfTurn < -10
                    then  RateOfTurn := -10;
                  LTurnButton^.Deselect;
                end;
            if RTurnButton^.ButtonHit( { ScrnX => } MouseX,
                                       { ScrnY => } MouseY )
              then
                begin
                  RateOfTurn := RateOfTurn + 1;
                  if RateOfTurn > 10
                    then  RateOfTurn := 10;
                  RTurnButton^.Deselect;
                end;
            if QuitButton^.ButtonHit( { ScrnX => } MouseX,
                                      { ScrnY => } MouseY )
              then
                Abort := true;
            GMouse.ShowMouse;
            repeat
              GMouse.GetPosition( { BtnStatus => } MouseButtons,
                                  { XPos      => } MouseX,
                                  { YPos      => } MouseY   );
              until MouseButtons = PrNone;
          end;
  ACHeading := ACHeading + RateOfTurn;
  if ACHeading >= 360
    then ACHeading := ACHeading - 360
    else
      if ACHeading < 0
        then ACHeading := ACHeading + 360;
      { now update the display........ }
  HeadingField^.ChangeLabel(
                  { LabelText  => } 'HDG: '+MakeStr(ACHeading));
  RealHeading := ACHeading * Pi / 180.0;
  SinHeading  := sin( RealHeading );
  CosHeading  := cos( RealHeading );
  ACEasting   := ACEasting + round( 150.0 * SinHeading );
  ACNorthing  := ACNorthing + round( 150.0 * CosHeading );
  GetViewSettings( { ViewPort => } OldVP );
  SetViewPort( { X1 => } XCoordIs,
               { Y1 => } YCoordIs,
               { X2 => } XCoordIs+SizeXIs,
               { Y2 => } YCoordIs+SizeYIs,
               { Clip => } true );
  Iterator := PFList.FirstNodeIs;
  while not PFList.AtEndOfList( Iterator ) do
    begin
```

```
              PPFListNode(Iterator^.NodeData)^.PtFeat^.Show(
                                  { XRef    => } ACEasting,
                                  { YRef    => } ACNorthing,
                                  { SOrient => } SinHeading,
                                  { COrient => } CosHeading,
                                  { DScale  => } DisplayScale );
            PFList.GoToNextNode( Iterator );
         end;    { iterator loop }
            { Draw aircraft symbol....... }
         XCenter := SizeXIs div 2;
         YCenter := SizeYIs div 2;
         Graph.SetColor( white );
         Graph.SetLineStyle( { LineStyle => } SolidLn,
                             { Pattern   => } 0,
                             { Thickness => } ThickWidth );
         Graph.Line(XCenter,YCenter-8,XCenter,YCenter+14);
         Graph.Line(XCenter-8,YCenter-3,XCenter+8,YCenter-3);
         Graph.Line(XCenter-4,YCenter+9,XCenter+4,YCenter+9);
         Graph.SetLineStyle( { LineStyle => } SolidLn,
                             { Pattern   => } 0,
                             { Thickness => } NormWidth );
         SetViewPort( { X1 => } OldVP.X1,   { Y1 => } OldVP.Y1,
                      { X2 => } OldVP.X2,   { Y2 => } OldVP.Y2,
                      { Clip => } OldVP.Clip );
       if keypressed
         then Abort := true;
    end;    { MapDisplay.Update }

{=======================================================================}
{                       No Initialization Code                          }

end.
```

of point feature (i.e., to which class) it is sending the message. This illustrates the second type of *polymorphism*. A message is sent to an unknown member of a class hierarchy with the knowledge that the receiving object knows how to respond to the specific command. In this case, all point feature types know how to display themselves, so the client does not have to worry about which one is getting the message. Each responds as is appropriate for its own type, drawing its own symbol on the screen.

THE MOVING MAP SYSTEM MAIN PROGRAM

As pointed out with previous examples, the main program should become relatively trivial. For this chapter's moving map system, the main program could hardly be simpler.

```
{ Program:     Aircraft Dash Panel simulator
  Author:      John R. Ellis
  Last Update: 25 August 1991
  Copyright (c) 1991 by John R. Ellis

  Description: This is a main line program which demonstrates
               extensive polymorphism.

               This program draws a digital map display on the
               screen and allows the user to "fly" through it.

  Requirements: This program's objects use graphics mode.
                                                                    }

program DashPanel;

  uses CRT,MapDsply,PtFeatur;

  var
        { object instance creation...... }
    TheMap         : MapDisplay;
        { other variables used by the program...... }
    Exit           : boolean;
begin
  TheMap.Init;
  { Pt Feature Def'n: PFType      PFEast  PFNorth   PFTag     PFColor }
  {                  ————   ——   ——   ——   ———— }
  TheMap.AddPFToList( NavCPntPF,  100000, 100000, ''       , Yellow  );
  TheMap.AddPFToList( SchoolPF,   107500,  95000, 'MELHI'  , Green   );
  TheMap.AddPFToList( StadiumPF,  107500,  98000, ''       , Green   );
  TheMap.AddPFToList( HospitalPF, 113000,  93000, 'HRMC'   , Green   );
  TheMap.AddPFToList( ChurchPF,   102500,  80500, 'PRESBY' , Green   );
  TheMap.AddPFToList( SchoolPF,   107500,  74000, 'PBHI'   , Green   );
  TheMap.AddPFToList( StadiumPF,  107500,  72000, ''       , Green   );
  TheMap.AddPFToList( AirportPF,  111500,  80000, 'VALKAR' , Green   );
  TheMap.AddPFToList( TallBldgPF, 110000,  86000, ''       , Green   );
  TheMap.AddPFToList( TallBldgPF, 111000,  86000, 'TWNTWR' , Green   );
  TheMap.AddPFToList( ChurchPF,   111500,  84000, 'METDST' , Green   );
  TheMap.AddPFToList( XmtTowerPF, 118000,  78000, 'WMMB'   , Green   );
  TheMap.AddPFToList( BridgePF,   120000,  82000, 'MLBCWY' , Green   );
  TheMap.AddPFToList( H2OTowerPF, 116000,  89000, ''       , Green   );
  TheMap.AddPFToList( BridgePF,   120500,  96000, ''       , Green   );
  TheMap.AddPFToList( RapidsPF,   121000, 101500, ''       , Green   );
  TheMap.AddPFToList( CemeteryPF, 115000, 105000, 'GRAVES' , Green   );
  TheMap.AddPFToList( LitHousePF, 127500, 106000, ''       , Green   );
  TheMap.AddPFToList( BridgePF,   120000, 112000, ''       , Green   );
  TheMap.AddPFToList( RapidsPF,   118000, 124000, ''       , Green   );
  TheMap.AddPFToList( XmtTowerPF,  92000, 121000, 'WMEL'   , Green   );
  TheMap.AddPFToList( ChimneyPF,   96000, 110000, 'COAL'   , Green   );
  TheMap.AddPFToList( AirportPF,   92000, 100500, 'MLB'    , Green   );
  TheMap.AddPFToList( AptTowerPF,  94000, 101000, ''       , Green   );
  TheMap.AddPFToList( ChurchPF,    94000,  95000, 'BAPTST' , Green   );
```

Figure 7.8.   Code listing: program DASHPNL3.PAS.

```
  TheMap.AddPFToList( CemeteryPF,   93000,  93000, ''       , Green     );
  TheMap.AddPFToList( TallBldgPF,   89000,  80000, 'HARRIS', Green     );
  TheMap.AddPFToList( TargetPF,     93000,  73000, 'AMMO'  , Magenta   );
  TheMap.AddPFToList( DestnPF,     106000, 118000, 'HOME'  , Yellow    );
  TheMap.AddPFToList( SAMSitePF,   124000, 120000, 'AFB'   , Red       );
  TheMap.AddPFToList( AAASitePF,    95000, 110000, ''       , Red       );
  repeat
    TheMap.Update( { Abort => } Exit );
    Delay(100);
    until Exit;
  TheMap.Done;
end.
```

DashPnl3.PAS (Dash Panel Simulator #3) instantiates a static instance of the *MapDisplay* class (*TheMap*) to become our moving map subsystem. First, a message is sent to *TheMap* to invoke its constructor *Init*. Initialization continues by building the point feature list with a series of messages to *TheMap* to *AddPFToList* ("add a point feature to the list"). With a data base to act on, the primary update loop is entered.

The update loop repeatedly sends a message to *TheMap* to invoke its *Update* method, causing simulated movement of the aircraft and refreshed symbol display on the map. When the user selects the *QuitButton*, the *Update* method returns the *Abort* parameter with a value of *true*. This causes the main program to exit its update loop.

Once out of the loop, a message is sent to *TheMap* requesting invocation of its destructor *Done*. The clean-up processing was described earlier. With clean-up completed, the program terminates normally.

SUMMARY

This chapter wrapped up coverage of the important characteristics of object-oriented programming, *polymorphism*. Polymorphism differs from Ada's static half-brother *overloading*. We discovered that *polymorphism* is a dynamic mechanism that allows objects within a hierarchy to share a method name while retaining the ability for each method to behave as required by its specific class.

We recalled how *virtual methods*, first introduced in Chapter 4, implement one type of *polymorphism*. Our program example, a simple digital moving map system, demonstrated the importance of virtual methods while drawing map symbols on the display and in the clean-up processing done by the class destructors.

Another form of *polymorphism* was demonstrated when the elements of a linked list of map symbols were individually asked to draw themselves. The tight loop that sent the "display" message to the list elements did not know precisely to which class the object belonged. However, because all the objects belonged to the same class hierarchy, polymorphic behavior sorted out their identities and allowed each to respond correctly to the general command.

PRACTICE

1. a. Extend the *PtFeatList* class described in this chapter by adding a method that, when invoked, returns a pointer to the closest "AirPort" point feature in the list. If there are no airports in the list, return *nil*. Hint: when interrogating nodes on the list, how can your method tell what type of point feature it is talking to? Who (what object) has this knowledge?

b. If you solved this problem by adding a field to *PtFeature* of the type *PFType*, set by the constructor *Init* and returned by a new access method, come up with an alternate solution that adds no new fields but requires objects of a class to return their own type. Hint: using virtual methods might help.

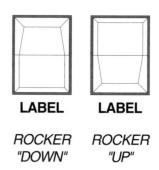

Figure 7.9.   Rocker switch objects.

2. Create an object that represents a rocker switch. A rocker switch may be in one of two states, as shown in Figure 7.9, indicating which way it last was pressed. A rocker switch could have a label above or below it. Selecting the left mouse button while the cursor is over the "UP" half of the switch will cause that side to rock "DOWN" and the state to change accordingly. Write a sample program that uses a rocker switch to turn a status box on and off.

3. Create a three-position toggle switch object (see Figure 7.10) similar to the rocker switches in Exercise 2. Allow a user-defined switch label to appear above or below the switch. Test your object with a three-way light object: off, dim, bright.

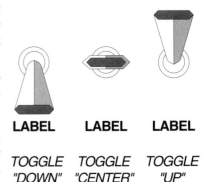

Figure 7.10.   Toggle switch object states.

She is in much trouble about the buzzard; says grass does not agree with it;
is afraid she can't raise it; thinks it was intended to live on decayed flesh.
The buzzard must get along the best it can with what is provided.
We cannot overturn the whole scheme to accommodate the buzzard.
— "The Diary of Adam and Eve," Mark Twain

Chapter *8*

Reusable Objects

Recall that in Chapter 1, I asserted that object-oriented development greatly enhances reuse. Through the subsequent chapters, objects were developed to support a variety of example problems. As the examples became more complex, they began to rely on objects that were introduced in the preceding chapters. Though the specific applications were different, the rewards for having defined the supporting objects in an application-independent manner were reaped. Hopefully, your solutions to the chapter exercises further demonstrated the benefits of reuse to you. Your reuse should have included not only the objects introduced in the chapter examples, but also objects you created in the chapter practice exercises.

In developing objects, as with any other software structure, there are three critical stages: analysis, design, and implementation. The examples and exercises until now have tended to downplay the first two stages. I have attempted to keep the objects required to solve the exercises intuitively obvious. However, I know, having taught the same type of material to seasoned software engineers, that identification of the objects in even these relatively straightforward instances is not a trivial matter for everybody. Selection of good candidate objects during analysis is critical to developing a successful software system. That is the primary thrust in Part II of this book.

So, if you have not found it easy to identify objects in the exercises, don't despair! Help is on the way. But before we address this issue, let's examine a few topics related to object-oriented programming and software reuse.

THE CASE FOR ITERATIVE/INCREMENTAL DEVELOPMENT

Through the sixties and seventies, a stepwise model for software development evolved and became the accepted standard. This model requires a sequence of development *phases*, each of which generates specific products that must be completed and verified by formal (or informal) review before the next phase may legally begin. Never at a loss for formalizing what it considers a better way, the Department of Defense (DOD) published a standard for software development (DOD-STD-2167) in June 1985 that elaborated stringent requirements for the application of this sequential development approach. Figure 8.1, based on a similar chart in the 1985 DOD standard, identifies the phases as horizontal bars that end with the corresponding reviews and then drop to the next bar down, which represents the next phase. This type of development model representation, where the phases stop abruptly and drop to the next phase, has led to the name popularly applied to the approach, the *Waterfall Model*.

Functional decomposition maps well to the Waterfall Model. One primary premise of functional decomposition is that all requirements for a software system can be collected, formalized, documented, reviewed, and frozen before design is permitted to begin. With the Waterfall Model, this happens during the Software Requirements Analysis phase. Only after the requirements are frozen (i.e., "baselined" and placed under formal configuration control) may the software designers proceed to create a software architecture that addresses the system's specific requirements. This first stage of design occurs during the preliminary design phase. When independent reviewers agree that the top-level design addresses all the specified requirements, the architecture is frozen and the designer is authorized to proceed with filling in the details of the design. Only after the detailed design has been blessed in yet another review are the programmers finally authorized to begin writing code.

Functional Decomposition first identifies the primary functions the system must perform. These high-level, and therefore generally somewhat abstract, functions are decomposed into successively more specific subfunctions until each lowest-level subfunction can be represented by a single algorithm whose description will be implemented as a single subroutine, procedure, or function (typically required to be 50 or fewer lines of source code).

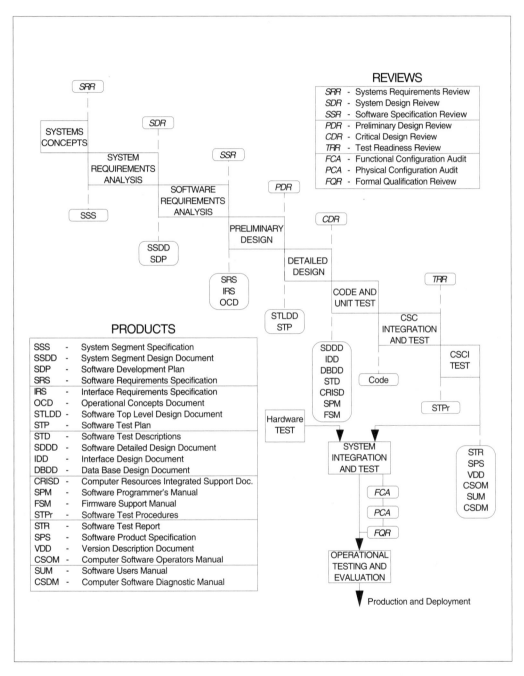

Figure 8.1.   A popular sequential development methodology.

Functionally decomposed systems seem to suffer badly when the requirements change. Seemingly trivial changes in top-level requirements can trickle down numerous branches of decomposed subfunctions and have impacts (although perhaps minor) across a significant breadth of the requirements definition model. Likewise, very low-level changes, such as those to hardware interfaces, can appear in numerous low-level subfunctions and again have a significant impact on the requirements model.

The basic assumption on which the Waterfall Model is built, i.e., that unchanging baselines can be established at each development phase, is almost always invalid. In reality, it is virtually impossible to fully identify all software requirements during the analysis phase and expect them never to change. Requirements are seldom fully understood during this very early phase. They may be incomplete, inconsistent, or misinterpreted. Often all implications of requirements cannot be completely assessed until implementations are considered. Finally, requirements always change. There are many sources for these changes: the customer, systems engineering, and hardware engineering, to name a few.

Systems evolve. As designs evolve, earlier decisions frequently need to be revisited. The embedded real-time system developer is sometimes myopic in failing to recognize that his *system* is really only a *subsystem* of some higher-level system. Such real-time systems are actually a collection of concurrently developed embedded subsystems. As the parent system evolves, the requirements passed down to the embedded subsystems will consequently change.

The embedded subsystems normally consist not only of software, but also of the hardware that becomes the final product and on which the software runs. As the concurrent design of the hardware evolves, software requirements, particularly those related to the hardware interface, will change. Design or implementation problems with the hardware often result in reallocation of requirements from hardware to software or introduce new software requirements to correct a troubled hardware implementation. Either way, the result is the same: the software requirements change.

Add to these inevitable sources of change customers who are frequently unsure of their requirements when the development begins. General Bernard P. Randolph, then Commander of the Air Force Systems Command, speaking at the Tri-Ada '89 conference in Pittsburgh, stated:

> In fact I just commissioned [a study] recently by the Air Force studies board to take a look at the problems and the thing that the board said was, one of the biggest problems we have in the Department of Defense was in the requirements area. We just can't sit still and define the requirements. The requirements continue to float while we're in the midst of designing

the programs and building the programs, and obviously that makes for an impossible job. And a good example is the Cheyenne Mountain Complex Upgrade Program for our missile warning and space surveillance systems: four years late, twice the original cost. And the reason, the studies board said, pure and simple, we just didn't sit down and freeze the requirements. . . . In fact, we rewrote the systems specs three different times. That's how bad it was. We're doing it to ourselves. We cannot baseline the requirements and I'm a big bug on that and that's one of the things we're pushing very, very hard now in the United States Air Force, and I'm sure in the other services. We've got to get our arms around the requirements before we start designing and building, and of course, we've got to do it right the first time. [Randolph, 1989]

Not all customer requirement definition problems are as bad as the ones General Randolph referenced, but my personal experience is that, for most projects, the customer will find the need to change or restate requirements in a manner that impacts the requirements definition model.

Therefore, any development model predicated on the up-front definition of unchanging requirements is consigned to ineffectively handling the inevitable changes of most real-world development projects. A better development model would accommodate change more gracefully.

Alternate development models that address change better than the Waterfall Model have begun to appear. Barry Boehm, in his 1986 article "A Spiral Model of Software Development and Enhancement" (*Software Engineering Notes*, August 1986), suggests an iterative approach in which development *spirals* through phases that develop and refine requirements. Approaches based on *rapid prototyping* encourage developing a "prototype" model to establish the *look* and *feel* of the final system to define requirements. In theory, the quickly developed prototype defines the criteria by which acceptable functionality and/or performance of the final system may be judged. If the final system behaves as the prototype does (in critical functions, interfaces, performance, or other facets around which the prototype was built), then the system is acceptable. The prototype itself is developed iteratively with the customer offering feedback at frequent review points.

More to the point of this book, identification of objects and their interactions is more properly an iterative and incremental process!

Three years after publishing its original software development standard, the DOD released a revised version (DOD-STD-2167A) that attempted to allow the developer more freedom in defining the software development methodology. Although the *waterfall* model was no longer specifically required, individual software units still had to undergo the same phases. Furthermore, inconsistencies in the revised standard still drove developers to use the waterfall model. As a result, the majority of today's software development projects still follow the waterfall model. Going into 1993, the DOD is developing a new software development standard to replace DOD-STD-2167A and offer development teams even greater lattitude in the software development process. The new standard (reportedly to be called MIL-STD-498) should make it easier to implement innovative approaches, such as an iterative and incremental object-oriented methodology.

OBJECTS AND ITERATIVE IMPLEMENTATION

Without going into the details of a specific object-oriented methodology (Part II of this book addresses one such methodology in considerable detail), we can consider a general strategy that illustrates the iterative nature of object identification. Objects can generally be regarded in two broad categories, those that are *discovered* by analysis of the problem and those that are *invented* to effect a solution. Discovered objects should generally precede invented objects, as demonstrated in the following strategic overview:

1. An initial reading of the system problem statement will immediately suggest some of the more essential objects of the system. These generally correspond to the important nouns in the specification text. These become the initial members of the *strawman* object set for the system. Recognize that critical system objects usually are derived from the vocabulary of the problem domain. Premature attempts to think about solution artifacts will prejudice the requirements of the system with preconceived solutions.

2. The interactions among the initial objects will identify some of the required object behaviors. Baseline the strawman objects with their initial behavior requirements (suggesting methods during implementation).

3. As the analysis of object interactions proceeds, the need for additional objects will arise. Add them and their expected behaviors to the baseline object set.

4. Examination of baseline set objects will identify groups that interact in such a manner to suggest that they be defined as an encompassing *mechanism* or *subsystem* (a more complex object). In other cases, baseline objects will be recognized as complex objects requiring decomposition into more primitive objects. Behaviors must be assigned to all new objects.

5. As implementations are considered for the baseline objects, new objects will be created to program a solution. Frequently, implementation details also will uncover new behaviors that are required from the baseline objects.

6. During the implementation process, objects will be reviewed and restructured to establish more efficient solutions.

7. During implementation testing, performance issues will be identified that require modifications to the model set.

As you read these steps, some of them should seem familiar based on your experience in working the chapter problem exercises. The steps that you have intuitively followed in solving relatively simple problems generally apply when addressing large, complex systems. The major difference is that you could hold most of the data for the chapter exercises either in your head or on a single sheet of paper. Real systems will often have orders of magnitude more objects to handle, and no one person can fully remember the volume of data needed to describe the multitude of objects of varying complexity and their sometimes complex interactions. Large systems need a more formalized process. However, the incremental, iterative concept prevails.

This argument could cause an engineer brought up on functional decomposition to have a heart attack! But the older structured programming techniques do not respond well to the inevitable changes. If object-oriented techniques could not accommodate such changes with ease and limit the spread of the impact from going outside the object itself, they would not be of any more value than the older techniques.

The answer lies in considering the types of changes that an object may undergo during the iterative development process and how the primary characteristics of object-oriented techniques reduce the system's sensitivity to such changes.

CHANGING OBJECTS DURING ITERATIVE DEVELOPMENT

The analysis methodology described in Part II of this book begins by identifying all objects necessary to satisfy the requirements of the problem domain. Primary emphasis is on identification of *objects* and not classes. Other approaches that place premature emphasis on classes divert attention from the specific requirements of the objects themselves.

Once the objects that sufficiently define the problem domain have been discovered, analysis of their required characteristics identifies the common traits (fields and methods), leading to a set of supporting class specifications. At the same time, the requirements of the objects may be compared to existing classes residing in available reuse libraries. Where reusable classes come sufficiently close to describing the required objects, they may be added to the emerging class hierarchies.

Because changing objects before baselining a set of class hierarchies has virtually no impact on the development process, I'll concentrate on changes to objects that are already mapped to classes from which they can be instantiated. The effects of changes on the overall system development depend largely on how well the principles of object-oriented development have been applied. Common types of changes that are likely to be required include:

1. **Adding a class.** It is not unusual to identify new required objects that do not map well to any existing class in the class hierarchies. This forces the creation of a new class, which may be descended from an existing class or independent of existing classes, for the new object. There is generally little or no impact to the system when adding new classes.

2. **Restructuring classes.** When a new class that is similar to an existing class is discovered, it may be advantageous to restructure the existing class to enhance inheritance. Those characteristics shared by the existing class and the new class may be extracted to an abstract class from which two descendents are immediately defined. One descendent class holds the remaining characteristics of the former existing class while the other contains those traits of the new class that are not inherited from the shared abstract ancestor class. The impact of such restructuring depends mainly on how well the existing class adheres to strong encapsulation principles. Be aware, though, that it is possible that implementation details cannot be split cleanly between the new abstract ancestor and its descendents. In general, because such restructuring is usually arbitrary, I recommend this type of change only after analysis quantifies the impact and shows the benefits to be greater than the cost.

3. **Adding a method to a class.** A common class change involves adding new behaviors to a class. There are two ways to do this. Generally, the specification of the new method is added directly to the interface section of the class declaration and the implementing code to the implementation section. However, if the class being extended by the new method(s) is a configuration-controlled, reused class, then it may be costly to retest a "certified" unit. In such instances, it is better to create a descendent class that adds the new method(s). There is seldom any real impact in making this type of change.

4. **Adding fields to a class.**   As more complex objects, perhaps representing mechanisms or subsystems, mature, it is not uncommon to discover new fields that are needed to retain state/value information related to the class. Adding fields is straightforward and seldom impacts other elements of the system. Generally, when new fields are added, new methods that input, process, or output the values of the field are also necessary. Likewise, there may be existing methods whose implementations require changes to use the new field values. Overall, adding fields to a class seldom has an impact beyond that class. Often, the best way to implement such changes is to create a descendent class that adds the new field.

5. **Changing the fields of a class.**   There are numerous reasons the fields, holding the state and/or value of the object, might be changed. For example, when a class represents a hardware device and its interface, it may retain a device-dependent representation of data or status in its fields. If the interface should change, or a new device with different data/status representations be substituted, those fields containing device-dependent information also must change. Another reason that class fields might be changed would be to improve memory efficiency. Fields might be "packed" to combine several values into the same memory byte or values could be "compressed" to require less memory when stored (access methods would have to decompress the returned field values).

The impact of class field changes depends on the degree to which encapsulation principles are followed. In general, the fields of a class should be invisible to clients. As long as clients do not exploit any incidental visibility that may result from use of a language that does not provide mechanisms to enforce strong encapsulation, the change impact is limited to the class and its descendents. If descendent classes are restrained from directly accessing any inherited visibility to the changing fields, then the impact is further restricted to the class methods that used direct access.

To minimize the effects of possible field changes, the implementation of class methods and descendent class methods should rely on access methods to read field values whenever possible.

6. **Changing the implementation of a class method.**   Class method implementations may require changes to correct deficiencies in their code. Such deficiencies range from improper execution (i.e., generation of an

incorrect or inaccurate answer, etc.) to inefficient execution. Other class changes, such as the addition of new fields or methods, may make better implementations possible. Proper encapsulation hides implementation details from the class's clients, so that the impact of such changes is usually minimal, often restricted to only the methods being changed.

7. **Changing the class interface.**   The most costly (and therefore least desirable) type of change is one that redefines an existing element of the class interface specification. For example, there could be a need to change the number or types of parameters in a method definition. Such changes are to be avoided as much as possible because they can have far-reaching impacts. For example, where the implementation language supports overloading, consider providing an overloaded method rather than changing an existing one. If a method parameter list must be changed, all clients that invoke the changed methods must be found and the invocations corrected to match the new parameter list. All descendent classes face possible impacts as well. If the changed method interface is for a virtual method, then all descendents that redefine the method must likewise change their interfaces (and possibly their implementations) to be consistent with the ancestor's new definition. In addition, inherited use of the changed method requires corrections to the parameter list wherever it is invoked. Other than to virtual methods, method interface changes in a descendent class seldom require changes in ancestor classes.

Thus, a system developed using good object-oriented principles, strong encapsulation in particular, is generally far less sensitive to changes than one developed using traditional functional decomposition and structured programming methodologies.

PERFORMANCE PENALTIES FOR OBJECT-ORIENTED TECHNIQUES

When I present the concepts of object-oriented programming to battle-weary embedded real-time system developers, they are immediately skeptical of the performance penalty associated with strict application of strong encapsulation. To use an access method takes extra machine cycles to go through a procedure/function call to read a value from memory. If values were globally visible (as has been "accepted practice" for many years), each client could directly read the necessary field values. To that type of concern I have several responses.

First, execution efficiency is often not the most important criterion of system acceptance. If a system's development cannot be completed in a reasonable time and for a reasonable cost, the system will often die regardless of how great its performance might have been. This is especially important in the commercial market where late arrival to market may be the stroke of death to a product. The ability to accommodate change will normally far outweigh the minor performance loss from enforcing encapsulation. General Bernard P. Randolph, in the same Tri-Ada '89 speech, observed:

> When you look at the marvelous improvement in the hardware, it's just fantastic. You know we can process a million lines of code today in the same time we could process one line twenty-five years ago. So when you stop and think about all of the things that we've done, if we had done that kind of improvement in automobiles, you know what a Rolls Royce would cost today? Two dollars and seventy-five cents. And, in fact, it would run something like three million miles on a gallon of gas. Even the microprocessors today, if we were talking about automobiles, would give us ten times better gas mileage while cruising at 250 miles per hour, which is kind of the speed I think my staff car goes sometimes. But the fact is that the machines, the hardware, have really improved. It's the software that's the problem. If you take that same comparison, that million to one over that period, and then you talk about productivity in software, the improvement has been about thirteen to one over that same twenty-five year period. But the part that bothers me is not so much that the productivity hasn't improved so much, it's that when you start looking at the productivity offshore, like in Japan, and you just take a look at the rates of generating completely debugged source code, per person, per month, and the typical U.S. average is like 100 to 500, as you know, and in Japan it's like 500 to 800. And, in fact, if you talk about reuse code, that number goes up to twenty-five hundred to three thousand. So we've got problems folks! [Randolph, 1989]

General Randolph made two important points. First, software development productivity has to improve. That improvement may come at the expense of execution efficiency in some cases, but it must come. Second, execution performance has become less of an issue as each successive generation of processing hardware arrives. Frequently, even with a slight loss of execution efficiency, the system still responds within its performance requirements. In such cases, it's the developer's personal desire to extract maximum performance that unintentionally drives the development schedule and cost. Managers must curtail such discretionary actions by the development team and insist on adherence to standards that improve productivity, reliability, and maintainability.

Advances in compiler technology can help recover some "lost" performance. The Ada language, for instance, includes a compiler directive to *in-line* a procedure rather than generating the code associated with a procedure call. C++ offers two ways to direct a function to be compiled *in-line*. Beyond such user-controlled optimization, modern compiler code optimization can automatically *in-line* a procedure if the procedure/function code is smaller than the overhead needed to invoke it. Such optimization allows the developer to provide enforced encapsulation while the compiler cleans up the executable code and acts as if the values had global visibility.

Finally, when performance really is a problem in a system, it is almost never a global problem. Most real-time systems spend 90% (or more) of their time in 10% (or less) of their code and 50% of their time in 5% of their code. It is nonproductive for the developer to worry about efficiency throughout the system. A good general guideline for developing software is: *design for functionality, tune for performance*. Once the system has been built, integration testing will show where the performance bottlenecks exist. Then, those problem sections of the system may be targeted for refinement. If the bottleneck is due to repeated access to an object's data via an access method, then that specific section of code can be modified to directly access the object field. There is no reason to make wholesale changes to the system to offer global visibility to other clients. Minimize the points at which strict encapsulation must be relaxed.

Don't make performance an artificial issue or use it as a general excuse not to use object-oriented techniques. The advantages of object-oriented development are sufficient to make it the standard from which exceptions are authorized for individual, justifiable cases. Make engineers prove that violation of good object-oriented principles is necessary! The same concern about execution performance greeted mandated use of higher-order languages. Even today, certain sectors of the software development community (such as those who write software for flight control systems) argue that code must be generated using assembly language to achieve necessary performance. Just as the inertia from such pockets of developers not to change is being overcome by strong customer mandates, the same must happen to those who decry the use of object-oriented development methods.

TUNING FOR PERFORMANCE

The included unit *Dates* has evolved from several systems I have developed over the last few years. Examination of its *DateObj* class specification bears witness to some of the types of systems in which it has been used. For example, its ability to format a date in military standard format (i.e., day-month-year; 20 September 1991) comes from a system that prints program listings for inclusion in military standard documents. On the other hand, the computation of the current age of a person born on a specified date comes from a data base system I wrote for the registration of members of a statewide sporting organization.

```
DateObj = object
  { ———— methods ———————- }
  constructor Init;          { sets defaults for today }
  procedure SetTodaysDate; { reads date from DOS }
  procedure SetDate(TheYear,TheMonth,TheDay : word);
  function StdFormatDateIs   : DateString;
                             { format: May 12, 1990 }
  function MILFormatDateIs   : DateString;
                             { format: 12 May 1990  }
  function ShortFormDateIs   : DateString;
                             { format: 5/12/90      }
  function AgeIs( BirthYear, BirthMonth,
                      BirthDay : word ) : integer;
  function TodayIs      : DateString; {format: Sunday}
  function TomorrowIs   : DateString; {format: Monday}
  function YesterdayWas: DateString; {format:Saturday}
  destructor Done; virtual;
private
  Year          : word;    { format: 1990 }
  Month         : word;    { range: 1..12 }
  Day           : word;    { range: 1..31 }
  DOW           : word;    { range: 0..6, 0=Sunday }
end;   { object: DateObj }
```

This object class uses the DOS clock to determine the current date, as in the *SetTodaysDate* method. In the method *SetDate*, it also uses the DOS clock date-setting function to determine the day of week for a specified date. The implementation of these methods follows:

```
procedure DateObj.SetTodaysDate;
  { reads date from unit DOS procedure 'GetDate' }
  begin
    GetDate( Year, Month, Day, DOW );
  end;   { DateObj.SetTodaysDate }

procedure DateObj.SetDate( TheYear, TheMonth,
                                TheDay : word );
  var
    tYear, tMonth, tDay, tDOW : word;
  begin
    { save the current DOS date/time setting }
    GetDate( tYear, tMonth, tDay, tDOW );
     { set new DOS date }
    DOS.SetDate( TheYear, TheMonth, TheDay );
      { return with day-of-week }
    GetDate( Year, Month, Day, DOW );
      { restore DOS date }
    DOS.SetDate( tYear, tMonth, tDay );
  end;   { DateObj.SetDate }
```

These methods use the Turbo Pascal *DOS* unit procedures *GetDate* and *SetDate* to interface with the MS-DOS software. This is a suitable implementation for all systems in which I have used this object class, and for all others that I could imagine needing date information. However, imagine a hypothetical system that needs to send messages to a *DateObj* object instance at an extremely high frequency, such that the overhead of going through the Turbo Pascal *DOS* unit procedures becomes unacceptable.

The system's initial implementation should reuse the existing object without modification! Only after analysis of the operational software clearly shows that the performance bottleneck is truly centered in the *DOS* procedure overhead should modifications be made. In this case, the overhead may be reduced by interfacing directly with DOS, bypassing the Turbo Pascal interface procedures. This change can be implemented by modifying the *hidden* implementation of the two methods with code such as:

```
procedure DateObj.SetTodaysDate;
  { reads date directly from DOS }
  const
    BIOSIntr  = $21;    { BIOS service interrupt }
    GetDateFct = $2A;   { GetDate function code }
  var
    Regs : registers;
  begin
    Regs.AH := GetDateFct;
    Intr( BIOSIntr, Regs );
    Year  := Regs.CX;
    Month := Regs.DH;
    Day   := Regs.DL;
    DOW   := Regs.AL;
  end;   { DateObj.SetTodaysDate }

procedure DateObj.SetDate( TheYear, TheMonth,
                                   TheDay : word );
  const
    BIOSIntr  = $21;    { BIOS service interrupt }
    GetDateFct = $2A;   { GetDate function code }
    SetDateFct = $2B;   { SetDate function code }
  var
    Regs : registers;
    tYear, tMonth, tDay, tDOW : word;
  begin
      { save current DOS date }
    Regs.AH := GetDateFct;
    Intr( BIOSIntr, Regs );
    tYear  := Regs.CX;
    tMonth := Regs.DH;
    tDay   := Regs.DL;
    tDOW   := Regs.AL;
      { set new DOS date }
    Regs.AH := SetDateFct;
```

```
          Regs.CX := TheYear;
          Regs.DH := TheMonth;
          Regs.DL := TheDay;
          Intr( BIOSIntr, Regs );
            { return with day-of-week }
          Year   := Regs.CX;
          Regs.AH := GetDateFct;
          Intr( BIOSIntr, Regs );
          Month := Regs.DH;
          Day    := Regs.DL;
          DOW    := Regs.AL;
          Regs.AH := SetDateFct;    { restore DOS date }
          Regs.CX := tYear;
          Regs.DH := tMonth;
          Regs.DL := tDay;
          Intr( BIOSIntr, Regs );
     end;    { DateObj.SetDate }
```

Although the performance gain is very modest, about 9% for *SetTodaysDate* and just under 5% for *SetDate*, this is typical of the magnitude of performance improvement for many types of implementation modifications. Dropping to in-line assembly code, an option with Turbo Pascal and many other languages, would provide even slightly more of a performance improvement. Although the performance gain is slight, this is at least enough to cover the loss due to the effects of encapsulation.

Notice how this type of modification to method implementations has no impact on the client, other than running marginally faster. The cost of the change is minimized by localizing the impact to the hidden implementations.

Once the changes are made, the modified version is returned to the reuse library so future applications may take advantage of the improved performance. One of those future systems could include a retrofit to an earlier system using this object.

```
UNIT Dates;

{ Program:      Dates - an object manager for setting dates
  Author:       John R. Ellis
  Last Update:  23 September 1991
  Copyright (c) 1991 by John R. Ellis

  Summary:      This UNIT provides a toolbox of low level routines which
                allow Turbo Pascal programs to generate formatted dates
                for ASCII output.
```

Figure 8.2.   Code listing: unit DATES.PAS.   *(continued)*

```
   Requirements: None.                                                }

interface

type

   DateString = String[20];


  {===================================================================}
  {                        Object Declarations                        }
  {===================================================================}
   DateObj = object
         { ————— methods ————————- }
         constructor Init;           { sets defaults for today }
         procedure SetTodaysDate; { reads date from DOS }
         procedure SetDate( TheYear, TheMonth, TheDay : word );
         function StdFormatDateIs   : DateString; { format: May 12, 1990 }
         function MILFormatDateIs    : DateString; { format: 12 May 1990  }
         function ShortFormDateIs  : DateString; { format: 5/12/90       }
         function AgeIs( BirthYear, BirthMonth,
                                   BirthDay : word ) : integer;
         function TodayIs           : DateString; { format: Sunday       }
         function TomorrowIs        : DateString; { format: Monday       }
         function YesterdayWas      : DateString; { format: Saturday     }
         destructor Done; virtual;
       private
         Year           : word;    { format: 1990 }
         Month          : word;    { range: 1..12 }
         Day            : word;    { range: 1..31 }
         DOW            : word;    { range: 0..6, 0=Sunday }
       end;    { object: DateObj }

implementation

  uses DOS;

  const
           { names of the months }
    TheMonths : array[1..12] of string[9]
              = ( 'January',    'February',   'March',      'April',
                  'May',          'June',       'July',       'August',
                  'September',  'October',    'November',  'December' );
            { names of the days }
    TheDays   : array[0..6] of string[9]
              = ( 'Sunday',     'Monday',   'Tuesday',  'Wednesday',
                  'Thursday',  'Friday',   'Saturday' );

  {===================================================================}
  {               Local Free Subprogram Definition                    }
  {===================================================================}
```

```
function MakeStr( i : integer) : String;
  { This function converts an integer into a string. }
var
  s    : String;
begin
  str( i,s );
  MakeStr := s;
 end;      { object utility: MakeStr }


{=================================================================}
{               Method Definitions for: DateObj                   }
{=================================================================}


constructor DateObj.Init;
 { sets defaults for today, to make sure some valid values are there }
  begin
    SetTodaysDate;
  end;   { DateObj.Init }

procedure DateObj.SetTodaysDate;
 { reads date from DOS procedure 'GetDate' }
  begin
    GetDate( Year, Month, Day, DOW );
  end;   { DateObj.SetTodaysDate }

procedure DateObj.SetDate( TheYear, TheMonth, TheDay : word );
  var
    tYear, tMonth, tDay, tDOW : word;   { hold DOS date setting }
  begin
    GetDate( tYear, tMonth, tDay, tDOW );
    DOS.SetDate( TheYear, TheMonth, TheDay ); { set new DOS date }
    GetDate( Year, Month, Day, DOW );     { return with day-of-week }
    DOS.SetDate( tYear, tMonth, tDay );      { restore DOS date }
  end;   { DateObj.SetDate }

function DateObj.StdFormatDateIs  : DateString;
 { return format: May 12, 1990 }
  begin
    StdFormatDateIs := TheMonths[Month] + ' ' +
                       MakeStr( Day ) + ', ' + MakeStr( Year );
  end;   { DateObj.StdFormatDateIs }

function DateObj.MILFormatDateIs  : DateString;
 { return format: 12 May 1990  }
  begin
    MILFormatDateIs := MakeStr( Day ) + ' ' + TheMonths[Month] + ' ' +
                       MakeStr( Year );
  end;   { DateObj.MILFormatDateIs }
function DateObj.ShortFormDateIs  : DateString;
```

(continued)

```
     { return format: 5/12/90      }
     begin
       ShortFormDateIs := MakeStr( Month ) + '/' + MakeStr( Day ) +
                   '/' + MakeStr( Year mod 100 );
     end;   { DateObj.ShortFormDateIs }

   function DateObj.AgeIs( BirthYear, BirthMonth, BirthDay : word ) : inte-
ger;
     { returns today's age of a person born on the date passed.  Assumes
       the object date is today's date.                                }
     var
       T_Age  : integer;
     begin
       if BirthYear < 100           { if year is passed modulo 100.... }
         then
           T_Age := Year - ( 1900 + BirthYear )
         else                       { no, year is of form 19xx }
           T_Age := Year - BirthYear;
       if ( Month < BirthMonth ) or
                         (( Month = BirthMonth ) and ( Day < BirthDay ))
         then
           T_Age := T_Age - 1;
       AgeIs := T_Age
     end;    { DateObj.AgeIs }


   function DateObj.TodayIs           : DateString;
   { return format: Sunday       }
     begin
       TodayIs := TheDays[ DOW ];
     end;   { DateObj.TodayIs }

   function DateObj.TomorrowIs         : DateString;
   { return format: Monday       }
     begin
       TomorrowIs := TheDays[ ( DOW + 1 ) mod 7 ];
     end;   { DateObj.TomorrowIs }

   function DateObj.YesterdayWas       : DateString;
   { return format: Saturday     }
     begin
       YesterdayWas := TheDays[ ( DOW + 6 ) mod 7 ];
     end;   { DateObj.YesterdayWas }

   destructor DateObj.Done;
     begin
     end;   { DateObj.Done }

   {===========================================================}

 end.
```

BUILDING A REUSE LIBRARY SYSTEM

Numerous issues are associated with building reuse libraries, some of which are technical while others are questions of law. There is only one primary motivation for worrying about these issues: The potential return on investment is, to say the least, significant.

Starting a reuse library seems easy enough. At the conclusion of a development project, place all of the programs and their supporting documents into a data base somewhere. As long as the number of programs remains small, there is no problem. But as additional projects are completed and their programs and documents are added to the data base, management of the data base becomes much more difficult. When a library reaches hundreds, thousands, or even tens of thousands of classes, there must be a mechanism by which a potential reuser can quickly identify the classes that are candidates for reuse in a new system. This suggests that the library be structured and that a search mechanism be invented.

If the "prologue" headers of all programs were written in some standard format, with key sections organized in a standard order or set off by standard section-identifying keywords, then a parser could be written to extract the data necessary to create indexes into the program library. Probably the most important field by which an object could be identified in a search would be a list of keywords that characterize the object and its use. In addition to choosing from a list of standard keywords, the developer should be permitted to specify arbitrary keywords. For example, our *Mouse* objects from Chapter 5 might have keywords like: *mouse, cursor, user interface, screen device, graphics user interface, graphics tools*, and *screen text*. The parser could build a file holding only the keywords with key descriptive information (unit name, language, text description from header, latest update date, etc.). An index file could link a master keyword list to the corresponding files. The actual source code files could be stored in a compressed format to conserve disk space.

When a new system is to be developed, the software analyst or designer could query the reuse data base by specifying keywords that suggest the essential characteristics of the needed classes. The reuse library system would first return the general descriptive information about the units that match the specified keyword patterns. If the unit descriptions suggest a possible match for the developer's needs, then the actual source files could be decompressed and presented for further consideration.

The data base might best be segmented by general categories to improve access performance. For example, user interface classes might be sorted and tracked separately from objects of the various problem subdomains and specialty areas.

When software is developed according to a rigorous methodology, it emerges with a type of *certification*. During the program development, each of the completed and reviewed documents is normally placed under project-level configuration control. This protects the customer from unmonitored, arbitrary changes that might not be completely tested or introduce unauthorized functions (perhaps even a virus).

At the end of the project, copies of all documentation and source and object programs are delivered to the customer. Local copies of the documentation and code are frequently put on a shelf someplace and promptly forgotten.

Organizations that want to institute a reuse program must establish a project-independent configuration control plan. This plan must identify an organization to assume responsibility for the completed project products and administer possible changes needed to library units. Because this function may not be funded by specific projects, it must often be funded as an overhead operation. This means a company must be willing to commit resources to operate a useful reuse library.

Because the delivered products may be considered *certified*, the reuse library configuration manager must be responsible for controlling future changes so as not to invalidate the certification. The primary function in maintaining certification is verification that the documentation accurately includes all changes and that the new units have been tested with documented results. When a developer pulls a reusable unit from the library, he should be able to paste the design documentation into the new system design documents without further development. More important, further unit testing can be avoided because the unit comes fully tested with supporting test drivers and documentation. It is through these savings in design and testing that the maximum benefits of reuse are derived. Plans that only allow for reuse of source code fall far short of the optimum return on investment for creating and administering a reuse library. In fact, I suspect that merely reusing code would not justify the administrative expense for maintaining a reuse library.

LEGAL ISSUES ASSOCIATED WITH REUSE

A little imagination, coupled with sound data base management techniques and concern for continuous configuration management, can solve the technical issues associated with creating an operational reuse library. Addressing legal issues may not be as easy. First, I warn you that it is well beyond the scope of this book to consider all the legal ramifications of software copyrights, patents, and licenses. My objective is to warn those planning reuse libraries of possible legal hurdles that must be cleared. Beyond that, let me suggest the type of legal problems that must be considered.

The easiest case to address is the commercial company that develops software for its own products. In this case, the company probably owns the rights to the software it develops and is therefore entitled to reuse it in future products/systems as it sees fit. In fact, any software that a company develops using its internal funds normally belongs to that company and may be reused at the company's own choosing.

This consideration could prompt a company to invest some of its internal research and development funds to establish key units solely for inclusion in the reuse library. Besides simplifying issues concerning the legal rights to such software, it permits the developer to concentrate on optimizing the units for reuse. This investment should be recoverable through the improved chance to win future contracts with lower proposal costs, thanks to not having to develop these reused units.

For the next easiest case, a company that develops software for a Government agency (such as for NASA, the Department of Defense, or the Federal Aviation Agency) does so fully knowing that the Government owns rights to that software. Such Government-owned software may normally be used freely on future Government contract projects.

The most sensitive situation involves a company that develops software under a commercial contract. If Company A contracted and funded me to develop a software system, they would justifiably object to my using some of the software they paid to develop in a future system for Company B, one of their competitors. In such commercial applications, it is important to clearly establish reuse rights at the time the contract is signed. The contract could include terms that trade future reuse of the code to be developed against reuse of code developed on previous projects. Alternatively, a royalty agreement could be tied to future reuse of the code being developed on that contract.

The number of possible cases, such as reusing software from commercial library vendors or "public domain" libraries, is vast and requires qualified professional legal guidance to sort through. There may be units in the reuse library that are limited to future application in only restricted categories of projects.

SUMMARY

One of the strongest justifications for using object-oriented software techniques has been the promise of reusing well-designed, well-constructed, and well-tested objects. Effective reuse depends heavily on ease of modification, because few objects move between system implementations without at least minor changes. This chapter considered how well-structured objects are generally resilient to various types of changes. An example of a heavily reused object was introduced, and then additional modifications to improve its execution performance were proposed.

Then, consideration was given to the performance price associated with using good object-oriented programming principles. Suggestions were made to show how performance might be recovered when using object-oriented techniques does reduce performance below acceptable levels.

Finally, technical and legal issues associated with creating an operational reuse library were addressed. The technical issues center on structuring a potentially large data base to facilitate access to candidates for reuse in a particular system. The legal issues revolve around ownership rights to developed software and their effect on the legal permission to reuse it on future projects.

PRACTICE

1. For each of the units introduced as examples, and for the units you created in the exercises in Chapters 2 through 8, assign meaningful keywords. Then build a master keyword list that maps each keyword to all corresponding units. Finally, imagine an application that uses a graphic user interface and perform a keyword search from your master list to identify candidate units that could be used in building your new system. Does your search come up with all of the reusable objects that apply? Can you suggest some guidelines in assigning key-words to units?

2. Create an avionics control panel "mechanism" similar to that shown in Figure 8.3. This complex object should use existing objects to the maximum extent practical. Use your keyword list from Exercise 1 to search for the units and classes you might use. How few new lines can you get by with and still imple-ment all of the indicated functions?

3. Create a "CAUTION AND WARNING" Enunciator Panel mechanism similar to that shown in Figure 8.4. As the panel is provided a new alert message, it is placed in a queue according to its priority (alert [highest], warning, or caution [lowest]). The (up to) eight highest priority messages must be displayed in the panel text fields 1 through 8, using color to specify the priority (alert => red, warning => yellow, and caution => gray). The panel must track an indefinite number of messages. The user may "acknowledge" any of the displayed mes-sages by using the left mouse button with the cursor over the ACK button cor-responding to the message being acknowledged. An acknowledged message is removed from the display and all lower-priority messages are moved up one position. Consider using the "generic" linked list object for the priority queue needed in the program. You can get by with one list if you define your descen-dent class's ordering method to swap only if the higher-priority message is behind a lower-priority message.

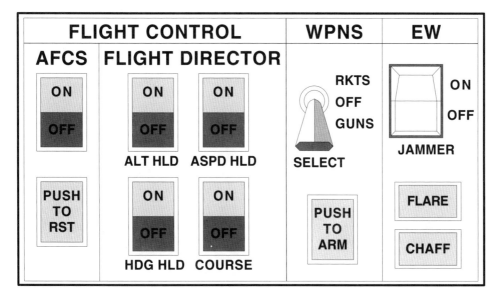

Figure 8.3. An avionics control panel.

This is an important consideration. Whether to use one queue for each priority, or one list with the messages sorted by priority, should be a design decision and neither approach should be specified as a *requirement*. Remember this example when you read Part II of this book.

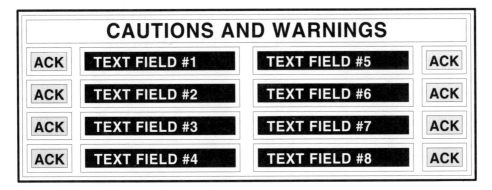

Figure 8.4. A caution and warning panel.

Specifying a System
the Object-Oriented Way

Your attitude, your approach, the sense of confidence and purpose (no hesitation) you bring to your activity is what people observe when they say you are "good at it." Zen is a practice for life; in Zen first comes the technique, practiced so many times that it is forgotten. Then you begin to use it. It is when you do not think about it anymore that you do it so well. Zen is no more than that.

— Introduction to *The Book of Five Rings*

Chapter **9**

Software Requirements Definition

If you have faithfully studied the concepts of object-oriented programming and worked the chapter exercises through Part I of this book, you have begun to see the world from the object viewpoint. In Part II you will learn how to apply this mindset to the specification of real-time systems.

Modern real-time software systems are far too complex to rush headlong into coding and testing. Without a clear concept of what a new system is to do and the criteria by which its performance will be judged acceptable, vast amounts of money can be spent developing the wrong system! In Chapter 8, General Bernard P. Randolph related how the *Cheyenne Mountain Complex Upgrade Program* was plagued by the program's inability to freeze requirements. Congressman John Murtha, then Chairman of the House Appropriations Defense Subcommittee, addressed this same project from his perspective in his keynote address at the Tri-Ada '89 conference:

Cheyenne Mountain is our nuclear fall-back communications system, retaliation, in case we were attacked by nuclear attack. They started telling us a couple of years ago that they had problems. One of the problems, software problems. We're beginning to see that when somebody tells us we have a software problem we're beginning to believe them. Even an old infantryman like myself is beginning to believe that this is a little more complicated than when they just say software and brush it off. We think, "Geez, how much is this going to cost us to take care of?" We've spent, right now, trying to straighten out Cheyenne Mountain, three quarters of a billion dollars. It's going to double. It's going to cost us twice as much. You want to know something? It's been going on for six and seven years. We don't have one system operating at Cheyenne Mountain! Good thing we're not going to be attacked tomorrow. It's a good thing Gorbachev took another route because we'd be in deep trouble if we were trying to use Cheyenne Mountain for the reason that we expect it to be used.

[Murtha, 1989]

General Randolph emphasized the cost effect of poorly specified and designed systems:

You understand better than I that it costs thirty-six times more money to get rid of errors during the operation [phase] rather than fixing all of those problems during the design phase. And, of course, 80% of the errors, according to the study that was done for me, 80% of those errors are due to a lack of understanding or a misunderstanding of the requirements. So therein lies the problem. And as we've heard, we've got to get away from the business of black art and get into the science.

[Randolph, 1989]

In 1987, General Randolph's Air Force Systems Command published a pamphlet (AFSCP 800-14) describing "Software Quality Indicators." Table 9.1 is one of the tables from that pamphlet. This table suggests that requirements analysis and specification is typically allocated 5% of the development budget. However, it suggests that correcting a requirements error will cost three to five times more even during the following design phase and up to 67 times as much when corrected during validation testing.

It would appear that a significant return on investment could be realized if additional resources were applied to requirements analysis and specification. If an approach, call it a *methodology*, accurately identifies the system requirements, i.e., its functions and performance, then the costly correction of requirements-based

**Table 9.1.   Relative costs of correcting software errors.
(Source: Air Force Systems Command Software Quality Indicators;
AFSCP 800-14; 20 January 1987.)**

Software life cycle activities	Percent of software development cost	Relative cost to correct errors
Requirements (analysis and specification)	5	0.3
Design (preliminary and detailed)	25	1.0–1.5
Implementation (coding and compilation	10	1.5–2.5
Integration and test (including unit test)	50	2.0–5.0
Validation and documentation	10	5.0–20.0

errors later in development (or, even worse, after deployment) can be reduced. Such a methodology should present the requirements in a form that allows easy verification. Just as an architect's blueprints may be reviewed for accuracy, so should the representation of a system's requirements be easily reviewable.

Carrying this example a step further, many engineering disciplines create models of a product before building it. Architects draw blueprints and "concept" drawings and build scale models. Aeronautical engineers build scale models for wind tunnel testing. Automotive engineers build clay scale models for the same reasons and to verify ergometric characteristics. Why not apply a conceptually equivalent system modeling to software systems?

SOFTWARE SYSTEM MODELS

When attempting to communicate the essential characteristics of a system, ideally we would merely demonstrate the actual system. This simple idea is the basis for the emerging use of *rapid prototyping*. This approach can be very expensive if the prototype must be developed from scratch. Object-oriented software development offers future benefits for software system prototyping. As *objects* from completed systems in the common problem domain find their way into a reuse library, building inexpensive prototypes based on those existing objects becomes practical. By merging reused objects with some basic prototyping tools, the analyst can show the user a prototype that has the *look* and *feel* of the final system. If the user does not like the way the prototype behaves, make quick fixes and eventually converge on a system with the user's approval.

In many cases, particularly with large or complex systems, prototypes may not be practical. An alternative type of model, more like the architect's drawings or electrical engineer's block diagrams, is needed. To be useful, the model of a system must accurately relate the essential characteristics of that system. Because we are not addressing a model with the physical traits of our system (as would the aeronautical engineer's wind tunnel scale model), our model must necessarily be an abstraction of the system. My goal in this book is to provide a modeling technique that represents the essential requirements abstraction of the software system to be constructed.

The idea of such models is not new. In the 1970s, Ed Yourdon and Tom DeMarco introduced *Data Flow Diagrams* as the basis of *Structured Analysis*. A decade later Paul Ward and Stephen Mellor, among others, suggested extensions that better represent real-time system requirements. My contributions build on the foundation of these efforts by introducing object orientation to the techniques of Ward/Mellor's real-time system models.

Although I specifically address software systems, modeling techniques described here may be applied more broadly to a variety of real-time systems.

SEPARATING REQUIREMENTS FROM IMPLEMENTATION

First recognize the distinction between a system's requirements and its design based on a specific implementation approach. To emphasize the distinction, different models are constructed to capture the essential data associated with each.

Requirements Model: describes the essential requirements of a system; describes what the system must do, how it must perform, and how it must interact with its environment.

Design Model: defines the design structure of the system; identifies the logical and physical elements of the implementation with their associated data structures and behaviors.

This may seem an exaggerated concern, but for many systems it's not. Once requirements have been baselined, changing them involves formal "change requests" processed by the project configuration control board and then revision to one or more requirements documents. Every documented *requirement* must be validated by formal tests. Because formal test documents are normally prepared in parallel to the software product development, changes to requirements affect the test documents as well. If arbitrary design decisions are documented as requirements and later development evolution leads to an alternate implementation, the cost associated with changing the requirements baseline becomes an unnecessary burden on the project. Therefore, make separation of requirements from design an early and continuing concern.

Table 9.2.   **Understand the distinction between the problem statement and specification of an implementation approach.**

	The problem	The solution
Determined by:	Systems Analysis	Systems Design
Model:	Requirements Model	Design Model
Model type:	Logical System Model	Physical System Model
Documented in:	Requirements Document	Design Document
Model represents:	Essence of the system: • required activities • required data	Implementation (incarnation) of the system

This separation of models is the same distinction found in differentiating the definition of the problem from its solution suggested by various scientific problem-solving strategies. Table 9.2 illustrates the essence of this difference.

Let's look at a hypothetical system. Consider a new development project to place an intelligent guidance package on our hypothetical 3.0" Air-Launched Rocket (ALR) system (see example program in Chapter 6). This intelligent guidance system (which we will call the Radar Acquisition and Target System, or RATS) is to identify a ground radar emitter's signal, determine the source of the signal, maneuver the rocket toward that source, and destroy the radar antenna. An antiaircraft battery without "eyes" won't be able to detect your aircraft as a target, so the skies become safe. You are assigned to the RATS project to produce the Software Requirements Specification (SRS).

Your associates from the systems engineering and hardware engineering teams have already developed a conceptual design (illustrated in Figure 9.1). This baseline design requires a pair of orthogonal, highly directional antennas and a small, omnidirectional antenna mounted in the nose of the guidance package. The omnidirectional antenna is tied to a receiver that is tuned to recognize the radar signal frequencies. When the energy in certain bands exceeds preset thresholds, a target is identified. One of the directional antennas is aimed to receive signals from directly ahead of the missile while the other receives signals orthogonal to the missile's travel. Each of these antennas feeds a receiver that conditions and normalizes the signal levels between the receivers. When these two receivers are "triggered" by the Radar Signal Detector, they pass their respective signal outputs to the Digital Signal Processor (DSP). These quadrature signals are approximately proportional to the sine and cosine of the bearing to the radar emitter's signal. Software in the DSP filters the signals to remove common noise and computes the

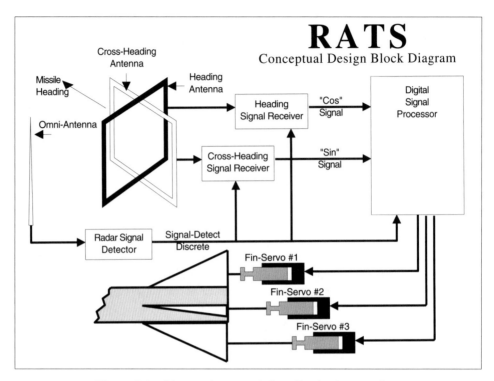

Figure 9.1.   Your project team's baseline implementation.

arctangent of the signals' ratio to determine an azimuth, relative to the missile heading, to the target source. Using theory for a closed loop control system, this azimuth is used as an *error signal* giving the deviation from the desired heading. The DSP software computes correction commands to control servo mechanisms that drive the missile's guidance fins. The software continually makes corrections until the missile is headed directly at the signal source and tracks it into the target.

This conceptual design quickly leads the designers to specify some additional details. For example, the Signal-Detect Discrete will be tied to an interrupt at the DSP. The Heading and Cross-Heading Receiver signals will be passed through an analog-to-digital converter and then presented to the DSP as a 32-bit integer via a pair of memory-mapped sample and hold hardware registers. The system analyst has determined that, owing to the missile velocity and its responsiveness to control commands, the output servo commands must be updated at 25 times per second (minimum) and changes to the servo positions must be rate-limited between updates. Two weeks later, the system analyst decides that the software must avoid attempting to control the servos if the azimuth exceeds 47° from the missile heading because the missile cannot respond sufficiently to converge on a target that far from the missile's heading.

Next, your customer informs your team that if, after a radar source has been identified, the radar signal disappears (as when the operators turn their radar off because they realize it is under attack), the missile must proceed to the last computed source.

As the concept and the customer's understanding of the requirements mature, the system continues to grow and change, in both requirements and design. From my personal experience, such evolution is typical of real systems. From a software requirements analyst's viewpoint, it is your job to sort the requirements from the design decisions (see Exercise 1 at the end of this chapter). Also, certain design decisions outside your control are actually requirements to the software!

When discussing requirements, three types of requirements must be considered:

Allocated Requirements: requirements directly traced to a requirement in a "higher-level," customer-provided or -approved specification. It is an essential part of the requirements verification process to ensure that all specification requirements are allocated to at least one target entity. "System" specification requirements are normally allocated to one or more hardware and/or software specifications. It is always possible to point explicitly to the source of an allocated requirement.

Derived Requirements: requirements that are the direct and logical consequence of a requirement from a "higher-level," customer-provided or -approved specification. Derived requirements, sometimes called "implied" requirements, differ from allocated requirements in that derived requirements are not directly stated in the higher-level specification. Although the derived requirement is not a direct allocation from the source requirement, a person who truly understands the source requirement logically concludes the implied existence of the derived requirement.

Self-Imposed Requirements: requirements not traceable as allocated or derived requirements from any requirement in a "higher-level," customer-provided or -approved specification. Self-imposed requirements normally result from design decisions made by other disciplines of the development team (e.g., systems engineering, hardware engineering, etc.).

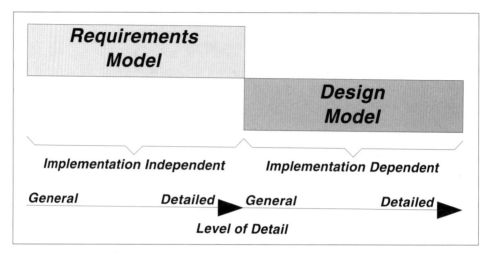

Figure 9.2. Model phasing with the Waterfall Model.

When identifying requirements for publication in a SRS, each requirement should be clearly identified by its type. The precise source of each allocated and derived requirement must be stated. For many systems, it is best to minimize the number of self-imposed requirements. Information that is often introduced as *self-imposed* requirements frequently would better be provided later in the design documentation.

By now you should begin to realize that practical systems are not developed in purely sequential steps (i.e., according to the "Waterfall" development model introduced in Chapter 8 and illustrated in Figure 8.1). This development approach separates creation of the Requirements Model (an activity of the Software Requirements Analysis phase) from building the Design Model (an activity of the Preliminary Design phase), as shown in Figure 9.2. Our brief description of the RATS "requirements" definition process illustrates a typical scenario for the concurrent maturing of the Requirements Model and consideration of the Design Model. Realistically, engineers overlap these two model developments (even if they do not commit the Design Model to paper or disk file) even when they are directed to use a *Waterfall* methodology!

What is important is not that the Requirements and Design Models be developed sequentially, but that they be consciously developed as separate products with distinctive information in each. The software engineer must recognize to which model current decisions contribute. The idea of bouncing between the two models is consistent with our heuristic of developing object-oriented systems in an iterative and incremental manner, as depicted in Figure 9.3.

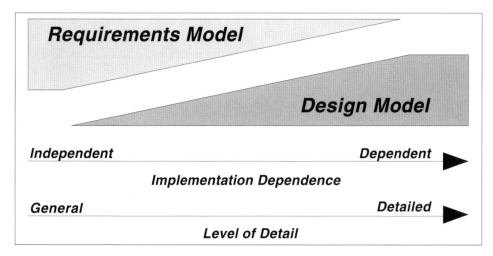

Figure 9.3. More-practical overlapping model development.

Some engineers tend to equate generalities with requirements and details with design. This is not strictly true. For example, our RATS may have a requirement to identify the azimuth to within ± 0.0625 degrees, while the whole approach of computing the azimuth from quadrature components may be a design decision. Perhaps the customer's requirements might be satisfied equally well by employing a movable directional antenna that is slewed until it provides the maximum strength signal.

CHARACTERISTICS OF A GOOD REQUIREMENTS MODEL

For many years, software developers attempted to write extremely detailed SRSs, usually heavily infiltrated by numerous design decisions. So precise were these specifications that only a single implementation could possibly satisfy the requirements. By securing customer approval of this specification, developers felt relieved of responsibility for how the system worked. If the customer were to object to some facet when the system was completed and first demonstrated, developers pointed to the specification and showed that the software reflected exactly the specification the customer had approved. It was a trap! It was a way to get the customer to take responsibility for an arbitrary design approach. But the requirement representations were so complicated, and often so abstract, that it was impossible for the customer to understand fully the implications of all that was "approved."

The trend is swinging the other way. Now customers are rightfully demanding that requirements specification be limited to the *essential* characteristics, the minimum acceptable functional and performance requirements, of the system to be constructed. The customer generally is not interested in how the developers accomplish their feat, merely that they come up with the proper results. The SRS should, as much as possible, identify the *whats* while excluding the *hows*. This may be tempered by situations when a customer has already done the research and requires a specific algorithm or implementation approach (e.g., to be compatible with other parts of the greater system).

A good Requirements Model is the heart of the SRS and the first step to a successful system development. So, how can you tell a good Requirements Model? One way is merely to throw out all the bad ones and what are left are the good ones. The bad ones are obviously those that led to unsuccessful systems. Well, maybe that approach won't help you create a good model, but it should give you cause to think about your model during its development to consider whether or not it is one of the *bad* ones.

A Requirements Model that is based on arbitrary implementation decisions usually does not adequately showcase the customer's concept of the system's necessary functions and performance. Minimize misdirection of attention by omitting implementation details that drive a technology selection. Such self-imposed requirements obscure the true requirements. The selection of an implementation technology and development of supporting design details will appear later in the Design Model.

The Requirements Model should, as much as practical, be expressed in the vocabulary of the problem domain. This will help the analyst avoid specifying implementation artifacts as part of the problem statement. Words and phrases have unique meanings to different people depending on their frame of reference.

Take the simple word *secure*. In a course I recently taught, I asked a student who was also an Air Force officer what he would do if I told him to *secure* something. He said he would place it in a safe and lock the safe. A Marine friend told me that he would *secure* something by rushing it with automatic weapons and making it free of hostile threats. A sailor *secures* something by lashing it to the deck so it won't wash overboard in high seas. To a software engineer, *securing* a system implies guarantees that unauthorized users will not be able to access classified information. An investment counselor will have even a different reaction if asked to *secure* your investments. This one word has completely different meanings to different people.

When preparing the Requirements Model, study the vocabulary of the problem domain and attempt to discuss requirements using its terminology. Treat this almost as if you were learning a foreign language. Be suspect of even the simplest statements by experts from the problem domain (such as end users). Do not confuse the issue by interjecting esoteric software or computer terminology. Your customer (or at least his users) wants to consider the system you build the same way most drivers look at their cars. They aren't interested in whether you use two or four bolt-connecting rods or the diameter and flow characteristics of the valves. Drivers judge a car by how it reacts to pressure on the throttle and brake and the response to changes in the position of the steering wheel. If it feels right and is reliable, that is all they care about. Believe it or not, most embedded computer system users want no more than that! Double buffering is a solution to meet throughput requirements. The buffers are normally not required by the customer, who is interested only in the throughput.

The Requirements Model should be the smallest complete model of the system to be built. Large models can obscure important facets of the system and, regardless of the presentation mechanism, are difficult for anyone other than the author to understand. The smaller and simpler the Requirements Model can be made, the more likely reviewers will be able to understand it and identify requirements errors before they are implemented and become expensive to fix.

In addition, the smaller the Requirements Model, the easier becomes the task of validating the completed system against its requirements. However important "small" may be, "complete" is even more important.

A good Requirements Model should be easily understood by the customer. If you were having a custom house built, you would spend endless hours bent over the architectural drawings to make sure that everything will be as you want it. During construction, you visit your new homesite to make sure that construction matches those prints. Several summers ago, one of my close friends had his builder replace a window box and move several walls that the carpenters had not built according to the design prints. He could do that because those prints had a common meaning to both him and his builder. In the end he got the house that he had contracted.

The Requirements Model must provide common understanding between the customer and the developer, as the design prints did between my friend and his builder. Normally the developer selects the type of model to be used, so it is the developer's responsibility to make sure the customer understands it. That is easier if the model does not use too many icons or icons that have different meanings in different diagrams.

The Requirements Model must be verifiable. All requirements must be testable. Ambiguous or arbitrary requirements, such as "The system shall be *user friendly,*" are likely to fail subjective evaluation by the customer. Only fast talking can possibly verify a requirement that your system be "infinitely expandable." There is no point in placing untestable requirements in the model. Design goals or design objectives may specify anything to help guide the developer in making arbitrary design decisions, but carry no weight during system validation.

REQUIREMENTS SPECIFICATIONS AND TECHNOLOGY LIMITATIONS

Only in the imagination of a Gene Roddenberry (*Star Trek*) or George Lucas (*Star Wars* and others) can one specify systems without regard for limitations of available technology. However, it is our nature to push the thresholds of technology by creating the need for new inventions.

The early 1980s saw the introduction of inexpensive 16-bit microprocessors: the Intel 8086, Zilog Z8000, and Motorola 68000. Before this advance in technology, it was inconceivable, for example, to build a full-digital helicopter Automated Flight Control System (AFCS). The eight-bit 8080, Z-80, and M6800 did not have sufficient throughput or address range. However, the new 16-bit microprocessor technology allowed Harris Corporation's Government Aerospace Systems Division to build the Augusta A-129 *Mangusta* (Mongoose) antitank helicopter Integrated Multiplex System (IMS). Each IMS box was delivered with four 200-KIPS (thousands of instructions per second) Z8000 processors programmed for eighteen different subsystems. These subsystems included AFCS (running on one dedicated processor), Navigation, Communications, Stores Management, Fire Control, and monitoring of Electric, Hydraulic, Engine, Rotor and Transmission, and other aircraft elements. Internal aircraft subsystem communications were carried on a 1 megabit per second MIL-STD-1553B coax serial data bus. For many years following its release, the A-129 IMS was the most highly integrated avionics suite in the world and the only fully digital AFCS on a helicopter (there were many that were largely digital but with analog inner control loop implementations).

As advanced as the IMS was a few years ago, it would be foolish to use its technology to limit the specifications for the avionics of the Boeing/Sikorsky RAH-66 *Comanche* helicopter. The avionics of the *Comanche* will be built around versions of the Intel 32-bit 80960 (i960) processors. An i960 processes up to 11.5 MIPS (million instructions per second) while data will travel around the aircraft on 100 megabit per second fiber optic high-speed data busses. The additional throughput will allow much more complex functions for the 1990s deployable *Comanche* than would be available with A-129 (1980s) era hardware. Not to push technology will result in system obsolescence before the aircraft is even deployed.

So, while on the one hand there is a relationship between requirements and technology, analysts must be careful not to unduly limit a customer's requirements by too conservatively estimating available implementation technology. Adopt a *problem-domain-based* orientation when identifying requirements, initially not considering technology limitations. Ask, "What must this system do to be successful?" Lack of concern for technology limitations has resulted in such marvels as the Mach 3, stealthy YF-12 interceptor (later produced as the reconnaissance SR-71 *Blackbird*) developed by Kelly Johnson at Lockheed in the early 1960s! Most regard this aircraft as outside the technological limitations of its day.

Our revised development life-cycle model that permits concurrent development of the Requirements and Design Models allows iteration between technology-free requirements specification and concurrent consideration of implementation feasibility by modeling the design. In many systems, technological capability should be considered merely another capacity against which the essential specification must be measured. Often, the limitation can be tied to the cost of using existing technology or inventing more expensive new technology.

Before proceeding with modeling techniques for real-time systems, let's characterize real-time systems.

WHAT ARE REAL-TIME SYSTEMS?

Through the first part of this book, I have relied on your intuitive notion of real-time systems. However, before describing a methodology to support analysis of real-time systems, I would like to establish a common understanding of the nature of real-time software systems by offering a definition and identifying the essential characteristics of such systems. Our methodology must consider each of these characteristics when specifying a real-time system. Conversely, any methodology that fails to consider the essential characteristics of real-time systems will generate an inadequate system specification.

James Martin's 1967 *Design of Real-Time Computer Systems* provides a definition of real-time systems with which I have trouble finding fault even today:

> **Real-Time System:** A real-time computer system may be defined as one which controls an environment by receiving data, processing them, and taking action or returning results sufficiently quickly to affect the functioning of the environment at that time.   [Martin, 1967]

Within this definition, we find that real-time systems generally share the following characteristics:

1. Modern real-time systems are usually embedded in devices or mechanisms for which the software must monitor data and issue controlling commands.

2. Many real-time systems interact with a "user" for whom they perform a needed function. This is important when addressing the requirements for a real-time system because meaningful requirements should be stated in the vocabulary of the problem domain, that is, using terms normally familiar to the intended user.

3. Real-time systems frequently require the concurrent processing of multiple inputs. Beyond the most trivial examples, real-time systems include both periodic (traditionally called "cyclic") processing at multiple frequencies and aperiodic (driven by sporadic events) processing. This concept is important because it is the basis on which I build the requirements model, concentrating on events and the system's required responses.

4. Real-time systems are frequently constrained by physical limitations. These normally include processor resources (memory and throughput), response times, input/output channel bandwidths, storage device capacities and transfer rates, and so forth. These limitations, as well as the essential system functions that must be performed, need to be explicitly considered when defining real-time system requirements.

5. Real-time systems frequently have various sensor and intersystem interfaces that provide continuous or periodic input and actuator output or intersystem interfaces that must be driven periodically. The sampling interval tolerances, event response intervals, and response precision are often critical. Permitted variances in responses are often required to be small as well.

6. The reliability of the software in such systems usually must be very high. This may seem obvious when considering military systems, but the cost of correcting a software problem in a microwave oven controller or automobile engine controller is overwhelming after a million units have been sold and distributed nationwide.

In your lifetime you have already seen the number and complexity of embedded real-time systems grow by orders of magnitude. Things that were impossible 20 years ago seldom draw a second thought. For example, the significance of aerodynamics has become secondary to radar signatures in the design of modern military aircraft. When the engineers at Lockheed's famous "Skunkworks" in Burbank, California began work on the stealth fighter, the only computer simulations they had characterized the radar reflections off flat surfaces. Their design, now recognized as the F-117A (Figure 9.4) is made up of triangular sections with no curved surfaces. This configuration would be impossible to fly without the responsiveness of a computer-controlled "fly-by-wire" system to overcome the poor aerodynamics of the design.

Likewise, Northrop first flew the "flying-wing" bomber design with the propeller driven XB-35 in June of 1946 and then with the larger YB-49 model a few

Figure 9.4. Early stealth aircraft design relegated aerodynamic behaviors
secondary to radar reflection characteristics.

years later. This design has also proved to be a low observable shape to radar, but
is again inherently unstable. So unstable was the design that the postwar program
was cancelled following the fatal crash of one of the two prototypes when its pilot
lost control. With the addition of a computer aided stability augmentation system,
the basic design has been reincarnated as the B-2 shown in Figure 9.5.

The new element of uncertainty in embedded real-time systems, when compared to other types of computer systems, is *time* itself. As John R. Garman
described the software problem that delayed the initial Shuttle launch in "The
'Bug' Heard 'Round the World" (*ACM Software Engineering Notes*, October
1981). The specific bug was traced to time, "that nemesis of real-time systems and
concurrent processing, that concept which though pervasive in our lives is difficult
to conceptualize in many contexts" [Garman, 1981]. Faults of this nature are
rarely anticipated adequately. The race condition that introduced a 1 in 67 chance
of failure in the Shuttle was ultimately traced to a change in a delay timing constant
in a seemingly unrelated program a full year before the launch.

Such time bombs are often inadvertently designed into systems. When they are
encountered during testing, they are often attributed to immature hardware and
never traced to their sources because the problem doesn't recur when the tests are
rerun, even several times. I speak from experience!

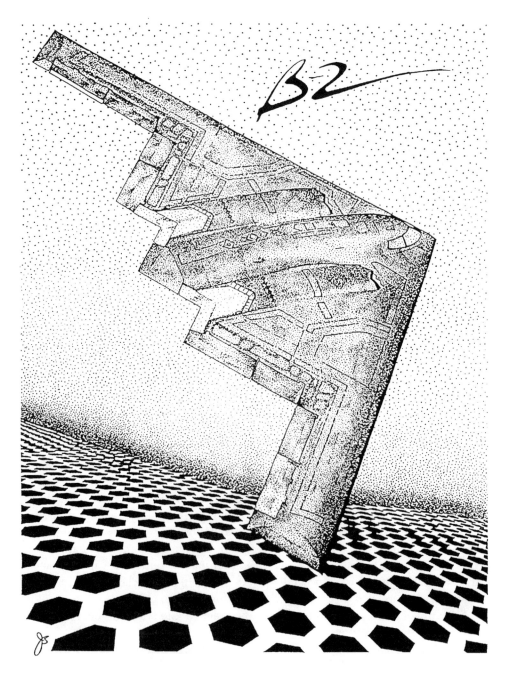

Figure 9.5. The B-2 couldn't fly without computer assist.

SUMMARY

This chapter laid the foundation for developing a Requirements Model. In it, we considered the importance of getting the requirements right early in the program. The idea of using a model to create an abstract representation of a system not yet built introduced two types of models: one to capture the required functions and performance of the system (i.e., the *Requirements Model*) and another to represent the structure of the system as it will be built (i.e., the *Design Model*). Considerable emphasis was given to the importance of separating the information describing the problem, the heart of the Requirements Model, from information describing an implementation approach, the basis of the Design Model.

Three types of requirements were defined: allocated, derived, and self-imposed. Identifying the type of a requirement helps to discriminate between real requirements, which must be validated during formal testing, and arbitrary design choices. Although a separation of mindset is necessary between working on the Requirements and Design Models, the creation of the two models was recognized as likely to overlap. Characteristics of a *good* Requirements Model were considered to help the developer get into the right frame of mind to create a Requirements Model.

Finally, we looked at the unique characteristics of real-time systems, the target of our requirements modeling methodology.

PRACTICE

1. Consider the hypothetical *Radar Acquisition and Target System* (RATS) described in this chapter. List the essential software requirements, i.e., those that would be put into the Software Requirements Specification. Identify the type each requirement would likely be.

2. At the first design review, your RATS customer realizes that your proposed design (Figure 9.1) cannot detect up and down errors in the missile travel. To solve the problem, a third directional antenna must be added that is parallel to the ground. How do these changes affect the software requirements list developed in Exercise 1?

3. Imagine an Automatic Teller Machine (ATM) system. Based on your personal experience as a user of such systems, generate a set of requirements for your ATM system. Be careful to separate requirements from arbitrary design decisions.

4. Repeat Exercise 3 for an automobile cruise control system.

5. Repeat Exercise 3 for some other commercial product that you use frequently (e.g., a microwave oven, a Compact Disk [CD] player, a stereo tuner, a Video Cassette Recorder [VCR], a telephone answering machine, your favorite word processor or spreadsheet program, etc.).

Some of us think it wise to associate as much as possible with historians and cultivate their good will, though we always have the remedy which Winston Churchill once suggested when he prophesied during World War II that history would deal gently with us. "Because," Mr. Churchill said, "I intend to write it!"

— John F. Kennedy

Chapter **10**

The Requirements Model

A person is not capable of holding all the details of a system in his or her head when the system exceeds even a modest degree of complexity. Some people might be able to maintain a good overall understanding of the system but be unable to keep up with all the low-level details. Others might be able to remember the details for several elements of the problem and have only general knowledge of other aspects.

We need a notation that allows us to commit ideas to paper so analysts and developers can easily document and mutually understand a wide breadth of details. The notation should convey the requisite information without distracting the reader. It should be sufficiently rich to represent all the important information. There should be a certain intuitiveness in the notation so that extensive training is not needed and one who is away from the notation for some time can easily recall its meanings. The notation should be largely graphic-based (engineers seem to turn to diagrams to explain complex ideas). But because graphics get overly complex for relating many details, there must be a textual extension to carry the backup details (even engineers' diagrams need supporting explanations).

The notation must be able to represent the necessary characteristics of real-time systems introduced in Chapter 9. In particular, the modeling notation must convey the concepts of concurrent and repeated (e.g., periodic) processes and distinguish between continuous and ad hoc activities. Data flows through a real-time system may be time-continuous, i.e., having significant values at all points in time and requiring sampling based on specific criteria (e.g., at regular intervals or based on another system event), or time-discrete, i.e., having significant values only at designated points in time.

The Ward/Mellor real-time model extensions to *Structured Analysis* (as documented in their three-volume book *Structured Development for Real-Time Systems*) do a reasonably good job of satisfying the above requirements. What their RTSA lacks is object orientation.

In the following chapters, I will reorient many of the basic ideas of the Ward/Mellor RTSA to become a Real-Time Object-Oriented Structured Analysis (RTOOSA).

THE REQUIREMENTS MODEL STRUCTURE

The RTOOSA Requirements Model actually consists of two integrated models, as illustrated in Figure 10.1. These top level constituent models of the Requirements Model are defined as follows:

Essential Requirements Model: an abstract system-wide model that captures the top-level essence of the system. The Essential Requirements Model is documented by three separate products: (1) External Interfaces Diagram (capturing the system's essential interfaces with the outside world), (2) External Events/Response List (identifying stimuli from the outside world to which the system must respond and the system's corresponding required responses), and (3) Object Relationship Diagrams (specifying the significant objects from the problem statement and their relationships).

Essential Objects Model: an abstract system-wide model that identifies the system's essential objects, including the behaviors and interactions that are necessary to satisfy the specifications of the Essential Requirements Model. The Essential Objects Model is documented by (1) Object Flow Diagrams, (2) Object Templates, and a (3) Data Dictionary.

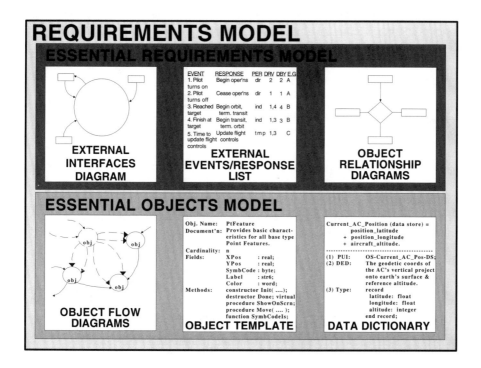

Figure 10.1.   The elements of the RTOOSA Requirements Model.

Developing these two parts of the Requirements Model will be, as with most object-oriented approaches, iterative and incremental. The process must always begin with the Essential Requirements Model. Only after a preliminary "baseline" Essential Requirements Model has been built should work on the Essential Objects Model begin. Thereafter, work on the Essential Objects Model may point out the need to revise the Essential Requirements Model. This should be considered healthy progress and ultimately flow back into the elements of the Essential Objects Model.

The analyst must understand that information will appear in different forms in the various elements of the essential models. Although the representations will be different, there must be consistency among those various representations.

For example, an *external event* from the External Events/Response List must correlate to an interface *flow* ("data" or "event," as will be explained in Chapter 11) represented on the External Interfaces Diagram. That same *flow* will appear in one or more Object Flow Diagrams and be explained in detail as a Data Dictionary

Element. If any of these representations are missing, then the overall Requirements Model is incomplete and/or inconsistent. A model that is missing elements or has inconsistencies is considered erroneous.

> **Erroneous Requirements Model:** a Requirements Model that is incomplete or contains elements that are inconsistent or contradictory. An erroneous model must ultimately be completed or corrected to prevent the problems from propagating to the design and implementation.

In the following chapters, each constituent element of the Requirements Model will be addressed individually. These chapters will concentrate on the syntax and semantics of the notations associated with the corresponding model element. Often, discussions of one model element will reference information that is derived from another element. Look for and remember the ways that model elements interrelate through common information in different representations.

To reduce the risk of creating an erroneous Requirements Model, the developer needs a plan addressing the creation of the model's specific elements. The plan must suggest the sequence in which the elements are developed and explicitly identify the interrelationships among the elements.

Unfortunately, it is not possible to establish hard-and-fast rules for the process of developing the Requirements Model elements of modern real-time systems. The diversity of system types with unique development environments would make it impossible to validate such rules even if they could be found. However, based on experiences with the programs that led to the evolution of the RTOOSA methodology, I can introduce some rules of thumb, or *heuristics*, that suggest an approach that is likely to lead to a successful model.

RTOOSA MODELING HEURISTICS

The heuristics for RTOOSA provide a set of ordered steps that lead to specific products, each an element of the Requirements Model, that attempt to capture the real requirements of a system. The success of this attempt will often translate directly to the success of the development project itself.

The heuristics for developing the RTOOSA Requirements Model must be specific enough to be useful. Guidelines that are too general (what I call "grand hand waving") may sound good when first introduced, but cannot answer the specific questions developers raise when attempting to apply them. On the other hand, these guidelines must be general enough to address the broad range of real-time systems to which they are to be applied. It would be easy to provide heuristics that address a very limited subset of possible systems, but be useless for many others.

The risk with heuristics that have too limited an application set lies in not being able to determine their lack of applicability until a considerable investment has been made attempting to apply them in an inappropriate situation. Keeping these limitations in mind, I provide the following heuristics for RTOOSA Requirements Model development:

1. **Establish the essential requirements model.** To do this, create the three elements of the Essential Requirements Model *in parallel*:

   External Interfaces Diagram (EID): defines the boundaries of the system and identifies what must cross those boundaries. In the EID, the system is represented by a single icon. Each of the external objects is represented by an icon. "Flow" icons define information and event signals that pass between the external objects and the system.

   External Events/Response List (EERL): defines the events from outside the system that require a response from the system and describes those responses. Every External Event specified in the EERL must be attributable either to an external object explicitly shown on the EID or to an implicit clock (which is often omitted from explicit representation on the EID). Dependencies among event/response pairs are explicitly defined and gathered in logical groups. Because all processing in a real-time system initiates in response to a stimulus from outside the system (assuming time is considered an external stimulus that may not be shown on the EID), the EERL becomes a structured summary of all functional requirements allocated to the system.

   Object Relationship Diagrams (ORD): identify the significant objects from the external environment and the key objects within the system and their relationships. Candidate objects are those that are identified in the descriptions of the event/response pairs in the EERL.

2. **Verify that all functional requirements allocated to the system are traceable to an event/response pair.** Because I propose to use the EERL as the basis for verification of completeness for the Requirements Model, it is essential to verify that the EERL accurately represents all of the allocated system functional and performance requirements. This is best accomplished by a *verification matrix* that maps each of the source document requirements to one or more of the event/response pairs. If a

requirement cannot be traced to an event/response pair, then expand the EERL to include the appropriate requirements.

3. **Verify consistency among the elements of the Essential Requirements Model.** Consistency among the three elements of the Essential Requirements Model suggests completeness sufficient to establish an initial baseline for the Requirements Model. *This baseline must be set before proceeding.*

4. **Establish the Essential Objects Model.** To do this, in parallel, create the three elements of the Essential Objects Model:

Object Flow Diagrams (OFD): a hierarchical set of diagrams that identify the key (essential) objects from the problem domain and establish their needed behaviors and interactions. Each object identified also must be explicitly declared by an Object Template. OFDs are the RTOOSA counterparts for the Structured Analysis Data Flow Diagrams. Each complex object (mechanism or subsystem) must be decomposed in a lower-level OFD. Each primitive object must be decomposed in a base-level OFD that identifies the essential fields and methods of the object. The structure of each field must be expanded as an element in the Data Dictionary and the processing requirements of each method must be specified in an appropriate form.

Object Template (OT): provides the essential structure of the key (essential) objects in terms of their needed fields and methods. Each object identified in an OFD requires explicit definition in an OT. Each field must correspond to an icon in a primitive object's OFD and be explicitly defined as a Data Dictionary Element in the Data Dictionary. Each method must be explicitly expanded in the backup to the corresponding primitive object OFD in a manner appropriate to the required processing.

Data Dictionary (DD): provides a structured textual definition for each of the "flows" identified in the EID and OFDs and for each field from a primitive object OFD. Each Data Dictionary Element (DDE) definition identifies any constituent components of the DDE and defines its key characteristics and attributes.

5. **Verify consistency among these Essential Object Model elements and the elements of the Essential Requirements Model.** This may require

revisiting the EID, EERL, and ORDs. Such iteration, when needed, is considered a constructive part of the development process.

The Essential Objects Model specifies the *essential* objects of the problem domain. This will map to a subset of all objects that will be implemented in response to the Design Model. *Do not attempt to introduce objects into the Requirements Model if they do not contribute to the statement of the problem.*

One important step in the verification of essential objects is to track a logical processing *flow* corresponding to each event/response pair in the EERL among the objects on the OFDs. Every object identified in each OFD must be "touched" in support of at least one of the event/response pairs or its removal from the Requirements Model is probably justified. Conversely, all objects necessary to provide the processing specified or implied by each event/response pair must appear on the appropriate OFDs. Required processing that cannot be associated with a specific object must either be added as a method to an existing object or assigned to a new object, if necessary. Only when each event/response pair can be completely traced through the OFDs can the Requirements Model be considered complete. Later, several ways to document this verification will be suggested.

The Requirements Model addresses the specific *objects* that are necessary to bound the system requirements. This model does not consider the classes from which such objects may be instantiated. Identification of suitable classes for the essential objects will be considered part of the design process discussed further in Chapter 17. In addition, the Essential Objects Model should consider only the behaviors necessary to specify the specific system to be developed. The methods identified in the primitive object OFDs and OTs are only those that contribute to the requirements of the system under development. When objects are later associated with classes, some of those classes may include methods not explicitly defined in this Requirements Model. This will very likely occur if an object is associated with a class from a reuse library. Reuse of such a class may carry fields and methods not required by the current system, but are a reasonable cost for enjoying the benefits of reuse! It is also possible that the Design Model may define additional methods for certain objects as part of an arbitrary implementation approach. It is not necessary (and generally not desirable) to include implementation-dependent object characteristics in the Requirements Model.

Although mapping the objects identified in the Requirements Model to objects in the Design Model will be considered in Chapter 17, many of the elements of this mapping should be intuitively obvious. If you think about the objects that appeared in the example programs in Part I of this book, you are likely to see the elements of the corresponding system's Requirements Model (were we to create one) that would have led to the implementation objects.

CASE STUDIES PROVIDE EXAMPLE SYSTEMS TO MODEL

Frequently software development methodologies are introduced with trivial systems (such as Automatic Teller Machine [ATM] systems and automobile Cruise Control systems) to illustrate application of the new methodology. Although use of simple systems prevents examples from becoming tedious, and thereby possibly obscuring the key points being explained, it also often results in assertions that the methodologies cannot be "scaled up" to address the larger systems that solve real-world problems. Another significant problem caused by using trivial systems comes from such systems being inherently simple and not addressing the complex situations that "real" systems invariably introduce. Engineers who attempt to use the new methodology are forced to invent solutions that are often not compatible with other aspects of the methodology and may not be consistent with solutions that other developers invented for other parts of the same system.

There will be places in the coming chapters where I will use simple systems, including ATM and Cruise Control, because their requirements are few. Because most readers will have had common experiences with these types of systems, I will not describe the system being modeled. However, for the reasons given above, three more significant systems will be used to demonstrate the various concepts as well:

1. A hypothetical navigation system for a converted C-130 cargo aircraft adapted for duty as a Gunship (and renamed the AC-130). The Gunship conversion consists of cutting away gun ports on the left side of the aircraft and mounting a complement of guns, ranging from 20-caliber miniguns to a 105-mm Howitzer. To fire the guns, the aircraft must fly a circular "orbit" around the ground target point at up to 10,000 feet altitude. A more detailed description of our AC-130 Gunship's requirements is provided in Appendix C.

2. A hypothetical Audio/Video Distribution System (AVDS) for the Space Station Freedom. The AVDS links various Audio/Video input devices (cameras, Video Tape Recorders [VTR], etc.) with various output devices (monitors, VTRs, etc.) in the six modules on-board the Space Station and via a data link to the ground station. A more complete description of the hypothetical AVDS is provided in Appendix D.

3. A hypothetical Doppler navigation system for a light, antitank attack helicopter. An aircraft's Doppler radar operates on the same principles as the radar "guns" used by police to measure automobile speeds. An aircraft Doppler radar uses multiple beams aimed in a specific pattern

to be able to measure velocity in three dimensions. By integrating velocity over time, displacement from a known starting position is updated iteratively. Finally, the computed aircraft position can be compared to a planned flight path to determine how far the aircraft is from its ideal position and heading. These "error" values can be fed to the flight control system, which commands the aircraft back onto the desired flight path. A more complete description of the Doppler navigator requirements is included in Appendix C.

Although these case studies bear certain similarities to systems on which I have worked over the years, they are sufficiently abstracted or generalized so as not to divulge any proprietary information. Significant details have been omitted intentionally to prevent the cases from being overly complex. This does not detract from their usefulness in illustrating the application of RTOOSA to the types of real-world systems for which the methodology is intended.

I recommend that the reader browse the appendices associated with these case studies to become familiar with their general requirements. As Requirements Model elements are constructed for these case study systems, consult the corresponding appendix to consider all of the stated "requirements" that the element must address.

SUMMARY

This chapter introduced the top-level structure of the RTOOSA Requirements Model by identifying the two constituent second-level models: the Essential Requirements Model and the Essential Objects Model. Then, the primary elements of the second-level models were individually defined.

There is little value in having the model elements without guidelines for their development. Unable to specify infallible rules that can cover every conceivable type of system, this chapter describes a set of heuristics that establish a sequence for developing the individual Requirement Model's elements and includes checkpoints at which the consistency and completeness of the model may be verified.

Finally, this chapter introduces three significant system case studies that will be used in the following chapters to illustrate application of the various model elements.

The following chapters introduce the details of each of the individual Requirements Model elements in turn.

Nobody can really guarantee the future. The best we can do is size up the chances, calculate the risks involved, estimate our ability to deal with them, and then make our plans with confidence.

— Henry Ford II

Chapter *11*

The External Interfaces Diagram

There are three elements of the Essential Requirements Model: the *External Interfaces Diagram* (EID), the *External Events/Response List* (EERL), and the *Object Relationship Diagrams* (ORDs). Developing these elements is addressed respectively in this and the next two chapters. Although each element is considered in turn, all three must be developed concurrently. This point cannot be over-emphasized!

Each "system" will have a single EID. Usually a *system* represents a product (software, hardware, or a combination of the two) that is managed as a single entity for configuration management purposes. Several factors drive the selection of such "configuration items." These include traditional tests for coupling and cohesion, modularity based on elements likely to undergo future changes, and deployed system modularity. For a software system developed according to military standards, a

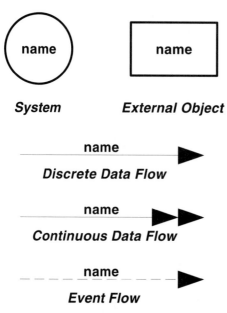

System *External Object*

Discrete Data Flow

Continuous Data Flow

Event Flow

Figure 11.1. External Interfaces Diagram icons.

system equates to a Computer Software Configuration Item (CSCI). Such a CSCI may include all the software running on a single processor, a single program executing on a multiprogrammed processor, tightly coupled software running on multiple processors, or any other combination that minimizes maintenance costs during the product's operational phase. A worthy maintenance goal is to have to change only single configuration items wherever possible, thereby limiting such cost drivers as regression testing. Later in this chapter, we will consider evolving the definition of the *system*.

The purpose of the EID is to bound the *system* by identifying all objects that are explicitly outside the system. Each object outside the system will have only specifically defined interfaces (i.e., the *external interfaces*) to the system. These too are shown on an EID.

An EID is restricted to the five icons illustrated in Figure 11.1. Figure 11.2 shows a sample EID for an extremely simple automobile Cruise Control system, illustrating the use of each of the EID icons. In this model, the driver has a switch or button that turns the unit on and off. By some other mechanism, the driver specifies the speed that the car is to maintain. The *system* must compare the desired speed to the current road speed and command corrections to the throttle control. As an exercise at the end of this chapter, you will be asked to develop an EID for a more complete cruise control system that is more representative of commercial units on the market today.

THE EID ICONS

At the center of an EID is its *system* icon. An EID must have one and only one *system* icon. The name of the *system* (which may actually be considered a subsystem in some other context) must appear on the icon.

The icon's circle outline suggests the boundary of the system the icon represents. Everything that is part of the system falls within the boundaries of the *system* icon. Anything not within the system falls outside the system and therefore must be shown with *external object* icons, with the appropriate data and event flow interfaces to the *system*. Sometimes establishing the system's boundaries is nontrivial. Shortly, we will consider options in specifying system boundaries and suggest some guidelines to aid in making such decisions. At other times it is difficult to specify how external entities should be grouped as objects, as external objects may also be complex entities.

Anything that is necessary to the statement of the system's requirements, but is not included within the boundaries of the system, must be related to an external object. Each external object is represented on the EID by the rectangular *external object* icon.

> **External Object:** any software or hardware system, subsystem, component, device, or shared data element that is not considered part of the subject system, but with which the subject system must interface.

Alternatively, it is acceptable to substitute an icon suggesting a specific external object (e.g., a keyboard and monitor for a "terminal" or a "dish" for an antenna) in lieu of the default rectangle icon. Use of appropriate graphics can greatly enhance recognition of the specific external object.

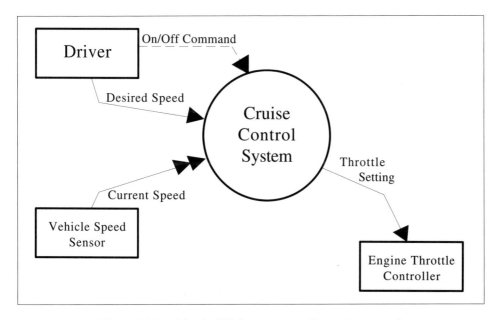

Figure 11.2.   Simple EID for an automotive cruise control.

In some methodologies, the rectangular *external object* icon (i.e., the *terminator* icon of Ward/Mellor RTSA) is restricted to use on the EID equivalent diagram (i.e., Ward/Mellor *Context Schema*, etc.). I believe that this is done to maintain consistency in the flow-down of interfaces from one level diagram to another. Each lower-level diagram uses flow icons unconnected on one end to represent flows whose source/sinks are defined on a higher-level diagram (this concept will be explained more fully in later chapters). However, in an object-oriented analysis, there are system *objects* that fully define the interfaces to a single external object. In such cases, it is helpful to show the icon for the external object on the appropriate lower-level diagrams as well. Therefore, RTOOSA does not restrict use of the *external object* icon to the EID. However, many existing CASE tools implement RTSA conventions that may prevent drawing the rectangular icon on any diagrams but the EID (called by some methodologies the "Context Diagram").

As you will see shortly, properly identifying External Objects involves several decisions about the nature of the real-world entities to which the system interfaces. For example, the Cruise Control system illustrated in Figure 11.2 identifies the Driver as an *External Object*. There are good reasons the driver was chosen as the *External Object*, rather than using the control panel through which the driver enters commands or the electrical interface that makes the control panel signals available to the software. Shortly, we will discuss guidelines to help select the proper *External Object*.

On the EID, every *External Object* icon must be connected by one or more *flow* icons to the *System* icon. Furthermore, all *flow* icons must connect an *External Object* to the *System* icon. Specifically, there must never be *flow* icons directly interconnecting the *External Object* icons. The purpose of the EID is to identify the external interfaces of the subject system. Interconnections among the external objects are irrelevant to this purpose.

There are three types of *flows* to describe the interfaces between the *External Objects* and the *System*: Discrete Data Flows, Continuous Data Flows, and Event Flows. The lines that are used to build the icons for these flow types have traditionally been drawn as curved segments. Because not all CASE tools support the curved flow lines, it is overly restrictive for the notation to be confined to them. Alternatively, a flow icon can be represented using connected straight-line segments, as used throughout this book. Either will be considered acceptable with RTOOSA.

The *Discrete Data Flow* icon represents data that are available at discrete points in time, often tied to an event that notifies the system of the data's presence. For example, a terminal operator presses the return key and a string of characters representing a mode change command becomes available for software processing. This command is not present until the final operator action of pressing the return key and may be replaced by a future message in the input message buffer if it is not processed within time limits specified by its interface protocol. Often the availability of data for processing is announced to the system by an interrupt, which may or may not be directly associated with the data source. Otherwise, the system must poll the input channel for new messages to ensure recognition before future messages can overwrite earlier ones. The *Driver* external object in Figure 11.2 provides the *Cruise Control System* with a *Desired Speed* (i.e., the speed that the *Cruise Control System* should maintain) only from time to time when a new speed is desired. This type of flow is shown as discrete on the EID.

The *Continuous Data Flow* icon represents data that are continuously available for processing. The meaning of "continuous" in this context deserves additional consideration. In the strictest sense, only an analog signal is truly continuous, such as a voltage that represents vehicle speed, where zero volts might correspond to 0 MPH and 10 volts to 100 MPH. When dealing with digital signals, there is no real continuous data flow. When an analog signal is converted to digital, there is a discrete time at which the analog value is sampled (by a circuit called a "sample and hold") and converted to a digital equivalent. Changes to the analog signal are ignored until the previous conversion is complete, when the cycle repeats and the next value is converted. A continuous signal is approximated by frequent sampling that, if the sample interval is short enough, closely tracks the actual continuous value.

In considering our system interfaces, we distinguish continuous from discrete data flows based on the following definitions.

Continuous Data Flow: a data flow, the frequency of whose autonomous update is equal to or greater than the fastest frequency at which the system must process it.

Discrete Data Flow: a data flow at precisely the required processing rate (i.e., each input value must be processed individually).

There is no adverse impact to the system if some (or even many) of the continuous data values are ignored, as long as the system operates at its designed processing frequency.

The *Cruise Control System* illustrated in Figure 11.2 shows the *Current Speed* as a *Continuous Data Flow* into the *System* icon. This suggests that the *Vehicle Speed Sensor* is continually sampling the *Current Speed* and making such data available to the *Cruise Control System*. The system will not be required to capture and process every individual value for *Current Speed*, which may be many times the required processing rate. This flow will be sampled as needed to determine its difference from the *Desired Speed* and the computation of the proper *Throttle Setting* to correct the difference. The *Throttle Setting* must be computed at some regular interval. Hence, its output to the *Engine Throttle Controller* is shown with a *Discrete Data Flow* icon.

The final *flow* type is called an event flow:

Event Flow: a flow that carries no explicit data with it.

Normally, an event flow from an external object corresponds to a system interrupt. The presence of the event whose name adorns the *Event Flow* icon is signaled by the raising of the corresponding interrupt. The event may be used to trigger the input of other data, as our *Cruise Control System* might use the *On/Off Command* event to read the *Desired Speed*. The event itself conveys only knowledge that the *On/Off Command* has been triggered by the *Driver*.

Figure 11.3 shows an EID on which all flows are represented as *Event Flows*. Intuitively, throwing a light switch can be considered a signal of one of two events, corresponding to the direction in which the switch has been thrown. No other data are necessary. The *Light Bulb Controller* system then uses the specific event, coupled with the current state of the system, to determine whether the bulb should be on or off. Finally, a discrete event is signaled to put the bulb into the proper state. This rather trivial example should reinforce your understanding of event flows and how they differ from data flows.

Readers who may be familiar with the Ward/Mellor RTSA may notice that RTOOSA excludes the *data store* icon (to be addressed later) from appearing on the EID. The focus of RTOOSA is on objects (which loosely correspond to data elements in traditional software systems). A "data store" is a representation that will later be used to specify an object's field(s). Because a data store corresponds to an object, it must either be an object within the system's domain or represented as an external object.

Frequently, an external data store actually corresponds to some type of shared or global memory data structure. Using object-oriented principles, we must encapsulate that object to control its access by clients within the system. It therefore becomes an object within the system. But it is an object with an interesting side effect. Although it is encapsulated with regard to the *system*, it is visible to one or more external objects. This requires special attention during analysis to ensure that a proper protocol for access is defined. Fortunately, implementation of the external protocol will be isolated to methods within the single object representing the global data store, and its encapsulation will provide clients with a single, consistent access approach. For these reasons, *Data Store* icons are not considered valid on the EID.

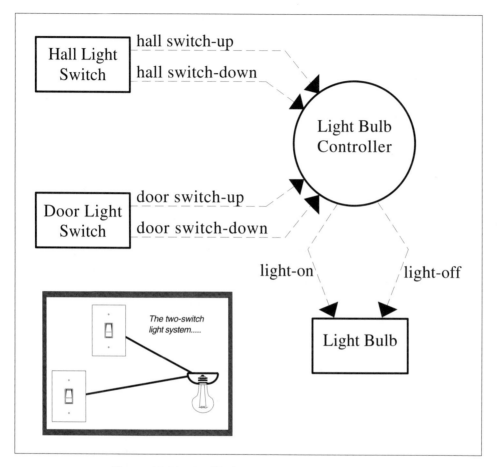

Figure 11.3. An EID for a dual-switch light system.

Frequently, system boundaries for an embedded "software system" will have been determined before the software requirements analyst becomes involved with the project. During the project's earlier phases (i.e., system analysis and/or system design), the system architects often partition the highest-level "system" into its constituent hardware and software elements and identify the essential interfaces among those elements. The job for the software requirements analyst is to validate those interface and allocation decisions and to flesh out the crude interface skeletons with successively greater detail. In the following section I suggest an approach by which such validations may be done.

IDENTIFYING EXTERNAL OBJECTS

It is helpful to consider the universe in which the system exists as the layers of an onion's skin surrounding the *system* at its core, as illustrated in Figure 11.4. Contact with the *system* requires penetration of each layer in turn. The outermost layer represents the abstract space in which the entity exists as a perception or action. The *system* can only be cognizant of the Perception/Action if there exist sensors that detect what is to be perceived and actors to cause the action. The Sensor/Actor layer therefore lies between the Perception/Action layer and the *system*. However, information can only travel between the *system* and its sensors and actors through appropriate interfaces. The Interface layer is therefore the innermost layer surrounding the core *system*.

Table 11.1 gives examples of each of these universe layers for two of our case study systems. The concept of aircraft movement is only perceived by means of an appropriate movement sensor, such as a Doppler Velocity Sensor (based on using a Doppler Radar to measure the Doppler frequency shift in the returned signal resulting from the aircraft's movement relative to the motionless reflecting ground surface), Inertial Measurement Unit (based on using accelerometers to measure accelerations from which the velocities are derived), Air Data Systems (which can determine aircraft movement relative to the air mass in which it flies), and a variety of radio and satellite navigation systems. Each such sensor set provides velocity data in a form unique to the phenomenon that it measures. For example, a Doppler Velocity Sensor may only provide velocity components relative to the aircraft frame of reference (i.e., velocity along the longitudinal axis, relative to the orthogonal axis out the right wing, and orthogonal vertical axis). On the other hand, because inertial navigation systems have their accelerometers mounted on an attitude-stabilized platform, their velocity components are often relative to the local plane of the earth's surface.

The nature of the interface between the sensor and the *system* will normally be unique for each sensor type. Often the *system* must provide additional control commands and read additional data to drive the interface itself. This forces

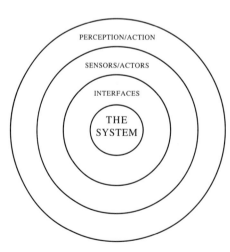

Figure 11.4. The universe as layers of an onion's skin.

Table 11.1.   Examples of the layers of an onion's skin.

Perception/action	Sensor/actor	Interface	System
Aircraft Velocity	Doppler Velocity Sensor	Avionics Data Bus	
	Air Data System	Avionics Data bus	Doppler
Aircraft Heading	Magnetic Compass	Syncro-to-Digital Converter	Navigation System
		Avionics Data Bus	
Point Camera	Camera Assembly/ Pan and Tilt Assembly	Object-Oriented Operating System; Control Bus; Camera I/F Unit; Fiberoptic Xmtr; Camera Assembly	
			AVDS
Camera Position	Camera Assembly/ Pan and Tilt Assembly	Camera Assembly; Fiberoptic Rcvr; Camera I/F Unit; Control Bus; Operating System;	

the analyst to make additional decisions in identifying External Objects and their interfacing flows.

Let's assume that our Doppler navigator uses a Doppler Velocity Sensor (DVS) to measure the aircraft velocity (the perception) in an aircraft referenced coordinate system. The DVS interfaces to the *system* through a MIL-STD-1553B (1 megabit per second) coaxial serial avionics data bus. The *system* must program the MIL-STD-1553B avionics bus controller to make it poll the DVS and then read the bus controller status after each transaction to verify that correct data transfer has occurred. From this slice through our onion skin, what layer(s) should be represented on the EID as an *External Object*?

There is no easy answer. Selecting the Perception/Action entity (in our example, Aircraft Velocity) as the External Object emphasizes the problem domain and tends to decouple the analysis from specific solution decisions. Choosing the Sensor/Actor (the DVS in our example), on the other hand, emphasizes the solution technology. Making the interface (such as our bus controller) the External Object buries the analysis even further into the solution domain. Do not read any negative connotation into any of these options. There are systems where each of these options best applies.

For example, consider an extremely complex avionics system for which your company is developing a Graphics Display Driver (GDD). For your analysis, the GDD is the *system*. The GDD interfaces to much of the rest of the avionics suite through a high-speed avionics bus. During specific mission modes, different external system elements are given control to supply the commands to the GDD to create displays that support specific mission activities. The GDD has no specific knowledge of the mission mode, merely responding to the commands being sent to it by whichever device is currently in control. In this case, the bus controller should be identified as the External Object. To the GDD, the bus controller appears to be the source of its graphics commands, not knowing what person or electronics box on the other end of the bus actually originated the commands. Furthermore, it serves no purpose in analyzing the requirements for the GDD to identify any entity other than the bus controller as the command source.

Table 11.2 provides some guidelines that the analyst might use to choose among Perception/Action entities, Sensor/Actor devices, and Interface devices in selecting the system's *External Objects*. The columns in this table correspond to the potential External Objects (which map to the layers of the onion skin model depicted in Figure 11.4) that could be chosen to appear as the EID *External Object*. The rows specify evaluation criteria relating specific system characteristics to these choices. For each of the table's rows, the analyst must consider the applicability of the corresponding characteristic to each potential External Object. If the analyst agrees that the "yes" response applies, that candidate is given one *vote*.

This evaluation will probably show that the candidate external objects' *votes* will not unanimously fall in any one of the columns. If they should, the choice is obvious. Lacking such a clear choice, the "best selection" can be the candidate with the most *votes*. However, I am not suggesting that democratic rule automatically applies. Deciding on the applicability for many of these evaluation characteristics may be subjective, resulting in a *vote* that is debatable. The most you can sometimes hope for is to use the table to eliminate an option. Thereafter, the choice falls to engineering judgment, guided by the *voting*.

In the Graphics Display Driver (GDD) case previously cited, the interface device (the bus controller) is probably the optimum external object because commands may originate from multiple sources. A human may be involved with originating some (e.g., selecting a display mode), but not all (e.g., software-generated parameter update) commands. So the operator is only ambiguously the Perception/Action entity. Because it is not important for the GDD to recognize the

Table 11.2. Guidelines for selecting External Objects.

Problem characteristics	External Object		
	Perception/ action entities	Sensor/actor devices	Interface devices
Interface directly involves a human	Yes	N/A	N/A
Identity of External Object is critical to problem statement	Yes	Yes	Yes
The External Object Technology is related to the application	N/A	Yes	Yes
The External Object Technology is well-defined	Yes	Yes	Yes
The External Object is active controlled by the system	N/A	Yes	Yes
Data depends on technology choice	N/A	Yes	Yes
	(Problem-space oriented)	(Implementation-space oriented)	

command source or perception, the interface falls out as the optimum external object.

Considering another example, some key elements of a digital map system (as described in Chapter 7) are the elevation and cultural data bases. It is almost impossible to describe such a map system without identifying these data bases. Therefore, these data bases are probably important external objects that belong on a digital map system EID.

Though the *External Object* icon on the EID must represent only a single object, it implicitly includes other layers inward to the *system*. For example, the top of Figure 11.5 shows the Astronaut as the external object for the hypothetical Space Station Audio/Video Distribution System (AVDS), consistent with the

Table 11.2 table criteria. Since the Astronaut is selected as the important external object, that object must encompass everything related to the Astronaut that is external to the *system*. That includes several discrete activities related to the Sensor/Actor Device (keyboard and display) and Interface Device (control bus

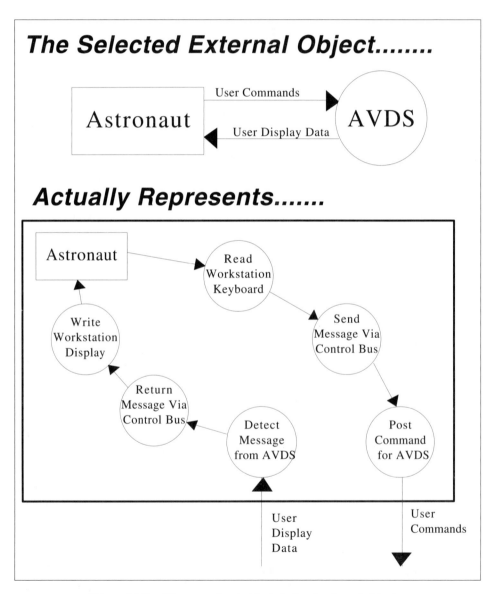

Figure 11.5. The meaning behind abstract external objects.

and the processor's bus controller). The "expansion" of the Astronaut icon at the bottom of Figure 11.5 shows how the icon implies all layers from the Astronaut inward.

In Figure 11.6, the Magnetic Compass (a sensor) has been chosen as the external object to provide the Magnetic Heading (a perception) to the Doppler Navigator. In this case, the compass data must be digitized and transmitted to the Doppler Navigator.

So, although the EID is kept simple by abstracting each external object to a single entity, none of the underlying details is ever lost.

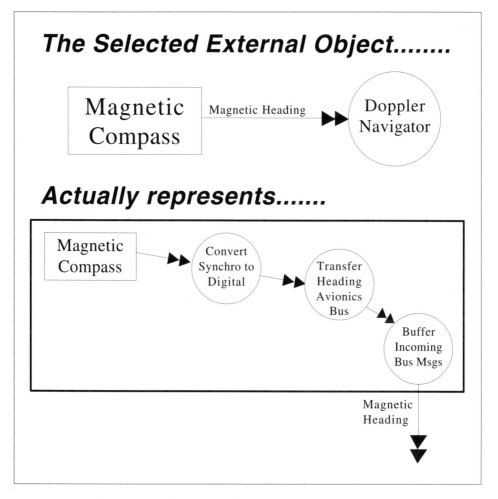

Figure 11.6. Expansion of another abstract external object.

DEALING WITH COMPLEX EXTERNAL OBJECTS

Frequently the problem description, perhaps in an "operations concept" document or a "system specification," will describe a relatively large number of entities that appear to be *external objects*. Closer examination of these objects may show that many may be physically or logically joined in some manner. Now the analyst must decide whether the EID should depict each detailed entity or combinations of entities that represent a more complex object.

On the one extreme, showing every detailed entity may result in a drawing that is very busy and obscures the important characteristics of the system interfaces. At the other extreme, joining unrelated objects in order to reduce EID complexity may obscure essential interfaces in a manner that fails to expose essential system behaviors needed to complete the behavioral analysis.

Consider again the Cruise Control System EID provided in Figure 11.2. That EID showed the *Vehicle Speed Sensor* and the *Engine Throttle Controller* as separate external objects. This partitioning differentiates between a sensor associated with the drive train and an actor associated with the engine. Another approach could be to specify a single external object called the "automobile" with *Current Speed* and *Throttle Setting* as the corresponding data flows. Why did I introduce Figure 11.2 with the two external objects? And would there ever be a case when a single *automobile* external object would be more appropriate?

As I have stated before, the products of RTOOSA are elements of an abstract model. The purpose of any abstract model is to provide important characteristics while hiding unimportant information. So, the fundamental question the analyst must answer is: "Which approach best describes the essential characteristics of the system?" The EID (and the other RTOOSA products) must communicate to the model's users. The analyst must always choose the representation that best conveys the important characteristics of the system.

In the Cruise Control System example, all interfaces, other than those to the driver, are with elements of the automobile. No purpose is served by depicting the obvious. Rather, a better representation shows to which elements of the automobile the *system* must interface. On the other hand, a system that interfaces with various objects, one of which is the automobile, might depict the *automobile* as an external object.

EXPANDING AND CONTRACTING THE SYSTEM CONTEXT

It is sometimes easier to find the proper *External Objects* for a system through an iterative refinement of the EID itself. First create an initial candidate EID by reading the project's system specification, operations concept document, and/or statement of work. Evaluation of the initial candidate objects and their interactions, coupled with application of the guidelines previously discussed in Table 11.2, leads to successive iterations of the EID. The EID should be baselined when an EID is achieved that correlates with the information of the External Events/Response List (EERL) and Object Relationship Diagrams (ORDs) being developed concurrently (as described in Chapter 10).

Let's consider a *Flight Control System* for a new-generation attack helicopter. On first reading of the system specification, we establish an initial EID as shown in Figure 11.7. Our helicopter requires fuel to feed its engines, which drive the rotor blades that create lift. That lift acts on the air mass to cause the aircraft to fly. The movement through the air mass provides a reference from which speed may be determined. The *Pilot* provides command information to the system.

You need not consider such a first effort for long before realizing that it is much too general. For one thing, the aircraft's engine is seldom considered part of a *Flight Control System* and should be moved outside of the *system*, as shown in Figure 11.8. The engine, and its coupling through the transmission to the rotor,

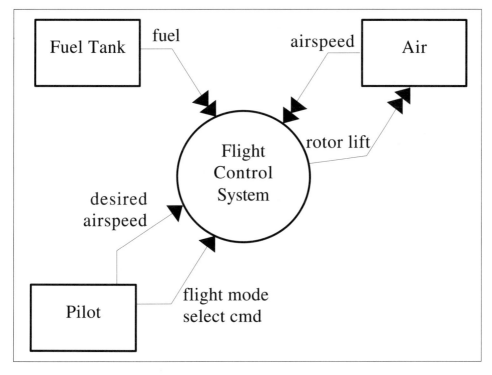

Figure 11.7. First cut at an EID for a Flight Control System.

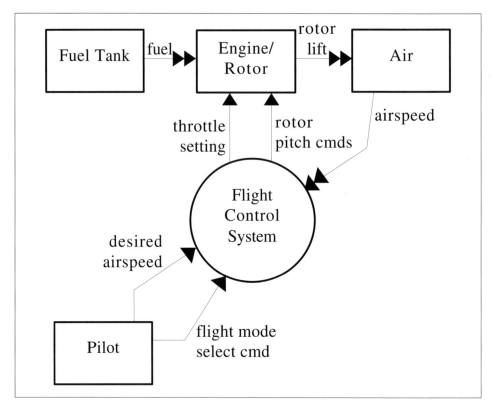

Figure 11.8. First refinement of the EID.

provides the lift identified in the first effort. Fuel flows directly from the tank to the *Engine/Rotor* object. Our *Flight Control System* must provide throttle setting and rotor pitch commands to the *Engine/Rotor* object. Although this EID is a significant improvement over the first effort, it contains several technical problems. For example, the only interfaces permitted on an EID are those between the *External Object* icons and the *system*. So the *Continuous Data Flow* icons from the *Fuel Tank* to the *Engine/Rotor* and between the *Engine/Rotor* and the *Air* should be removed. This leaves the *Fuel Tank* with no identified interfaces. It should therefore also be removed from the EID.

The next iteration, shown in Figure 11.9, incorporates these corrections. Also, the *Air* object (a "perception") is relatively unimportant when compared to the *Air Data System* (a "sensor") needed to measure and provide the craft's Airspeed. Table 11.2 suggests that the *Air Data System* is a better *External Object* than the *Air*. Meanwhile, the interfaces to the engine and main rotor's actuators (the

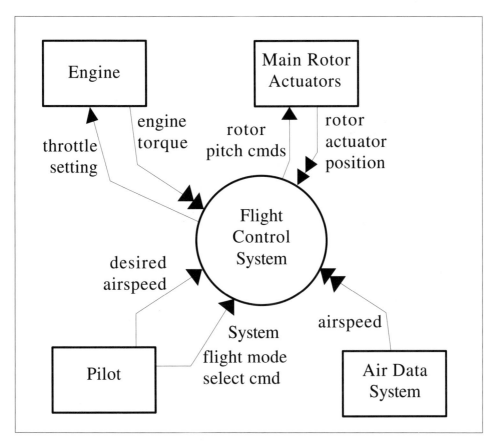

Figure 11.9. Additional refinements remove technical faults.

mechanical devices that control the pitch of the rotor blades and therefore the amount of lift induced) are distinct from one another. Because the purpose of the EID is to identify all of the interfaces to the *system*, we provide an icon for both the *Engine* and the *Main Rotor Actuators*.

The EID now appears to be converging on its final form. However, further analysis shows that the helicopter also must control its yaw axis by controlling the *Tail Rotor's Actuators* (counteracts the torque action of the main rotor rotation that attempts to spin the aircraft around the axis of the main rotor shaft). Furthermore, controlling the aircraft's attitude requires very accurate measures of the current *pitch*, *roll*, and *yaw* attitudes, as commonly provided by gyroscopes. By filling in the EID with these additional requirements in the same iterative manner as demonstrated in Figures 11.7 through 11.9, a baseline EID (see Figure 11.10) can be established.

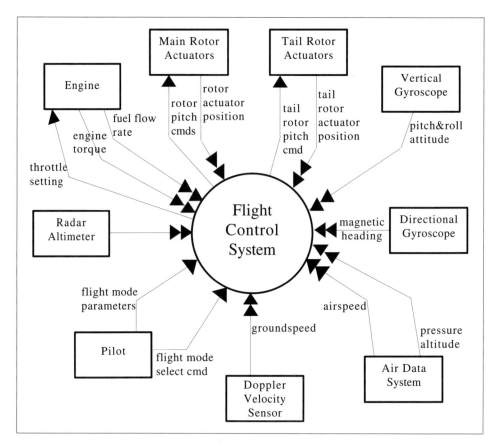

Figure 11.10.   Finally, an initial baseline EID.

SPLITTING EIDS

When all of the interfaces are finally identified for a specific system, the EID can become very busy. This in itself can be a warning that the system being defined (i.e., the configuration item) will be very complex. Often, it is wise to heed this as a warning and partition such a system into major subsystems (each perhaps to be managed as a separate configuration item). When this is done, you can imagine a *system* icon for each of the major subsystems, as is suggested by Figure 11.11. However, by definition, the EID may have only one *system* icon. So each *system* icon establishes a new EID, with the other subsystem(s) represented as new *External Objects*. Figure 11.12 shows the resulting *Automated Flight Control Subsystem* EID, on which the removed functions of the *Navigation Subsystem* are

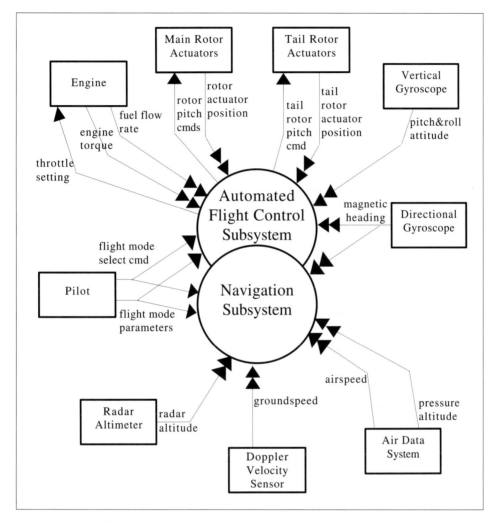

Figure 11.11. Partitioning the system into subsystems.

represented by a new *External Object* icon. Likewise, Figure 11.13 shows the *Navigation Subsystem* EID, on which the *Automated Flight Control Subsystem* is represented by an *External Object* icon.

You could split the system to minimize the interfaces between the resulting subsystems (remembering the desirability of highly cohesive and loosely coupled elements). In the *Flight Control System* example, the *Navigation Subsystem* computes the current deviations from the desired flight path and heading for use by

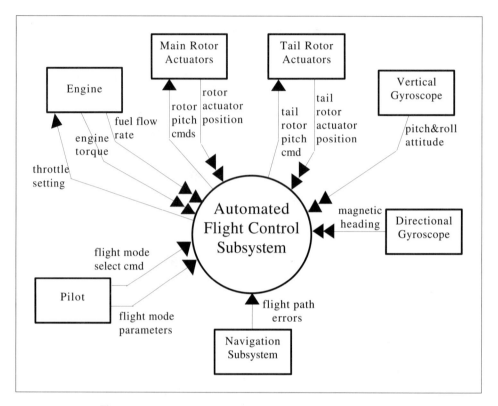

Figure 11.12. The partitioned Flight Control Subsystem.

the *Automated Flight Control Subsystem* in computing the rotor actuator commands needed to return to that desired flight path. Failure to simplify such inter-subsystem interfaces can cause the subsystems to be too tightly coupled for effective maintenance once the system is deployed. Such partitioning, by nature of its minimized interfaces, becomes the basis for assignment of processes to multiple processors when it becomes necessary.

In reality, many of the steps suggested by the sequence of figures in this chapter may be done in the analyst's mind, resulting in fewer iterative steps. However, facts driving the definition of the EID are not restricted to consideration of the EID alone. Realistically, work on the External Events/Response List and Object Relationship Diagrams will initiate changes to the EID while developing the initial Essential Requirements Model. Later, when working on the Essential Objects Model, even more iterations to the EID may be identified.

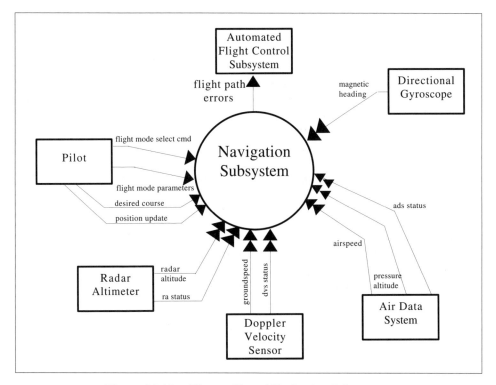

Figure 11.13. The partitioned Navigation Subsystem.

SUMMARY

This chapter introduces the External Interfaces Diagram (EID) as the first critical element of the Requirements Model. The EID establishes the boundaries of the *system* and graphically documents the interfaces with all pertinent *External Objects*. Each of the icons used on the EID was individually considered.

Because the exact system boundaries and the characterization of external objects is not always obvious, guidelines were presented to assist the software analyst. Where the *External Object* icon represents an abstract entity, such as the Perception or Action entity, then examples illustrated how the icon actually is made to represent several layers of relationship between the *system* and the *External Object* named on the icon.

Finally, the manner of iterative refinement of an evolving EID was presented through an extended example.

Practice

1. Starting with the EID given in Figure 11.2, add your personal experiences with commercial automobile cruise control systems to develop an EID for the embedded software of a system that more accurately reflects the type of commercial product you might buy. Remember such safety features as disengaging when the brake is pressed or when the engine speed exceeds a preset threshold (as when driving on ice or when the clutch is disengaged with a manual transmission and increasing throttle cannot make the needed speed correction).

2. Using the requirements list generated in Exercises 1 and 2 of Chapter 9, develop a corresponding EID for the Radar Acquisition and Tracking System (RATS).

3. Based on your personal experience with Automatic Teller Machines (ATMs), develop an EID for the embedded software of such an ATM system. Consider all of the available user options and the interfaces required to support them. Use the requirements list generated in Exercise 3 of Chapter 9.

4. Review the requirements list for the commercial product selected for Exercise 5 of Chapter 9. For that system, develop an EID for its embedded software system. Try to consider all the essential features of the product and what is required to support each.

5. Develop an EID for the Low Cost Doppler Navigation System (LoCoDoNS) described in Appendix C.

A group can spark an idea, but only an individual can have one. As former President Griswold of Yale has so aptly asked: "Could Hamlet have been written by a committee? Or the Mona Lisa painted by a club?"

— W. John Upjohn

Chapter **12**

The External Events/Response List

One flaw I find with most current object-oriented analysis methodologies is their total preoccupation with identifying objects to the exclusion of formally recognizing functional requirements. This produces several significant problems in managing the software development process:

1. Customers are predominantly concerned with *what* their new system must do. Statements of work and high-level system specifications invariably specify required functions and performance. Mapping allocated requirements only to objects and their assigned behaviors makes it difficult for the customer to verify that all requirements will be addressed during the new system's development.

2. Most formal requirements documents, including all current Government Standards' Software Requirements Specifications (SRSs), are

structured to identify requirements allocated to specific *capabilities* (another way of saying "functions"). Traditional methodologies that decompose functions map easily to the capability-based sections of the requirements documents. For example, each Ward/Mellor *transformation schema* identifies a system capability. Because object-oriented decomposition is orthogonal to functional decomposition, objects tend not to map easily to capabilities. This makes "standard" requirements specification documents difficult to prepare.

3. Formal Qualification Testing (FQT), or equivalent formal testing of the final product to validate satisfaction of specified requirements, naturally traces to functionality and performance. Most such formal testing is done as *black box* (also called "data driven") testing. With this type of testing, the product is fed data via its external interfaces and the results are observed at the external interfaces. The internal structure of the product is normally of no specific concern. Requirements stated in terms of objects and their behaviors become difficult to validate. Formal testing of a system's objects will probably not convince the customer that a functioning system is being delivered.

A software development methodology must include a means of formally stating functional and performance requirements, if for no other reason than to capture and communicate required functionality and performance back to the customer to confirm a common understanding of system requirements. For RTOOSA, this mechanism is the *External Events/Response List* (EERL).

As will become clear through references to the EERL in future chapters, the EERL is a cornerstone for RTOOSA. The EERL drives the behavioral definitions of objects during development of the Object Flow Diagrams (OFDs). In the same vein, it provides the criteria by which the baseline OFDs are measured for completeness and accuracy. Elements of the EERL become the basis by which the incremental *builds* are scheduled through coding and testing. Finally, the EERL provides a natural foundation from which to derive the plans and procedures for formal testing.

A complete, accurate EERL is perhaps the single most important product of the RTOOSA Requirements Model. Therefore, this chapter is, in some respects, the most important of this book!

EXTERNAL EVENTS AND EMBEDDED REAL-TIME SYSTEMS

All processing in embedded real-time systems is in direct or indirect response to events initiated outside the system. Relative to the *system*, these events occurring in the environment are considered *External Events*. If we include system start-up and time-based events (e.g., expiration of a periodic clock or delay timer, regardless of their implementations) as initiated in the environment, then all processing of embedded real-time systems is in response to *External Events*. This is the premise upon which I use the EERL as the basis of model verification.

First, let's formalize the concept of the *External Event*.

> **External Event:** a "happening" that occurs outside the system at a definable instant in time and to which the system must respond. System start-up and time-based events are considered External Events for requirements analysis purposes, regardless of their specific implementations.

The system may perceive an External Event in one of three ways: as either directly perceived, indirectly perceived, or temporally perceived.

> **Directly Perceived Event:** an event that is immediately known to the system without the system having to perform any processing to distinguish it from other possible events.

An EID event flow usually is the source of a directly perceived event. It is also possible to identify EID data flows that represent directly perceived events. Furthermore, by convention, system start-up is normally considered a directly perceived event, regardless of its hardware or software mechanism.

> **Indirectly Perceived Event:** an event that requires the system to analyze externally provided data to differentiate specific events or to determine the specific instant at which the event occurs.

Some EID discrete data flows and many continuous data flows are the source of indirectly perceived events. EID discrete data flows are usually composite data elements (i.e., elements that are defined as a composite of other data elements). For example, an EID will often show a "user commands" discrete data flow between an external object representing the system operator and the *system*. However, the arrival of each distinct command is normally a separate External Event. Because the *system* must interpret each incoming message to determine which command the specific instance of the data flow contains, the event associated with each such command is indirectly perceived. When a continuous data flow is being monitored, it is not uncommon to specify requirements based on specific thresholds. For example, the battery monitor for a notebook computer may need to sample the voltage level periodically and raise an alarm when the voltage drops below a predetermined level. The voltage dropping below the threshold is considered an indirectly perceived event.

> **Temporally Perceived Event:** an event that depends on the passing of a period of time. Periodic processing is considered to be initiated by a temporally perceived event, as is processing that is initiated after a finite time delay.

The most common type of temporal events are driven by a system clock, often at a regular interval. For example, a real-time display with moving objects is typically refreshed at a steady 30 times per second to provide the illusion of smooth continuous motion. Irregular display refresh can cause an annoying jitter in the image, while refreshing at too slow a rate can cause an object to move in small jumps rather than smoothly.

Distinguishing among the three types of events can sometimes be confusing. Consider a few additional examples to try to clear up the confusion.

Assume a software system receives messages from a data bus. The arrival of each new message is announced by an interrupt from the bus controller to the processor. Then "arrival of a new message" becomes a directly perceived event. When the interrupt service routine associated with the bus-message interrupt executes, no processing is required for the system to know that a new message has arrived. However, if the system operator's commands are embedded in those bus messages, then the arrival of any specific message (e.g., "list document command received") would be an indirectly perceived event because the contents of the message must be examined to determine which precise event has occurred.

The distinction between directly and indirectly perceived events becomes important later when identifying essential objects and their behaviors. Indirect event perception requires processing of an associated object (e.g., interpretation of received messages in the bus-message example). This necessary object behavior, and the associated ability to activate other processing, must be allocated when defining the essential objects.

As with any other element of analysis, identification of pertinent External Events is very important. The criteria for a "good" External Event are derived from the definition provided above. Table 12.1 offers some examples, both good and bad, of External Events.

It is sometimes difficult to identify the perception of an External Event without considering the context of the system. Consider Event 3 in Table 12.1. The table identifies this as a directly perceived event because it assumes an interface such as a control panel button that is tied to a system interrupt. If, on the other

Table 12.1. Examples of External Events.

No.	Candidate External Event	Good/Bad
1.	The user decides to enter a new command.	Bad. The system doesn't have to respond. Unless it is telepathic, it can't even know that this event has happened.
2.	The system finishes validating the user's identity.	Bad. This event doesn't occur outside the system.
3.	The user selects "Display Airspeed."	Good. (Direct Perception)
4.	The engine temperature goes above the safe operating threshold.	Good. (Indirect Perception)
5.	Target has been "lock" for two seconds.	Good. (Temporal Perception)
6.	Directional Gyro fails.	Depends. This is a good event if the system is required to respond to the failure, bad if it is extraneous information to which there is no required response.

hand, "Display Airspeed" is one of several available messages from a remote interface unit, then its arrival is an indirectly perceived event because processing is necessary to distinguish it from other possible messages.

Temporal events might otherwise be considered directly perceived (e.g., an interrupt service routine linked to a clock-driven interrupt) or indirectly perceived (e.g., a task that is scheduled every n^{th} occurrence of a clock-driven interrupt). It is more important to establish the time-based requirement, creating a reminder to provide an associated timing mechanism object during later stages of analysis.

Event 6 of Table 12.1 illustrates the importance of selecting only relevant events. If there is no requirement to provide a response, then the event is not significant and should not be included in the events list.

If the EERL is to be used as a comprehensive summary of the system's functional requirements, the external events should be precise. This means that, for most systems, there will be a fairly large proportion of indirectly perceived events. For example, the "arrival of a new message" event is only important when the system must implement the communications protocol and respond to messages independent of their information content. It is usually more important to consider each message (or message type) as a distinct event and specify the corresponding responses.

The primary importance for correctly identifying External Events is to map each such event to the response required by the system. Figure 12.1 illustrates the EID for a simple heating/air conditioning thermostat and suggests a corresponding

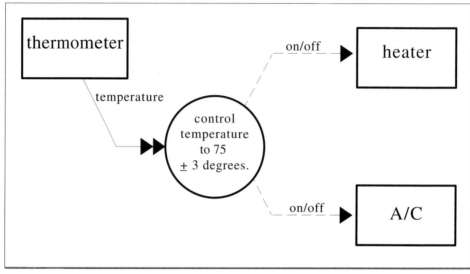

Figure 12.1.   A simple list of events and their responses.

No.	Event	Response	Perc.
1.	Temperature drops below 72 degrees	Turn heater on	Indirect
2.	Temperature enters range 72–78 degrees	Turn heater and A/C off	Indirect
3.	Temperature rises above 78 degrees	Turn A/C on	Indirect

list of External Events and their required responses. Notice that because all events are based on analysis of the continuous data flow input *temperature*, recognition of each event is indirectly perceived.

Figure 12.1 also illustrates the interdependence between the EID and its corresponding EERL. When working on the EERL, it is not unusual to have to modify the EID. Consistency between the EERL and the corresponding EID will be addressed in greater detail later in this chapter.

Once the External Events have been identified, the analyst must provide the functional and performance requirements associated with each event.

CAPTURING THE REQUIRED RESPONSES TO EXTERNAL EVENTS

An External Event is only significant because the *system* must respond to it. It follows there must be an identifiable response associated with each listed event. Conversely, any event to which a specific response cannot be assigned is not significant and should not be included in the EERL.

In all but the most trivial examples, the response to an External Event is seldom a single action. More commonly, External Events require a series of activities to take place. The easiest way to represent such a sequence of actions is to specify them in a numbered list.

Event responses can sometimes become lengthy. This is not necessarily bad. However, the function of the response specification is not to describe the *design* of an implementing program.

The analyst might be tempted to define a sequence of processing states and then map each state to an event/response pair. This is improper for state changes that cannot be attributed to External Events.

For example, most embedded real-time systems require a series of activities at system start-up. The code for this software is usually stored in a "bootstrap PROM" (Programmable Read Only Memory) and is treated as an independent configuration item (i.e., a separate *system*). Typically, the processing required by this system might include the sequence: (1) perform a start-up Built-In-Test (BIT) to confirm minimal system operations; (2) initialize network interfaces; (3) download the operational program; (4) set default operating modes and control parameters; (5) generate a default display; (6) initiate background BIT; and (7) pass control to the operational program.

I knew an analyst who had to define such a start-up processing system. He first listed each step as a separate "response." Then he worked backward to find a suitable event. The External Event assigned to the first response was (correctly) "system power applied." However, for the "initialize network interfaces" response, he created an event called "start-up BIT completed." However, completion of start-up BIT is not initiated outside the system and therefore cannot be an External Event. This response is merely the second step in sequence responding to the "system power applied" event.

Completing the network interface initialization may or may not involve an External Event, depending on the specific network protocol. If, as is often the case, network initialization requires only setting some control registers to default values with no network interaction, then the completion of network initialization may not be used as an External Event. On the other hand, if the specific network initialization protocol requires sending an *"I_am_here"* message onto the network and waiting for an acknowledging message, then the arrival of the acknowledgment is an External Event that may be considered to conclude network initialization. Such an event may be used as the second "external event," to which "Initiate operational program download" is the required response.

Loading the operational program undoubtedly requires interaction with an External Object, perhaps over the network or from a mass storage unit (disk drive, etc.). Typically, the operational program arrives in blocks that are checked for

Table 12.2. Bootstrap start-up system events and responses.

No.	Event	Response
1.	System power applied.	1. Perform start-up BIT. 2. Initialize network interfaces.
2.	Network initialization ACK message received.	1. Initiate operational program download.
3.	Operational program download complete.	1. Set default operating modes and control parameters. 2. Generate control display. 3. Initialize background BIT. 4. Pass control to operational program.

errors and may even be explicitly moved from a buffer area to the program store area. The software loading the program must be able to identify the last such block (e.g., based on a block counter or an end-of-file marker). Therefore, "Operational program download complete" is usually an indirectly perceived external event that may be used to trigger a series of steps in response, including "Set default operating modes and control parameters," and so forth.

Table 12.2 suggests a possible list of events and responses for the bootstrap start-up system. This list cannot be blindly applied to all systems of this type because every system will implement its interfaces a little differently. Events that may be external in one system will often be internal in others. Consider carefully the validity of each candidate External Event. This is usually easier if the analyst begins with the potential events and considers how the system must respond, not by attempting to work from candidate responses back to events.

Specification of responses may be complicated further by other factors (such as a system state or operating mode) that may make required actions conditional. Consider a flight control program, for example. Assume such a system recognizes the External Event "altitude update message arrival." Such a system probably has, among others, an operating mode called *Altitude Hold*. The system's required response to the arrival of an updated altitude value will depend on whether or not the *Altitude Hold* mode is engaged. Table 12.3 suggests how the operating mode might be integrated into the response. Here, the mode independent steps are listed, followed by a conditional step: "Command aerosurfaces to correct for differences between new altitude and reference altitude" that is applied only "If Altitude Hold mode is engaged."

This approach works well when much (or most) of the response is independent of the conditional statement and only a small amount depends on the condi-

Table 12.3. Conditional expression in the response.

No.	Event	Response
1.	Altitude Update message arrival.	1. Display new altitude value for crew use. 2. Compute and display new rate of altitude change (Rate of Climb). 3. If Altitude Hold mode is engaged. a. Command aerosurfaces to correct for differences between new altitude and reference altutude.

tion. However, frequently most of the response for a specific event is highly dependent on the single condition. In such cases, it is convenient to create two events that are each qualified by the mutually exclusive states. Table 12.4 suggests how this approach might be applied to the flight controller. In this presentation, the "Altitude Update message arrival" with the Altitude Hold mode engaged is treated as a distinct event from the arrival of the same message with the mode not engaged. Required processing that is independent of the Altitude Hold mode must be listed in the response to both events. This explains why you might not want to use this approach if there is considerable common processing and only a few unique requirements are associated with the mode.

Three underlying goals are associated with specification of event responses:

1. The response field should present processing requirements in an easily understood manner. Specific rules of presentation should be of less concern than the clarity of the information being presented.

Table 12.4. Qualifying the event to simplify responses.

No.	Event	Response
1.	Altitude Update message arrival and Altitude Hold mode not engaged.	1. Display new altitude value for crew use. 2. Compute and display new rate of altitude change (Rate of Climb).
2.	Altitude Update message arrival and Altitude Hold mode engaged.	1. Display new altitude value for crew use. 2. Compute and display new rate of altitude change (Rate of Climb). 3. Command aerosurfaces to correct for differences between new altitude and reference altitude.

2. The response list should include all required responses. This list will be used to check other elements of the Requirements Model for completeness. If elements of the response are missing, then the associated requirements may not be tracked properly and may be implemented improperly or not at all.

3. Required responses should be presented in a sufficiently general manner. The details of the required processing are better provided in other sections of the system's requirements specification document. Keep the response field brief and to the point.

Although the events and their corresponding responses are the primary elements of the EERL, there are others that we will now consider.

CONTENTS OF AN EXTERNAL EVENTS/RESPONSE LIST

The External Events/Response List is a structured presentation of functional (and optionally performance) requirements for a real-time system. Figure 12.2 suggests a form for specification of an EERL. Each element from this format has significance to the overall Requirements Model.

The first column provides a sequential number to identify each External Event and its required Response (i.e., an "event/response pair"), listed respectively in the next two columns. The contents of the Event and Response columns have been discussed in the preceding paragraphs.

The fourth column shown in Figure 12.2 is optionally included to list any performance requirements associated with the event and its response. In some systems, there are specifications for the maximum time permitted between an event

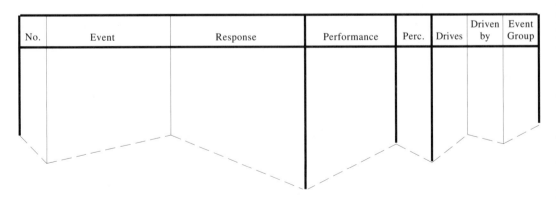

No.	Event	Response	Performance	Perc.	Drives	Driven by	Event Group

Figure 12.2.   Format for an External Events/Responses List.

and completion of its designated response processing. For example, the system may be required to acknowledge a user command within 50 milliseconds. For systems with this type of response timing requirement, the performance column neatly associates the performance requirement with the appropriate event/response pair. This aids in validation test planning.

The next EERL column specifies the event perception: direct, indirect, or temporal.

The sixth and seventh columns address sequencing dependencies that frequently occur among events in systems. For example, the first event for most systems (generally numbered "1" in the "No." column of the EERL) might be named "power applied to module" or "system turned on." For most systems, no other listed events have meaning until this event occurs. In this respect, the start-up event *drives* all of the other events in the system. Conversely, when considering those other system events, we can say that they are *driven by* the start-up event. Likewise, the start-up event is seldom *driven by* any other event because it depends on no other listed event to be valid.

The terms *drives* and *driven by* have meaning only relative to the "current" event, the event being defined by the current row. Formally, these terms are defined as follows:

Drives Event: when the "current" event drives another event, that event will not be recognized unless the "current" event has first occurred.

Driven By Event: when the "current" event is driven by another event, that event must already have occurred before the "current" event can be recognized. The absence of a prior occurrence of the "driven by" event inhibits the response to the "current" event.

The column labeled "Drives" lists all the events (by their assigned numbers) that depend on occurrence of the specified event. The "Driven by" column lists all the events that are prerequisites for the specified event. It may be inconvenient to actually list all events for either category. For example, the start-up event might list "all" in its "Drives" column rather than listing each event individually. It may also be necessary to specify the prerequisite events in the "Driven by" column as a Boolean expression. For example, event number 12 may require the occurrence of events 1, 3, and then either 5 or 9. This should be represented in event 12's "Driven by" column as "1,3,(5 or 9)".

The final column is labeled "Event Group," which we define as follows:

Event Group: identifies events bound by arbitrary analyst-selected criteria.

This binding could include interdependent "drives" and "driven by" relationships, similarity of requirements, assignment to development teams, assignment to integration "builds," mapping to requirement specification paragraph numbers, mapping to formal test cases, and so forth. Event groups are typically named by alphabetic characters, but alternate naming conventions are acceptable. If useful, more than one "Event Group" column could be provided to support several of the suggested uses for this field. Events (e.g., the start-up event) may belong to more than one group.

EXAMPLE OF AN **EERL** IN ACTION

Exercise 5 in Chapter 11 asked the reader to develop an EID for the Low Cost Doppler Navigation System (LoCoDoNS). Based on the information provided in Appendix E, with no further criteria for analysis yet, the resulting EID should resemble the one in Figure 12.3. Table 12.5 suggests a companion EERL for the LoCoDoNS EID.

Notice first that this EERL includes no explicit "start-up" event. One might argue that there must be a *derived* requirement to initialize some processing parameters to default values. In this case, such a requirement would better be called *self-imposed* than *derived*. Based on the problem statement in Appendix C, there is no clear need for parameter initialization. One might also expect the crew to enter an initial aircraft position before attempting updates. But the computed aircraft position could be maintained in a nonvolatile memory (e.g., battery powered). Because Appendix C does not explicitly specify a power-up position requirement, it would be presumptuous to carry it as a requirement at this point. This does not preclude adding such a requirement as the result of additional analysis or during later customer requirements negotiations.

The description of LoCoDoNS processing requirements in Appendix C clearly presents an iterative solution. Every so often, the software must use the current velocity to estimate how far the aircraft has gone since the last update. The distance-traveled estimate must be added to the last computed position to achieve a new estimate of the aircraft position. An engineer knowledgeable in navigation systems recognizes that such systems are typically implemented using a constant interval between these update computations. This establishes the basis for a *derived requirement* to provide periodic update computations. After consultation with the project's hardware engineer, an interrupt is assigned to control the periodic navigation processing. Hence, events 1 through 3 and 7 are based on the expiration of the periodic navigation timer (a temporal event).

The Appendix C processing descriptions for the navigation function identify three distinct modes: (1) when the Doppler Velocity Sensor (DVS) is functioning;

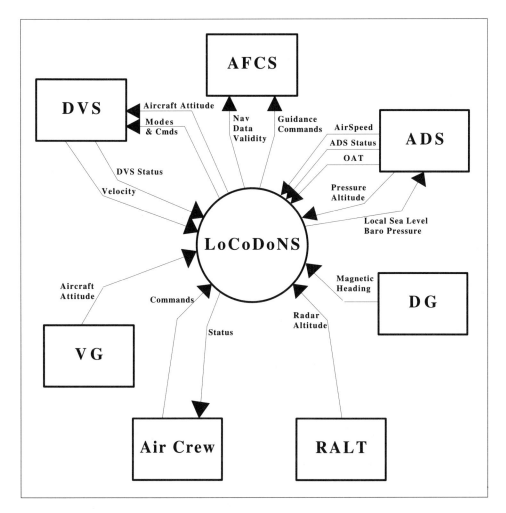

Figure 12.3.   Preliminary LoCoDoNS EID.

(2) when the DVS is not providing valid data but the Air Data System (ADS) is; and (3) when neither the DVS nor the ADS is providing good data. Because the processing requirements are different for each of these *modes*, each has been used to qualify the *Periodic Nav timer lapse* event to create EERL events numbered 1, 2, and 3, respectively. Notice how the mutually exclusive processing requirements of these *modes* map well to the unique descriptions in the "response" column. When later developing formal test plans, each of these events will naturally drive a different set of test cases.

Table 12.5. Candidate LoCoDoNS EERL.

No.	Event	Response	Perc.	Drives	Driven by	Event Group
1.	Periodic Nav timer lapse (DVS providing good data).	**1.** Use groundspeed data from DVS to update computed current aircraft position. **2.** If ADS providing good data, use difference of ground-speed from DVS and airspeed from ADS to estimate current windspeed vector. **3.** Set Nav Data Validity = "Normal."	temprl	6	18, 19, 21, 22	A
2.	Periodic Nav timer lapse (DVS not providing good data, but ADS is).	**1.** Use airspeed data from ADS with the current wind-speed vector estimate to estimate groundspeed. **2.** Use the estimated ground-speed to update the computed current aircraft position. **3.** Set Nav Data Validity = "Backup."	temprl	6	17, 21, 22	A
3.	Periodic Nav timer lapse (neither DVS nor ADS providing good data).	**1.** Inhibit flight plan following. **2.** Set Nav Data Validity = "Invalid."	temprl		17, 20	A
4.	Crew commands pinpoint update.	**1.** Change the computed current position to the position provided by the crew.	indir			A
5.	Crew selects a flight plan to follow.	**1.** Load selected flight plan from the data base as the active flight plan. **2.** Select first waypoint in the active flight plan as current target waypoint.	indir	6		B
6.	Crew selects guidance function. (flight plan following).	If a flight plan has been selected AND Nav Data Validity not "Invalid," then **1.** Enable periodic computa-tion of Guidance Commands and output to automated flight controls. **2.** Activate guidance mode indicator.	dir	7	(1 or 2) & 5	B

No.	Event	Response	Perc.	Drives	Driven by	Event Group
7.	Periodic Nav timer lapse (estimated position update complete and guidance command computation enabled).	1. Compare the current estimated aircraft position to the ideal course to the current target waypoint to compute cross-track error. 2. Compare the current aircraft heading to the ideal course bearing to the current target waypoint to compute track-angle error. 3. Send cross-track error, track-angle error, and Nav Data Validity to automated flight controls.	temprl	8, 9	6	B
8.	Aircraft approaches current target waypoint, which is not the last waypoint in the active flight plan.	1. Signal crew that waypoint is reached. 2. Select next waypoint in the active flight plan as the new current target waypoint.	indir		7	B
9.	Aircraft approaches last waypoint in the active flight plan.	1. Signal crew that final waypoint has been reached and flight plan following mode has been disengaged. 2. Continue along same bearing followed along last leg into the final waypoint.	indir		7	B
10.	Crew deselects guidance function (flight plan following).	1. Disable periodic computation of Guidance Commands and output to automated flight controls. 2. Deactivate guidance mode indicator.	dir			B
11.	Crew enters command to add/delete/edit a waypoint in the Waypoint data base.	If the waypoint is not part of the active flight plan. 1. Make commanded change to the designated waypoint. 2. Update the Waypoint data base.	indir			C

(continued)

Table 12.5 (continued)

No.	Event	Response	Perc.	Drives	Driven by	Event Group
12.	Crew enters command to add/delete/edit a Flight Plan in Flight Plan data base.	If the Flight Plan is not part of the active flight plan. **1.** Make commanded change to the designated Flight Plan. **2.** Update the Flight Plan data base.	indir			C
13.	Crew commands location fix.	**1.** Create a new waypoint with current aircraft position. **2.** Set waypoint label to "FIX" and sequential identifier. **3.** Set Symbol code for default "FIX." **4.** Store new waypoint in Waypoint data base.	dir			C
14.	Crew enters command to set modes and parameters of DVS.	**1.** Send command to DVS.	indir			D
15.	Crew enters command to set modes and parameters of ADS.	**1.** Send command to ADS.	indir			D
16.	Crew enters local sea level barometric altitude.	**1.** Send value to ADS.	indir			D
17.	DVS fails or stops providing good data.	**1.** Stop using DVS velocities for aircraft position update computations.	indir	2, 3		E
18.	DVS resumes providing good data.	**1.** Resume using DVS velocities for aircraft position update computations.	indir	1		E
19.	ADS fails or stops providing good data (DVS providing good data).	**1.** Stop using ADS velocities to update estimated wind vector.	indir	1		E
20.	ADS fails or stops providing good data (DVS not providing good data).	**1.** Stop using ADS velocities for aircraft position update computations.	indir	3		E

No.	Event	Response	Perc.	Drives	Driven by	Event Group
21.	ADS resumes providing good data.	**1.** Resume using ADS velocities for updates to estimated wind vector for for updates to estimated aircraft position.	indir	1, 2		E
22.	DG fails.	**1.** Inhibit navigation and guidance functions.	indir	1, 2		E

In Table 12.5, the response to event number 1 contains a conditional qualifier as well. When the DVS is used to compute the updated aircraft position, the ADS velocities are used to estimate the current wind direction and velocity (if the ADS is also operational). It would be acceptable to divide event number 1 into two events: one for the case when both the DVS and ADS are providing valid data and a separate event for when the DVS is providing valid data but the ADS is not. However, the approach illustrated was chosen because the primary function (updating the aircraft position based on DVS velocities) applies whether the ADS is operational or not. The secondary processing of the ADS data is meant to be subservient and is therefore presented as such.

Evaluating such situations is very subjective and reflects the analyst's personal engineering judgment. Either approach is technically valid. It becomes a matter of emphasis. Remember that not all requirements are created equal. It may be useful to relegate some requirements to a subservient presentation to provide a desired emphasis on others. This in no way relieves the developer from implementing such secondary requirements.

Events 1 through 4 are the only ones directly associated with the *navigation function* (i.e., determining the aircraft position). These four events have been designated as a separate event group (called "A") based on this functional commonality. This grouping could be used for such purposes as identifying a section of the requirements document, assigning team responsibility for implementation, identifying qualification test cases, and others. Groups such as these can be helpful management aids.

Similarly, the Group B events in Table 12.5 describe the requirements for the LoCoDoNS *guidance function* (i.e., determining the aircraft's deviation from a desired course). Definition of the event/response pairs in this group requires somewhat more engineering judgment than was needed for those of Group A. The guiding requirements' source document seldom is structured to provide easy identification of the desired event/response pairs. Although many requirements are directly identifiable, you often must "read between the lines" for the *derived requirements*. However, as previously suggested, be careful not to read too much into the requirements!

For example, the Event 5 responses fall into this category. Appendix C provides an explicit requirement that the crew be able to select the desired flight plan from the Flight Plan data base. The Appendix does not specify the actions to be taken when the crew exercises this option. It is perfectly reasonable to assume this action should cause the specified flight plan to be "loaded" (whatever that may mean in the context of this system) from the data base. It might not be as obvious that this action should also provide certain initialization processing associated with selecting a new flight plan, such as identifying the first waypoint in the new flight plan as the initial target for guidance processing. Appendix C defines a flight plan as "an ordered sequence of [waypoints]." A reasonable engineer would assume that an ordered list would require that the aircraft fly to the waypoints in the indicated order, beginning with the first. Engineering judgment only associates this *derived* requirement with the response to Event 5.

Similarly, Appendix C explicitly identifies the requirement that the crew be able to select and deselect the guidance function. Engineering judgment places restrictions on the system permitting this to happen. The response to Event 6 provides a conditional clause that enables the guidance function only if a flight plan has been selected and the navigation function is providing valid aircraft position updates. Although Appendix C has not placed such restrictions, it is reasonable to prevent the crew from attempting to follow a flight plan if none has been selected. Perhaps a little more subtle is an implicit requirement not to allow the software to fly the aircraft if the navigation function doesn't know where the aircraft is. In such a case, it may take an engineer knowledgeable in navigation systems (or a pilot) to recognize the potential for serious danger and establish such a *derived* requirement! This dependency is reflected by the event numbers in the *Driven by* column.

Once the guidance function has been selected, as the result of responding to Event 6, the periodic nav timer drives the guidance function to compute the deviations from the desired course (Event 7).

As described above, the derivation of the EERL is more than merely restating requirements provided by the source requirements document. For example, Appendix C describes the guidance function as following a flight plan. Consequently, the aircraft must sequence from one leg to the next as each waypoint is reached. So there is an implied event that the aircraft, following each leg of the flight plan, will reach its immediate target. In Table 12.5, this event is shown as Event 8. But what must the system do at that point? It would be a logical conclusion that the system sequence to the next waypoint as the new target and proceed to the next leg. For one navigation system on which I worked, the customer did not want the software automatically to make such decisions. That system had to notify the crew that the waypoint was reached and wait for the crew to authorize proceeding to the next leg. Our LoCoDoNS specification does not state any such requirement. However, it might be reasonable to notify the crew. Would this requirement be *derived* or *self-imposed*? Because an expert suggests that this would be a typical system reaction due to reasonable and safe operational considerations, it should remain and be considered a *derived* requirement. The criteria for such determination should be the reason a statement is considered a requirement.

Event 8 addresses reaching the target waypoint for most situations. However, at the end of the final leg, there is no *next* waypoint. Therefore, reaching the final waypoint is a unique event that requires a different response than reaching the waypoint for any of the preceding legs. Again, the source specification (Appendix C) offers no hint how this event should be handled. Probably the worst thing to do would be merely to turn off the guidance function without any crew notification. If the crew did not expect such a change, then, quite literally, nobody would be flying the plane. It is reasonable to assume a *derived* requirement to notify the crew, as listed as the first step in the response to Event 9. But what else should the system do?

When there is no formal guidance regarding specific situations, the analyst has several options, such as:

1. Take the source specification literally and specify nothing.

2. Acknowledge the need for an as yet unspecified requirement by listing "tbd" (to be determined). This acts as a flag for where specific information will be substituted when it becomes available.

3. Provide a *derived* requirement when sufficient expertise is available to make a reasonable assessment of what is required, based on general practice, published standards, or previous experience.

4. Attempt to resolve the missing requirements interactively with the customer as they are encountered.

These options may all apply to a single project in differing situations. Likewise, one or two may be best suited to specific supplier/customer relationships. Clearly, all requirements must ultimately be approved by the customer. The choice of an interim solution for missing requirements must be based on expediency to minimize the overall development cost. If your development organization includes a domain expert, then the third option often becomes the easiest to manage. The underlying problem with going to the customer directly is that the *customer* often has a disparate organization and it may take considerable time to get to the right individual to make a specific decision. Such communications channels are often not planned and are relatively inefficient.

The response to Event 9 in Table 12.5 takes a conservative position. Rather than shutting the guidance function off without the crew being involved, the aircraft will be commanded to continue along its last computed bearing until the crew commands deselection of the guidance function (Event 10).

Events 11 and 12 illustrate how several similar events with similar responses might be combined in a single EERL event. For Event 11, for example, the commands to add, delete, or edit (change) a waypoint in the Waypoint Data Base are all considered the same event. For presenting summary requirements in the EERL, this seems adequate. The *derived* conditional test in the response, again provided by the domain expert as a safety concern, prevents any changes to waypoints that are part of the active flight plan. The primary concern when combining events in such cases is to ensure that no required action is missed.

The Group D event/response pairs are again derived requirements associated with the control of the specified navigation equipment. In cases such as these, often no explicit requirement is provided directing control of the external equipment. However, the analyst should realize that the availability of useful data from such equipment requires that the equipment be placed in the appropriate operating modes and perhaps provided with specific control parameters.

The Group E event/response pairs are associated with fault detection for the associated equipment. The requirement for the loss of certain equipment's data is well described in the specification of Appendix C. For example, the loss of valid data from the DVS dictates use of the ADS data as a backup. The specification describes the nature of the DVS as temporarily losing its radar return signal during certain aircraft maneuvers. This suggests a requirement that the system be able to detect when good data from the DVS return. Hence, we not only have Event 17 upon the loss of good data, but also have Event 18 detecting the return of good data. Again, a knowledgeable navigation engineer recognizes the loss of accuracy during the absence of the DVS data and the need to return to the "normal" mode as quickly as possible.

Event 22 is an example of the subtle requirements that an analyst without specific domain experience might miss. The general requirements for dead-reckoning navigation relate to knowing the direction and velocity of travel. Appendix C spends considerable attention in addressing the source of the velocity data: how the ADS data must be used to estimate the prevailing winds and then used with the most recent wind computations to estimate groundspeed in the absence of DVS data. Nothing is ever specified regarding the heading data. Without the direction of travel, it is equally impossible to compute the updated aircraft position. The analyst must identify all such requirements and specify their interdependencies with other requirements.

The EERL of Table 12.5 is still relatively short. It satisfies the need to capture the general requirements of the system. As should be obvious, it does not attempt to identify the detailed requirements associated with either the events or their corresponding responses. EERLs may be considerably longer than this example. Do not attempt to place artificial limits on the size of the EERL. Let it be as long or short as the requirements of the specific system dictate.

CONSISTENCY BETWEEN THE EID AND EERL

The External Interfaces Diagram and External Events/Response List have a common theme. Each is concerned with the relationship between the *system* and its environment. As you might expect, each of these will address external interface issues from a different perspective. There must be consistency between these two Essential Requirements Model products.

In general, consistency between the EID and EERL dictates that each interface on the EID be questioned as to whether or not it carries (directly or indirectly) an external event. Conversely, each external event (other than system start-up and maybe clock- or timer-related events) must be traceable to an interface on the EID. After all, if an event is *external*, there must be an interface shown on the EID that specifies the source of the event and its actual interface to the system.

The following checklist should be used to verify EID/EERL consistency. If the answer to any of the questions is no, a correction is required:

1. Can every *event flow* on the EID be tracked to a directly perceived event in the EERL?

2. Are all "complex" *discrete data flows* (which can be decomposed to several alternatives, each requiring a specific response) tracked to a specific indirectly perceived event for each alternative value in the EERL?

3. Can all other *discrete data flows* on the EID be tracked to either an event or a process associated with a "response" in the EERL?

4. Are all EID *continuous data flows* for which there are specified threshold values tracked to one or more indirectly perceived events in the EERL?

5. Can all other EID *continuous data flows* be tracked to a process associated with a "response" in the EERL?

6. Can every event (except possibly some temporal events) in the EERL be traced to an interface between an *External Object* and the *system* in the EID?

7. Do all "external data" needed by all "responses" in the EERL appear as part or all of a data flow on the EID?

8. Are all necessary start-up and/or shut-down conditions covered?

Special attention needs to be paid to EID data flows for possible associated events. If a discrete data flow can be decomposed to a number of alternatives, such as an EID flow called "command messages" that consists of a *turn_on_command* or a *turn_off_command* or a *set_speed_command* or a *resume_speed_command*, then the arrival of each of the alternative message types initiates processing specific to that message and therefore should be regarded as a separate External Event.

As demonstrated by the heating/air-conditioning thermostat example introduced in Figure 12.1, there may also be multiple events associated with specific thresholds applied to continuous data flows.

REQUIREMENTS TRACEABILITY MATRIX

To ensure a complete requirements model, it is important that all functional requirements be associated with one or more event/response pairs. Whenever doing an audit, such as checking to verify that all source document requirements are addressed by event/response pairs, it is a good practice to document the findings. A tool that works well in doing this is a matrix that maps system requirements to EERL event/response pairs.

Table 12.6 suggests how such a matrix might appear for some of the requirements of the LoCoDoNS case study. Along the top of this matrix are column headings that identify, by number, each event/response pair (refer to Table 12.5 for the LoCoDoNS EERL with corresponding event/response pair identification). Down the left column of the matrix are the functional requirements, in this case extracted from the text of Appendix C. Along each row, "X" is used to indicate where that requirement is addressed in full, or in part, by the event/response pair of the corresponding column(s).

USE OF THE EERL IN FORMAL REQUIREMENTS DOCUMENTS

In the opening paragraphs of this chapter, I identified a need to capture a system's functional and, when applicable, performance requirements. For many customers, such as the various U.S. Government agencies (DOD, NASA, FAA, etc.), this is

Table 12.6. LoCoDoNS functional requirements versus EERL cross-reference matrix.

	1	2	3	4	5	6	7	8	9	10	11	12	13	14	15	16	17	18	19	20	21	22
...employs dead reckoning nav with position updating by flyover.	X	X	X	X																		
...use velocity data from DVS or ADS and heading data from DG.	X	X																				
...maintain a data base to fly pre-determined flight plans and drive pilot's instruments and displays.				X							X	X										
...use flyover pin-pointing to per-form position up-dating.			X																			
...support location fixing by flyover.													X									
...signal from crew cause capture of aircraft position & assign to crew pro-vided label.													X									
...determine rela-tive error from a predetermined flight plan.				X	X																	
...provide AFCS with cross track error and track angle error.					X	X																
...primary velocity measurements provided by DVS system.	X												X			X	X					

more than merely a need, it is a project management requirement. Usually the presentation format for these requirements is strictly controlled. The system's software requirements document is usually called the Software Requirements Specification (SRS). Because most SRS formats (both Government and commercial) resemble that used by the Department of Defense (DOD), I will suggest how the EERL can be used to structure the requirements presentation for a DOD-type SRS.

The DOD currently requires software development according to a standard called DOD-STD-2167A, *Defense System Software Development*. This standard identifies a series of documents that are required for the development to be compliant. A Data Item Description (DID) defines the exact format and content for each of these documents. The DID governing the 2167A SRS is called DI-MCCR-80025A. That is the format I refer to below. An outline of a DI-MCCR-80025A compliant SRS is included in Appendix D.

The SRS DID divides the document into four major sections. The first is a document and system introduction. It identifies the name and configuration identification number of the software configuration item to which the SRS applies, how that software fits into its overall operating environment, and other overview descriptions. The contents of Section 1 are considered informational only and cannot be used to specify system requirements.

The second SRS section contains a list of other documents related to the contents of the specification. At a minimum, this section must identify the source documents from which the SRS requirements are allocated and derived.

Section 3 is the requirements section and Section 4 contains the software quality requirements. There is a final section in which the developer lists acronyms and abbreviations used in the document and other notes that may be useful to the SRS user.

SRS Section 3 is where you should put the EID and EERL for the system. The DID requires that the external interfaces be explicitly identified in Paragraph 3.1 and suggests that a diagram be provided. The EID is such an interface diagram. The DID also specifies that each external interface be given a name and a Project Unique Identifier (PUI, an alphanumeric code that uniquely identifies each element of the system). Because the EID only names the data and control flows that make up the interfaces and not the interfaces themselves, the analyst will need to add a name and PUI to each interface. Most CASE tools support ad hoc comments on their flow diagrams, so adding interface names should not present any particular problem.

The remainder of the SRS Section 3 is designated for the presentation of the system's required *capabilities* and their associated requirements. The EERL can be used to map into the system's capabilities. A separate subparagraph of Paragraph 3.2 (numbered 3.2.1, 3.2.2, 3.2.3, etc.) must be provided for each capability. Each capability should relate directly to one or more of the event/response pairs from the EERL. Using the LoCoDoNS as an example, the primary capabilities might be identified as: (1) the navigation capability, (2) the guidance capability, (3) the data base management capability, (4) the navigation equipment control capability, and (5) the equipment status monitoring capability. Not coincidentally, these capabilities happen to map directly to the event groups shown in the last column of the EERL. You may not always choose to use the EERL event groups as the major capabilities, but they certainly can be used as a point of departure.

SUMMARY

This chapter introduces the External Events/Response List (EERL) as possibly the most important product of the analysis process. Attempts to use a poor EERL can cause a considerable number of problems and possibly project failure. The EERL captures and structures the functional and performance requirements for the system under development. The importance of capturing functional requirements, even with an object-oriented development paradigm, was highlighted.

Considerable effort was spent identifying the contents of a proper EERL. Using the hypothetical Doppler navigation system described in Appendix C as an example, the process of extracting the system functional requirements was pursued. The subtle derivation of several of the requirements used in this example EERL was considered and offered as the type of process that the analyst must use.

The need to ensure consistency between the External Interface Diagram (EID) and the EERL was emphasized. This included a set of guidelines that may be used to evaluate the consistency between a system's EID and its companion EERL.

Use of a matrix to cross-reference source document requirements to the individual event/response pairs was suggested as a means of ensuring that the EERL is complete.

Finally, the incorporation of functional requirements, as guided by the contents of an EERL, into a Department of Defense Software Requirements Specification (SRS) was presented. Because many Government and commercial organizations use the DOD-type SRS as a model, the products of the analysis effort should easily map directly into the required presentation format.

PRACTICE

1. Beginning with the EID you developed for the automobile cruise control system as Exercise 1 in Chapter 11, provide an accompanying EERL. Ensure consistency between the EID and EERL. Modify the EID if necessary.

2. Work from the EID you generated for the Radar Acquisition and Target System (RATS) in Exercise 2 in Chapter 11 to create an EERL. Ensure consistency between the EID and EERL.

3. Beginning with the Automatic Teller Machine (ATM) EID you developed for Exercise 3 in Chapter 11, provide an accompanying EERL. Ensure consistency between the EID and EERL.

4. Using the EID you developed for the commercial product in Exercise 4 in Chapter 11, provide an accompanying EERL. Ensure consistency between the EID and EERL.

5. In parallel, develop a consistent EID and EERL for the Space Station Audio/Video Control System described in Appendix B.

Chapter *13*

Object Relationship Diagrams

The third and final product of the Essential Requirements Model is the *Object Relationship Diagram* (ORD). Each system's Essential Requirements Model will include one or more ORDs to define the system's essential objects and their relationships. If I haven't stressed its importance strongly enough to this point, let me emphasize again that proper analysis requires that all three elements of the Essential Requirements Model (the EID, EERL, and ORDs) be developed concurrently. Further, a balanced baseline Essential Requirements Model is a prerequisite for progressing to the Essential Objects Model.

The ORD serves two important functions.

1. The ORDs highlight interdependencies among *objects* in the problem space. They capture static snapshots of the system and its environment in terms of its essential objects. The ORDs do not differentiate between objects inside and outside the *system*. In some cases, ORDs can better describe the essence of the system than the other model products that exclude elements external to the system. Many times these diagrams will show closed-loop relationships that illustrate subtle system behaviors or spot potential disasters from open loops.

2. The objects identified in the ORDs (both internal and external) become candidates for object modeling in the Object Flow Diagrams. The defined relationships among the ORD objects suggest behaviors that drive the definitions of the object fields and methods.

Data modeling concepts are not particularly new, dating back at least to work done by Peter Chen [e.g., Chen, 1976] in the mid-1970s and later refined by Matt Flavin [Flavin, 1981] and others. Paul Ward and Stephen Mellor [Ward/Mellor, 1985] suggest using Chen-type diagrams to help define the events list in the absence of a well-defined EID (which they call the *Context Schema*) in their Real-Time Structured Analysis methodology. Variations of Chen's Entity Relationship Diagrams (ERDs) are supported by numerous CASE tools on the market today.

I attach special importance to developing ORDs because they represent the first formal recognition of objects in the Essential Requirements Model. The ORD information complements, and therefore must be consistent with, the data of the EID and EERL. Because these three elements are developed concurrently, information discovered during creation of the ORDs may drive changes to the EID and EERL. This is part of the incremental, iterative nature of object-oriented software development. For example, identifying the objects for an ORD may help isolate an abstract external object for the EID. Likewise, objects are likely to be suggested by the narratives in the EERL event responses (and vice versa).

In the remainder of this chapter, I address the syntax and semantics of the ORDs.

LOOKING AT OBJECT RELATIONSHIP DIAGRAMS

Object Relationship Diagrams are constructed from three basic icons, illustrated in Figure 13.1. Figure 13.2 illustrates application of these icons to represent a relationship between two objects.

The rectangular icon represents an *object* of significance in the problem space. These *objects* encompass the common qualities of a group of real-world entities in the same sense as a *class* in the object-oriented programming paradigm. These *objects* also may have differences that are of no consequence in the problem domain. For example, the *caller* identified in Figure 13.2 might be male or female, young or old, tall or short. Should one or more of these characteristics make a difference in dialing the telephone, such as affecting the specification of the key size, then the *object* should be decomposed into lower-level objects that share common significant characteristics. In this example, there may be a *class* that represents those very young or very old callers that require oversized keys.

The objects of significance may either be part of the *system* or may be identifiable as part of the system's external environment. External objects are of interest because, as I will explain in Chapter 15, external objects almost always have internal counterparts that embody the system's knowledge of the external objects. Each object icon must include a unique name.

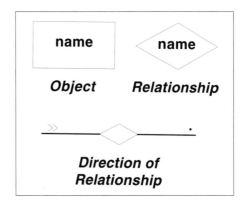

Figure 13.1. Object Relationship Diagram icons.

The *relationship* between two objects is represented by the diamond-shaped icon in Figure 13.2. The *relationship* must be a single, unique relationship described by the required relationship name shown on the icon. The relationship name should be a verb (or verb followed by a preposition) that, when read between the names of the two objects, describes the objects and their relationship.

The named *relationship* may include multiple specific associations that apply commonly to the corresponding objects. In the Figure 13.2 example, the *dial* relationship may include rotary-dial, touch-tone, or electronic autodialer if it is unimportant in the problem specification to differentiate among these.

The interconnecting lines that bind the relationship icon to the two object icons are adorned with symbology that indicate the direction in which the relationship is to be read. Usually the direction to read the relationship is apparent. For example, even without the additional symbology, Figure 13.2 is obviously read "*a caller dials a telephone.*" I doubt anybody would mistakenly read this relationship as "*a telephone dials a caller.*"

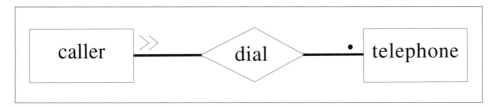

Figure 13.2. A simple Object Relationship Diagram.

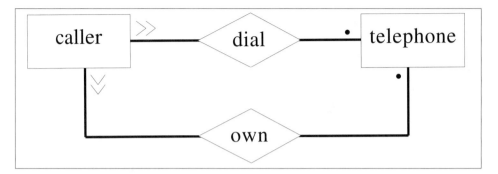

Figure 13.3. An ORD with multiple relationships between two objects.

When the problem statement identifies multiple relationships between two objects, then each of the relationships requires a separate icon. Do not attempt to force the definition of an unnatural relationship that could be conveyed clearly by two relationships. Figure 13.3 shows how there may be other relationships between callers and telephones, such as callers owning their telephones.

Figure 13.4 illustrates how multiple similar objects may be bound by a single relationship icon. In this case, both the *hall switch* and the *door switch* are equally bound to the *light bulb*. Presumably, for the specific problem being modeled, there is some significant difference between the two switches that necessitates them being depicted as separate objects. Otherwise, it might be better to represent both with a single object icon, representing multiple instances of the same *class*.

In Figure 13.5, the *pilot* is associated with multiple objects. On the one hand, the *pilot reads* the aircraft *altitude*, probably from some type of altimeter. In response to the indicated reading, the *pilot adjusts* the aircraft *pitch attitude*. Although these relationships are true, there is a cause-and-effect relationship that is not apparent. When the *pilot* changes the *pitch attitude*, it should cause a change in the aircraft's *altitude*. Further, the *pilot* cannot directly *read* the *altitude*. An instrument that displays the aircraft's altitude is a necessary intermediary. Figure 13.6 better ties together all the critical elements. When multiple relationships form a closed-loop association, then the ORD should clearly show a continuous closed set of relationships. The *pilot* in this example changes the *altitude* based on the current reading. You could take this example a step further and provide the *pilot* with the source of the desired altitude. If the pilot is changing the *altitude*, then there must be a target altitude that he is trying to achieve or an "error" value that needs to be removed. Figure 13.7 is a more complete ORD.

In this more advanced sample ORD, one or more *mission planners* create the *flight plan* that the aircraft is to follow. I identify the presence of a *navigator* who

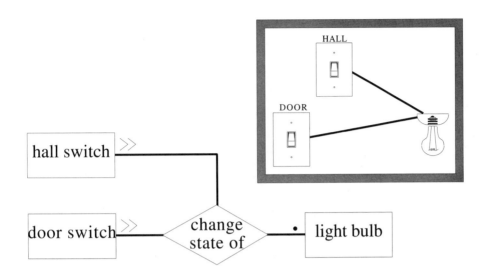

Figure 13.4. An ORD with a common relationship among multiple objects.

references the *flight plan* to determine the proper aircraft altitude at any point in time. The *navigator* determines the *altitude errors* by comparing the ideal altitude to the aircraft's current altitude, read from an *altimeter*. Using these *altitude errors*, probably given in feet above or below the ideal altitude, the *pilot* commands the actuator that sets the position of the control surfaces. These changes cause the aircraft to change altitude and the whole process begins again.

This example contains six objects (i.e., *pilot, altitude errors, navigator, altimeter, altitude,* and *aerosurface actuator*) in the closed loop. The system reaction

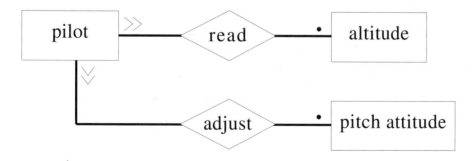

Figure 13.5. An ORD with a common object sharing multiple relationships with two other objects.

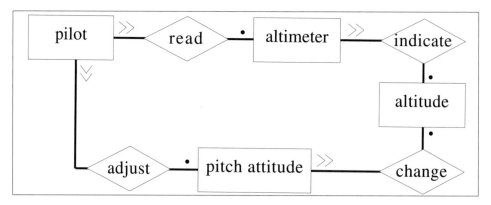

Figure 13.6. The pilot control ORD showing a closed-loop control relationship.

depends on each of those objects. Were the altimeter to contain a noisy output (the way an automobile speedometer needle bounces when the cable gets old and dry) or be biased (be different from the real value, as most automotive speedometers tend to read low), then the *navigator* will have to compensate for these error sources when computing the *altitude errors*. Timing also drives the behavior of closed-loop relationships. If it takes the *navigator* two minutes to determine the *altitude errors*, then this system will probably never be able to maintain the desired altitude. By the time the *pilot* corrects for the computed *altitude errors*, enough time will have passed that those values would bear no relationship to the actual errors at the time the correction was applied. Such a loop would be unstable.

Because this ORD contains *all* objects of significance to the problem, not only those that are in the system, the analyst can recognize the presence of this closed-loop relationship and address all the associated requirements in the analysis. Of all RTOOSA models, this is the only one that clearly identifies such relationships. Many other methodologies would fail to identify such a relationship altogether.

Notice that the ORD is a requirements analysis tool. It does not specify, or even suggest, an implementation for its objects. The *pilot* object, for example, could be human, an older-style analog autopilot, a digital computer executing an autopilot algorithm, or a neural network. In fact, at one extreme, this ORD could represent a system with no computers (or software). At the other extreme, this system could be for a remotely piloted vehicle and have no humans in its implementation. At this stage of requirements analysis, the primary objective is to define the essential relationships among objects. Later an implementation technology can be chosen to satisfy the essential requirements.

At the beginning of this chapter, I restricted ORD objects to those of significance in the problem space. The analyst must be careful not to be too hasty in dismissing objects whose significance may be less than obvious. My discussion of Figure 13.7 has concentrated on the closed-loop relationship that includes most of the objects shown in the ORD. One might conclude that the *mission planner* object is not significant and should be removed from the diagram. This would be a mistake. The computations of the altitude-hold system require the flight plan to include altitude data. This requirement drives the *mission planner* to provide such data in the flight plan. Not all *mission planners* support three-dimensional navigation. The presence of the *mission planner* recognizes an important indirect interface in the problem space that might otherwise be overlooked. Do not be too quick to disregard objects in the problem domain.

In Figure 13.7, we also see for the first time that an object (the *mission planner*) has a relationship with itself. Such relationships are permissible. In this case, *mission planners* might consult with one another in developing a *flight plan*.

This example illustrates the broad spectrum of objects that are possible. An object may be an abstraction, such as *altitude*, or exist only as information or data,

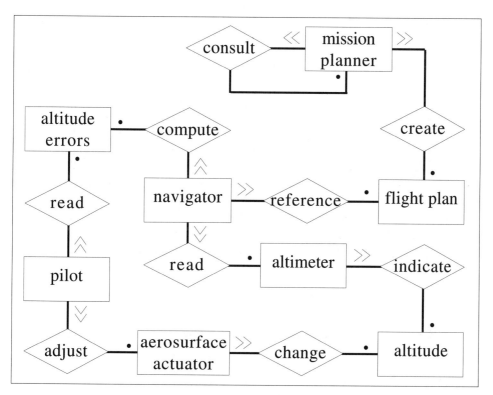

Figure 13.7. An ORD depicting the altitude channel of a simple autopilot.

such as the *flight plan* and *altitude errors*. The object may be a physical entity with undetermined form, such as the *pilot, navigator,* and *mission planner*. Or it may have very specific form dictated by the problem space, such as the *aerosurface actuator* and the *altimeter*. The analyst must be able to identify problem space objects in their many forms.

Remember that the ORD is not an active model. It illustrates the associations among the categories of objects within the problem space. The next two chapters will introduce Object Flow Diagrams (OFDs) as the mechanism that represents the dynamic interactions among objects.

Although it may be intuitively obvious that there will be many commonalities between the objects identified on ORDs and those to appear in the OFDs (and later implemented in actual code), it may be surprising to discover that the *relationship* icons also can spawn objects. This can happen when the relationship suggests a state or value that cannot properly be attributed to either object in the association. This is the basis for defining an *associative object*.

THE ASSOCIATIVE OBJECT

When considering a relationship between two objects, there may occasionally be the need to store data about the relationship that cannot be attributed specifically to either of the objects.

Consider a reconnaissance aircraft equipped with a set of cameras to photograph potential targets. On first reading, the analyst might generate a relationship between the camera and its targets as illustrated in Figure 13.8. However, the *camera* will take several photographs of various potential *targets*, so it is important to be able to relate specific exposures to each target. One way to do this is to remember, for each camera, which exposure (by number) was made of each target.

Assuming each camera carries a single roll of film, there needs to be some tie between the exposure and the camera. However, the camera will take many exposures of several targets on that same roll of film. On the other hand, if we tie the exposure to the target, it will be inadequate because several cameras may have

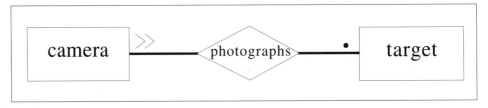

Figure 13.8.   An ORD that illustrates the need for an associative object.

photographed that target. If the exposure number cannot be maintained with either object, where does it belong?

In this example, the exposure number belongs to the association of a specific camera (and its roll of film) to a specific target. That is, it belongs to the *relationship* and not to either of the objects. To handle this type of situation, we define a special type of object called an *associative object*. An associative object "objectifies" the relationship by pulling its name from the relationship icon, changing its verb form to a noun, and inserting it into an object icon with the proper keys to the associated objects. Figure 13.9 illustrates that the *photographs* (verb form) relationship is moved to the *photo* (noun form) object. Also shown on the *photo* object icon are the three key data elements of this associative object. First is the exposure number. This is only of significance relative to the camera (and its roll of film) that took the specific photo, so a reference (pointer or index) to the specific camera is included. Finally, a reference to the specific target is also provided. This associative object now fully expresses the relationship between the camera and its targets.

One fundamental requirement of associative objects is that they specify the references to the objects that they bind. In this example, a photo is defined in terms of the camera that took the picture (*@camera_number*) and the target at which it was aimed (*@target_number*), as well as the exposure number and perhaps other pertinent information (e.g., aircraft position and altitude when the photograph was taken, lens zoom setting, etc.).

Figure 13.10 suggests another first-look analysis, this time of a missile launch

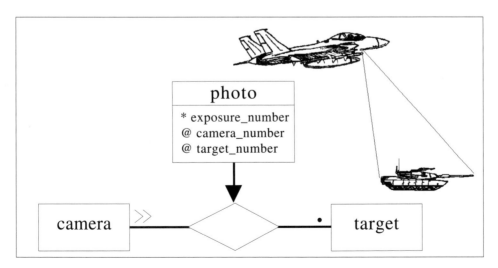

Figure 13.9. An associative object captures the values or states associated with the relationship but not tied to either object.

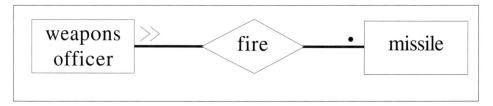

Figure 13.10.   Another ORD in need of an associative object.

system. A *weapons officer fires a missile*. However, further consideration of the relationship suggests there is another object that needs to be represented: the *target*. Presumably the *weapons officer* would not *fire* the *missile* without a *target*. One advantage of an associative object is that it can reference more than two objects, as shown in Figure 13.11. The associative firing object (noun form of *fire*) includes references to the weapons officer (@*weapons_officer_name*), missile (@*missile_type*), and target (@*target_ID*), as well as other pertinent information

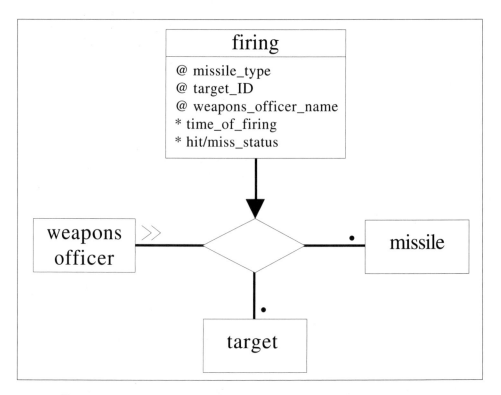

Figure 13.11.   Using an associative object to reference multiple objects.

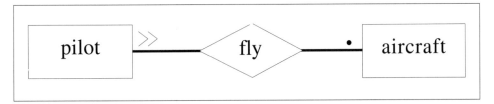

Figure 13.12. Another ORD lacking a unique relationship.

about the firing. This could include, as illustrated, the time of the firing and an indication of the success of the missile finding its target.

Associative objects serve another important function. The relationship between two objects must be unique. Consider the *pilot flies an aircraft* relationship shown in Figure 13.12. Because a pilot may have many flights in a given aircraft, the pilot-to-aircraft relationship is not unique. To satisfy the uniqueness criteria, additional information must be associated with the *flying* relationship. One way to do this is to create an associative object (Figure 13.13) for this relationship, call it *flight*, and provide the references and the additional data needed to make the relationship unique. For this example, identifying the date and time of the take-off would be sufficient.

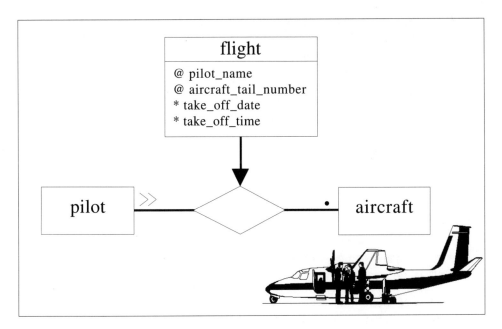

Figure 13.13. Using an associative object to make the relationship unique.

Associative objects, which essentially embody the relationship between other objects, suggest additional objects that require consideration during implementation. The analyst must take the time to recognize when relationships warrant the generation of an associative object.

ORD GUIDELINES

For an ORD to be considered internally consistent and correct, the following rules must be obeyed:

1. Each *object* in the ORD must have a unique name.

2. Each *relationship* between two *objects* must be unique relative only to those *objects*. A similar relationship may exist between other *objects* in the ORD. Where several relationships exist between the same *objects*, unambiguous names are required.

3. Each instance of each *object* must be uniquely identifiable. When necessary, provide a data element or *associative object* that creates uniquely identifiable *objects*.

4. Remove all *relationships* that do not or cannot exist in the problem domain. For example, in Figure 13.7, there can be no *relationship* between the *mission planner* and *altitude errors*.

5. After careful consideration, remove all *relationships* that are not significant in the problem domain. The *pilot* and *navigator* in Figure 13.7 might be neighbors, but an "is neighbor of" *relationship* is extraneous to the problem space.

6. Remove all *objects* that contain no data element except that needed to identify the individual *object* instances. Normally other objects that have a *relationship* with such *objects* can extend their data elements to include the identity of the removed *object*.

7. If an *object* contains data elements that do not apply to all instances of the *object*, decompose the *object* to an ancestor/descendent type of relationship.

8. Data elements that seem to apply jointly to a combination of *objects* suggest a missing *associative object*.

9. Remove any *associative objects* that are related to only one *object*. Any

data elements from the removed *associative object* should be added to the related *object*.

Semantic clarity requires that the analyst choose *objects* wisely. If unimportant aspects are elevated to *object* status, the significance of other *objects* may be lost. If important objects are not elevated to *object* status, then the significance of those *objects* is lost.

A set of quality ORDs enhances the value of the *Essential Requirements Model*.

RELATIONSHIPS BETWEEN ORDS, THE EID, AND THE EERL

I have found that software analysts who use traditional structured analysis techniques tend to concentrate on the algorithmic requirements of the system and consider the data requirements as an afterthought, if at all. This has seldom hindered the system specification or implementation significantly when using methodologies based on functional decomposition.

With RTOOSA, I have extended emphasis of the ORD to become an equal partner with the EID and EERL. In the next chapter, we will begin decomposing the *system* (visualized as the central icon on the EID) into its essential objects and define their structure and behaviors. The three major sources of objects we will consider will be the EID, EERL, and the ORDs. Because all three of these products contribute to the creation of the *Essential Objects Model*, they must provide consistent data. For example, the names of *External Objects* on the EID should be identifiable on the ORDs. The names need not be identical (that would be an unnecessary restriction) but should clearly trace back and forth. In addition, the terminology used in the EERL must be consistent with the *objects* and *relationships* specified in the ORDs. In reality, the EERL will normally identify many of the elements that appear on the ORDs and therefore should help guide in selecting the names for the *objects* and *relationships*.

The EERL also will identify mutually exclusive operating modes. For example, the LoCoDoNS case study EERL developed in Chapter 12 highlights three modes based on the validity of data from the sensors: (1) both the ADS and DVS are providing good data; (2) the ADS is providing good data, but the DVS isn't; and (3) neither the ADS nor the DVS is providing good data. Because the relationships among objects change for each mode, it is usually a good idea to provide a separate set of ORDs for each such mode. Separate ORDs tend to declutter the diagrams and bring out the mutually exclusive relationships associated with the modes.

The ORD is a natural mechanism for identifying the essential objects of the problem domain. The analyst must be careful to restrict ORD *objects* to those that represent the requirements of the problem. This is often easier than working through algorithmic decomposition because, usually, specific algorithms are not part of the essential requirements. The developer is left to choose any algorithm that fulfills the functional and performance requirements of the specific problem. Analysis emphasis on algorithms quickly becomes mired in implementation decisions. The concurrent development of the EID, EERL, and ORDs produces a more pure requirements model.

SUMMARY

This chapter provides a detailed description of the final product in the Essential Requirements Model, the Object Relationship Diagram (ORD). Each ORD is a snapshot in time that captures the essential objects of the problem space and explicitly defines the relationships among those objects.

The graphic representation of ORDs is intentionally kept very simple. Usually, interconnected icons represent the two related objects and another icon specifies the relationship. A special type of object, the *associative*, is needed when the relationship presumes information that cannot be properly attributed to either object alone. The identification and use of associative objects is considered.

Finally, the importance of maintaining consistency among the elements of the Essential Requirements Model, the EID, EERL, and ORDs, is emphasized. The development of these products tends to provide a more pure requirements model than concentrating on algorithms so early in the analysis process.

PRACTICE

1. Working from the EID and EERL developed, respectively, for Exercise 1 of Chapters 11 and 12, provide an ORD that identifies the essential objects and their relationships for the automobile cruise control system. If necessary, refine the EID and EERL to arrive at a complete, consistent Essential Requirements Model for this system.

2. Working from the EID and EERL developed, respectively, for Exercise 2 of Chapters 11 and 12, provide an ORD that identifies the essential objects and their relationships for the Radar Acquisition and Target System (RATS). If necessary, refine the EID and EERL to arrive at a complete, consistent Essential Requirements Model for the RATS.

3. Working from the EID and EERL developed, respectively, for Exercise 3 of Chapters 11 and 12, provide an ORD that identifies the essential objects and their relationships for the Automatic Teller Machine (ATM) system. If necessary, refine the EID and EERL to arrive at a complete, consistent Essential Requirements Model for the ATM.

4. Working from the EID and EERL developed, respectively, for Exercise 4 of Chapters 11 and 12, provide an ORD that identifies the essential objects and their relationships for the commercial product of your choice. If necessary, refine the EID and EERL to arrive at a complete, consistent Essential Requirements Model for your system.

5. Generate one or more ORDs to identify the essential objects and their relationships for the LoCoDoNS presented in Chapter 12. Are there any *external objects* shown in the EID of Figure 12.3 for which no requirements have been established? If so, update the EID to retain only the required external objects and their interfaces.

6. Generate an Essential Requirements Model for the gunship navigation system specified in Appendix A.

*One of the most dangerous forms of human error
is forgetting what one is trying to achieve.*
— Paul Nitze

Chapter **14**

Object Flow Diagram Notation

If you have faithfully completed the three elements of the Essential Requirements Model described in the three preceding chapters, you have reached a critical point in the analysis process. The information captured in the Essential Requirements Model remains fairly abstract. There is no clear relationship between the abstractions thus identified and the logical/physical entities that will be realized during design and implementation of the modeled system. However, when we begin constructing the Essential Objects Model, some entities we identify will later be directly recognizable as implementation entities in the design model.

The distinction between analysis abstractions and design entities begins to blur with the building of the Object Flow Diagrams (OFDs). The objects that you draw on an OFD will often lead directly to the classes you will implement in the system's Object-Oriented Programming Language (OOPL). When an OFD object icon is elaborated into its stores and processes on a lower-level OFD, those stores will often map directly to the fields and the processes to the methods of the implemented class. This extremely close relationship between the icons of the OFDs and the OOPL entities in the implementation space suggests that the OFDs bear directly on the system design.

Grady Booch, in his keynote address at the Harris Corporation OBJECTive.92 (Object-Oriented Technology seminar) on June 8, 1992, likened the process of analysis to discovery and that of design to invention. I find this helpful in explaining the mindset while generating OFDs.

The OFDs for a system must reflect the objects necessary to describe the required behavior of the system. These objects will be *discovered* by analysis of the products of the Essential Requirements Model. The OFD objects may not be sufficient to implement a working system. The design process will often add *invented* objects that are needed to create a working system. Many of these invented objects are needed to support the implementation architecture. The OFD does not illustrate the implementation architecture. It does, however, identify requirements for concurrency, preemption, resource allocation, and so forth that the architecture must satisfy.

So, although the objects identified on OFDs may directly map to classes and objects in the implementation space, they are not sufficient to specify the software design. For this reason alone, the creation of the OFDs remains part of the analysis process. Admittedly, there is overlap with design, but this is to the developer's advantage. The OFD provides an excellent foundation from which to build a working design model.

I therefore assign two important missions to the Essential Objects Model:

1. The detailed behavioral analysis that generates the Essential Objects Model provides insight into holes, inconsistencies, or other deficiencies in the Essential Requirements Model. The corrections to these problems are flowed back up to corresponding updates to the Essential Requirements Model. The result is an Essential Requirements Model that carries greater confidence as being complete and consistent.

2. The Essential Objects Model suggests many of the objects that must be accounted for in the design model. The Essential Objects Model therefore provides a natural bridge from analysis to design. A smooth transition from analysis to design reduces the risk of designing a system that fails to satisfy its specified requirements. This bridge provides inherent traceability between requirements and design.

This chapter and the next will describe how to build OFDs and their corresponding Object Templates (OTs). First, this chapter introduces the notation and associated semantics of OFDs. Chapter 15 describes a process for taking the elements of Essential Requirements Model and building the consistent OFDs and OTs for a system.

THE ELEMENTS OF OBJECT FLOW DIAGRAM NOTATION

Figure 14.1 illustrates the icons used in constructing Object Flow Diagrams. These icons allow considerable flexibility in the specification of a system. They support a purely object-oriented analysis, a purely functional decomposition analysis, or a hybrid of these two approaches. This chapter describes using these icons to support any of these analysis strategies. The next chapter will describe their application specifically to an object-oriented analysis. The greater flexibility of this notation allows the system analyst to choose an approach that best matches a specific system. There are times when it makes sense to consider nonobject entities. Many OOPLs (e.g., C/C++, Turbo Pascal, etc.) accommodate combinations of object and nonobject structures. From a pragmatic point of view, there is no compelling reason to make everything in a system an object. You will discover that a vast majority of what you must create in software is best represented by objects. But you need not force the rest into an object mold. The notation described in this chapter allows the analyst to merge elements of object-oriented analysis with nonobject entities (functions).

Objects and Messages

Because RTOOSA concentrates primarily on objects and their interactions, the two icons most heavily used will be the *Object* icon and the *Object/Object Message* icon.

The *Object* icon must contain the name of the object and the tag *obj*.

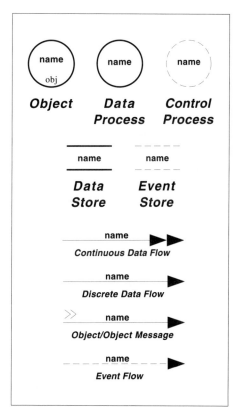

Figure 14.1.   Object Flow Diagram icons.

Some CASE tools will not permit writing the *obj* tag onto the icon itself. In such cases, an alternate form, such as putting the comment "*obj*" beside the circular icon, is acceptable. In this book, I use the "tag on the icon" convention.

The named *Object* icon carries all the connotations of an object developed through Part I of this book. In particular, the *Object* icon represents a specific instance of a class and implicitly includes the fields and methods of that yet-to-be-defined class. RTOOSA uses the specific field/method requirements of individual objects to establish the requirements for classes. The *Object* icon can *always* be decomposed. If the icon represents a mechanism or a subsystem (as defined in Chapter 6), then the *Object* icon is decomposed by another OFD that shows the lower-level objects whose cooperative behavior defines the mechanism or subsystem. Otherwise, the *Object* icon is decomposed by an OFD that exposes the constituent fields (using *Data Store* and *Event Store* icons) and methods (using *Data Process* and *Control Process* icons). There are also cases, such as the *ALauncher* class illustrated in Figure 6.8, where the object decomposition introduces other objects as fields. The OFD of a decomposed object may therefore include *Data Stores*, *Data Processes*, and *Object* icons. Object decomposition will be considered further in the next chapter.

Recall how Chapter 2 introduced the *message* as the paradigm by which objects communicate with one another. A message is initiated by an object method and is sent to a method in another object. The *Object/Object Message* icon uses a double-caret symbol to point in the direction of the message flow. A message serves one of four possible functions: (1) supplies information, (2) requests the return of information, (3) both supplies and requests information, or (4) requests the object to invoke a behavior (method) without a direct flow of information. The arrowhead at the end of the message icon line indicates the *primary* direction of information flow. Parameters passed in a message requesting information may often be considered secondary data and left off of the message icon. The returned information is the primary information flow. If the passed parameter must be stored by the object in a field, then its flow is usually worth depicting as well.

Figure 14.2 illustrates an object, *Navigator*, that sends four messages to a second object, *Inertial_Measurement_Unit*. The double-caret symbol on each message icon shows that all four messages flow from the *Navigator* to the *Inertial_Measurement_Unit*. The first message provides data (*IMU_Mode*) to the *Inertial_Measurement_Unit* object. In the second message, the *Navigator* requests return of data (*Current_IMU_Position*) from the *Inertial_Measurement_Unit* object. The third message provides data (*IMU_Mode*) to the *Inertial_Measurement_Unit* and receives data (*IMU_Status*) in return. Via the final message, the *Navigator* requests the *Inertial_Measurement_Unit* to *Run_BIT* (Built-In-Test). Notice that the *name* on the fourth message is preceded by an optional underscore

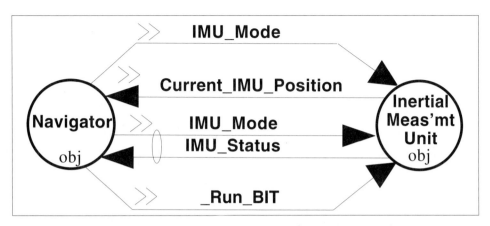

Figure 14.2. Messages passed between two objects.

character that may be used to distinguish the request to invoke a method for a non-data-flow-related behavior from a message bearing an information flow.

Data and Event Stores

There are two icons that represent stored *information*. These *stores* are defined as follows:

Data Store: that which holds information to be acted upon by one or more data processes without altering that information.

Event Store: that which records occurrences of event flows in a First In/First Out (FIFO) order.

A data store is a source and/or sink of persistent, discrete data. A data store may be implemented as a single data element, such as a Boolean, an integer, or a floating point number; a compound data structure, such as a record (C++ "struct") or an array; or a complex data structure, such as a linked list or a stack. Its persistence must extend beyond the local scope of a single language structure, but not necessarily beyond the life of the program. A data value that exists only as a passed parameter should never be represented as a data store.

Discrete data flows must be used to show data being written into a data store. Because the data store is a passive entity that makes its stored value available at all times, a continuous data flow must be used to show data being read from a data store. In addition, the data flow arrows clearly illustrate whether the data store access is read, write, or read/write. *A data flow may enter or leave a data store only through a data process.* For example, data flows directly between data stores are not permitted. The data flow icon to/from a data store may or may not include a name label. If there is no label, then the flow is assumed to access all elements of the data

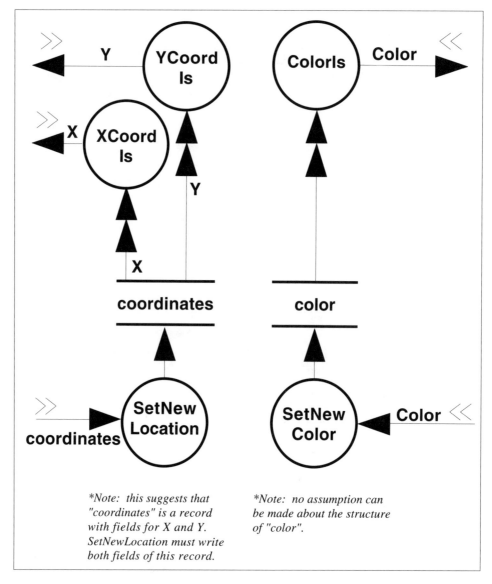

Figure 14.3. Legal access to data stores.

store. If only part of the data store is to be accessed, then the name of the applicable part(s) must be shown as the flow name. Figures 14.3 and 14.4 illustrate some rules regarding data stores and their access. In Figure 14.3, the data flow from the data process *Set New Location* to the data store *coordinates* is unlabeled. If this is a valid OFD segment, then the data process must write the entire data store structure. The read access data flows show an *X* and a *Y* component coming from the data store. Because these are the only read accesses, then (from a requirements point of view) *coordinates* must be a compound data structure (such as a record) that contains at least *X* and *Y* components. The data store *color* is always read and written as a complete structure, so no assumptions may be made regarding its make-up. *Color* could be a single byte, a three-element record containing the intensities of the red, green, and blue components, or any other means of representing color (such as "hue, intensity, and saturation"). This diagram offers no hint as to how *color* is defined. That can be determined only by looking up *color* in the Data Dictionary (as described in Chapter 16).

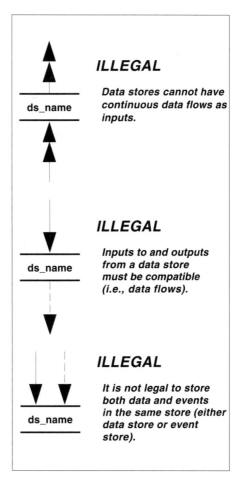

Figure 14.4. Some violations of data store syntax.

Figure 14.4 illustrates some illegal data store accesses. Any access to a data store that is not a *discrete* data flow in or a continuous data flow out is illegal.

From an object-oriented viewpoint, the *data store* has all the characteristics of an object field. It can retain an object's state or value while being acted upon by one or more data processes, which can correspond to object methods. When we later decompose a single *object* icon on a separate OFD, the object's fields will be represented by data (and sometimes event) stores.

The *event store* is similar to a *data store* in that it retains information. As the data store captures information from data flows, the event store captures event flows. However, there are significant differences between an event store and a data store.

Remember that in Chapter 11 we defined an event flow on an External Interface Diagram as *a flow that carries no explicit data*. The same basic concept applies to OFD *event flows*. Because it carries no explicit data, the only significance of an event flow is its occurrence. The event store therefore stores only the history of the chronological arrivals of events. This time ordering of events suggests implementation with a First-In-First-Out (FIFO) queue.

Implicit in writing to an event store is the enqueuing of the event, while reading from the event store implicitly includes the function of dequeuing an event. Dequeuing an event from an event store is a destructive read (not generally true when reading data from a data store). Because of these implicit enqueue/dequeue functions, event flows may be directly connected to an event store without an intervening process icon. This contrasts to the *random access* nature of the data store.

Data and Control Processes

There are two icons that represent "processes" that act upon data and event flows. These processes are defined as follows:

> **Data Process:** a "process" that transforms one or more (data or event flow) inputs into one or more (data or event flow) outputs.

> **Control Process:** a "process" that accepts only event flows as inputs and produces only event flows as outputs.

Data and control processes are the active elements of a system. The required name on the process icons will normally be an active verb phrase (i.e., verb–object) describing the process. Although the process icons may be used anywhere on OFDs, in a purely object-oriented analysis model, they can be restricted to representing object methods or the functionally decomposed elements of a method. When a process icon is used to represent an object's method, the process name should be the name of the method.

Because an implicit execution is associated with a process, there must be a way to "activate" it and thereby initiate its processing. A process may be activated in two ways. One is by the arrival of a discrete data flow, event flow, or object message. The other is by an explicit "activation" event. In Figure 14.5, the data process *Compute Course to Waypoint* is activated by the arrival of the *AC_position* data flow. The data process can access the target waypoint location from the *target*

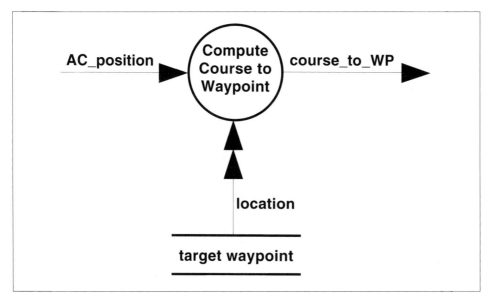

Figure 14.5.   A data process activated by the AC_position discrete data flow.

waypoint data store, but the continuous *location* data flow can never activate the *Compute Course to Waypoint* process because a data store can never initiate a flow. The data process computes the required course between the aircraft position (*AC_position*) and the target waypoint and provides the result as the discrete data flow *course_to_WP*. The data process *Compute Course to Waypoint* is implicitly deactivated when its discrete function is completed and the *course_to_WP* flow has been generated. Then the data process receiving the *course_to_WP* flow is activated.

Because the arrival of a discrete flow carries an implicit process activation, the lowest-level processes (determined by hierarchical decomposition) must have no more than one time-discrete input flow. A series of data processes connected by discrete flows establishes a *causal interface relationship* leading to sequential activation among those processes. In Figure 14.6, for example, the data flow output from the *Determine Filter Setting* data process causes the *Send Filter Gain to Rcvr* data process to activate. These two data processes have a "causal relationship" with sequential activations.

Figure 14.7 illustrates a "noncausal relationship." This OFD shows part of a system that updates screen images based on a regular, hardware-driven redraw rate (typically on the order of 30 Hz). The *Draw Nav Feature* data process is activated by the arrival of a *draw request* discrete data flow. Such new information could

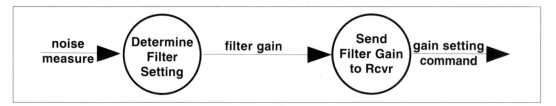

Figure 14.6. A "causal relationship" between data processes.

arrive at any time during the processing cycle. This data process writes the *plot commands* to the data store *Plot Command Buffer*. The execution of the *Draw Nav Feature* has no immediate effect on the process *Write Plot Cmds to Screen*. In such a system, the hardware can only accept draw commands at a specific point during data processing. So, when the hardware-generated *frame trigger* event arrives, it activates the *Write Plot Cmds to Screen* data process, which reads the previously generated *plot commands* from the *Plot Command Buffer* and generates the discrete data flow output *plot cmds*. These two data processes execute asynchronously.

It is important for the analyst to recognize when *causal* and *noncausal* relationships exist between data processes to represent the corresponding requirements for concurrency. Typically, two processes with a *causal* relationship are part of the same thread of execution, while *noncausal* relationships suggest separate, concurrent threads of execution.

Figure 14.8 illustrates the problem of a data process with two activating discrete data flow inputs. When should the *Stuff Envelopes* data process be activated? Does activation require the presence of both *letters* and *addressed envelopes* or just

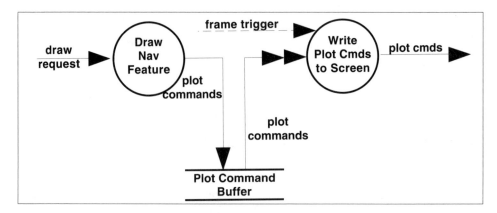

Figure 14.7. A "noncausal relationship" between data processes.

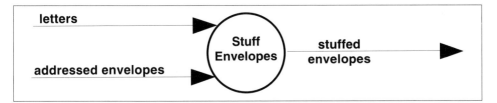

Figure 14.8. Ambiguous activation of a data process.

either of these inputs? Each of these cases can be represented unambiguously.

Consider first the asynchronous arrival example in Figure 14.9. This figure shows the decomposition of the data process *Stuff Envelopes* to a lower-level OFD wherein a separate lower-level data process accepts each of the data flows. The asynchronous arrival of either *letters* or *addressed envelopes* activates a lower-level data process that attempts to match the new input with its counterpart from a data store. If a match is not achieved, the new input is moved to a data store. If a match is made, then the *matched letter and envelope* flow activates the *Stuff One Envelope* process to generate the *stuffed envelopes* output data flow.

If simultaneous availability of the *letter* and the *addressed envelope* is required

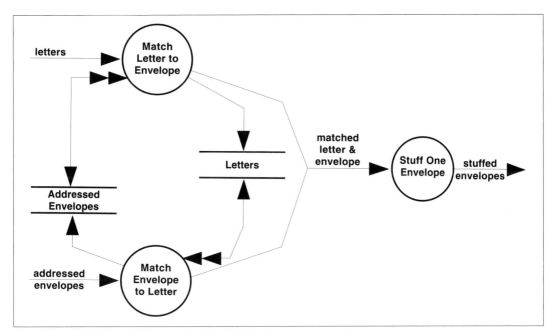

Figure 14.9. An unambiguous OFD depicting asynchronous data arrival.

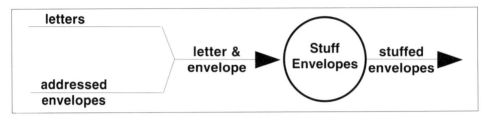

Figure 14.10.   An unambiguous OFD depicting synchronous data arrival.

to activate *Stuff Envelopes*, then a different representation is needed. Figure 14.10 shows how the merged data flows depict the requirement for synchronous data arrival to activate *Stuff Envelopes*.

If these examples seem to be a sleight of hand, there are some conventions associated with data flow notation that explain the apparent trick. Figure 14.11 illustrates these conventions. In Figure 14.9, the merged data flows represent the same flow being initiated by two different processes. This corresponds to the top example in Figure 14.11. Figure 14.10 shows merged data flows where each flow contributes a subset of the merged flow, as in the second example in Figure 14.11. Unfortunately, not all CASE tools support the notation for merged and split data flows.

The second type of process activation involves specific types of event flows. These labeled event flows include:

Process Activation: an event flow, labeled "activate" or "enable," that enables the continuous/repeated or discrete execution of a process.

Process Deactivation: an event flow, labeled "deactivate" or "disable," that disables the continuous or repeated execution of a process.

Figure 14.12 depicts a generic system that has distinct processing requirements based on its operating mode. Specifically, the *Toggle Mode Command* (perhaps controlled by a push button on a control panel) causes the *Select Operating Mode* control process alternately to activate the data processes associated with the active mode. When the *Process for Mode A* is enabled, the *Process for Mode B* is disabled, and vice versa. A disabled process will not respond to the discrete data flow *Environment Parameter*. In this OFD, the output *Control Command* is always generated in response to the *Environmental Parameter* input. However, the data process that generates the output depends on the operating mode as controlled by *Select Operating Mode*.

While Figure 14.12 illustrates activation/deactivation of repeated executions,

Figure 14.13 shows an unpaired activation for a single execution. In this example, the data store *Sample Rate* specifies the number of interrupts between samples. When the *Select Needed Sample* process, activated by the *50 Hz Interrupt* event, counts down the *Sample Rate*, it *activates* the *Sample Azimuth* data process to read the current value of the continuous data flow *Azimuth*. That sampled value is placed in the *Azimuth Samples* data store for access by other data processes. The total effect of this segment of an OFD is to generate azimuth samples at a fixed data rate for asynchronous access by unspecified clients.

While a *Data Process* may accept any combination of data flows and event flows, a *Control Process* may only accept or issue event flows. The control process behaves much the same as a finite-state machine, using knowledge of previous

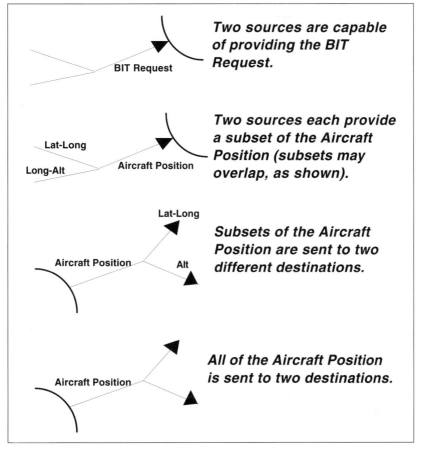

BIT Request — Two sources are capable of providing the BIT Request.

Lat-Long / Long-Alt / Aircraft Position — Two sources each provide a subset of the Aircraft Position (subsets may overlap, as shown).

Lat-Long / Aircraft Position / Alt — Subsets of the Aircraft Position are sent to two different destinations.

Aircraft Position — All of the Aircraft Position is sent to two destinations.

Figure 14.11. Data flow conventions: merged and split data flows.

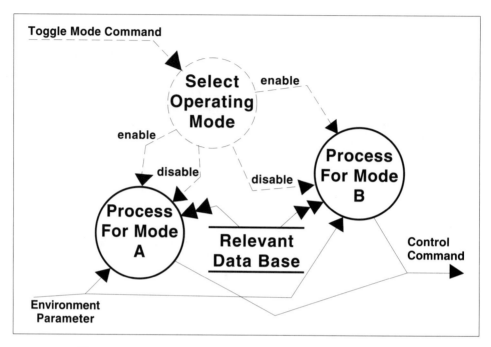

Figure 14.12.   Paired activation/deactivation of data processes.

event arrivals to produce its outputs. A control process assumes that one event has been processed before the next can arrive. If it is possible to violate this assumption when considering the event flows of a specific system, then the event flows must be buffered by an event store (with its implicit enqueue and dequeue functions).

Figure 14.14 illustrates a simple system that implements a common pull-cord electric lamp. The logic of the *Control Lamp* control process could be represented by a state transition diagram with two states (*Lamp On* and *Lamp Off*). Each new *Cord Pulled* event causes a state change to the opposite state, generating the corresponding output event flow. This OFD illustrates how a control process includes an implied internal memory, suggesting it could be implemented as an object:

```
Light = object
    constructor Init;    {init to default state}
    destructor Done;  virtual;
    procedure ToggleState; {response to cord-pull}
    function LightIsOn : boolean;
  private
    CurrentState    : boolean; {true = on}
  end;    { object = Light }
```

The data process *Monitor Current Speed* at the top of Figure 14.15 has two major problems. First, there is no way it can be activated, so it can never process the available inputs *desired speed* and *current speed*. Further, it is a data sink in that it has no outputs. This violates the basic definition of a data process, which states that a data process transforms inputs to outputs.

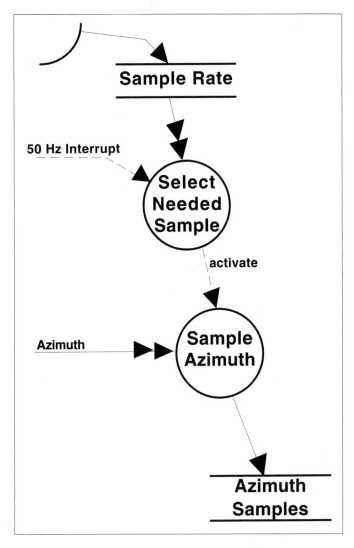

Figure 14.13.   Explicit unpaired activation of a data process.

Data processes that have outputs but no inputs are generally illegal as well. However, there may be rare exceptions, such as a random number generator that periodically turns out a random value. Such cases are extremely rare. Carefully evaluate all "output only" data processes for reasonableness in the context of the system requirements.

The control process *Process A* at the bottom of Figure 14.15 violates the definition of a control process because it has a data flow as an input. Control processes may only have event flows as inputs and outputs.

The processes defined in OFDs need to capture the behavioral requirements of the system. It is therefore important that each process be associated with the proper inputs and outputs. In Figure 14.16, the top OFD illustrates a data process that is illegal because it lacks sufficient inputs to generate the indicated output. On the other hand, the bottom OFD contains a data process that has a superfluous input data flow (*Y-Temperature*) that is not necessary to generate the specified output. Although this situation is not illegal, it is undesirable. A data process should

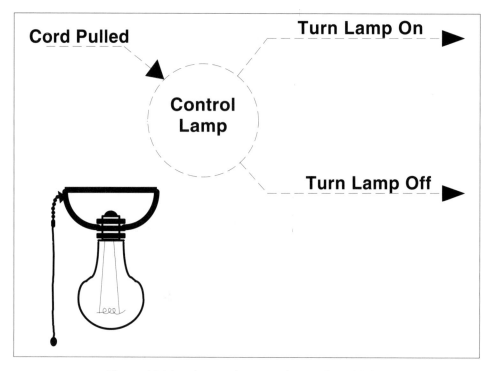

Figure 14.14.   A control process for a pull-cord light.

have exactly the inputs needed to generate the required output and no more or less.

Just as we need to consider cases of ambiguous process activation due to multiple discrete inputs, so must we ensure that a process generates unambiguous discrete outputs. Consider the data process *Take Square Root* in Figure 14.17. The general rule is that if there are multiple discrete outputs from a process, they must be mutually exclusive such that only one may be generated by each "execution" of the process. *Take Square Root* generates three discrete outputs. Although the *input negative* event flow (perhaps implemented by an *exception* in a language such as Ada or C++) is mutually exclusive of the two output data flows, those two flows

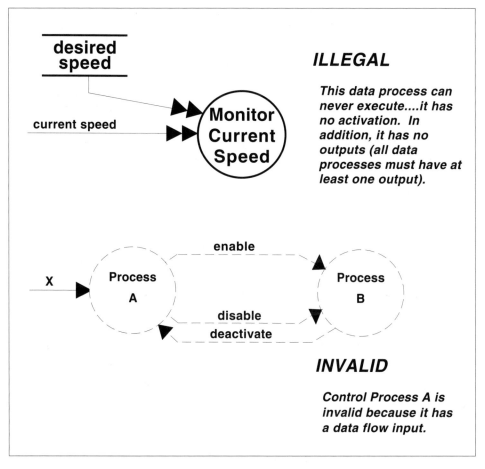

Figure 14.15. Illegal process syntax examples.

are both generated when a nonnegative input X is received. The ambiguity lies in the undefined sequence or manner in which these flows activate other processes.

Assuming the two data flows from *Take Square Root* in Figure 14.17 actually go to the same process, those two outputs should be combined into a compound data element as illustrated in Figure 14.18. The actual structure of *square root data* must be defined by an entry in the data dictionary (as discussed in Chapter 16).

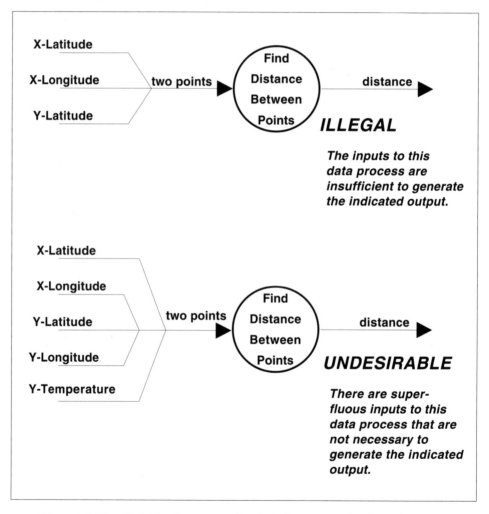

Figure 14.16.   Matching the process inputs to its computational requirements.

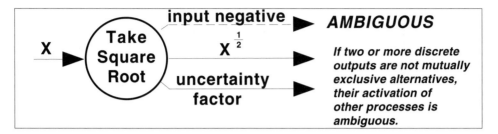

Figure 14.17. Ambiguous data process' discrete outputs.

DECOMPOSING OBJECTS

Object Flow Diagrams capture the computational requirements for a system by depicting the system's essential objects and their required interactions. Consider the *Targets* program developed to illustrate application of the geometric objects hierarchy of classes in Chapter 3. The listing for the *Targets* program was provided in Figure 3.11. An OFD that captures part of the initialization processing for this program is shown in Figure 14.19.

This OFD shows data processes sending messages to three of the objects required by this program: *APoint*, the *Target*, and the *Sight*. Based solely on this OFD, *APoint* must be able to respond to two distinct messages, suggesting two methods. One is identified as *_INIT* and the other sets three object *APoint* fields with the point coordinates and color and draws the point. *APoint* can be assumed to contain, at a minimum, two visible methods and three fields. This structure can be captured by generating a lower-level OFD that decomposes the *APoint* object icon. Figure 14.20 illustrates a decomposition of *APoint* that reflects these

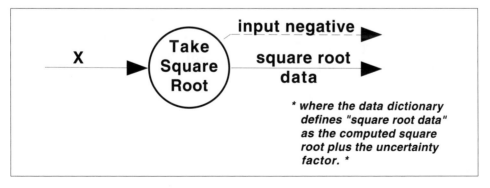

Figure 14.18. Proper data process outputs.

required elements. This decomposed object OFD shows two incoming messages with an unspecified source (i.e., attached to no process at the source end of the message flow). When an object is decomposed, all unattached messages are assumed to be resolved at the higher-level OFD showing the use of the object. It is

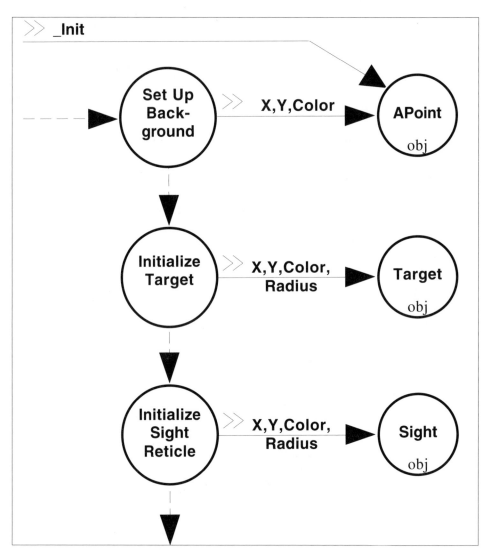

Figure 14.19.   Part of an OFD depicting the start-up processing for TARGETS.PAS (Figure 3.11).

therefore important that the decomposed object OFD *balance* with the higher-level OFD by having exactly the same message interfaces. Figures 14.19 and 14.20 are *balanced* for the *APoint* object interfaces. Additional OFDs would be needed to decompose the objects *Target* and *Sight* and thereby completely *balance* the OFD in Figure 14.19.

Because Figure 14.19 shows the only requirements for *APoint* in the entire *Targets* program, the OFD in Figure 14.20 should be considered complete (for analysis purposes). Nothing else should be added arbitrarily to the requirements for *APoint. Analysis must be restricted to identifying the minimum requirements of the system's essential objects. It must not try to anticipate the general requirements for a class that could satisfy the needs of many applications.* After all individual object requirements have been collected from all similar objects, a composite OFD can be created to identify the structure of a class that could instantiate those various objects. This design step must be kept distinct from the identification of individual object requirements.

There is another way to use the individual object OFDs like that shown in

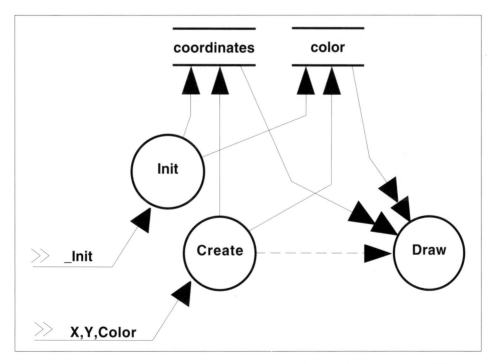

Figure 14.20. OFD showing required elements of *APoint* for the previous OFD.

Figure 14.20. If your organization has a well-documented reuse library, the OFDs of individual objects can be matched to OFDs that capture the structures of existing classes in that library. For example, Figure 14.21 describes the class structure of the *Point* class defined in the *Geo_Objs* unit (see Figure 4.5). Comparative analysis of Figures 14.20 and 14.21 shows that the *Geo_Objs.Point* class easily generates the object *APoint*. Admittedly, the traceability in this example is strong because, in the *Targets* program, *APoint* is declared as an instance of the class *Geo_Objs.Point*. Normally the analyst will have to search deeper to determine whether a class can be used to instantiate a required object. In fact, it often requires reconsidering the object to see whether its structure could be restated in an equivalent form that more closely matches an available class. I consider the matching of essential objects to existing or new class designs as part of the design process. This will be addressed further in Chapter 17.

In general, all object icons must be decomposed. If an object is actually a mechanism or subsystem consisting of or containing other objects, then a separate OFD is needed to illustrate how these lower-level objects interact. If the object is a base object not made up of other objects, then a separate OFD that exposes the fields and methods of that object is required.

DECOMPOSING CONTROL PROCESSES

A *Control Process* has been previously defined as a process that accepts only event flows as inputs and produces only event flows as outputs. The processing requirements for a control process can always be specified by a *State Transition Diagram* (STD). There are numerous conventions for representing STDs. The one I have chosen to present here is based on the description by Ward/Mellor in Volume 1 of *Structured Development for Real-Time Systems*. This notation is supported by many commonly available CASE tools.

First, consider the following definitions:

State: a stable condition wherein processing remains constant until an event occurs.

State Transition: a change from one state to another in response to an event.

Conditions: a description of the event that causes a state transition.

Associated Actions: processing that must occur as part of a state transition.

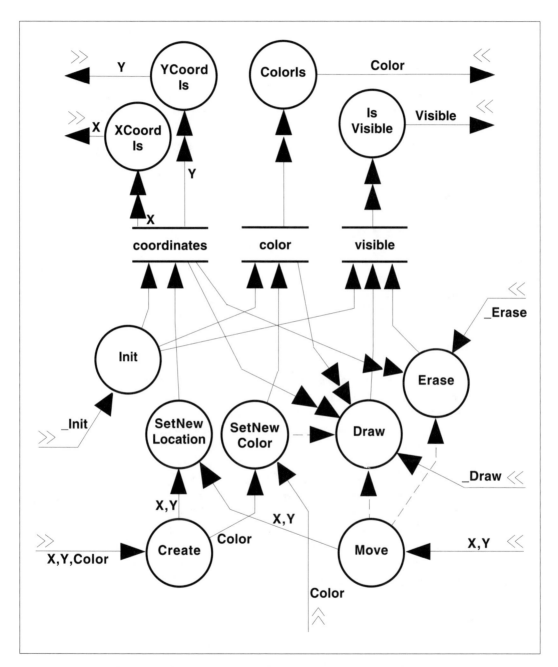

Figure 14.21. OFD for the Geometric Objects unit *Point* class.

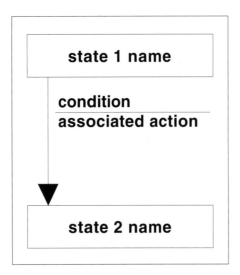

Figure 14.22.   The essentials of a State Transition Diagram.

Figure 14.22 illustrates these STD elements. Each state must have a name that describes the *mode* of system processing associated with that state. Each state is connected to one or more states (possibly including itself) by directed lines. The arrows on these lines point to the new state resulting from the associated state transition. Each transition line must explicitly identify the condition(s) that initiate the state transition. The *associated actions* identified for a state transition are executed in response to the stated conditions *before* the new state is achieved. These actions are assumed to occur instantaneously and, where more than one action is identified, simultaneously.

Consider the OFD for a very simple automobile cruise control system, as shown in Figure 14.23. In this system, when the driver turns the system on (*turn on* event), the system captures the *current speed* as the speed to be maintained and saves it in the *desired speed* data store. Once a *desired speed* has been established, the process *Monitor Current Speed* is activated to compare the *current speed* to the *desired speed* and determine when the difference goes out of or returns to within a predetermined (but unspecified) tolerance. This data process raises the corresponding events back to the *Control Vehicle Speed* control process. *Control Vehicle Speed* activates the *Adjust Speed* data process when the speed goes out of tolerance and deactivates it when the speed returns to within tolerance. *Adjust Speed* generates *throttle setting* commands to attempt to change the vehicle speed. This simple system has no additional features for coast/resume or increase/decrease speed as found on most commercial systems. This system must be turned off and back on to set a new *desired speed*. Although this may not be a sufficient set of features for a viable commercial product, it reduces the complexity to allow its use as a teaching aid. Defining a more complete system is left as an exercise for the student (see Exercise 1 at the end of this chapter).

Figure 14.24 provides the STD for the *Control Vehicle Speed* control process of this simple cruise control system. This diagram shows four states: *off*, *setting desired speed*, *speed in tolerance*, and *adjusting speed*. The initial state, *off*, is entered by application of system power, depicted by the **activation** condition.

When a system has a specific initial state, you may show a single transition into the initial state that occurs with the system start-up. The condition for that transition may be anything that suggests a start-up event. In this case, *activation* was chosen as the start-up condition description.

Notice that the state transition *conditions* map directly to the event flows into the *Control Vehicle Speed* control process and that the *associated actions* for the state transitions correspond to event flows initiated by the *Control Vehicle Speed* control process. A proper STD will account for all the event flows into and out of the corresponding control process. As illustrated by this example, the STD defines the relationships among the event flows in and out of a control process. The

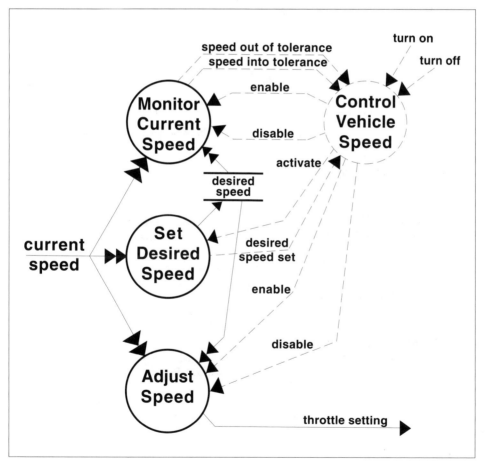

Figure 14.23. An OFD for a simple automotive cruise control.

control process "remembers" the current state so it knows how to respond to the next input. Any input for which there is no corresponding state transition from the current state is ignored.

Figure 14.25 suggests another OFD, this time for the familiar two-switch controlled light. Although this OFD appears very simple, the corresponding STD could be fairly complex, as illustrated by Figure 14.26. Because the problem statement didn't specify an initial state, there are two possible STDs: one if the light is

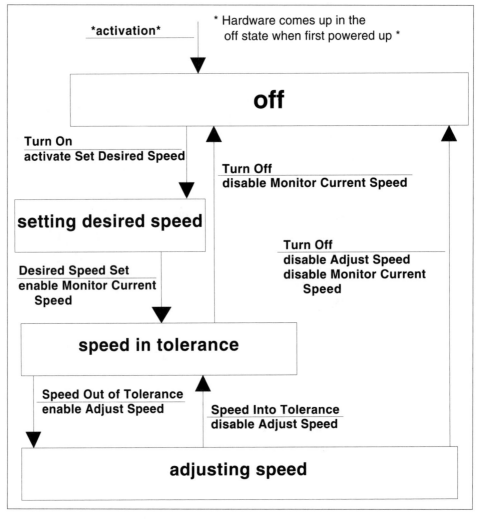

Figure 14.24.   An STD for a simple automotive cruise control.

off when both switches are down and the other if the light is on when both switches are down. If an initial state were specified, then only one of the STDs would be necessary as the states of the two STDs are mutually exclusive.

Because the initial state of this system is not specified, an alternate OFD might be considered that is insensitive to either possible initial state. Figure 14.27 suggests such an OFD. In this model, any time a switch event arrives, a *toggle light* event is dispatched to the *control the light* control process, which alternates the light between on and off. With two control processes, a separate STD is required for each. Figure 14.28 suggests corresponding STDs. Notice how this strategy decouples the control process definition from the initial state. Whatever it might be, these STDs will accommodate it.

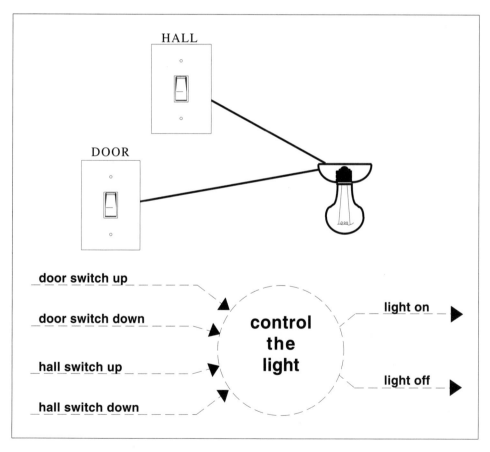

Figure 14.25. The OFD for a two-switch light "system."

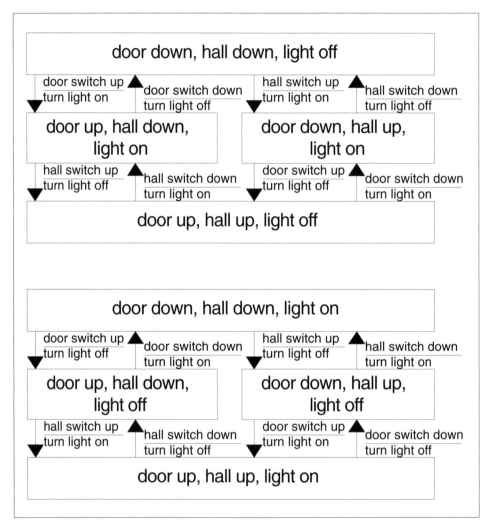

Figure 14.26.   A State Transition Diagram for the two-switch light "system."

This process could be carried a step further, and the OFD shown in Figure 14.29 developed. In this case, each switch is handled by a separate control process, requiring a separate STD. Figure 14.30 suggests the STDs for these three control processes. Although using three control processes to define this simple system, already shown to be definable with either one or two control processes, may seem excessive, it has a certain elegance when considered from an object-oriented system developer's viewpoint. First, the three control processes map directly to the

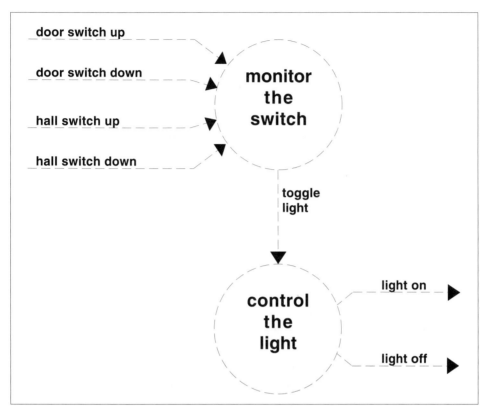

Figure 14.27. An alternate OFD for the two-switch light "system."

three physical entities in the problem environment: two switches and the light. Then consider that the behaviors of the two switches are identical. This suggests that they might be implemented as two instances of the same class. The implementors need worry about only two very simple STDs. The final system should be more reliable, more understandable, and far more maintainable. For example, in each of the above cases, what is required to add a third or fourth switch to the system?

One danger with partitioning control processes as described above is the potential for creating states that cannot exist in the system's real-world counterpart. Assume, for example, that an initial state had been specified back in the first problem statement for the two-switch light system. In that case, only one or the other of the STDs in Figure 14.26 would accurately depict the valid states of the system. All subsequent STDs considered by partitioning the control processes

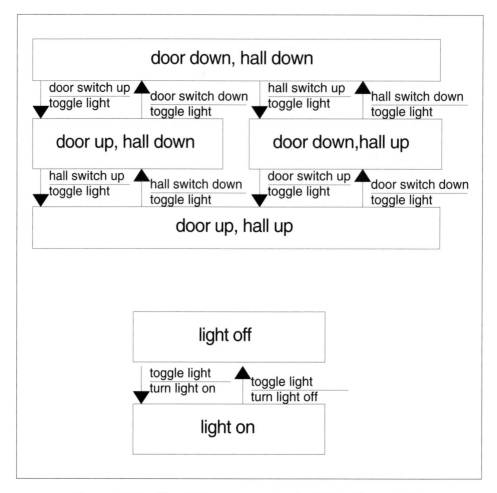

Figure 14.28. The STDs accompanying the OFD in Figure 14.27.

would suggest invalid states and therefore be erroneous. This would be a flawed model because it would not map into the real world. The analyst must recognize all requirements levied on the system and ensure that the derived models exactly represent those requirements. Conversely, the analyst must not impose requirements that unduly restrict the requirements model (or implementation). In our example, the absence of an initial state requirement makes the model and the implementation much cleaner!

Because control processes may only be decomposed into STDs, their consideration is much less complex than that of data processes, which follows.

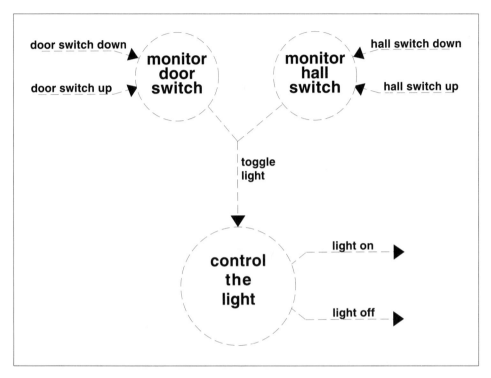

Figure 14.29.   A more "object-oriented" OFD.

DECOMPOSING DATA PROCESSES

OFDs are developed hierarchically. Each process icon on an OFD requires further elaboration. If the icon represents a control process, then the control process must be expanded with a STD, as just described. If the icon represents a data process that might be considered relatively complex, then it is usually best to represent the functions of the data process in another OFD. For example, Figure 14.31 shows part of an OFD with a data process named *Determine Wind Speed*. If this process were relatively straightforward, then it would be best to define the processing requirements of this process directly. If, on the other hand, this process contained several discrete and somewhat complex steps, then it would be better first to provide another OFD to identify those subprocesses.

Figure 14.32 suggests how the *Determine Wind Speed* data process might be represented by four processes. If these lower-level processes are sufficiently primitive, then further levels of OFD elaboration are not warranted and individual process definition can begin.

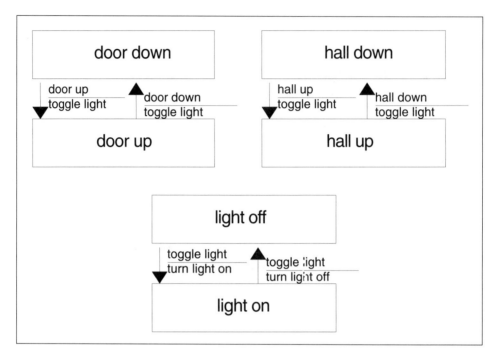

Figure 14.30.   The STDs to accompany the control processes of the more "object-oriented" OFD.

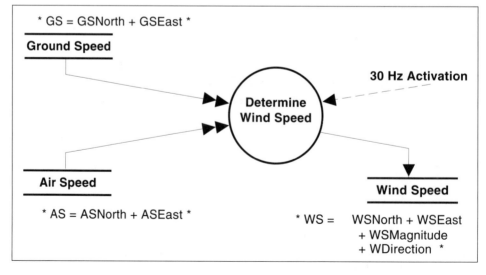

Figure 14.31.   A data process that would better be further elaborated by another OFD.

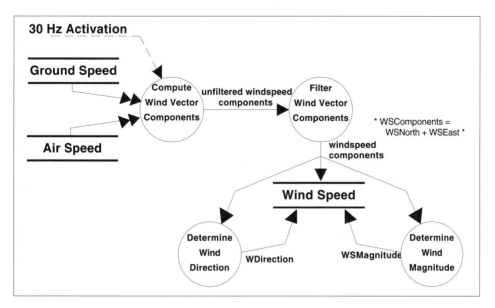

Figure 14.32. The elaboration of the data process *Determine Wind Speed.*

An overriding requirement for the levels of OFD elaboration is that each level *balance* with the icon it represents on the next higher-level OFD. In the wind speed computation example, the three data stores and the external event *30 Hz Activation* on Figure 14.31 are again recognizable in Figure 14.32. It is also apparent that *30 Hz Activation* must be tied to a source on an OFD at a level higher than that shown in Figure 14.31, where the source is also unspecified.

The other way that a data process icon can be elaborated is by providing the definition of the process in a way that is appropriate for that particular process. There are many ways available, including PDL ("Process" or "Program" Design Language), decision trees, truth tables, State Transition Diagrams, Preprocess/Postprocess specifications, and so forth.

For example, the *Compute Wind Vector Components* data process might best be represented by PDL:

```
begin
  — Compute North component
  WSNorth := GSNorth - ASNorth;
  — Compute East component
  WSEast  := GSEast  - ASEast;
end;
```

Other processes could be represented by PDL or some other technique. The computation of the wind direction from the wind speed components might be clear enough using PDL:

```
begin
  if abs( WSNorth ) >> abs( WSEast ) then
    Wind_Dir := arctan( WSEast / WSNorth );
  elsif abs( WSNorth ) = abs( WSEast ) then
    if WSNorth = WSEast then
      Wind_Dir := 45 degrees;
    else
      Wind_Dir := -45 degrees;
    end if;
  else   - abs( WSNorth ) < abs( WSEast )
    Wind_Dir := arccot( WSNorth / WSEast );
  end if;
  if WSNorth < 0  then   - direction is southerly
    Wind_Dir := Wind_Dir - 180 degrees;
  endif;
end;
```

Or it could be presented in a form that doesn't suggest the sequence of operations, such as the decision tree shown in Figure 14.33.

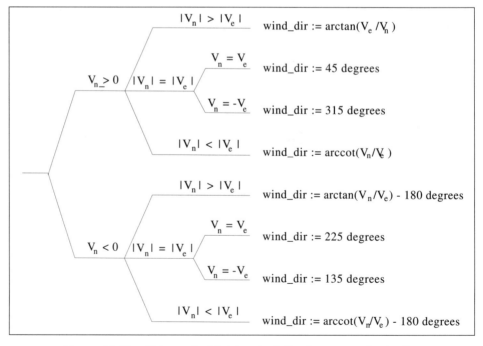

Figure 14.33.   Using a decision tree to define the processing for the *Determine Wind Direction* data process.

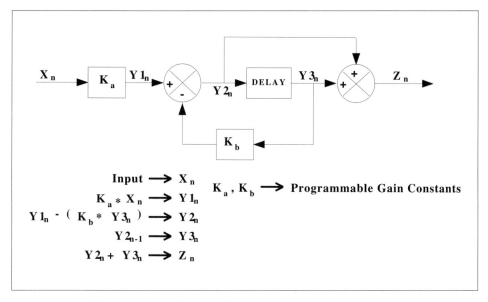

Figure 14.34. Control theory notation for a low-pass filter.

The *Filter Wind Vector Components* might best represent the filter definition with notation used by control theorists to show a digital filter. Figure 14.34 shows such a control theorist's notation for a low-pass filter. Although this representation may appear foreign to a software engineer, using this notation may be more meaningful to the system analyst who is expected to review the software requirements model. Figure 14.35 shows how the clever software engineer would build a *LPFilter* class to implement such an object.

Try another example. The *input decimal value* data process in Figure 14.36 could be defined by pseudocode (another name for PDL):

```
begin
  Initialize decimal_value to 0;
  loop
    read next character;
    if character is in [0..9] then
      decimal_value := (decimal_value * 10) + digit;
    else
      if character = "enter" then
        return decimal_value
      else
        return "invalid input message"
      end if
    end if
  end loop
end;
```

```
unit DigFlter;

{ Program:    Digital Filter — an object class for a low pass filter;
  Author:     John R. Ellis
  Last Update: 30 June 1992
  Copyright (c) 1992 by John R. Ellis

  Description:  This unit provides a object class that implements a low
                pass digital filter.  The filter used is:

                               _____
                              |                  |
             ____             |        _____    |         _v_
    Xn      |    |  Y1n   /\ /\|       |      |   | Y3n   /\+/\   Zn
   —— >| Ka |————>|+ X  |——— >| DELAY |——— >|+ X  |———>
         |____|        \/-\/  Y2n  |_____|   |       \/_\/
                        ^                     |
                        |          ____       |
                        |         |    |      |
                        ————————| Kb |<————
                                  |____|

                    input —> Xn          Ka, Kb are gain constants
                    Ka * Xn —> Y1n
          Y1n - ( Kb * Y3n ) —> Y2n
                    Y2[n-1] —> Y3n
                    Y2n + Y3n —> Zn

  Requirements: None.
                                                                        }
interface

   type

      {===================================================================}
      {                        Object Declarations                        }
      {===================================================================}

      LPFilter = object
         constructor Init( ConstKa, ConstKb : real { gain constants } );
         function Cycle( Xn : real ) : real;
         destructor Done;
       private
         Ka      : real;   { filter gain constant Ka }
         Kb      : real;   { filter gain constant Kb }
         Y2n     : real;   { Y2n from previous pass }
         Y3n     : real;   { Y3n from previous pass }
      end;        { object = LPFilter }

{——————— end of interface section ———————-}
implementation
```

Figure 14.35. Code listing: unit DIGFLTER.PAS.

```
{========================================================================}
{                   Method Definitions for: LPFilter                     }
{========================================================================}
  constructor LPFilter.Init( ConstKa, ConstKb : real { gain constants } );
    begin
      Ka  := ConstKa;
      Kb  := ConstKb;
      Y2n := 0.0;
      Y3n := 0.0;
    end;    { LPFilter.Init }

  function LPFilter.Cycle( Xn : real ) : real;
    var
      OldY2   : real;
    begin
      OldY2 := Y2n;                         { Y2(n-1) }
      Y2n   := (Ka * Xn) - (Kb * Y3n);
      Y3n   := OldY2;     { save Y2(n-1) as Y3n for next pass }
      Cycle := Y2n + Y3n;
    end;    { LPFilter.Cycle }

  destructor LPFilter.Done;
    begin
    end;    { LPFilter.Done }

{========================================================================}
{                        No Initialization Code                          }
end.
```

Or this logic could be represented by the State Transition Diagram shown in Figure 14.37. Because this STD is not representing a control process, there is no correlation between the *conditions/associated actions* and event flows as there was with STDs representing control processes. In this diagram, the *conditions* are associated with indirectly perceived events based on the *characters* data flow.

SUMMARY

Object Flow Diagrams (OFDs) become the first RTOOSA product containing elements that will trace directly to design and implementation entities. The objects identified on OFDs represent the essential objects necessary to define the required behavior of the system. The behaviors associated with these essential objects represent only those needed to satisfy the specific requirements of the specific problem space.

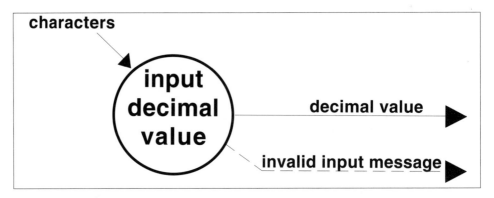

Figure 14.36.   A data process ready for definition.

The notation used for OFDs consists of icons for objects, nonobject processes, stores, and the various flows that interconnect them. OFDs are constructed hierarchically, whereby a single icon will be represented by another OFD that exposes that icon's next lower-level structure.

This chapter described the syntax and semantics for each of the OFD icons. Examples illustrated common mistakes made with their use.

When OFD object icons representing mechanisms or subsystems have been elaborated to their base object structure, the base-level object icons must each be elaborated by an OFD containing data/event stores and data/control processes

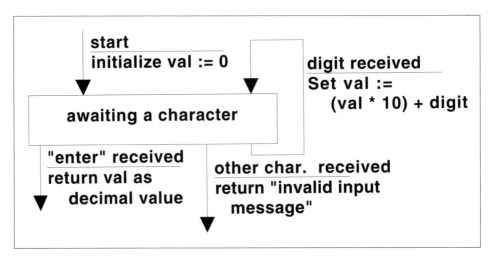

Figure 14.37.   Defining a data prodess with a STD.

that correspond to the object's required fields and methods, respectively. Remember that this process identifies essential objects and does not worry about the structures of classes that might be used to instantiate such objects.

When control processes are identified on an OFD, then the control logic of these processes must be defined by corresponding State Transition Diagrams (STDs). The conditions and associated actions of the STDs map directly to the event flows in and out of the corresponding control processes.

Data processes are elaborated hierarchically until the base-level processes are at a level of complexity easily understood. These base-level processes must each be defined in a manner befitting the associated function. Some process definition techniques illustrated include PDL, STD, decision trees, control theory diagrams, and so forth.

PRACTICE

1. Extend the OFD provided in Figure 14.23 to include the features found on most commercial automobile cruise control systems, such as coast/resume, increase/decrease speed, and so forth. Derive a new STD that incorporates the states not present in Figure 14.24.

2. Develop an OFD containing control processes that define the required behavior of a light controlled by three switches. Provide a STD for each of the control processes identified on the OFD.

3. Develop an OFD for the Automatic Teller Machine (ATM) system for which you completed the Essential Requirements Model in Exercise 3 of Chapter 12. Imagine what objects are necessary to define the behavior of such a system. Decompose each object icon on a separate OFD to show the object's fields with stores and methods with processes.

4. Develop an OFD for the Gunship navigation system. Work from the Essential Requirements Model developed in Exercise 6 of Chapter 13.

Yabu o tsutsuite hebi o dasu.
[Poking at the brush drives out a snake.]
— Old Japanese Saying

Chapter **15**

Building
Object Flow Diagrams

Chapter 14 introduced the notation for Object Flow Diagrams (OFDs). However, merely understanding the syntax and semantics of OFDs does not guarantee that an analyst can generate a complete, consistent, and meaningful OFD network for a specific problem. In this chapter, I will introduce heuristics to guide the analyst through the creation of an OFD network.

The three criteria of goodness suggested above must underlie the object model. The OFDs must capture the *minimum* set of objects that completely defines the required behavior of the system. Such a model is *complete* only if the essence of each requirement allocated to the system can be mapped to a subset of the objects within the model. The model is *consistent* if it suggests no contradictory behaviors. Finally, a *meaningful* model easily maps the products of the requirements analysis to an implementable design model. If the requirements allocated to the OFD objects cannot be implemented, there is little point in expending resources generating such a model.

Stated another way, a requirements model that does not accurately predict the behavior of the subject system is, at best, useless, and may be counterproductive. Because the OFD network reflects the behavior of the system as allocated to essential objects from the problem space, using the products of the Essential Requirements Model for guidance helps identify these objects and their behaviors.

Because the OFDs depend on the products of the Essential Requirements Model, the analyst must establish a baseline Essential Requirements Model (i.e., External Interface Diagram, External Events/Response List [EERL], and Object Relationship Diagrams) before beginning the OFDs! That's not to say that the products of the Essential Requirements Model won't change during development of the Essential Objects Model. To the contrary, knowledge gained during the creation of the OFD network may drive numerous modifications to the Essential Requirements Model products. For example, when considering the allocation of system behaviors to objects, it may become apparent there are situations not covered by the Essential Requirements Model or that two or more behaviors are contradictory. Part of the function of the Essential Objects Model is to identify such flaws in the model and drive them to resolution before too much effort is wasted on work that may need to be backed out of the model. *Although the Essential Requirements Model must be baselined before work on the Essential Objects Model begins, it cannot be finalized until the Essential Objects Model is complete.*

THE STRATEGY FOR OFD MODEL DEVELOPMENT

Before going too deeply into the details of the OFD generation heuristics, let's first consider the general strategy that will drive this process. Each of the steps will be covered in more detail in the remainder of this chapter.

1. From the Essential Requirements Model, use the ORD(s), supported by the EID and EERL, to create a preliminary OFD network.

    a. Objects and associative objects identified on the ORDs are often objects on the OFDs as well.

    b. Other external objects not represented as objects on the ORDs (e.g., corresponding to interface objects to EID external objects) may still require one or more objects on the OFD.

    c. Additional objects may be suggested by nouns in the EERLs.

2. Using each event/response pair on the EERL, "execute" the preliminary OFD network. This process should begin with the object that perceives the corresponding event and *traces* through each object necessary to provide the required response. If objects needed to provide the required event detection or responses are missing, add them.

3. When all event/response pairs have been traced through the objects on the OFDs, examine the structure of the resulting essential objects. Restructure as needed to enhance the object model based on information hiding and model consistency criteria.

4. Because the OFDs generated will probably entail many objects, the preliminary OFDs may be complex. Restructure the OFD network to create a hierarchy of objects that reduces the presentation complexity.

5. Iterate the above process as necessary to achieve a baseline top-level OFD.

6. Proceed to *decompose* the top-level OFD until each base object is decomposed on a separate OFD showing its fields and methods structure.

7. Specify each method (data process) as appropriate for the specific functions of the method.

The RTOOSA strategy concentrates on *objects*, as opposed to *classes*, that are important in the system's problem space. Each discovered object is represented by an object icon on the OFD network. All base objects, i.e., those that cannot be considered mechanisms that further decompose as interacting objects, decompose to their primitive elements (fields and methods) on a separate OFD. After all base objects have been defined, then the similarities among defined objects and between objects defined by the model and *classes* available from the reuse library may be undertaken as part of the design process.

Recall that the difference between requirements analysis and design is more one of mindset than of the order in which they are done. Analysis may be considered "making the right system" while design is "making the system right." At this point, do not permit existing classes to drive the requirements expressed in the OFDs. Do not add requirements to OFD objects merely because an existing class supports certain functions. Ensure that the OFDs reflect the minimum set of object requirements needed to specify the system.

Although the OFDs bear a physical resemblance to the data flow diagrams (or equivalent) of other real-time structured analysis methodologies, the above strategy departs from the *functional* or *algorithmic* decomposition required to generate their non-object-oriented cousins. To successfully generate a good OFD network, the analyst must first adopt the object-oriented mindset developed in Part I of this book.

This strategy also obviates the need to perform both functional and object-oriented analyses, as required by some hybrid methodologies. For example, the Ada Design Approach for Real-Time Systems (ADARTS) requires that the analyst first complete functional decomposition using any established methodology (Ward/Mellor RTSA, etc.). Then, three sets of guidelines based on information hiding and execution behaviors map the leaf node functional "bubbles" into object-like modules. Although this approach is useful for those not trained in object-oriented methodologies, it delays the inevitable adoption of an object-oriented mindset.

THE INITIAL TOP-LEVEL OFD NETWORK

The top-level Object Flow Diagram should contain all the key abstractions (objects and mechanisms) of the problem space and show their primary interactions. Begin with a blank sheet of paper (whiteboard, CASE tool, etc.). Make sure your sheet is big enough that you don't have to worry about limiting the number of objects you might discover during the early stages. Later refinements will merge some objects into abstractions to make the top-level OFD more manageable.

Begin placing object icons onto your sheet by considering first the objects identified in the Object Relationship Diagrams of the Essential Requirements Model. During this step, show only the object icons and do not worry about their interconnections.

1. If an ORD object corresponds to an external object on the EID, perhaps including the interface of the object to the system, draw a corresponding object icon on the top-level OFD to represent that object. Later analysis may cause you to separate the interface into a distinct object, but resist doing so at this early stage.

2. If an ORD object corresponds to an abstract object (e.g., "altitude error"), even if it cannot be directly identified in the environment, draw a corresponding object icon for the abstract object on the top-level OFD to represent that object.

3. If an ORD object corresponds to a necessary data base (e.g., "flight plan"), then draw an object icon on the top-level OFD to represent this object.

4. If an ORD object corresponds to an abstract notion of *modes* of operation, draw a control process icon on the top-level OFD to represent this

object. Chapter 14 showed how control processes are natural candidates for implementation as objects.

5. Apply your engineering judgment (*intuition*) to the remaining ORD objects. If an object is needed to describe the system's required behavior (e.g., the object is mentioned in the response column of the EERL), then add an object icon to the top-level OFD for this object.

6. Finally, consider the relationships (i.e., the diamond icons) on the ORDs:

   a. If a relationship suggests an object to retain state (e.g., remember parameters associated with an operation, etc.) or an object required to perform the operation (e.g., a table needed to determine operational parameters), then draw an object icon on the top-level OFD to represent the object.

   b. If the relationship merely suggests an operation that may be associated with one of the objects to which it relates, then the operation will be part of the behavior of that object. Do not show this as an object icon on the top-level OFD.

Again, the objects identified on the top-level OFD represent discrete entities, real or abstract, in the problem space. Do not prematurely restrict your understanding of the specific system's objects by pouring them into existing class molds. The purpose of requirements analysis is to specify a single system's requirements.

Figure 15.1 (External Interface Diagram), Table 15.1 (External Events/Response List), and Figure 15.3 (Object Relationship Diagram) suggest an Essential Requirements Model for the Space Station Freedom Audio/Video Distribution System (AVDS) case study described in Appendix D. (The dedicated student will have created a similar EID and EERL in response to Exercise 5 in Chapter 12.) A corresponding initial top-level OFD, shown in Figure 15.3, contains object icons for each of the objects identified in the ORD. Notice that the "Switch Routing" associative object on the ORD became a "Routing Tables" object in the OFD. Such renaming is perfectly acceptable as long as the relationship is easily recognized (or explicitly documented in the specification).

CAPTURING OBJECT DEFINITIONS

The ancient Chinese are credited with the saying that a picture is worth ten thousand words. There is much truth in this. When an engineer tries to explain some aspect of a complex system, invariably some type of diagram is quickly sketched on

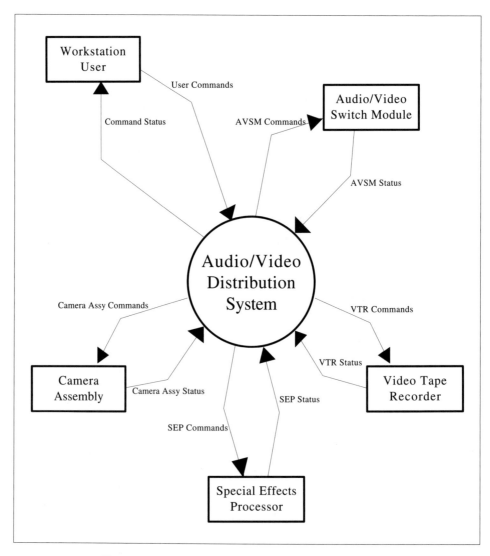

Figure 15.1. External Interface Diagram for the AVDS.

a sheet of scrap paper or a nearby blackboard to make the elements of the system and their relationships clear. However, the problem with relying on pictures to convey ideas is that two people may look at the same picture and each sees ten thousand words worth of different ideas. That is the nature of art. Viewing art is a personal and individual process. The engineer's quick diagrams work only because they are accompanied by a verbal explanation. Unfortunately, as engineers, we

Table 15.1. External Events/Response List for the AVDS.

No.	Event	Response	Perc.	Drives	Driven by	Event Group
1.	System initialization.	**1.** Indicate that all devices are unallocated. **2.** Indicate that all AVSM ports are unallocated. **3.** Poll all devices for health and status. Update status tables accordingly. **4.** Clear the Path Allocation Table to show no paths allocated.	dir	(all)		A, B, C
2.	User requests path set-up (not private).	**1.** Verify specified signal source and sink(s) are healthy and available. (If not, notify user.) **2.** Determine AVSM routing and allocate inter-AVSM port assignments. (If none available, notify user.) **3.** Send configuration map commands to the AVSM(s). **4.** Verify AVSM(s) configured as commanded. (If not, notify user.) **5.** Notify user path set-up is complete.	ind	4–9	1	A
3.	User requests path set-up (private).	**1.** Verify specified signal source and sink(s) are healthy and available. (If not, notify user.) **2.** AVDS temporarily substitutes the bar generator for the designated signal source **3.** Determine AVSM routing and allocate inter-AVSM port assignments. (If none available, notify user.) **4.** Disconnect any residual signal sinks on any of the allocated paths by connecting them to the bar generator. (Notify user of disconnects.) **5.** Send configuration map commands to the AVSM(s). **6.** Verify AVSM(s) configured as commanded. (If not, notify user.) **7.** Send configuration map command to the signal source AVSM to disconnect the bar generator and connect the designated signal source. **8.** Verify AVSM configured as commanded. **9.** Notify user private path set-up is complete.	ind	4–9	1	A

(continued)

Table 15.1. (continued)

No.	Event	Response	Perc.	Drives	Driven by	Event Group
4.	User commands camera assembly parameter(s).	1. Validate command (legal parameters, existing camera assembly, etc.). (Notify user if invalid command.) 2. Format command for camera assy. processing. 3. Send camera assy. command to the AVSM Camera Interface Unit via the Control Bus for transmission to the camera assy. on a video channel. 4. Determine AVSM routing and allocate inter-AVSM port assignments to send camera signal to camera I/F unit. 5. Send configuration map command to the AVSM(s). 6. Verify AVSM(s) configured as commanded. 7. Accept camera assembly command echo and verify against original command. (If fails to match, notify user.) 8. Notify user that command successfully sent to camera assembly.	ind		2 or 3	B
5.	User commands camera assembly built-in-test.	1. Validate command (existing camera assembly). (Notify user if invalid command.) 2. Send BIT command to the AVSM Camera Interface Unit via the Control Bus for transmission to the camera assy on a video channel. 3. Determine AVSM routing and allocate inter-AVSM port assignments to send camera signal to camera I/F unit. 4. Send configuration map command to the AVSM(s). 5. Verify AVSM(s) configured as commanded. 6. Accept camera assembly health and status data. 7. Compare health and status data to nominal value to identify fault conditions. Mark camera assembly Go/NoGo status accordingly. 8. Return camera assembly health and status data to user.	ind		2 or 3	B

No.	Event	Response	Perc.	Drives	Driven by	Event Group
6.	User commands VTR controls.	**1.** Validate command (legal parameters, existing VTR, etc.). (Notify user if invalid command.) **2.** Format command for VTR processing. **3.** Send VTR command to the VTRI driving the specified VTR. **4.** Send command to the VTR to read current status. **5.** Accept VTR status data. **6.** Compare current parameters to those commanded. (If fails to match, notify user.) **7.** Notify user that command successfully sent to VTR.	ind		2 or 3	B
7.	User commands VTR built-in-test.	**1.** Validate command (existing VTR). (Notify user if invalid command.) **2.** Send BIT command to the VTRI driving the specified VTR. **3.** Send command to VTR to read current status. **4.** Accept VTR health and status data. **5.** Compare health and status data to nominal values to identify fault conditions. Mark VTR Go/NoGo status accordingly. **6.** Return VTR health and status data to user.	ind		2 or 3	B
8.	User commands SEP controls.	**1.** Validate command (legal parameters, existing SEP, etc.). (Notify user if invalid command.) **2.** Format command for SEP processing. **3.** Send SEP command to the specified SEP. **4.** Send command to SEP to read current status. **5.** Accept SEP status data. **6.** Compare current parameters to those commanded. (If fails to match, notify user.) **7.** Notify user that command successfully sent to SEP.	ind		2 or 3	B

(continued)

Table 15.1 (continued)

No.	Event	Response	Perc.	Drives	Driven by	Event Group
9.	User commands SEP built-in-test.	**1.** Validate command (existing SEP). (Notify user if invalid command.) **2.** Send BIT command to the specified SEP. **3.** Send command to SEP to read current status. **4.** Accept SEP health and status data. **5.** Compare health and status data to nominal values to identify fault conditions. Mark SEP Go/NoGo status accordingly. **6.** Return SEP health and status data to user.	ind		2 or 3	B
10.	60-second timer interval lapse.	**1.** Interrogate each AVSM, SEP, VTR, and camera assembly (in turn) for health and status. **2.** Compare health and status data to nominal values to identify fault conditions. Mark device Go/NoGo status accordingly. **3.** Notify user of devices with changed status to "Go."	tmp	11–16	1	C
11.	AVSM fault, affects all ports.	**1.** Attempt to reroute "pass-thru" paths through other AVSM(s). **2.** Notify user of failed device.	ind		10	C
12.	AVSM fault, not on all ports.	**1.** Attempt to reroute "pass-thru" paths on alternate ports. **2.** If unable to reroute thru same AVSM on alternate ports, attempt to reroute through other AVSM(s). **3.** Notify user of failed device.	ind		10	C
13.	Camera Interface Unit fault.	**1.** Notify user of failed device.	ind		10	C
14.	SEP fault.	**1.** Notify user of failed device.	ind		9 or 10	C
15.	VTR fault.	**1.** Notify user of failed device.	ind		7 or 10	C
16.	Camera Assembly fault.	**1.** Notify user of failed device.	ind		5 or 10	C

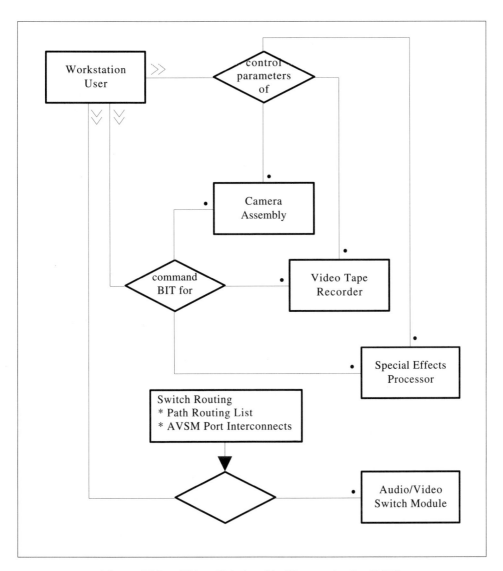

Figure 15.2.   Object Relationship Diagram for the AVDS.

cannot trust individual interpretations to pervade the viewing of pictures used to represent engineering data.

I have sat in software reviews in which data flow diagrams (DFDs) were presented. Because the presenter thought a particular DFD spoke for itself, it was accompanied by little verbal elaboration. Everyone in the room nodded agreement

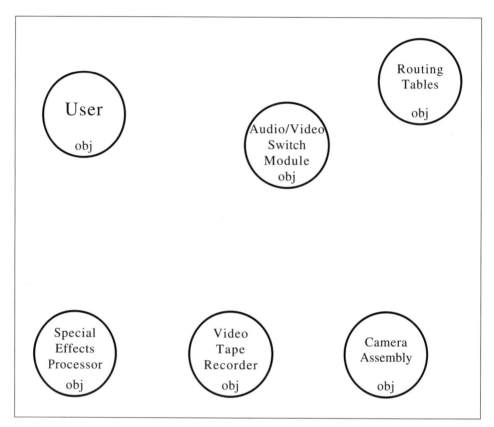

Figure 15.3.   Initial top-level OFD for the AVDS based on objects identified on the ORD.

that the meaning was obvious. However, when a problem arose later, reexamination of the DFD revealed that everybody's obvious understanding of the diagram reflected several conflicting interpretations.

Some engineering organizations try to short-cut the data flow diagram process by eliminating the specification of the processing underlying the leaf node processes. Such a decision introduces risk because the "obvious" meanings of these processes are not always commonly understood by all users of the diagram.

At this stage of OFD generation, the analyst is sitting in front of a (big) sheet showing unconnected object icons. Nothing specific has been assumed regarding content of those objects. To prevent future confusion about assumptions made concerning a specific object's structure or behaviors, RTOOSA provides a way to capture such assumptions.

For each object identified on the preliminary top-level OFD, take a blank 4" x 6" card, sheet of paper, or electronic equivalent. These cards will capture the essential characteristics of the system objects as *Object Templates* (OTs). First, identify the object at the top of the card. On each card, you will define the data structures (fields) and behaviors (methods) assigned to the corresponding object as such data becomes known. Now, assume that each object must have a constructor (assigned a constructor name determined by convention), so list it on the card under the object name. The resulting cards, showing the initial OTs for the AVDS case study, appear in Figure 15.4.

Throughout the remaining OFD generation, each decision affecting the data

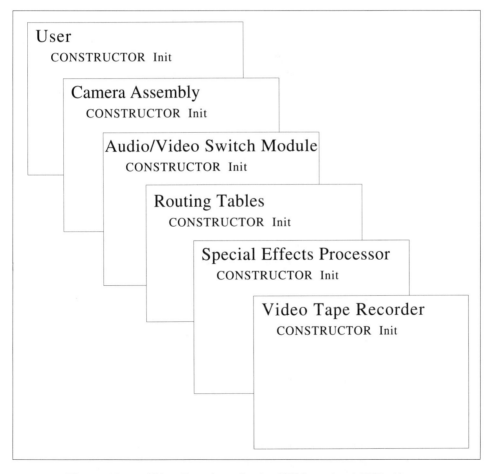

Figure 15.4. Object Templates for the AVDS top-level OFD objects.

structure or procedures and functions (methods) associated with the object should be captured immediately on the corresponding OT. I have found that failing to capture key decisions as they are made often results in later confusion when, under the weight of a multitude of other information and decisions, the basis of a key element becomes forgotten and forever lost. It is all too easy to forget completely the underlying foundation of an object in a complex system. Don't trust your memory to generate the backup data weeks, days, or even hours later.

INITIAL OBJECT EVALUATIONS

Emphasis in the top-level OFD generation now shifts from the information provided by the ORD to that provided by the EERL. The EERL describes what the system must do in response to events occurring in the system's environment. As already concluded, everything an embedded real-time system does is in response to events in its environment. Therefore, the EERL should provide a comprehensive guide, and later confirming checklist, for the completeness of the OFD network.

There are two primary elements of object specification when considering an event/response pair from the EERL. First, there must be one or more objects that allow the system to recognize the occurrence of the specific event. Then, there are the objects associated with the response to that event. The analysis strategy for each event/response pair on the EERL is as follows:

1. If the external event perception is *direct* or *indirect*, identify the object(s) responsible for event recognition. Normally, this object represents the EID external object from which the event emanates. If the event is *temporal*, identify the object that is assigned responsibility for initiating the time-based "thread of execution." This object will usually have some type of "system clock" input event.

2. Trace the EERL narrative of the event's response from object to object, ensuring that each object required to contribute to the specified response is depicted. Add any necessary objects that are not already present.

3. As this process visits the various objects on the OFD, add a brief note to the corresponding OTs to describe the nature of the visit (e.g., "to cause computation of the updated windspeed," "to retrieve the current value of the wind speed," "to determine the bearing to the next Navigation Point and return the value," etc.). Later, these expressions will be converted to method names and specified with the appropriate formal parameter list.

4. As you travel from object to object on the OFD, draw the appropriate messages or data/event flows to illustrate the interobject interfaces.

To illustrate this process, consider Event 2 from the AVDS EERL (see Table 15.1). The EID (Figure 15.1) shows that *User_Commands* arrive from the external object *Workstation User* as discrete data flows. It is reasonable to assume that the "User request" for a "path set-up" called out as Event 2 will be one of these *User_Commands* (to be formalized in the *User_Commands* Data Dictionary Element defintion). Therefore, this discrete data flow is carried down to the preliminary OFD and shown as an input to the *User* object there. This allocation assigns responsibility for recognizing this indirectly perceived event to the *User* object. With event recognition complete, proceed to the required responses for this event.

The first response to Event 2 is to "Verify specified signal source and sink(s) are healthy and available. (If not, notify user)." There are several ways that the analyst may proceed at this point. For example, maintaining knowledge of the system configuration could be allocated to the *User* object, and the *User* could interrogate the various devices directly. However, the *User* is only coincidentally interested in specific configuration data and therefore an unlikely candidate to which to allocate such responsibility. The *Audio/Video Switch Module (AVSM)*, on the other hand, must maintain a record of device assignments and interconnections (i.e., the switch settings that establish the device interconnections). It would be reasonable to expect the *AVSM* object also to remember the health status of those devices. If the maintenance of device status is allocated to the *AVSM* object, the *User* object must work through the *AVSM* object to report device health status. In fact, it doesn't take much thought to conclude that, if the *User* object were to send the path set-up request to the *AVSM* object, then the *AVSM* could worry about checking the health and availability of the associated devices and return status data to the *User* object in case a requested object was unavailable for the requested set-up. For this to happen, a message, such as *path_setup_req*, must be sent by the *User* to the *AVSM*. Then, for the *AVSM* object to check and update the status of the various devices, it must send messages requesting each object to return its status. Figure 15.5 shows these message interfaces among the OFD objects. Our imaginary "execution" ends up (unless there is a fault) with the *AVSM* object.

The second response to Event 2 is to "Determine AVSM routing and allocate inter-AVSM port assignments." To perform this event, the *AVSM* must know how the various AVSMs are interconnected. Two questions must be answered to perform this function. First, there must be some way to represent all possible routing between any two AVSMs. For example, in some cases two AVSMs are directly connected while other AVSMs may require connections through one or more

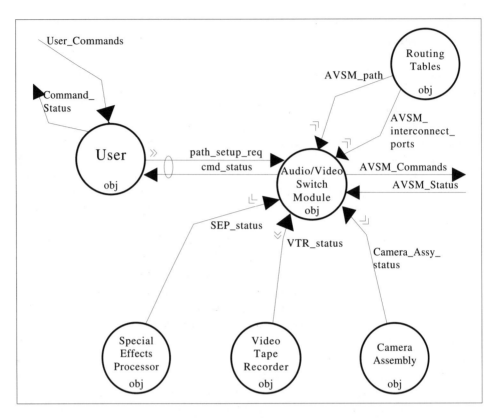

Figure 15.5. Top-level OFD for the AVDS after adding object/object messages for EERL Events 2 and 3.

intervening AVSMs. A second data set must identify the input/output port interconnections between adjacent AVSMs. These two appear to be the key data structures of the *Routing Tables* object. Our analysis concludes that the *AVSM* must send messages to the *Routing Tables* object requesting first an *AVSM_path* and then the *AVSM_interconnect_ports* to establish that path from the source device to the sink device AVSM(s). Finally, the internal data structures of the *AVSM* must be updated to reflect the allocations. However, this is internal to the *AVSM* object and does not show on the top-level OFD.

The third response to Event 2 is to "Send configuration map commands to the AVSM(s)." This response appears as the *AVSM_Commands* output from the *AVSM* object to the external object *Audio/Video Switch Module* (shown on the EID, Figure 15.1).

The fourth response to Event 2 is to "Verify AVSM(s) configured as commanded. (If not, notify user.)" The AVSM performs this operation by accepting the discrete input *AVSM_Status* from the *Audio/Video Switch Module* (again, shown on the EID) and comparing it to the commanded state. Failures are reflected by the *cmd_status* returned to the *User* for output as *Command_Status*.

The final response to Event 2 is to "Notify user path set-up is complete." This requires the *AVSM* object to return the successful *cmd_status* to the *User* object, which, in turn, sends the *Command_Status discrete* output to the *Workstation User*.

Analysis for recognition for Event 3 and its responses discovers no additional object interfaces. However, some additional behaviors must be added to the *AVSM* object. For example, there is the requirement to "unallocate" paths and ports to establish privacy. Figure 15.5 captures the state of the emerging top-level AVDS OFD following the consideration of Events 2 and 3.

Notice that the narrative carrying us through the above analysis allocated certain data structures to specific objects. Further, those allocations made assumptions regarding the contents and, in some cases, formats of those data structures. Being careful not to lose these decisions and assumptions, we immediately update the corresponding OTs. Figure 15.6 shows the two major data structures and three behaviors (in addition to the constructor) that have been allocated. Each of the data structures is also given a provisional definition. The notation used to represent the data structure contents will be introduced in Chapter 16 as that used to define Data Dictionary Elements.

Figure 15.7 provides a similar definition for the *Routing Tables* object with its two data structures, described in the narrative, and its required behaviors. Although the Data Dictionary Element notation may be concise, it may be less than easy to visualize. The analyst must not feel constrained to using formal notations in capturing the analysis decisions. For example, the *Routing Tables* object data structures might be more clearly shown as interconnection matrices. Figure 15.8 illustrates how the *AVSM_Routing_Table* data structure is more understandable when drawn to show how AVSMs (represented by the matrix rows) may be connected to the other AVSMs (represented by the matrix columns). Figure 15.9 provides a similar matrix that illustrates, for the direct AVSM-to-AVSM connections, which "from" AVSM output ports connect to which "to" AVSM input ports. Again, this representation is more meaningful to most engineers (excluding a few software engineers) and managers than the more formal Data Dictionary Element format. The primary objective of the analyst's efforts must be to capture the key data in a form that others can understand easily.

The process of tracing "execution" through event recognition and response processing must eventually include every event on the EERL. Figure 15.10 shows the state of the top-level OFD following consideration of Event 4 ("User commands camera assembly parameter(s)."). Notice that a new object, the *Camera Interface Unit*, was discovered during the analysis of this event/response pair and now appears on the top-level OFD.

Figure 15.11 shows the state of the top-level OFD following analysis of Event 5 ("User commands camera assembly built-in-test."). While analyzing this event/response pair, similarities to the messages defined in the previous step were

Audio/Video Switch Module

```
Device_Data_Table = (data store)
    {   Device_Type              * enumerated type*
      + System_Device_ID         * integer 1..n *
      + Device_Name              * of form: "VTR#2" *
      + AVSM_and_Inp_Port        *  pair: (1..6, 0..15) *
      + AVSM_and_Out_Port        *  pair: (1..6, 0..15) *
      + Health                   * [ Go | NoGo ] *
      + Allocation               * [ Free | InUse ] *
      + Priviate                 * boolean *    }
Path_Allocation_Table = (data store)
    {   Logical_Path_ID          * integer 1..n *
      + Requester_ID             * format tbd *
      + Private                  * boolean *
      + 1{   AVSM_ID             * integer: 1..6 *
           + Inp_Port            * integer: 0..15*
           + Out_Port  }n        * integer: 0..15*    }
CONSTRUCTOR  Init
Run_BIT
Allocate_Path ( Mode : [Private | NotPrivate] )
Unallocate_Path
Unallocate_Port
```

Figure 15.6.   Object Template for the AVSM after considering EERL Events 2 and 3.

noted. Rather than carrying separate message flows for each, the similar messages were abstracted to a higher level *Camera_Assy_Cmd* and *Camera_Assy_Status*. The formal definition of these abstractions must be made as Data Dictionary Elements, as will be described in the next chapter.

Finally, Figure 15.12 represents the completed preliminary top-level OFD for the AVDS. The analyst can demonstrate how each event/response pair is fully considered by the behaviors of the objects shown individually and with one another. Before you get too frustrated trying to convince me that it fails in one or more

Routing Tables

```
AVSM_Routing_Table = ( data store )
   * table giving possible paths (direct or via intervening
     AVSMs) between source and sink device AVSMs  *
   1,1{  [  "None"                    * no interconnecting path *
         |[  "Direct"                 * AVSMs connect directly *
             |{ AVSM_ID } ]  ]  }6,6*  ordered list of AVSMs  *
AVSM_Interrconnect_Table = ( data store )
   * table lists physical connections between the output ports
     of one AVSM and the input ports of another  *
   1,1{  [  "None"                    * no interconnecting links *
         |{    Out_Port               * source AVSM output port *
           + Inp_Port } ] }6,6    * sink AVSM input port *
CONSTRUCTOR  Init
Find_AVSM_Path(  in       Source_AVSM : integer 1..6;
                 in       Sink_AVSM  : integer 1..6;
                out AVSM_List  : array of AVSM IDs )
Find_AVSM_Ports(  in       Source_AVSM : integer 1..6;
                  in       Sink_AVSM : integer 1..6;
                 out Source_AVSM_Output_Port : 0..15;
                 out Sink_AVSM_Input_Port:  0..15  )
```

Figure 15.7.   Object Template for the Routing Tables after considering EERL Events 2 and 3.

To AVSM # From AVSM #	**1**	**2**	**3**	**4**	**5**	**6**
1	None	Direct Via 3	Direct Via 2	Via 3 Via 2,3		
2	Direct	None	Direct	Via 3		
3		Direct	None	Direct		
4				None		
5					None	
6						None

Use whatever format best expresses the information!

Figure 15.8.   A graphic representation of the AVSM Routing Table.

cases, remember that you must have the corresponding OTs to understand the assumptions made while deriving this OFD.

BEGINNING TO CONSOLIDATE THE TOP-LEVEL OFD

I doubt that anyone will disagree with me if I say that Figure 15.12, the completed preliminary top-level OFD for the AVDS, is confusing. When an OFD contains too many objects or the number of inter-object interfaces becomes large, the value

From AVSM # \ To AVSM #	1	2	3	4	5	6
1	None	#7 -> #3 #8 -> #4	#9 -> #3 #10 -> #10 #11 -> #4	None		
2	#2 -> #7 #3 -> #9 #5 -> #13	None	#1 -> #2 #6 -> #5	None		
3		#5 -> #5 #7 -> #6 #8 -> #12	None	#6 -> #1 #9 -> #2		
4				None		
5					None	
6						None

Figure 15.9.   A graphic representation of a table that depicts the way AVSMs are interconnected.

of the OFD diminishes quickly because it becomes difficult to understand. Even the analyst who created such an OFD will begin to have problems recalling its meaning after a time. In general, the optimum amount of data can be gleaned from an OFD that has seven (plus or minus two) object and process icons (reference George Miller's often-cited paper "The Magical Number Seven, Plus or Minus Two: Some Limits on Our Capacity for Processing Information" [Miller, 1956]).

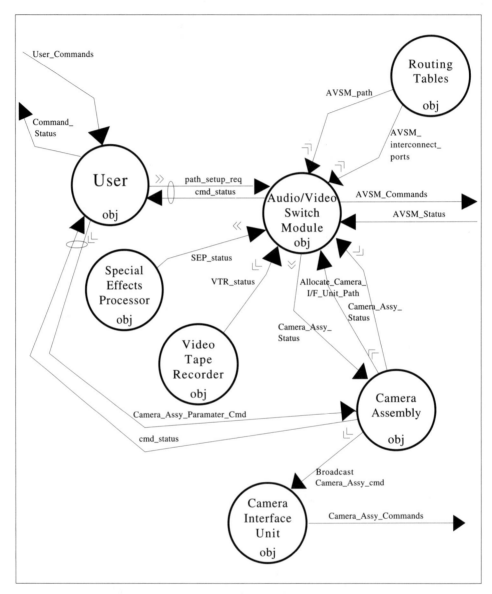

Figure 15.10.   Top-level AVDS OFD after EERL Event 4.

This rule-of-thumb becomes much more important when the number of flows among the icons becomes large and the pattern of those interfaces is somewhat random. OFD consolidation should proceed with a goal of controlling the number

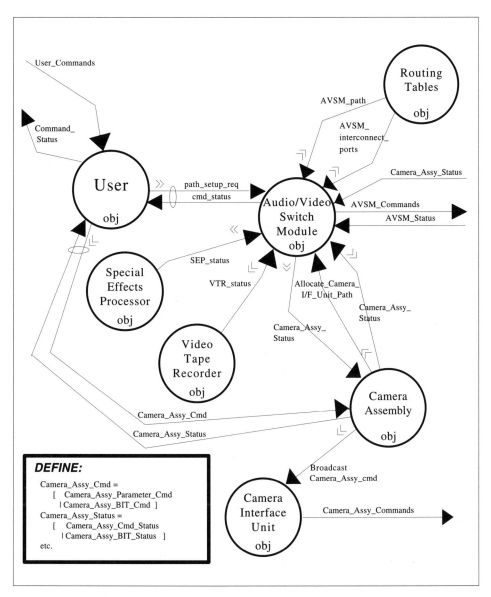

Figure 15.11. Top-level AVDS OFD after EERL Event 5.

of object and process icons and their interconnecting interfaces.

The general ways to consolidate objects in an OFD are demonstrated by the following guidelines:

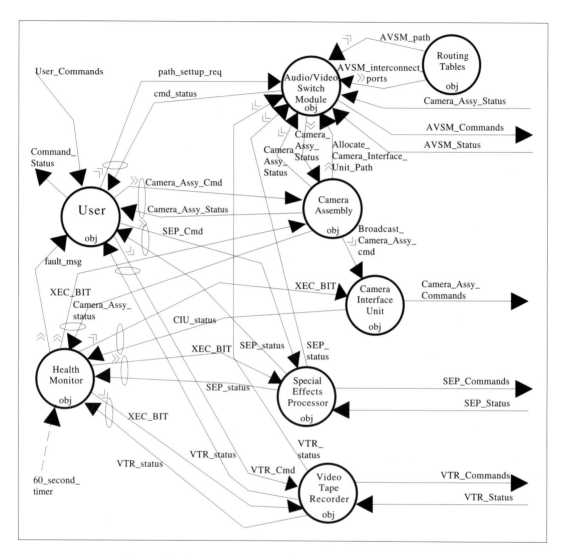

Figure 15.12. Preliminary top-level AVDS OFD—complete.

1. When a group of objects interact to emulate the behavior of a more complex object, substitute a single object icon for the newly defined mechanism on the top-level OFD. In very large systems, repeating this process by grouping multiple mechanisms can lead to abstract *objects* representing subsystems.

2. When a group of similar objects, with similar interfaces, can be identified on the top-level OFD, create an abstract object icon to represent the more specific descendent objects on the top-level OFD network. These objects need not always be implemented by an ancestor/descendents relationship.

Returning to the preliminary top-level OFD in Figure 15.12, consider the *Routing Tables* object. This object interfaces only with one other object, the *AVSM*. This is a relatively tight coupling that allows the two objects to be treated as a mechanism. The top of Figure 15.13 highlights the original two objects and their coupling. Using our first consolidation guideline, these interacting objects can be replaced by an object icon representing the equivalent mechanism (call it, perhaps, *AVSM Controller*) on the top-level OFD. The bottom of Figure 15.13 shows the icon for the resulting mechanism.

Further analysis of the preliminary top-level OFD shows considerable similarity among the various video device objects (camera assembly, SEP, VTR, etc.). Each video device object interfaces with other AVDS objects by accepting messages that command built-in-test or control device operational parameters and by sending messages that report the device status to the *Health Monitor* object. Figure 15.14 suggests an abstract object that might be used to replace the individual device objects on the top-level OFD.

After these substitutions are made on the top-level OFD, the revised OFD becomes considerably easier to understand. Figure 15.15 shows the resulting top-level OFD.

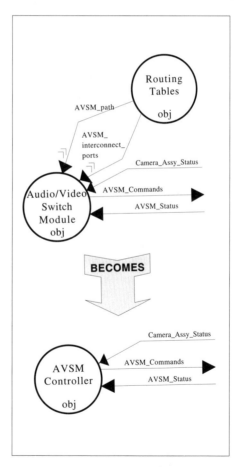

Figure 15.13.   Merging two objects to become a mechanism.

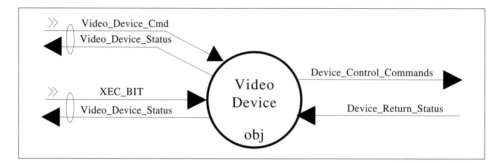

Figure 15.14. Capturing multiple similar objects in an abstract object.

Once the top-level OFD has been baselined, the objects representing subsystems, mechanisms, or generalized object abstractions must be expanded on separate OFDs to show their constituent elements. This process should not be difficult because much of this "decomposition" should be recovering the elements that were combined during the consolidation process.

DECOMPOSING THE TOP-LEVEL OFD NETWORK

Each object and data/control process on the OFDs must be expanded. The following guidelines suggest how this decomposition must proceed.

1. Nonbase objects (i.e., objects that represent subsystems, mechanisms, or groups of similar objects) must be decomposed by a lower-level OFD that exposes the constituent objects represented by the nonbase object icon.

2. Base objects (i.e., objects that do not represent subsystems, mechanisms, or groups of similar objects) should be decomposed by:

   a. An OFD that identifies the object *fields* as data and event stores and its *methods* as data processes, and

   b. An OT that captures the essential descriptive information for each object.

3. Nonbase control and data processes must be expanded by lower-level OFDs that expose the functional processes represented by the process icons on the higher-level OFD.

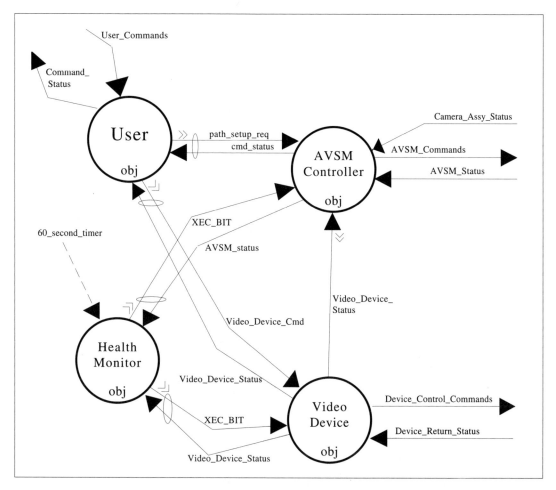

Figure 15.15.   Revised top-level OFD for the AVDS.

4. Control processes should be explained by a State Transition Diagram (STD).

5. Data processes at a sufficiently low level of abstraction should be expanded using a presentation that best explains the functional requirements. Some typical means of representing data processes include:

   a. Program Design Language (PDL), Process Specification (P-Spec), or equivalent structured English.

b. State Transition Diagram (STD).

c. Decision Tree.

d. Truth Table.

e. "Control Theory" Diagrams.

f. Preprocess/Postprocess Specification.

g. Other, application-dependent technique.

When a higher-level process or more abstract object is decomposed, the procedure must be repeated on the resulting OFDs until all icons are represented in an appropriate process definition.

REPRESENTING AN OBJECT WITH A SEPARATE OFD

Part of the analysis process involves exposing the essential requirement for each object. RTOOSA provides two ways to do this. Already, the OTs have gathered the field and method requirements for each object. Although the OT "cards" may use arbitrary graphic formats, they are generally text-based. The second representation is predominantly graphic. That is, an OFD base object icon can be decomposed by a separate OFD that shows the essential elements of the object consisting of object fields represented as data and event stores and methods shown as data processes.

The arguments for using graphic representations of model elements drive showing the decomposed object with an OFD. Further, the resulting OFD can be *balanced* with the higher-level diagram(s) that interface with the object to ensure that the OT is complete.

For each base object shown on an OFD, create another OFD that depicts the essential constituent elements of that object. Use the OT as a source of data for this OFD:

1. For each data field identified on the OT, draw a data store (or event store, if appropriate) on the OFD.

a. Using the notation provided in Chapter 16, add or update the Data Dictionary Element (DDE) corresponding to that data or event store. Decompose the DDE if it is a complex data structure.

b. These data stores will become class fields during the implementation of the objects.

2. For each method (i.e., procedure or function) identified on the OT, draw a data process on the OFD.

   a. These data processes will often become class methods during the implementation of the objects.

3. Consult the OFD on which the object appears as a single icon. Verify that all messages and data/event flows to and from the object appear as inputs/outputs to the data processes (or, in exceptional cases, data stores) on the object's OFD. Always ensure that the object interfaces from the higher-level OFD are consistent with those shown as off-page flows at the lower-level OFD.

4. Consult the ORD(s) for relationships between the subject object and other objects not accounted for by the processes on the OFD. Correct either the ORD or the OFD to ensure there is consistency between these requirements model elements.

5. Fill in the internal data/event flows on the object's OFD that are necessary to describe the essential object behavior. During the process of defining object behavior, the need for internal data/control processes may arise. In general, only internal processes (i.e., with no message or data/event flow interfaces outside the object) should be discovered at this stage. Be sure to update the Data Dictionary to include DDEs for each new data/event flow added.

6. Decompose the data/control processes as previously described (to lower-level OFDs, PDL, STD, etc.).

Let's consider another case study to illustrate the object decomposition process. Appendix A describes the requirements for a hypothetical autopilot system for the specialized gunship application. You may have generated an Essential Requirements Model for this system as Exercise 6 of Chapter 13. The gunship Essential Requirements Model should be similar to that illustrated in Figure 15.16 (External Interface Diagram), Table 15.2 (External Events/Response List), and 15.17 (Object Relationship Diagram). Using the top-level OFD strategy described in this chapter leads to an OFD such as that shown in Figure 15.18.

OFD decomposition suggests a hierarchical relationship among the various resulting OFDs. To administer the decomposition process better, we define an object/process numbering mechanism that depicts the relationship among icons on the various OFDs. First, each object and data/control process on the top-level OFD is assigned a top-level identification number of the form $X.0$ (where X is an integer). Figure 15.19 repeats the system top-level OFD with the object identification numbers added. When one of these objects is decomposed on a separate OFD, the identification number for each of the object/process icons on the resulting OFD will begin with the same integer used to identify the object from the top-level OFD, followed by successive second level integers.

To illustrate this mapping between OFDs, the object *INS* (Inertial Navigation System) on the top-level OFD (Figure 15.19) is assigned the identification number 1.0. When the object *INS* is decomposed by the OFD shown in Figure 15.20, each of its processes is numbered 1.*Y* (where *Y* is an integer). The OT for the *INS* object specifies two required behaviors and one field. The *Sample INS* method (identification number 1.1) is activated by a periodic event flow to have it read the continuously available *aircraft_position* and store a value in the *Current_INS_Aircraft_Position* field (data store). When the *AutoPilot* object (identifi-

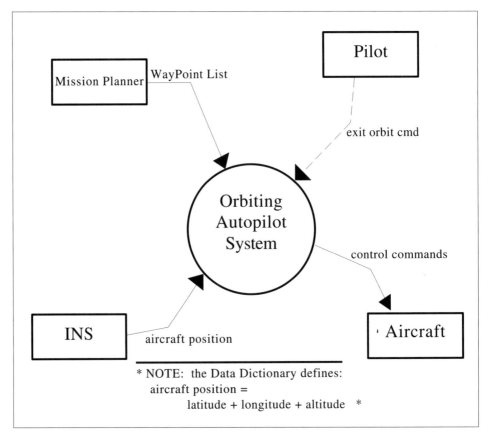

Figure 15.16. External Interface Diagram for the gunship's orbiting autopilot system.

cation number 5.0 on the top-level OFD) needs the current aircraft position, it sends a message that is processed by the *AirCraft Position Is* method (identification number 1.2), which returns *AC_position* to the requester.

Similarly, Figure 15.21 illustrates the decomposed *WayPoint List* object (identification number 2.0 on the top-level OFD). This object decomposes to the four methods and two fields shown in the figure. The behavior of this object is captured in the functions of the identified methods:

1. The *system initialization* event activates the *Import Waypoint List* method (identification number 2.1). This method copies the externally

Table 15.2. External Events/Response List for the gunship's orbiting autopilot system.

No.	Event	Response	Perc.	Drives	Driven by	Event Group
1.	Pilot activates the system.	**1.** Select the first waypoint from the Waypoint List. **2.** Determine a course from the aircraft current position and the first navpoint position. **3.** Begin generating control commands necessary to fly to the first waypoint.	dir	(all)		A
2.	Aircraft reaches waypoint.	**1.** From Waypoint List, for this waypoint, retrieve distance, elevation, and speed at which to orbit. **2.** Orbit the waypoint using the corresponding parameters.	ind		1	A
3.	Pilot commands "exit orbit" (not at last waypoint)	**1.** Select the next waypoint from the Waypoint List. **2.** Determine the course from the current waypoint position to the next waypoint position. **3.** Begin generating control commands necessary to fly to the next waypoint.	dir		2	A
4.	Pilot commands "exit orbit" (at last waypoint)	**1.** Notify pilot "at last waypoint." **2.** Continue orbit.	dir		2	A
5.	Pilot deactivates the system.	**1.** Cease generating control commands.	dir		1	A

provided *Waypoint List* shown on the system EID (Figure 15.16) to the object field data store *Waypoint List* shown on Figure 15.21.

2. As the system moves the aircraft from one waypoint to the next, it must sequence through the individual waypoints in the *Waypoint List* field. The method *Select Next WP* (identification number 2.2) is invoked by a message from outside the object, initially and when each waypoint is

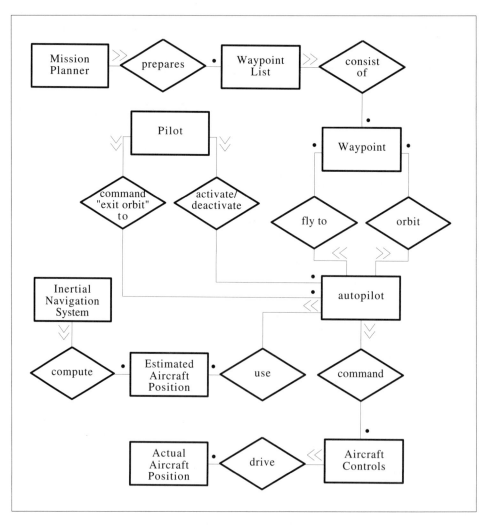

Figure 15.17. Object Relationship Diagram for the gunship's orbiting autopilot system.

reached, to select the next waypoint from the *Waypoint List* and store its identification in the *Current Target Waypoint* data store. Because other methods need knowledge of the current leg target, this datum is maintained as a separate field.

3. The *AutoPilot* object must draw an imaginary line to the current waypoint that has been selected as the current leg's target. When invoked by a message from the *AutoPilot* object, the *Course to WP Is* method (identification number 2.3) responds by returning the *Course_to_Waypoint*.

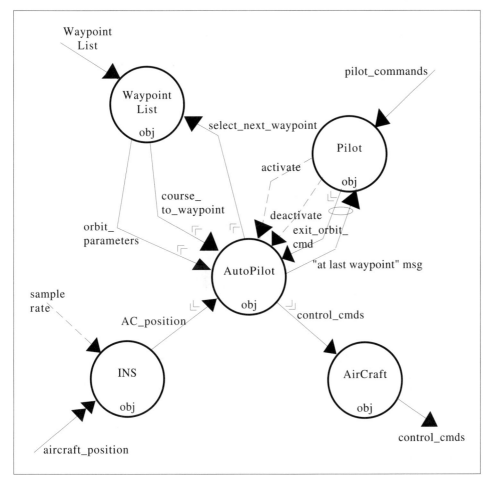

Figure 15.18. A top-level OFD for the Orbiting Autopilot System.

4. Finally, when the aircraft approaches the *Current Target Waypoint*, it must begin to orbit that waypoint. When the *AutoPilot* object determines the aircraft is sufficiently close to the waypoint, it sends a message to the method *Orbit Parameters Are* (identification number 2.4) requesting return of the waypoint's *orbit_parameters*.

The sufficiency of the requirements model must be examined at all levels of the analysis process. This is why the Essential Requirements Model cannot be finalized until the system behavior analysis is complete, determined by the comple-

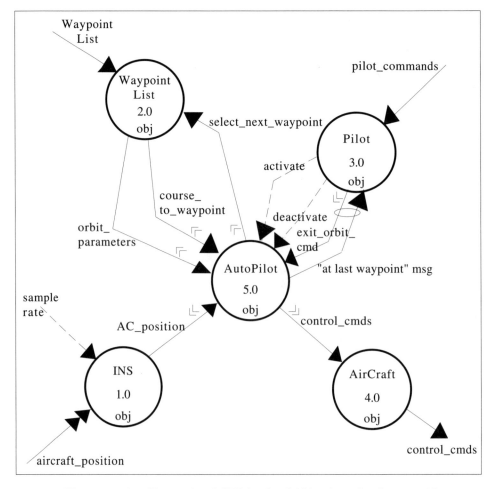

Figure 15.19. The top-level OFD for the Orbiting Autopilot System with Icon Identification numbers assigned.

tion of the Essential Objects Model. Often the analyst will not detect holes in the requirements until the behaviors of the individual methods have been defined.

Consider again the methods just described for the decomposed *Waypoint List* object. When attempting to specify the requirements for these four methods, the astute analyst discovers there are problems with the object as defined. Specifically, the following questions are unanswered:

1. The *Select Next WP* method will increment the index into the *Waypoint List* to identify the next list element as the new *Current Target Waypoint*. As this is specified, the method assumes there is a former *Current Target Waypoint* index that can be incremented. What is this object's requirement to handle the initialization problem of selecting the first waypoint in the list?

2. That same *Select Next WP* method can only increment the list index until it points to the last waypoint in the list. What is the object's required behavior when it is at the last waypoint and another *Select Next WP* message arrives?

3. The *Course to WP Is* method knows the target waypoint to which the imaginary flight path line must be drawn. However, what location should be used as the other end of that line?

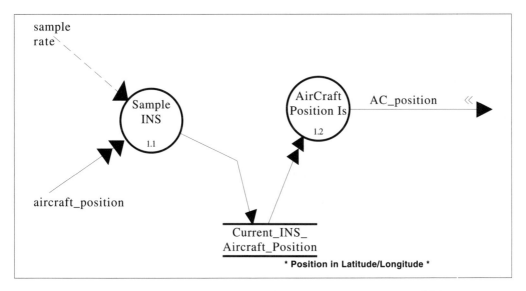

Figure 15.20. The decomposed "INS" object from the top-level OFD of the gunship's orbiting autopilot system.

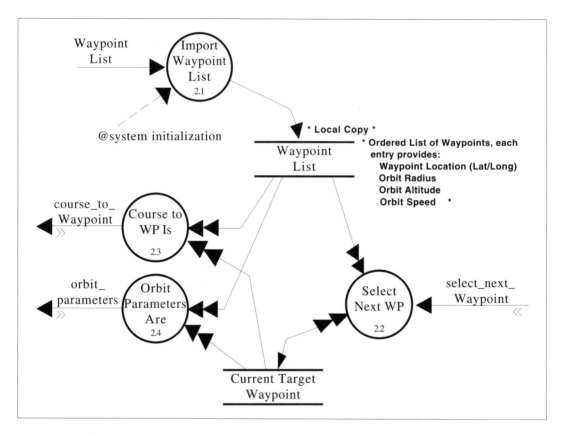

Figure 15.21. The decomposed "Waypoint" object from the top-level OFD of the gunship's orbiting autopilot system.

As such inconsistencies are encountered, the analyst must determine the required behavior. This new knowledge must then be added to the corresponding object definition. For example, a new method might be identified to answer the first question. As illustrated in Figure 15.22, a new method to *Select First WP* (identification number 2.5) allows the external client to initialize the flight path sequence by forcing entry at the first waypoint in the list. This new method also can address the previously unasked question "What happens if there is no *Waypoint List*?" A returned response *invalid_Waypoint* can notify the external client that the course cannot be used.

The second question can be addressed by having the *Select Next WP* method return a flag to indicate the *at_last_Waypoint* state. The selected solution to the third question requires the client to provide the *AC_position* to the *Course to WP*

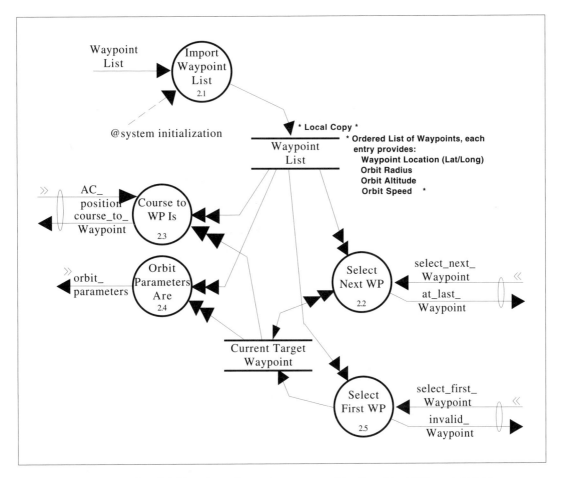

Figure 15.22. Additional requirements uncovered for the object "Waypoint List."

Is method. This defines a requirement for the computation always to be from the aircraft's current position to the *Current Target Waypoint*.

Adding messages or data/event flows to the object's interface definition, as we just did to solve deficiencies in the object behavior, makes this modified OFD inconsistent with the object's icon interface on the higher-level OFD. *Unbalanced* OFDs must be made again consistent by flowing the new interfaces to the higher-level OFD. Figure 15.23 shows how the top-level OFD is changed to make it again consistent with the new *Waypoint List* decomposed OFD.

When addressing deficiencies in the OFDs, the analyst walks a thin line between extracting additional *derived requirements* and injecting arbitrary *self-*

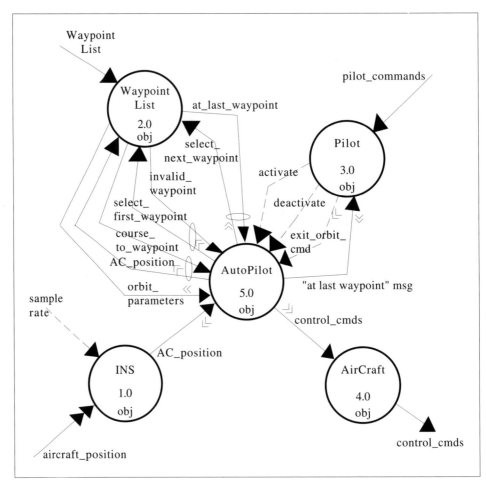

Figure 15.23.   Discovered requirements are elevated to the
Orbiting Autopilot System's top-level OFD.

imposed requirements into the requirements model. Chapter 9 defined the various types of requirements and described why *self-imposed requirements* are generally undesirable. The *customer* must understand that adding specific behaviors to the requirements model may unnecessarily restrict the developer's options through the remainder of the development cycle.

I consider the proposed responses to the first two questions examples of *derived requirements*. Any reasonable engineer must conclude that list processing must handle the special cases of the first and last entries in the list. Contrast these questions to the third. There is nothing intuitive about continually recomputing the course from the current aircraft position to the target waypoint. In fact, navigation systems seldom work this way! (See the LoCoDoNS definition in Appendix C for a more typical approach.) Calling the proposed solution a *derived requirement* violates our definition of this requirement type. This would clearly be a self-imposed requirement that faces the additional risk of being unacceptable to the system's ultimate user.

Locking down missing requirements is a two-edged sword. On the one hand, restricting the definition of the system's behavior prevents the developer from providing undesirable behaviors for otherwise unspecified situations. Having the customer define such previously missing requirements reduces the risk of the customer being surprised (and perhaps disappointed) by the implementor's arbitrary solution. Technically, a system that satisfies its stated requirements and arbitrarily addresses unspecified situations is contractually compliant. This will probably not pacify an unhappy customer, who may be unable to use the system as it is delivered.

On the other hand, if there are several acceptable approaches to an otherwise unspecified situation, a forced requirement may drive a more costly implementation than is necessary. The full impact of such arbitrary requirement decisions often cannot be determined until much later in the development cycle.

RELATING THE OFDS TO THE REQUIREMENTS SPECIFICATION

There is a fundamental contradiction between the products of any object-oriented analysis and the way software system requirements must be presented in a requirements specification document. The purpose of the requirements document is to capture the functional, performance, and quality requirements for the completed system. Therefore, the format for many commonly used Software Requirements Specifications (SRSs) includes major sections for functional and performance requirements (often Section 3) and for quality requirements (normally Section 4). The Section 3 requirements are usually structured around paragraphs that correspond to the system's individual capabilities or functions. Such requirements apply to the complete software system and not to some arbitrarily partitioned element, such as an object. From the customer's viewpoint (after all, that is for whom the requirements specification is written), it is the performance of the complete system —not that of constituent parts created by the developer's methodology—that is of prime importance.

When systems are decomposed using some variant of *functional decomposition*, the "bubbles" on the data flow diagrams usually correspond to the system functions. The decomposition of a bubble in subsequent diagrams introduces bubbles representing subfunctions of the higher-level function. These diagrams that identify and map functions fit cleanly into the SRS format. Developers can usually correlate the hierarchical identification numbers assigned to the data flow diagram bubbles to corresponding subparagraph numbers in Section 3 of the SRS. Because the bubbles on OFDs usually relate to objects rather than to functions, and objects may capture part of the behavior of several functions, the use of OFDs to illustrate functional requirements becomes a mistake.

For this reason, I caution the analyst not to attempt to use OFDs in exactly the same manner as traditional functional decomposition methodology data flow diagrams. OFDs do not directly identify the primary system functions. Each of those functions likely cuts across multiple objects, perhaps requiring several OFDs. The heuristics described in this chapter force the analyst to trace all of the system's required functions, defined by event/response pairs, across the OFD network. However, unless each of these "tracings" is captured in another graphic presentation, the relationship between OFDs and functional requirements will seldom be obvious. Few SRS readers will have the patience to verify the analyst's work. I recommend that the OFDs created to capture the system's behavioral requirements be attached as an appendix to the SRS. Additional appendices also should be added for the OTs and the Data Dictionary, which will be described in Chapter 16.

What then should be included in the SRS functional/performance requirements section? To be compliant with most customers' requirements for SRS format and content, requirements specifications must be organized by functions or capabilities. Because the External Events/Response List is the product of RTOOSA that captures functional requirements, it offers a requirements listing from which the SRS capabilities may be extracted.

Either individual event/response pairs or groups of closely related event/response pairs may be classified as the system's individual required capabilities. These capabilities may be stated in the form: "In response to [*insert event description*] the [*insert system name or mnemonic*] shall perform the following functions: [*insert list of required responses*]." In the remainder of the SRS paragraph dedicated to that capability, the more specific allocated and derived requirements, usually quoted or paraphrased from the original requirements statement in a higher-system-level requirements document, must be listed.

Requirements traceability is a growing concern to customers who purchase large, complex software systems. The specified software system must account for all the requirements allocated to it from the higher-level specification(s). To ensure proper traceability, the source paragraph number (or requirement number when available) from the higher-level requirements document should be given along side each SRS requirement as the requirement's source. The source of all SRS requirements must be known, whether allocated, derived, or self-imposed.

Because the OFDs capture the requirements for system behavior based on the behavioral requirements allocated to individual objects, many customers will want to see the relationship between the stated capabilities and the OFD model. To do this, the analyst can do one or both of the following:

1. For each event/response pair, the analyst can describe the way the objects shown on the OFD network interact to recognize the stated event and provide the behavior required by the stated response. This narrative captures the process the analyst used to verify that the OFD model was complete and sufficient.

2. For each event/response pair, the OFD network object and data/control process icons that support that specific event's detection and response processing requirements can be redrawn on a separate diagram to highlight the thread(s) of execution associated with the event/response pair. A diagram that captures the essence of a single event/response pair will be less cluttered than the full OFD network that captures the requirements of all event/response pairs.

Either (or both) of these techniques documents the traceability between functional requirements and the corresponding objects' behaviors. This traceability will become useful again during software integration if, as I will propose in Chapter 17, integration is based on the threads of execution associated with event/response pairs.

SUMMARY

This chapter suggests a set of heuristics for using the OFD notation introduced in Chapter 14 to develop an OFD network. These heuristics build on the products of the Essential Requirements Model, the EID, EERL, and ORD, for the identification of objects in the system problem space. As the individual OFDs are created, their contents must be balanced against one another and against the Essential Requirements Model products to ensure that the Requirements Model is internally consistent and complete. When the detailed behavior analysis discovers previously missing requirements, the new requirements must be incorporated and propagated to all other model products.

Finally, this chapter suggested how the OFD network data could be incorporated into the software system's formal requirements specification document.

PRACTICE

1. Work from the Essential Requirements Model for the Radar Acquisition and Target System (RATS) completed in Exercise 2 of Chapter 13 and create a corresponding OFD network. If the OFD analysis uncovers the need to change the products of the Essential Requirements Model, update the corresponding products to maintain complete model consistency.

2. Work from the Essential Requirements Model for your chosen commercial product, completed in Exercise 4 of Chapter 13. If the OFD analysis uncovers the need to change the products of the Essential Requirements Model, update the corresponding products to maintain complete model consistency.

3. Select another commercial product with which you are familiar. Create an Essential Requirements Model for that commercial product. If you have the operator's manual for your product, use it as the source of requirements. When your Essential Requirements Model is complete, apply the heuristics of this chapter to generate an OFD network. Show where the Essential Requirements Model was updated because of new requirements discovered while doing the OFD analysis.

4. Using the Essential Requirements Model completed in Exercise 5 of Chapter 13 for the LoCoDoNS (reference Appendix C), develop an OFD network for that system. Identify needed changes to the Essential Requirements Model as the result of new (or changed) requirements discovered during OFD analysis.

A vision without a task is but a dream.
A task without a vision is drudgery.
A vision with a task is the hope of the world.
— Carved on a church in Sussex, England, 1730

Chapter **16**

The Data Dictionary

We examined the symbology for *Object Flow Diagrams* in Chapter 14. Chapter 15 provided heuristics to aid in generating a complete, consistent, and meaningful OFD network. Those heuristics also specified using *Object Templates* to capture the allocation decisions for each object, including assigned object fields and methods. Data were added to the OTs as the corresponding analysis decisions and discoveries were made. The OTs provide textual data to support the information on each object's OFD. The final Essential Objects Model product, also needed to back up the OFD network, is the system's Data Dictionary.

It is usually apparent when examining an OFD (or its predecessor data flow diagrams) that the full specification of the system requirements is not complete merely by defining the data and control processes and objects (as described in Chapters 14 and 15). Some of the OFD symbology has not been fully defined. Those OFD icons not covered by definition procedures introduced so far include the data/event flows, object/object messages, and data/event stores. These OFD element definitions are provided in the system *Data Dictionary*. This chapter defines the Data Dictionary, the final RTOOSA product. The following definitions establish a foundation for discussing Data Dictionaries.

Data Dictionary: a set of Data Dictionary Element (DDE) definitions, normally arranged alphabetically by DDE name.

Data Dictionary Element: the formal definition of a data store, event store, data flow, event flow, or object/object message appearing on one or more OFDs; or of a constituent part of a Composite Data Dictionary Element.

Composite Data Dictionary Element: a Data Dictionary Element that is defined in terms of other Data Dictionary Elements.

Primitive Data Dictionary Element: a Data Dictionary Element that is not defined in terms of other Data Dictionary Elements. The definition of a primitive DDE is self-contained, not requiring reference to other DDEs.

The Data Dictionary (DD) is a type of data base containing the set of Data Dictionary Elements (DDEs). Most DD CASE tools are specialized data base management systems that include linkages to the graphic elements of other products of the CASE toolset. These linkages allow the analyst to "click" the mouse on a store or flow icon label and automatically open the corresponding DDE for review or modification. Many of the CASE toolsets have a special function that automatically creates new DDEs for any store or flow icon label not already in the DD. The user must then edit the new DDEs to fill in the pertinent data. All such CASE tools (to the best of my knowledge) will balance the graphic diagrams against the DD to verify that every store and flow icon label has a corresponding DDE defined.

The DD is often printed in an alphabetical list by the data element name and included as an appendix to various requirements and design documents. For Government-type Software Requirements Specifications (SRSs), the DD provides much of the specific data required by the document format/content specifications.

Figure 16.1 provides a more formal definition of the DDE. Each DDE definition has three primary sections. The first provides the DDE formal definition. The syntax for the formal definition is relatively rigid because many CASE tools parse this section. The next section lists the element attributes that describe the essential characteristics of the DDE. These attributes contain many of the physical characteristics that are essential in the formal definition of interfaces. The final section applies only to DDEs that define data stores used as fields in objects. For this object data, the third section of the DDE describes the methods (procedures and functions) associated with that specific data element.

DATA DICTIONARY ELEMENT FORMAL DEFINITIONS

The formal definition section of the DDE is only interesting for *composite data elements*. If the DDE is a *primitive data element*, then this specification is only the string: "* primitive element *." The important characteristics of a primitive data element are provided in the element attributes section of the DDE definition.

The formal definition of a composite data element identifies the other DDEs that contribute to the definition and their logical relationships. Figure 16.2 provides examples of some ways in which a composite data element might be defined.

DDEs as the Concatenation of Other DDEs

When a DDE is defined as the concatenation of other data elements, each of the concatenated elements is always present when the data element is used. In the Figure 16.2 example, a *Person_Identifier* is defined as the concatenation of the person's name (*Individual_Name*), address (*Home_Address*), phone number (*Home_Phone*), and so forth. Any data or message flow that has *Person_Identifier* as its label implicitly includes all of its concatenated elements.

If a data flow with the label *Person_Identifier* enters a data process that is decomposed on a lower-level OFD, then the lower-level OFD must have a data flow labeled *Person_Identifier* coming from off-page. If the constituent elements of the data flow are processed separately, the proper way to show the flow is to have the off-page flow *split* using the notation shown previously in Figure 14.11. However, some CASE tools will not support the flow merge/split notation. In such cases, the composite flow on the higher-level OFD may be shown as separate flows from off-page for each of the constituent elements on the lower-level OFD. Such CASE tools will recognize that the flow has been decomposed and most will check to ensure that all constituent elements are explicitly shown.

A DDE defined as the concatenation of other elements could be implemented by a C++ structure, Ada/Pascal record, or equivalent, having the constituent elements as fields.

DDEs as the Alternative of Other DDEs

A DDE that is defined as the alternative of several other elements has different characteristics than a concatenated element DDE. Referring to the second example in Figure 16.2, the *User_Command* is defined as either the *Turn_On_Cmd* or the *Turn_Off_Cmd* or the *Set_Speed_Cmd* or the *Resume_Speed_Cmd*. This type of element should be thought of as an *enumerated type* variable that could take on any of the specified values, but has only one of them at a time.

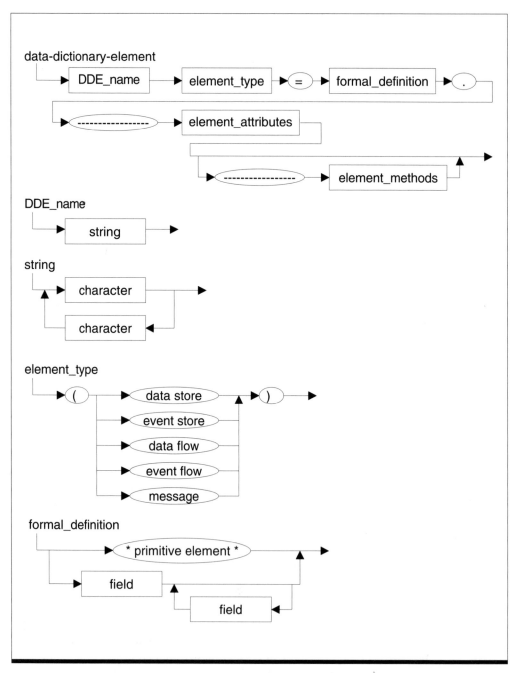

Figure 16.1. A formal definition of Data Dictionary Elements.

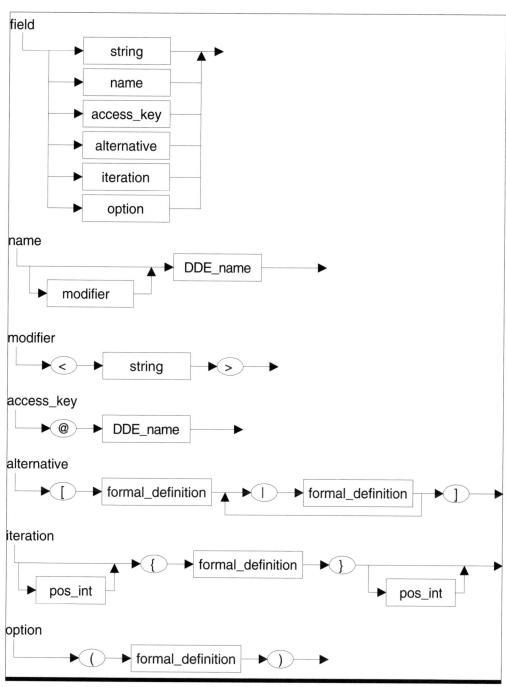

(continued)

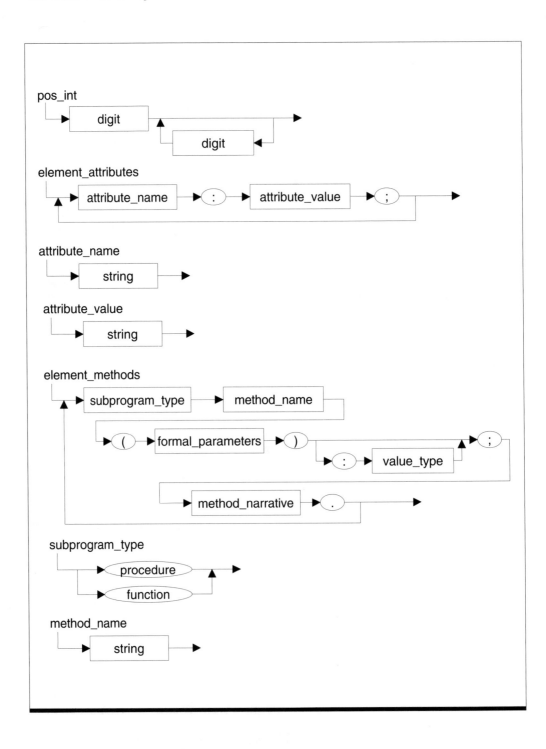

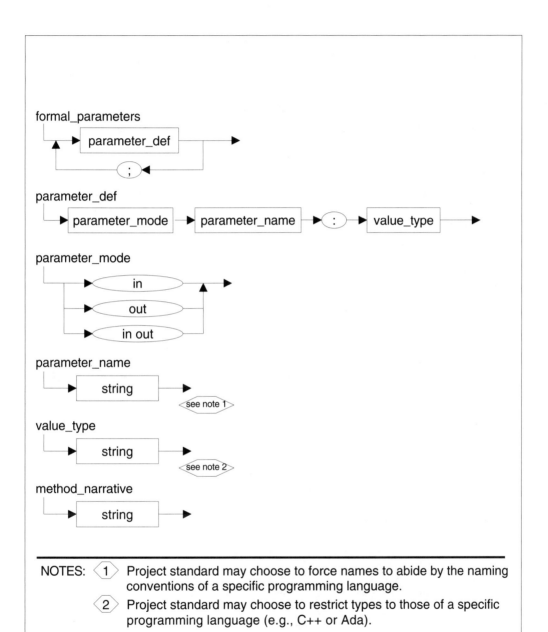

NOTES: 1   Project standard may choose to force names to abide by the naming conventions of a specific programming language.

   2   Project standard may choose to restrict types to those of a specific programming language (e.g., C++ or Ada).

If a data flow with the label *User_Command* enters a data process that is decomposed on a lower-level OFD, then the lower-level OFD may show the flow coming from off-page in either of two ways. It may have a single data flow labeled *User_Command* coming from off-page. Optionally, the alternative values of the *User_Command* may each be shown separately as flows coming from off-page. Figure 16.3 illustrates this approach. On the higher-level OFD (shown at the top of the figure), the data flow called *User_Command* enters the data process *Process User Cmds*. This process is decomposed in the lower part of the figure. Here, instead of a data flow called *User_Command* coming from off-page, each of the four possible values of *User_Command* (i.e., *Turn_On_Cmd*, *Turn_Off_Cmd*, etc.) is shown coming into a different lower-level data process. The lower-level OFD is not correct and balanced with the upper-level OFD unless every one of the alternatives is depicted.

DDEs with Modifiers

DDE *modifiers* provide a way to show the similarity among various DDEs. The definition of a modified DDE is specified as a simple relationship to another DDE. The third example in Figure 16.2, perhaps the definition of a DDE called *Previous_Person*, shows the DDE to be a particular instance of the DDE called *Person_Identifier*.

Normally, use of a DDE modifier suggests an implementation where two or more data items will be of the same type. In this example, the DDE definition says that this entry could be of the same type as the DDE for *Person_Identifier*.

DDEs as Access_Keys

DDE *access keys* convey the basic notion of *pointers* from languages such as C/C++. In Chapter 13, the access key notation was introduced when associative objects were defined. For example, Figures 13.9, 13.11, and 13.13 show how access keys are used to reference data in other objects.

DDEs as the Iteration of Other DDEs

A DDE that is defined as an *iteration* of another DDE suggests that the DDE represents a compound data structure. Such a data structure might be implemented as an array, a stack, a queue, or a list.

The basic notation for iterations specifies the minimum number of elements (the integer before the opening braces) and the maximum number of elements (the integer following the closing braces) that the DDE can contain. The bottom example in Figure 16.2 specifies that an *Employee_Team* must have at least one member and may have no more than twelve. Omitting the minimum or maximum number

Concatenation: Person_Identifier =
                Individual_Name
              + Home_Address
              + Home_Phone
              + Sex
              + Date_of_Birth
              + Social_Security_Number

Alternative: User_Command =
              [Turn_On_Cmd
               | Turn_Off_Cmd
               | Set_Speed_Cmd
               | Resume_Speed_Cmd]

Modifer: <previous>Person_Identifier

Access_Key: Employee_Identifer =
              @Employee_Number
              + Person_Identifier

Iteration: Employee_Team =
              1{ Employee_Identifer }12
            * 1 to 12 employees on the team *

Figure 16.2.   Examples of composite DDE definitions.

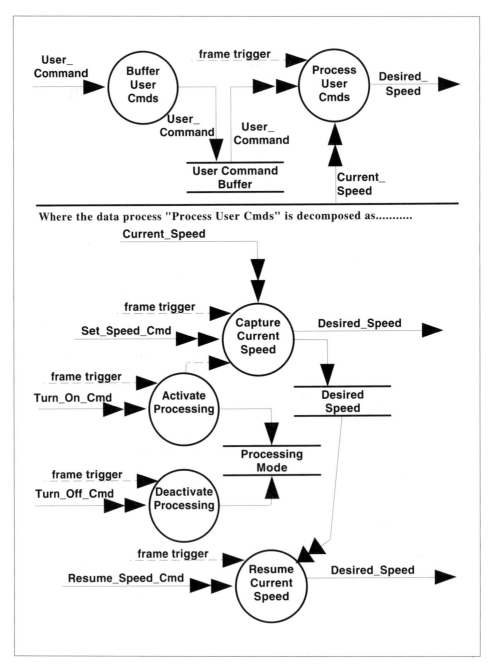

Where the data process "Process User Cmds" is decomposed as...........

Figure 16.3.   Expanding alternative data elements on lower-level Object Flow Diagrams.

of members in the iteration specification invokes defaults for these values. A missing minimum number is considered the same as "zero." A missing maximum number suggests no upper bound. Notice that omitting the maximum value may lead to some problems in determining system resource requirements because computers cannot handle infinitely large data structures. The value for the upper bound may determine the type of resources that the system needs to contain the data element. Try always to provide at least the upper bound for iteration definitions.

Figure 16.4 shows how iteration specifications should be interpreted when one or both of the iteration bounds are omitted from the specification. The *Waiting_for_Work_List* DDE may have no members or an unlimited number of members. (How would you allocate memory to hold this data element?) The *Command_Queue* is limited to a maximum of thirty-two instances of *User_Command*, but also may be empty (no instances). The *Football_Team* DDE specifies a minimum of eleven players but leaves the maximum number unspecified. (How many records should be allocated to hold player statistics in the data base system?)

The final example in Figure 16.4 expresses the very useful concept of an optional element. Using parentheses denotes the same specification as an iteration with a minimum number of instances equal to zero and a maximum number of one. That is, the specified element may be present (one instance) or not (no instance). The example shows that the *User_Password* data element is an optional part of the *Sign_On* data element.

DATA DICTIONARY ELEMENT ATTRIBUTES

Decomposing DDEs as various combinations of other DDEs is important. However, this process is not encompassing because, at some point, the characteristics of the primitive elements must be provided.

The type of information needed to characterize a particular data element often is project dependent. Figure 16.5 shows a list of candidate attributes that the analyst might typically use. This list includes all the attributes required by the Department of Defense standard for software development (DOD-STD-2617A) plus a few others that have proven useful in my personal experience.

The Project Unique Identifier (PUI) is particularly important on larger programs that may include several software configuration items. The PUI allows the creation of a single data base that guarantees that every element can be uniquely identified, even if several configuration items choose identical names for data elements (e.g., several systems might define a DDE for *User_Command*). Developments in strict compliance with the DOD standards must provide PUIs for all DDEs.

Iteration: Waiting_for_Work_List =
  (special cases)   { Person_Identifier }
                          * 0 or more on the list *

                      Command_Queue =
                            { User_Command }32
                          * 0 to 32 commands in queue *

                      Football_Team =
                            11{ Football_Players }
                          * at least 11 players on team *

                      Sign_On =
                            User_Name
                            + (User_Password)
                          * password may or may not be
                                                present *

Figure 16.4.   Examples of iteration DDEs.

The Data Element Description field is probably the most important and should be included as an attribute for all software projects. This field allows the analyst to explain the purpose and function of the DDE in free-text.

The next six attributes (Data Type, Size, Units of Measure, Limits/Range, Accuracy, and Precision/Resolution) are required by the DOD standard. These are the common data characteristics that are needed for many types of systems analysis, such as algorithm adequacy and error budget allocations, memory requirement analysis, and so forth.

The Frequency attribute is particularly important in real-time systems built around periodic processing. The update frequency requirements drive analysis of

(1) Project Unique Identifier: * DOD-STD-2167A required *
(2) Data Element Description: * free-text narrative *
(3) Data Type: * in an Ada-like sense *
(4) Size: * in bits, bytes, words, etc. *
(5) Units of Measure: * as applicable *
(6) Limits/Range: * as applicable *
(7) Accuracy: * determined by sensor or
     computations *

(8) Precision/Resolution: * value of least significant bit *
(9) Frequency: * update interval *
(10) Display Format: * user view of object value *
[If the DDE represents internal interface data, then add:]
(11) Internal Interface Data..............
     - Interface Name: * e.g. source-destination-name *
     - Interface PUI: * Project Unique Identifier *
     - Source Capability Name: * Originating process name *
     - Source Capability PUI: * Project Unique Identifer *
     - Dest Capability Name: * Target process name *
     - Dest Capabiltiy PUI: * Project Unique Identifer*

Figure 16.5. Candidates for data element attributes.

processor loading and process latency. The requirements derived from data element update frequencies also contribute to architectural decisions at the early states of the system implementation.

Display-based systems often attempt to standardize data presentation formats. In such a system, the Display Format attribute may be used to specify a standard format for the display of the data element. It is good system design practice always to show the user important data consistently. A pilot could easily get confused if sometimes aircraft altitude were shown in feet and at other times in meters or sometimes position were given in degrees, minutes, and seconds and at other times in degrees, minutes, and hundredths of a minute. Such inconsistencies invariably lead to user errors.

The Internal Interface Data attribute is listed for completeness. This attribute is specified by the DOD standard. It captures data that is already available (except for the PUIs) in graphic form on the OFDs. This information could be useful if the DD is placed into a data base. It would permit searching the DD to identify all processes affected by certain changes based on the DDEs that interface to it. For many systems, the user may choose not to provide the Internal Interface Data attribute. Inspection of OFDs will provide the same data with no additional work.

DATA DICTIONARY ELEMENT METHODS

When the DDE defines a data store that represents a future object field, it is useful to specify the required methods associated with the field data. These methods define how the data may be accessed, updated, displayed, and so forth. This section of the DDE definition does not apply to non-object field DDE types.

The method identification section contains a formal interface definition and a narrative description for each method. The formal interface definition is the equivalent of the procedure/function declaration provided for objects in the interface section of a unit. The interface to the method should include the method type (either "procedure" or "function"), the method name, and a formal parameter list. If the method is a function, then the type of the returned value also must be specified.

Another way to specify the methods associated with the DDE would be to identify the *object template* on which the applicable methods are defined. When RTOOSA is fully employed, this is the preferred approach. If the methodology is modified to exclude the use of OTs, then the methods section of the DDE definition must be provided.

PUTTING IT ALL TOGETHER

Figure 16.6 suggests some DDEs associated with the LoCoDoNS data element *Current_Aircraft_Position*. This list is based on the order in which the DDEs are introduced, not alphabetically.

The *Current_Aircraft_Position* is a composite element defined as the concatenation of three other DDEs: the *position_latitude*, *position_longitude*, and *aircraft_altitude*. Each of these DDEs is then defined as a primitive element.

For this example, the Internal Interface Data attribute was omitted and the element methods section split into two categories: Access Methods and Modifier Methods. The analyst should consider what data are necessary for complete

```
Current_Aircraft_Position  (data store) =
                  Position_Latitude
              + Position_Longitude
              + Aircraft_Altitude

    (1) Project Unique Identifier: L-Current_AC_Pos-DS;
    (2) Data Element Description:  The geodetic coordinates (latitude
                                   & longitude) of the aircraft's
                                   vertical projection onto the
                                   earth's surface, and the
                                   reference altitude.
    (3) Data Type:                 record
                                      latitude  : latitude_type  *flt*
                                      longitude : longitude_type *flt*
                                      altitude  : altitude_type  *int*
                                   end record;
    (4) Size:                      (3 * 4 bytes);
    (5) Units of Measure:          reference primitive elements;
    (6) Limits/Range:              reference primitive elements;
    (7) Accuracy:                  reference primitive elements;
    (8) Precision/Resolution:      reference primitive elements;
    (9) Frequency:                 latitude/longitude @15 Hz,
                                   altitude @ 5 Hz;
    (10) Display Format:           reference primitive elements;

    (11) Access Methods:
        function Current_AC_Latitude_Is () : latitude_type;
                   This method returns the geodetic latitude of the
                   aircraft's current position.
        function Current_AC_Longitude_Is () : longitude_type;
                   This method returns the geodetic longitude of the
                   aircraft's current position.
        function Current_AC_Altitude_Is ()  : altitude_type;
                   This method returns the aircraft's current
                   altitude.
    (12) Modifier Methods:
        procedure Reset_AC_Position
                       ( in     New_Latitude  : latitude_type,
                         in     New_Longitude : longitude_type );
                   This method is invoked when a crew member performs
                   a navigation fix to set the aircraft position to
                   its corrected value.
        procedure Update_AC_Position();
                   This method is invoked to update the current air-
                   craft position by accessing the assigned nav-
                   igation device.
        procedure Update_AC_Altitude();
                   This method is invoked to update the current air-
                   craft altitude by accessing the assigned altitude
                   device.
```

Figure 16.6. Sample Data Dictionary Elements.

(continued)

```
========================================================================
Aircraft_Altitude  (data store) =
                    * primitive element *
_____

     (1) Project Unique Identifier: L-Aircraft_Alt-DS;
     (2) Data Element Description:  The current aircraft altitude above
                                    the reference ellipsoid as provided
                                    by the GPS.
     (3) Data Type:                 integer.
     (4) Size:                      4 bytes
     (5) Units of Measure:          feet
     (6) Limits/Range:              -250 .. +99,999
     (7) Accuracy:                  +3 feet
     (8) Precision/Resolution:      lsb = 1 ft
     (9) Frequency:                 5 Hz
     (10) Display Format:           00000 FT ALT
     _____

     (11) Access Methods:
          function Display_Altitude(
                  in        Alt_Value : altitude_type ) : string;
                  This method returns the current aircraft altitude
                  in the specified display format, ready for output
                  to the display device.
     (12) Modifier Methods:
          none.




========================================================================
Position_Latitude  (data store) =
                    * primitive element *
_____

     (1) Project Unique Identifier: L-Pos_Lat-DS;
     (2) Data Element Description:  The geodetic latitude of a
                                    reference object.
     (3) Data Type:                 float;
     (4) Size:                      4 bytes;
     (5) Units of Measure:          degrees;
     (6) Limits/Range:              -90.0 .. +90.0;
     (7) Accuracy:                  .001 minutes;
     (8) Precision/Resolution:      floating point representation;
     (9) Frequency:                 * varies by update source *
     (10) Display Format:           default: LAT 00 00'00"
     _____

     (11) Access Methods:
          function Display_Latitude(
                  in        Lat_Value : latitude_type ) : string;
                  This method returns the current aircraft latitude
                  in the specified display format, ready for output
                  to the display device.
     (12) Modifier Methods:
          none.
```

```
========================================================================
Position_Longitude   (data store) =
                     * primitive element *
        _____

        (1) Project Unique Identifier: L-Pos_Long-DS;
        (2) Data Element Description:  The geodetic longitude of a
                                       reference object.
        (3) Data Type:                 float;
        (4) Size:                      4 bytes;
        (5) Units of Measure:          degrees;
        (6) Limits/Range:              -180.0 .. +180.0;
        (7) Accuracy:                  .001 minutes;
        (8) Precision/Resolution:      floating point representation;
        (9) Frequency:                 * varies by update source *
        (10) Display Format:           default: LON 00 00'00"
        _____

        (11) Access Methods:
             function Display_Longitude(
                        in        Lon_Value : longitude_type ) : string;
                     This method returns the current aircraft longitude
                     in the specified display format, ready for output
                     to the display device.
        (12) Modifier Methods:
             none.
```

specification of a particular system and modify the DDE definition requirements accordingly.

Collecting data in the DD must be a continual process. When a new store or flow is added to an OFD, generate a skeletal DDE entry for it and add a few critical notes. As the flows change, make the corresponding changes to the DD. Do not leave the DD as a final exercise after all of the OFDs are complete.

SUMMARY

This chapter introduces the final product of the Essential Objects Model, the Data Dictionary (DD). The DD is important because it provides a verbal backup to the graphic data of the OFDs. The DD is defined as a set of Data Dictionary Elements (DDEs). This chapter then described the format and contents by which DDEs should be defined.

PRACTICE

1. Create a DD for the Space Station Freedom Audio/Video Distribution System (AVDS) defined in Chapter 15. Be sure to create a DDE for every data store and event/data/message flow on the EID and all of the OFDs. Select the data element attributes that are important for the definition of this type of system.

2. Generate a DD for the Radar Acquisition and Target System (RATS), for which you generated OFDs as Exercise 1 of Chapter 15. Be sure to create a DDE for every data store and event/data/message flow on the EID and all of the OFDs. Select the data element attributes that are important for the definition of this type of system.

3. Create a DD for the gunship's orbiting autopilot system defined in Chapter 15. Be sure to create a DDE for every data store and event/data/message flow on the EID and all of the OFDs. Select the data element attributes that are important for the definition of this type of system. Is the list of attributes for this DD different from that in Exercise 1 for the AVDS? Should it be?

4. Generate DDs for the commercial product systems for which you created OFDs as Exercises 2 and 3 of Chapter 15. Again, select the data element attributes that are important for the definition of each type of system.

All truth passes through three stages.
First, it is ridiculed.
Second, it is violently opposed.
Third, it is accepted as being self-evident.
— Arthur Schopenhauer

Chapter *17*

Following Requirements Analysis

So far, this book has described an analysis methodology that leads to a complete, consistent, and meaningful requirements model. In Chapter 16, we developed the final product of this model. Perhaps you too gave a sigh of relief when we completed such a significant milestone.

While a poor Requirements Model all but ensures a poor product, a quality Requirements Model is merely the foundation of a successful system. It is far too early to celebrate very much. A good Requirements Model sets you off to a good start, but it is only the first leg of a long race. This chapter briefly suggests what must now follow to turn the quality Requirements Model into a quality system.

REVIEWING THE REQUIREMENTS MODEL

Before proceeding out of the software requirements analysis phase, your Requirements Model must be formally evaluated. This involves exposing your product to critical review, the objective of which is to find problems. These problems may include technical problems, such as inconsistencies or improper representation of requirements, practicality problems that address the feasibility and cost of implementing a compliant system, and contractual problems, such as misinterpreted requirements or overly restrictive self-imposed requirements. By finding such problems now, you can correct them before attempting to build a system based on a faulty model.

When the Requirements Model is complete, it is prudent to conduct a *formal* requirements review. The Government calls this review the *Software Specification Review* (SSR). The SSR presents the products of the software requirements analysis phase to up to five types of reviewers, each with a different interest in the project:

1. *The customer.* The customer needs to ensure that all of his/her requirements have been captured and that nothing has been overlooked. The presentation must expose the system requirements in a way that allows the customer to conclude that his/her requirements are properly understood without inconsistencies.

2. *Representatives of other engineering disciplines from the development team.* The software of an embedded system has explicit and implicit interfaces with other development disciplines. These groups include systems engineering and electrical design (hardware engineering), and sometimes other engineering organizations. Reviewers from these groups are concerned with algorithms, communications protocols, performance (response, latency, etc.), and low-level interfaces.

3. *One or more representatives of the development company's program management office.* Many projects become classified as failures because the development organization could not manage the development budget or schedule. Some consider it the nature of an engineer to provide more than is required. Requirements specifications can fill with the engineer's *self-imposed requirements*. This phenomenon is sometimes called *requirements creep.* The program manager wants to ensure that the analyst has not increased the scope of his program by creating new requirements that will impact cost and schedule.

4. *One or more independent reviewers with a strong background in software development and a firm understanding of the analysis methodology.* There is considerable interest within the software industry in achieving repeatable development processes. I was a member of a panel that administered a process maturity self-assessment for my division. One

finding that surprised me was how each of the nonsoftware organizations interviewed had the same impression: "The software organization has a process that they follow but I don't understand it." Perhaps it is unrealistic, especially as engineering processes become more complex for all disciplines, to expect anyone other than a software engineer to understand the software process. If you accept this premise, then the SSR review committee must include a software engineer who is not associated with the development team to determine whether the analysis process has been applied correctly.

5. *Members of the quality assurance team.* All companies have slightly different views of the role played by the software quality assurance (SQA) organization. Minimally, SQA must ensure that the development team abides by their Software Development Plan. Beyond that, they may review the quality of the requirements specification according to their organization's criteria.

Many companies conduct the SSR in two stages. First, all the developer company's reviewers convene for an *internal* SSR (Figure 17.1). The internal reviewers need to fulfill their individual review objectives and to verify that the products are suitable for presentation to the customer. When the presentation meets the company quality requirements and presents a unified company position, then the second stage of the review is conducted with the customer. Development team disagreements, some of which may be major, in front of the customer can create a bad image and erode confidence. Air your dirty laundry in private and present a professional image to the customer.

Military Standard for Technical Reviews and Audits for Systems, Equipments, and Computer Software (MIL-STD-1521B, 4 June 1985) states in Appendix A:

The SSR shall be a formal review of a CSCI's [Computer Software Configuration Item's] requirements as specified in the Software Requirements Specification(s). Normally, it shall be held after System Design Review but prior to the start of CSCI preliminary design. A collective SSR for a group of configuration items, treating each configuration item individually, may be held when such an approach is advantageous to the contracting agency. Its purpose is to establish the allocated baseline for preliminary CSCI design by demonstrating to the contracting agency the adequacy of the Software Requirements Specification (SRS), Interface Requirements Specification(s) (IRS), and Operational Concept Document (OCD). [MIL-STD-1521B]

Using the military standard as a guide, the following are among the items that should be reviewed at an SSR:

1. Mission requirements of the system and its associated operational and support environments.
2. All interface requirements between the CSCI and all other configuration items both internal and external to the system.
3. Functions and characteristics of the computer system within the overall system.
4. Functional overview of the CSCI, including inputs, processing, and outputs of each function.
5. Overall CSCI performance requirements, including those for execution time (processor loading), storage requirements, interface transfer rates, event response times, message latencies, and similar constraints.

These SSR requirements are addressed by the requirements analysis products described in this book. A full military standard SSR also must address other topics, such as special delivery requirements, quality factors, milestone schedules, updates to previously delivered documents, and so forth, which are beyond the scope of RTOOSA.

The SSR presenter must realize that the audience has a diverse background, different concerns, and will generally not follow a lot of esoteric software jargon. Notice that the items to be reviewed are primarily concerned with the *system* functions and performance. The presenter must not lose sight of most reviewers' needs to maintain a "big picture" perspective of requirements.

Though the system was analyzed using object-oriented decomposition, do not base the presentation on detailed consideration of isolated objects. The nonsoftware reviewers will not appreciate the essence of an Object Template or an object decomposing OFD. However, the External Interface

Figure 17.1.   The Software Specification Review is an open forum to examine the products of the Requirements Model.

Diagram, External Events/Response List, and Object Relationship Diagrams are valuable SSR presentation tools. When discussing the details of individual functions, use flow diagrams that trace the processing requirements through various objects.

To many, the SSR is treated as the proverbial *dog and pony show*. Too often, the strategy is to overwhelm the reviewers with technical detail and expect a bewildered committee and customer to rubber-stamp approval of the requirements document. It may be difficult to conduct preliminary or critical design reviews without becoming wrapped up in design notations and details, but the SSR presentation need not be so esoteric. Instill every presenter with an urgency to make the requirements presentation understandable. It is far better to uncover requirements problems during this phase than to proceed on false assumptions and build an invalid or merely unusable system. Presenters should take pride in requirement problems that are uncovered during the SSR! This can happen only if the form of the presentation is understood by the diverse audience.

The primary result of the SSR is a baseline requirements document (and model). Make that model as solid as the available data permits. Remember that one of the strengths of object-oriented technology is that it is more resilient to changes than more traditional methodologies. With your requirements baseline as firm as you can make it, proceed with confidence.

INCREMENTAL AND ITERATIVE SOFTWARE DEVELOPMENT

Grady Booch, in the opening chapter of his *Object Oriented Design with Applications*, reflects the generally held concept of object-oriented development being incremental and iterative:

> Clearly, there is no magic, no "silver bullet" [Brooks, F. April 1987. "No Silver Bullet: Essence and Accidents of Software Engineering." *IEEE Computer*, Vol. 20 (4)], that can unfailingly lead the software engineer down the path from requirements to the implementation of a complex software system. In fact, the design of complex software systems does not lend itself at all to cookbook approaches. Rather, . . . the design of such system involves an incremental and iterative process.   [Booch, 1991]

The traditional waterfall model described in Chapter 9 is the antithesis of incremental and iterative development. One of the significant problems for an organization wanting to adopt object-oriented technology is the cultural change that extends to management concepts and customer relationships. Company (and Government) standards are often based on the traditional sequential processes of the waterfall model (reference Figure 8.1). Sometimes the standards are tied to sequential phases in subtle ways. For example, standards may dictate that requirements documents be completed before any design is permitted. Other times, a review standard may require that the complete design architecture undergo a preliminary design review before detailed logic design may begin. Changing standards is seldom easy (not that it should be too easy).

Many organizations will resist making such cultural changes that must begin from the root level. However, there are real advantages to making the change to a development life-cycle model that recognizes incremental development. For example:

1. Seeing early increments of the system operate improves management confidence and development team morale.

2. Seeing early increments of the system operate permits earlier customer witness and acceptance of system functions. Problems can be fixed with less "sunk cost."

3. Early increments of the system implementation permit early performance evaluation and confirmation of resource utilization (memory, throughput, channel bandwidth, etc.).

4. Problems encountered in the early increments can limit the scope of changes needed for corrections.

5. With greater overlap of development activities comes more evenly distributed need for development facilities and equipment. This can reduce development costs and schedule risks.

The programmatic advantages of incremental development surely outweigh the difficulties and resistance facing such a change. If your customer is not familiar with this new approach, you may have another selling job to do. Remember that it is human nature to consider anything new, and therefore uncertain, a frightening risk.

Let's assume that these obstacles can be overcome and you pursue a planning strategy that features incremental software development.

Planning for Incremental/Iterative Development

As with any engineering process, incremental development must be manageable. Process management must include the following functions:

1. Identify specific development activities.

2. Determine the resources required for each development activity.

3. Allocate (i.e., assign) the required resources for each development activity.

4. Schedule the required activities and resources consistent with the overall program plan.

5. Measure progress against schedule milestones.

6. Take corrective actions when progress deviates from the plan.

The basic concepts of software management do not change for incremental development. The changes are in the structure of the development activities and how success is demonstrated. Activities will resemble those of multiple concurrent minidevelopments. A separate demonstration "sell-off" for each of the incremental minidevelopments provides iterative system maturity. Traditional system development terminates with a single demonstration of all capabilities.

Figure 17.2 provides a hypothetical program's incremental development schedule. This example illustrates several important characteristics of this development strategy.

First, the schedule shows the Requirements Model development being completed before any design begins. This may seem to contradict the overlapping analysis and design model developments proposed in Chapter 9 (see Figure 9.3). It does not. Figure 9.3 shows how the preliminary work on the design model must begin long before the Requirements Model is completed. The early work on the design model supports the analysis process and verifies that the requirements are implementable. The early design model work is included in the Requirements Model preparation task on the schedule.

One of the underlying principles of successful incremental development is that each increment should be individually demonstrable. This means that increments should not be based on classes or arbitrary groups of classes. Although a class captures the entire behavior of an object, it will seldom (if ever) provide end-to-end demonstration of a system capability. More likely, demonstration of a system capability slices across several object classes, but does not require all methods from most of those classes.

RTOOSA provides a convenient way to define the development increments. Each event/response pair on the External Events/Response List (EERL) specifies an end-to-end, demonstratable capability of the system. In most systems, there are intuitive groupings of events that become natural candidates for development

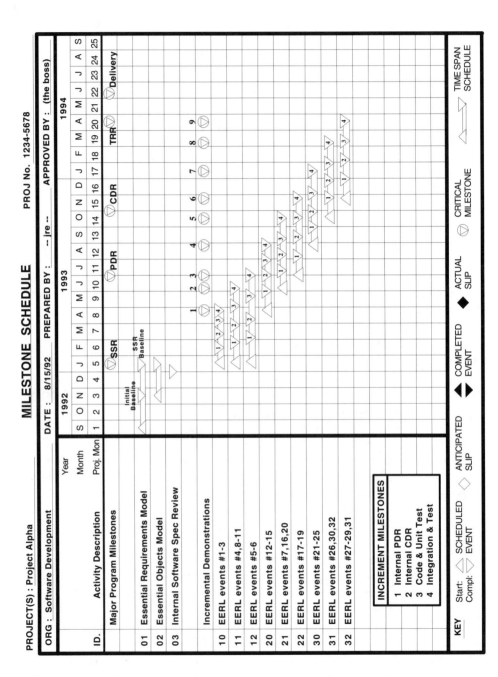

Figure 17.2. A schedule for a hypothetical program using an incremental development strategy.

increments. Figure 17.2 shows development increments identified by the corresponding assigned EERL events. One could also assign a descriptive name that captures the primary capabilities assigned to the increment. Regardless of how you name the increment, it is based on demonstrating specific EERL events.

Developing each increment is treated as a miniproject with its own phases and key milestones. The first phase, preliminary design, must identify the class and object elements required for the increment and all required control structures. The control and class/object structures should be verified by an internal (incremental) Preliminary Design Review (PDR). When the preliminary design has been approved, the detailed logic of the code may be designed. The detailed design should be verified by an internal (incremental) Critical Design Review (CDR). The third phase of the increment development is Code and Unit Test. This phase implements the individual classes/objects and verifies the logic of the individual units. The final increment phase integrates the various units to create a *minisystem* that demonstrates the assigned event/response pair(s).

A critical milestone is designated at the conclusion of each increment build to demonstrate the capabilities assigned to that increment. These milestones become a critical measure of development progress. The increment demonstrations provide the customer with early visibility into the capabilities of the final system.

Generally, the first increment should provide the system start-up processing, without which none of the later increments can execute. Further, either the first or second increment should implement the essential architecture control structure for the system. This is usually also required to demonstrate end-to-end processing.

On the schedule, I assigned task identification numbers that illustrate how multiple development teams may be assigned. The low-order digit identifies the development team and the high-order digit identifies its assignment. For example, the increment that implements *EERL events 1–3* has an identifier of 10. This identifier specifies that the increment is team zero's first assignment. When this team completes its increment 10, it is projected to implement the increment for *EERL events 12–15*, identified as 20. Task numbering of this type helps the manager track critical resources and quickly assess the impact of missed milestones.

Even on a program using incremental software development, many customers will insist on the traditional program milestones for Software Specification Review (SSR), Preliminary Design Review (PDR), Critical Design Review (CDR), and Test Readiness Review (TRR). These events historically marked the conclusion of corresponding waterfall model development phases (see Figure 8.1). As the schedule shows, it is difficult to correlate some of these milestones to the implementation activities of an incremental development. There are two ways to address this basic inconsistency between the customer's review requirements and the incremental development methodology.

The more straightforward (although often politically more difficult) approach is to "educate" your customer regarding your implementation strategy and how it offers greater insight into your development progress than traditional approaches. Then suggest that some or all of the increment demonstrations, supported by associated design documentation, be designated as incremental design reviews in lieu of the traditional PDR and CDR. If the customer desires greater insight, offer the customer participation during the internal PDR and/or CDR milestones of each increment.

If you cannot sell your customer on the spirit of incremental development, then tie the traditional reviews to significant stages of the incremental development. For example, schedule the PDR when you are ready to demonstrate approximately one-third of the development increments and schedule the CDR at approximately the two-thirds mark. By PDR, you would be able not only to review the architecture of the system, but to demonstrate its operation. By CDR, two-thirds of the system could be demonstrated while the remaining third would probably be well through its detailed design.

CLASS STRUCTURING

I have emphasized several times that the objects you have created in the OFD network are the essential *objects* in the problem space. To create the corresponding objects in the implementation space, the designer must first create *classes* from which the required objects may be instantiated. Some may consider the identification of classes as part of the analysis activity. Because *classes* are an element of the implementation space, I prefer to consider class identification a design activity.

There are two categories of objects for which classes must be defined. The Essential Objects Model identified the objects that were discovered while defining the required system behavior. These objects correspond directly to real and abstract objects in the problem space. The second set of objects are those that must be invented as part of the implementation space. Such objects as data structures (linked lists, queues, etc.) and process controllers that are needed to implement an operational system must be added to the system.

The OTs created as part of the Essential Objects Model provide the required characteristics of each problem space essential object. Similar definitions are needed for the architectural objects. These object definitions, specifying needed object fields and methods, establish the requirements for the classes that must instantiate them. The process of defining classes is based on sorting objects to find common (or at least very similar) field and method requirements. Care must be exercised to compare the characteristics of the fields and methods and not their names, which could be different.

1. If two or more objects have identical field requirements (though the field names are different), then consider a common class that includes the union of the methods from those objects.

2. If one object has fields that are a subset of those in another object, consider an ancestor/descendent class relationship with the ancestor having the common subset and the descendent the remainder.

3. If there is a common subset of fields and methods between two (or more) objects, consider an abstract class to define the common subset and a separate descendent class for each of the sets of objects that have additional requirements.

4. Iterate this process until a preliminary set of hierarchy trees has been created.

In addition to defining classes from the defined characteristics of the system's objects, the designer must also compare the required object characteristics with existing class definitions from whatever reuse libraries are available. The cost benefit of reuse cannot be overstated.

When reuse is being considered, include object design documentation and unit test drivers and documentation with the code. Because code generation is such a small part of the development process, code reuse alone cannot justify the costs associated with developing and maintaining reuse libraries!

When the object characteristics appear to require a superset of a library class, define a descendent of the library class to instantiate the object. If there is a common subset of fields and methods between an object and a library class, consider creating an abstract ancestor class from which will descend the remainder of the library class and a new class to instantiate the required object. Creating such new ancestor classes increase the likelihood of direct reuse in a future project.

It may be necessary to iterate until a complete set of objects has been created. Class hierarchies can be illustrated graphically as shown in Figure 17.3. Once a set of initial class hierarchy trees has been created, the designer must step back and consider the shape of the "forest." If the forest of hierarchy trees is wide and shallow, then the system may not capitalize on all the inheritance that may be available in the system. If, on the other hand, that forest is narrow and deep, then the system is rich in inheritance, but perhaps at the expense of excessive complexity. The proper shape is that which exploits good inheritance characteristics without becoming excessively complex. There is no unique formula for the shape of a system's hierarchy trees. Every system will have its own optimum shape. It is the designer's challenge to find it.

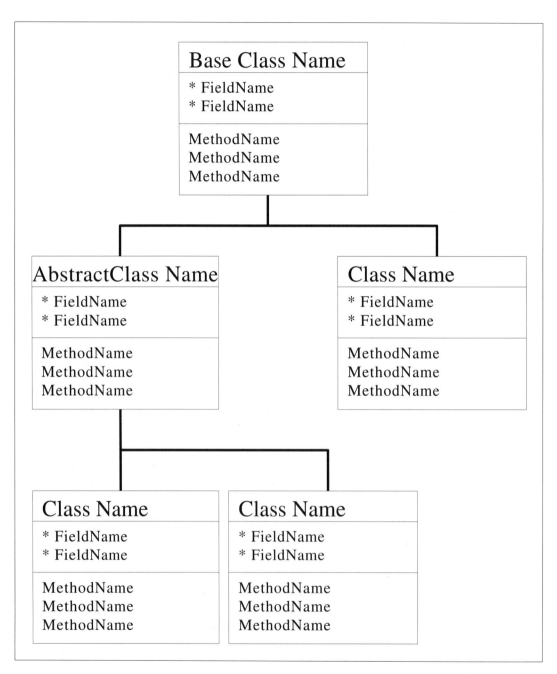

Figure 17.3. A framework for class hierarchy trees.

Often a company may concurrently develop several software systems (configuration items) as part of the same project. Once the hierarchy trees for each configuration item have been created, they should be compared to those for other parts of the project to determine whether additional commonality can be exploited. At a minimum, the following are candidates for shared use (and future reuse):

1. If the systems execute with the same processor environment, then objects associated with environment built-in-test (processor, memory, interfaces, etc.) are candidates for shared use.
2. If the systems have common interfaces (storage devices, communications busses, etc.), then the objects that implement those external objects are candidates for shared use.
3. If the systems share a common implementation architecture, then the invented implementation space objects are candidates for shared use.
4. If the systems have common algorithms from the problem space, then the objects that implement those algorithms are candidates for shared use.

There are undoubtedly other project-unique instances where classes could be shared. There are several advantages, beyond the obvious, for shared use of classes across multiple systems in a project. Consider, for example, the opportunity to use personnel with special experience or expertise (e.g., data base, graphics display, bus protocol, or kernels/executives) to implement specific objects for shared use across the project. I have seen this specific case applied to the design of an external object class that implements a particularly complex network bus protocol and another that implements built-in-test. There also may be an opportunity to use a development team from one system, because they are not on the critical path, to develop a shared class.

THE DESIGN MODEL

The purpose of the design phases is to create the Design Model. For this book, I don't propose any specific object-oriented design (OOD) methodology. However, the design approach you choose must account for all four aspects of the Design Model identified by Grady Booch [*Object-Oriented Design with Applications*]: logical/physical and static/dynamic.

The logical design process identifies the logical design entities: classes and objects. The physical design process assigns the logical entities to physical entities. The physical entities generally correspond to system files: Ada package specification and body files, C++ header (.h) and source (.cpp) files, Turbo Pascal units, and so forth. The files can be organized using the host development system's directory structure to correspond to a hierarchical ordering of the files.

The static perspective considers system characteristics such as class definitions and memory utilization while the dynamic perspective addresses topics such as object message passing, processor loading, concurrent process control, and so forth.

Figure 17.4 suggests how the products of the Requirements Model can feed a

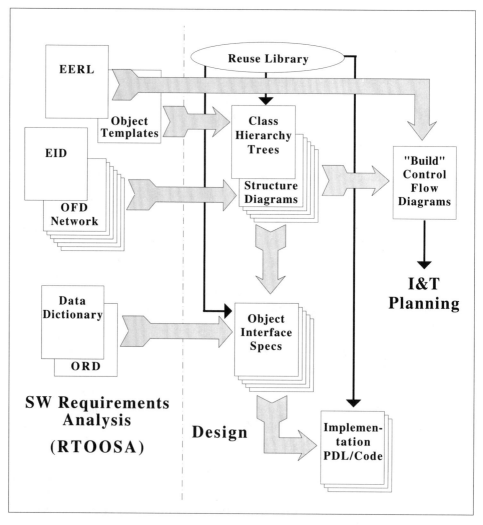

Figure 17.4. The flow of Requirements Model products into the implementation model.

Design Model. The OTs and reuse library, as previously described, are the primary sources of data for creating the class hierarchy trees. The design phase also assigns the logical design entities, including all the system's classes and objects, to physical entities. Most OOD methodologies represent the relationships among the logical design entities (e.g., message passing between objects, etc.) and among the physical design entities (i.e., their compilation dependencies) by some type of structure diagrams. The OFD network provides much of the information needed for the design of the logical object relationship structure diagrams. As the design matures, the designer must create the "code" specifications for the interface and later implementation sections of the classes.

The other design phase activity that ties to the analysis phase products is planning the integration and test (I&T) activities. If I&T is to be based on event/response groups (as I suggested earlier in this chapter), then the test team must determine which code segments are required for each increment's *build*. Increment planning often must go below the class level to identify the methods of each class required for each build. These data can be captured with control flow diagrams that identify graphically the methods and other code entities needed for each build. These diagrams feed planning for the code and test of each increment of the software.

If the Requirements Model is constructed properly, then its products should almost intuitively contribute to the Design Model. This is perhaps the best argument for an object-oriented analysis for a system to use OOD and OOP.

CLASS TESTING

If enhanced reuse is a real driving reason to adopt object-oriented technology, then testing in an object-oriented environment carries some special considerations. For example, if the *class* is to be a primary element of reuse, testing at the class level (i.e., for each method of the class) is mandatory. Further, because each descendent class carries the potential for requiring regression testing of its inherited methods, automated method testing is necessary if a cost benefit from reuse is to be realized.

Each *unit* (or language-dependent equivalent of the Turbo Pascal *unit*) should have its own class-testing program. That program should have one or more procedures to test each method of the class. The procedures should be constructed to direct the test results to a file. Once the proper execution of the class method under test has been confirmed, the corresponding test results-file must be placed under configuration control as the control against which the results of future tests can be measured. Comparing the results of a future test to the *control results-file* can be invoked automatically from within the test program or implemented as a manual procedure that invokes a utility to compare the contents of two text files.

This means that, for each class in a unit, the following support is required:

1. A *software test description* that identifies the individual test cases that must be applied to each method. This documentation should normally be available for formal review with the preliminary design of the corresponding unit(s).

2. A *software test procedure* that tells the tester what precisely must be done to test each method. If automated testing is used, the *test procedure* may be as simple as directing the execution of the corresponding test program procedure for each method.

3. A *testing program* that contains the coded procedures to test each of the methods in the class and capture the results of the tests to one or more result files.

4. A *control results-file* that provides the norm against which future results-files may be compared. The *control results-file* is usually generated as a results-file from the execution of the testing program and then manually verified as correct.

If changes to a system are made and regression testing of an existing class is considered necessary, the indicated approach provides fast and inexpensive testing. A similar strategy can be applied to the integration of the objects in the incremental builds. However, because integrated objects tend to be problem-specific, the cost benefit derived from future reuse is more limited. The decision to develop automated testing for the incremental builds must be based on the economics of the immediate system and generally should not be extended to possible reuse on future systems.

UPDATE THE REUSE LIBRARY

When a project has completed, it is important to immediately place all candidates for reuse into a reuse library that is maintained under strict configuration control. In many companies, configuration control is funded for each project. When a project concludes, the products of the project are "archived" for possible reuse. Archiving consists of nothing more than locking the master copies of all software and documents in a file cabinet, vault, or warehouse and permitting no further access. Nothing is catalogued for random searches seeking reusable components. Nothing is available, except the memories of the engineers who worked on the earlier project, to allow systematic reuse, even if the system was designed anticipating future reuse.

For a reuse library to have any practical value, all of the elements of reuse (e.g., classes) must be catalogued in a way that allows easy searches by future potential reusers. There must be a system that permits access based on key characteristics of the needed class, i.e., some type of data base query system. The library must be broad enough to contain all development data regarding the class: its design documentation, code, and the test support elements described above.

In addition to the system to maintain the reuse components, a company must be willing to allocate the resources to populate the library with candidate elements following the completion of each project. Closing out a project may require resolving cases where reused elements from the library were actually modified on the new project. Because the project is complete, the funding must often come from another source. Even after the library has been updated, it must be maintained under continuous, formal configuration control. Only in that way can a reused element be accepted on a new project without all the rigor of a new development. It can maintain its "certification" from its previous use only through continual configuration control.

A company must be willing to fund its commitment to software reuse.

SUMMARY

This chapter summarizes the activities that must follow completion of the Requirements Model. Although not a thorough treatment of any of these topics, this chapter provides an overview that should allow the software engineer to plan the remaining development activities.

First, following completion of the Requirements Model, its contents should be critically reviewed with a Software Specification Review (SSR). When all concerned parties concur on the validity of the gathered requirements, the development can formally proceed to design.

Object-oriented development suggests using an incremental and iterative development life cycle rather than the traditional sequential cycle, frequently called the *waterfall model*. The Requirement Model also can suggest how the increments should be defined and how their remaining development may be scheduled. This chapter suggests some guidance on how this can happen.

The RTOOSA Requirements Model identifies the essential objects and their required characteristics. An early part of the design process must identify *classes* from which the essential objects, and those need to implement the system architecture, may be instantiated. This chapter offers some guidance in defining object classes.

The class hierarchy is only one aspect of an object-oriented Design Model. Although I do not propose any specific design methodology in this book, several important characteristics of a good Design Model are described. The relationship between the products of the RTOOSA Requirements Model and those of a typical Design Model are presented.

This chapter suggests a strategy for unit testing by developing a testing program for each class. This program would contain procedures for each method to be tested. The results of such automated testing should be captured to a results-file, which will be compared to a *control results-file* containing the "correct" results. Such automated testing is an essential element of software reuse.

Finally, this chapter recommends updating the company's reuse library immediately upon completion of the project development. Some costs associated with populating and maintaining a reuse library are discussed.

PRACTICE

1. Create class hierarchy trees for the Space Station Freedom Audio/Video Distribution System (AVDS) and the Low Cost Doppler Navigation System (LoCoDoNS) Requirements Models developed over the preceding chapters.

2. Create incremental development schedules for the AVDS and LoCoDoNS. Assume an eighteen-month completion after "contract award."

3. Define the key characteristics of a reuse library management system. Identify what must be maintained in such a library, in what form it should be stored, what accesses should be provided, and so forth.

Glossary

Abstract Class: a class whose definition is based on generalities that may be used by multiple descendent classes; an abstract class is declared with the expectation that it will have no direct instances.

Access Method: a method whose purpose is to make an object's fields available for reading and writing through the process specified in each access method.

Allocated Requirements: requirements that are directly traced to a requirement in a "higher-level," customer-provided or -approved specification. It is an essential part of the requirements verification process to ensure that all specification requirements are allocated to at least one target entity. "System" specification requirements are normally allocated to one or more hardware and/or software specifications. It is always possible to point explicitly to the source of an allocated requirement.

Ancestor Class: a class from whom fields, methods, and/or type compatibility is inherited. Some refer to such a class as a "superclass," while it is known as the "base" class in C++.

Associated Actions: processing that must occur as part of a state transition.

Base Class: the first-level ancestor class in a class hierarchy tree; often an abstract class. A base class has no ancestor class.

Class: a common structure and behavior shared by a set of objects. Classes have an interface segment, describing the visible characteristics of member objects, and an implementation segment, defining the hidden implementation secrets of their behavior.

Client: any software (an object or otherwise) that invokes the services of an object is said to be a client of that object.

Composite Data Dictionary Element: a Data Dictionary Element that is defined in terms of other Data Dictionary Elements.

Conditions: a description of the event that causes a state transition.

Constructor: a class method that contains implicit code to link an object to its class's Virtual Method Table. The constructor must be invoked before any of the object's virtual methods or the system will fail (possibly indeterminately).

Continuous Data Flow: a data flow, the frequency of whose autonomous update is equal to or greater than the fastest frequency at which the system must process it.

Control Process: a "process" that accepts only event flows as inputs and produces only event flows as outputs.

Data Dictionary (DD): provides a structured textual definition for each of the "flows" identified in the EID and OFD and for each field from a primitive object OFD. Each Data Dictionary Element (DDE) definition identifies any constituent components of the DDE and defines its key characteristics and attributes.

Data Dictionary Element (DDE): the formal definition of a data store, event store, data flow, event flow, or object/object message appearing on one or more OFDs; or of a constituent part of a Composite Data Dictionary Element.

Data Process: a "process" that transforms one or more (data or event flow) inputs into one or more (data or event flow) outputs.

Data Store: that which holds information to be acted upon by one or more data processes without altering that information.

Derived Requirements: requirements that are the direct and logical consequence of a requirement from a "higher-level," customer-provided or -approved specification. Derived requirements, sometimes called "implied" requirements, differ from allocated requirements in that derived requirements are not directly stated in the higher-level specification. Although the derived requirement is not a direct allocation from the source requirement, a person who truly understands the source requirement logically concludes the implied existence of the derived requirement.

Descendent Class: a class that inherits fields, methods, and/or type compatibility from an ancestor class. Some refer to such a class as a "subclass," while it is known as a "base" class in C++.

Design Model: defines the design structure of the system; identifies the logical and physical elements of the implementation with their associated data structures and behaviors.

Destructor: a class method that, when used with the extended syntax of the dispose memory management procedure, allows for object clean-up and memory deallocation in a single step.

Directly Perceived Event: an event that is immediately known to the system without the system having to perform any processing to distinguish it from other possible events.

Discrete Data Flow: a data flow at precisely the required processing rate (i.e., each input value must be processed individually).

Driven By Event: when the "current" event is driven by another event, that event must already have occurred before the "current" event can be recognized. The absence of a prior occurrence of the "driven by" event inhibits the response to the "current" event.

Drives Event: when the "current" event drives another event, that event will not be recognized unless the "current" event has first occurred.

Early Binding: establishing the linkage to a method at compilation time, as applies to static methods. The entry address is "hard coded" in-line. The transfer of control is direct.

Element Attributes: describes the essential characteristics of a Data Dictionary Element (DDE).

Encapsulation: the mechanism of modularity by which the fields and methods of an object are structured to allow only explicitly defined access to the object's structure and behavior while hiding implementation details from the object's clients.

Erroneous Requirements Model: a Requirements Model that is incomplete or contains elements that are inconsistent or contradictory. An erroneous model must ultimately be completed or corrected to prevent the problems from propagating to the design and implementation.

Essential Objects Model: an abstract system-wide model that identifies the system's essential objects, including the behaviors and interactions that are necessary to satisfy the specifications of the Essential Requirements Model. The

Essential Objects Model is documented by (1) Object Flow Diagrams, (2) Object Templates, and (3) a Data Dictionary.

Essential Requirements Model: an abstract system-wide model that captures the top-level essence of the system. The Essential Requirements Model is documented by three separate products: (1) External Interfaces Diagram (capturing the system's essential interfaces with the outside world), (2) External Events/Response List (identifying stimuli from the outside world to which the system must respond and the system's corresponding required responses), and (3) Object Relationship Diagrams (specifying the significant objects from the problem statement and their relationships).

Event Flow: a flow that carries no explicit data with it.

Event Group: events that are bound by arbitrary user-selected criteria. This could include interdependent "drives" and "driven by" relationships, similarity of requirements, etc. Event groups are named by alphabetic characters. A single event (e.g., the start-up event) may belong to more than one group.

Event/Response Pair: an External Event and its associated required Response defined in the External Events/Response List (EERL).

Event Store: that which records occurrences of event flows in a First In/First Out (FIFO) order.

External Event: a "happening" that occurs outside the system at a definable instant in time, and to which the system must respond. System start-up and time-based events are considered External Events for requirements analysis purposes, regardless of their specific implementations.

External Events/Response List (EERL): defines the events from outside the system that require a response from the system and describes those responses. Every External Event specified in the EERL must be attributable to either an external object explicitly shown on the EID or to an implicit clock (which is often omitted from explicit representation on the EID). Dependencies among event/response pairs are explicitly defined and gathered in logical groups. Because all processing in a real-time system initiates in response to a stimulus from outside the system (assuming time is considered an external stimulus that may not be shown on the EID), the EERL becomes a structured summary of all functional requirements allocated to the system.

External Interfaces Diagram (EID): defines the boundaries of the system and identifies what must cross those boundaries. In the EID, the system is represented by a single icon. Each of the external objects is represented by an icon. "Flow" icons define information and event signals that pass between the external objects and the system.

External Object: any software or hardware system, subsystem, component, device, or shared data element that is not considered part of the subject system, but with which the subject system must interface.

Field: a data structure that retains the state or value of an object.

Free Subprogram: a procedure/function that provides a utility operation that is best not assigned as a method to a single class.

Identity: the nature of objects by which each instance exists as a unique entity with ownership of its fields and methods. The definition of an object's fields and methods are declared as a class, from which multiple unique instances may be declared.

Indirectly Perceived Event: an event that requires the system to analyze externally provided data to differentiate specific events or to determine the specific instant at which the event occurs.

Inheritance: a relationship between objects wherein one object automatically acquires fields (data structures) and methods (procedures and functions that define the object's behavior) from one or more other objects. Inheritance is illustrated by hierarchy diagrams that show ancestor/descendent relationships in the same manner as a family tree.

Late Binding: establishing the linkage to a method at runtime, as applies to virtual methods. The entry address is stored in the Virtual Method Table. The transfer of control is indirect through the VMT entry.

Mechanism: a complex object, consisting largely of other objects interacting in some well-defined manner to represent an entity in the real world.

Method: a procedure or function that is invoked to implement some aspect of the object's behavior.

Modifier Method: a method that causes a change of state or value for one or more of an object's fields or otherwise operates on an object's fields.

Object: a logical programming entity that encapsulates state or value in data fields and predefined behavior in methods. Each object is an instance of a class, but has unique identity distinct from all other objects. Fields and methods may either be defined by the object's class or be inherited from ancestor classes.

Object Flow Diagrams (OFD): a hierarchical set of diagrams that identify the key (essential) objects from the problem domain and establish their needed behaviors and interactions. Each object identified also must be explicitly declared by an Object Template. OFDs are the RTOOSA counterparts for the Structured Analysis Data Flow Diagrams. Each complex object (mechanism or subsystem) must be decomposed in a lower-level OFD. Each primitive object must be decomposed in a base-level OFD that identifies the essential fields and methods of the object. The structure of each field must be expanded as an element in the Data Dictionary, and the processing requirements of each method must be specified in an appropriate form.

Object Relationship Diagrams (ORD): identify the significant objects from the external environment and the key objects within the system and their relationships. Candidate objects are those that are identified in the descriptions of the event/response pairs in the EERL.

Object Template (OT): provides the essential structure of the key (essential) objects in terms of their needed fields and methods. Each object identified in an OFD requires explicit definition in an OT. Each field must correspond to an icon in a primitive object's OFD and be explicitly defined as a Data Dictionary Element in the Data Dictionary. Each method must be explicitly expanded in the back-up to the corresponding primitive object OFD in a manner appropriate to the required processing.

Polymorphism: the property by which objects in a hierarchy can share a single method name, wherein each object implements the method in a manner dictated by its unique requirements.

Primitive Data Dictionary Element: a Data Dictionary Element that is not defined in terms of other Data Dictionary Elements. The definition of a primitive DDE is self-contained, not requiring reference to other DDEs.

Private: fields and/or methods that are known to the methods of the declaring class, but hidden from descendent objects and external clients.

Process Activation: an event flow, labeled "activate" or "enable," that enables the continuous/repeated or discrete execution of a process.

Process Deactivation: an event flow, labeled "deactivate" or "disable," that disables the continuous or repeated execution of a process.

Protected: fields and/or methods that are known to the methods of the declaring class and all of its descendents, but hidden from all external clients.

Public: fields and/or methods that are globally visible and therefore are directly accessible by all clients. This level represents a lack of protection. The only level of encapsulation is that provided by the programmer's discipline.

Real-Time System: a system that controls an environment by receiving data, processing them, and taking action or returning results sufficiently quickly to affect the functioning of the environment at that time. [Martin, 1967]

Requirements Model: describes the essential requirements of a system; describes what the system must do, how it must perform, and how it must interact with its environment.

Self-Imposed Requirements: requirements not traceable as allocated or derived requirements from any requirement in a "higher-level," customer-provided or -approved specification. Self-imposed requirements normally result from design decisions made by other disciplines of the development team (e.g., systems engineering, hardware engineering, etc.).

State: a stable condition wherein processing remains constant until an event occurs.

State Transition: a change from one state to another in response to an event.

Subsystem: a complex abstract object, consisting largely of other objects that have a logical relationship. A subsystem may be thought of as a collection of objects that relate to a common function. Avionics subsystems traditionally include: navigation, communications, flight controls, fire control, hydraulics, and so forth.

Temporally Perceived Event: an event that depends on the passing of a period of time. Periodic processing is considered to be initiated by a temporally perceived event, as is processing that is initiated after a finite time delay.

Virtual Method: a class method whose entry is achieved indirectly through a pointer stored in the class's Virtual Method Table.

Virtual Method Table (VMT): a data structure, assigned to a class with declared or inherited virtual methods, which holds (among other things) pointers to the virtual method execution entry point. At runtime, control is passed to virtual methods through their pointers in the VMT.

Appendices

An invasion of armies can be resisted,
but not an idea whose time has come.
— Victor Hugo

Appendix **A**

Case Study:
Gunship Orbiting Autopilot

The use of side-mounted guns for shooting at targets on the ground dates back to World War I planes equipped with swivel-mounted machine guns. Following that war, 1st Lt. Fred Nelson successfully experimented with fixed-mounted, side-firing .30 calibre machine guns. Lieutenant Nelson introduced the use of the pylon turn to establish a constant target sighting reference. The pylon turn, a term popularized by air racers, puts the plane into a left bank and follows a circular orbit around a fixed reference point. By using the pylon turn, Lt. Nelson could sight through an aiming device on a wing strut to the target on the ground. Except for a reference in a 1939 Air Corps Tactical School thesis by Capt. Carl J. Crane proposing a weapon system based on Nelson's successes, the ideas laid dormant until World War II.

In early 1942, 1st Lt. Gilmour Craig MacDonald, of the 95th Coast Artillery, suggested using a side-firing pylon-turn maneuver to maintain constant fire on enemy submarines and thereby prevent them from using their antiaircraft guns for defense. A normal forward-firing aircraft could only make a pass and then spend several minutes positioning for another pass. Nothing came of Lt. MacDonald's proposal. Near the end of the war, MacDonald attempted to revive the idea, but that proposal also died.

In September 1961, MacDonald (then promoted to Air Force lieutenant colonel) submitted a new proposal, entitled the "Transverse Firing of Rockets and Guns," in response to the new limited war problems faced by the Air Force. His basic premise was that "by flying in a banked circle, the airplane can keep the gun pointed continuously at a target, and by flying with one wing low, limited longitudinal strafing can be done without worrying about pullout." Again, MacDonald's idea was dismissed.

But then in late 1961, Lt. Col. MacDonald met Ralph E. Flexman, an Assistant Chief Engineer with Bell Aerospace Company, at Eglin Air Force Base, Florida. Bell held several Government contracts related to limited war and counterinsurgency problems. Flexman considered the side-firing pylon-turn concept and proposed the idea at a Bell brainstorming session in late 1962. This led to a letter to Dr. Gordon A. Eckstrand at Wright-Patterson Air Force Base, Ohio describing ideas that he and his associates at Bell were working on. Among these ideas:

> . . . with respect to aircraft, we believe that lateral firing, while making a pylon turn, will prove effective in controlling ground fire from many AA [antiaircraft] units. In theory at least, this should more than triple the efficiency of conventional aircraft on reconnaissance and destructive missions.

The problem facing the pilots in Vietnam was that they were losing their targets between first sighting and the time of the second pass. An aircraft that could bank into a pylon turn could maintain sight of the target and immediately assume an attitude from which to provide effective fire. However, there were still unanswered questions about this tactic. What would be the dispersion pattern of the ballistics? How well can a pilot maintain sighting and fire the weapon? How well can a pilot make the transition from the initial sighting point into the pylon turn? Captain John C. Simons adopted Flexman's cause and proposed a test program to prove the concepts to Wright-Patterson offices interested in limited war and counterinsurgency development. Concerns about the ballistics of side-firing weapons led to rejection of the proposal as technically unsound.

Flexman wrote Capt. Simons in 1963 referencing work by Dr. W. H. T. Loh, Associate Chief Engineer at Bell Aerosystems, that provided ballistic equations that could be programmed into computers to control weapons for a side-firing pylon-turn aircraft. After several more rejections, Capt. Simons finally arranged a set of tests that proved the concept. First, he proved that a pilot could easily acquire and orbit a target. Then, tests were conducted using cameras mounted in a C-131B instead of guns.

The third test pilot in the program was Capt. Ronald W. Terry, who in the spring of 1963 had served on an Air Force Systems Command team in South Vietnam. Captain Terry envisioned application of the concept to the Southeast Asia theater, disregarded the ballistics skeptics, and became a strong advocate of the dragging test program. Finally, a 6,000-rounds-per-minute General Electric SUU-11A gun pod (Gatling gun) was mounted in the cargo compartment of the C-131 for the first live firings during the late summer of 1964. The results exceeded expectations.

The test results caught the attention of personnel from the 1st Combat Application Group at Eglin Air Force Base. They questioned using Air Force Special Forces aircraft already deployed to Southeast Asia, such as the C-47 or C-123. Captain Terry supervised the installation of three Gatling guns in a C-47 cargo compartment and repeated the test successes he had with the C-131. He became a salesman for the new weapons system, eventually pitching all the way to Air Force Chief of Staff Gen. Curtis E. LeMay. General LeMay was impressed and ordered a team to go to Vietnam, modify a C-47, and test the concept in combat. Captain Terry's test team arrived in December 1964, and the test aircraft were each configured with six Gatling guns. After crew orientation training, the first test mission was flown within two weeks of the team arrival, with the first night mission a week later. The system was an immediate success. In May 1965 the Air Staff selected the C-47 for the gunship role in Southeast Asia. It didn't take long before the renamed FC-47 became affectionately known as "Puff, the Magic Dragon" and "dragonship."

An evolution of improvements followed to illumination, sensors, guns, and targeting systems. By late 1966, consideration was being given to a heavier aircraft to replace the AC-47, as the attack version of the C-47 was dubbed. A heavier aircraft could carry a variety of weapons of different calibers and a larger ammunition load. It could fire longer and obtain better fire patterns. Better sensors for target identification and tracking could be added. Stronger armor plate could protect the crew. It also could fly at altitudes up to 10,000 feet, above the threat of small-arms fire from the ground.

During the spring of 1967, a C-130A was selected for modification and evaluation as the new-generation gunship. The C-130 high-wing configuration made it ideal as a gunship, putting the wing well above the line-of-fire. It was outfitted with 20-mm cannon that could be used at altitudes of 6,000 to 10,000 feet and with 7.62-mm Gatling guns. Its sensors included infrared and radar. By fall, the prototype arrived in Vietnam for evaluation. After its final test mission in early

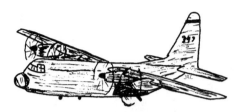

Figure A.1. The high-winged C-130 made an excellent platform for a heavier gunship that could carry a wider variety of guns at a higher altitude.

December 1967, it served operationally until November 1968, when it returned to Wright-Patterson with extensive equipment malfunctions. Upon its return, analysis showed the AC-130 prototype "to be one of the most cost effective close air support and interdiction systems in the Air Force inventory." [Ballard, 1982]

Despite the success of the AC-130 prototype, the C-119K Flying Boxcar was ultimately chosen for the production gunship. The C-130 airframes were judged too important as transports to be converted for gunship use. However, a limited number of AC-130 gunships were produced.

Following Vietnam, the AC-130 survived as the Special Forces fixed-wing gunship. It has been used in such recent actions as Grenada, Panama, and the Gulf War. There have been several upgrades to the sensor and gun systems. The most recent version includes 20-mm miniguns, 40-mm cannons, and a 105-mm Howitzer (an Army artillery piece).

For this case study, we will assume another upgrade to the AC-130 gunship is being undertaken by the Air Force. Our project is concerned only with the navigator subsystem of the upgrade.

THE GUNSHIP NAVIGATION PROBLEM

A mission planner, acting on intelligence data from various sources, creates a list of waypoints, each corresponding to a target. The waypoint list is called the mission's flight plan. When fed into the gunship's navigation computer, the aircraft flies to each waypoint in turn.

As the aircraft approaches a waypoint, the navigator must make the transition from straight flight to a pylon turn to orbit the target, as illustrated in Figure A.2. As the navigator holds the aircraft in a specified orbit (e.g., with a given radius and altitude), the gunner can train the guns on the target and control their firing. When the target has been neutralized, the pilot issues a command that terminates the orbiting maneuver and initiates travel to the next waypoint.

The navigator is constantly updated with new aircraft position data (latitude, longitude, and altitude) from an Inertial Navigation System (INS). The navigator generates commands that are output to the aircraft control surfaces. These control commands determine the direction and attitude of the aircraft's travel.

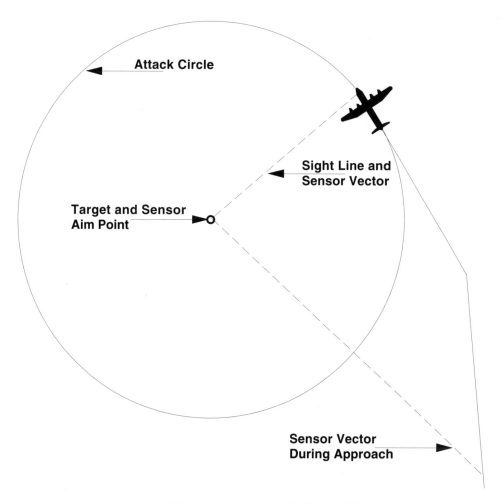

Figure A.2.   Basic gunship firing geometry (no wind). Source: *Development and Employment of Fixed-Wing Gunships 1962–1972* by Jack S. Ballard (Office of Air Force History, USAF, Washington, D.C., 1982)

This hypothetical autopilot system for a hypothetical gunship upgrade program has been kept simple to provide the student with a manageable problem. The advanced student should consider incorporating other elements of navigation provided in Appendix C to the gunship problem. Further expansion of the problem could include interaction between the navigator and the sensor operators, who can greatly refine the target location data.

There is just one thing I can promise you about the outer-space program: Your tax dollar will go farther.
— Wernher von Braun

Appendix **B**

Case Study: The Audio/Video Distribution System

This appendix provides the general specifications for a hypothetical system to distribute audio and video communications aboard the Space Station Freedom, currently under development by NASA. These specifications reflect obvious requirements for the distribution of communications aboard the Freedom and not the actual NASA requirements for the system currently under development. There are, however, certain similarities to the NASA system. The specifications in this appendix could be applied to many complex audio/video systems, such as those used by the television networks to broadcast major sporting events (Olympic coverage, professional football games, major auto races, etc.).

The Space Station Freedom will provide a habitat for extended missions in

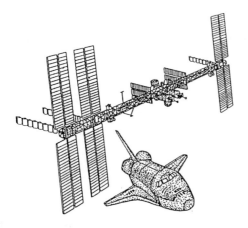

Figure B.1. AVDS is a hypothetical system of the Space Station Freedom.

earth orbit, initially to conduct scientific experiments and, perhaps eventually, for light industry. It will be constructed incrementally of modules carried to space by the NASA Space Shuttle Fleet. Each module will be configured for specific uses. Some will serve as living quarters, others as laboratories, and others to support the station operations. The individual modules will be integrated into a life-sustaining structure with all their interconnecting communications components. The crew will need to communicate among themselves throughout the Freedom and with ground controllers (and others on the ground). Some operations will require live video to support remote control.

Let's call the system that controls the distribution of the various audio and video signals the Audio/Video Distribution System (AVDS). This system must interconnect various audio and video signal input devices (such as video cameras and microphones, video tape recorders [VTRs], intercoms, etc.) to signal output devices (such as video monitors at crew workstations, VTRs, etc.). The on-board system is also connected by a radio data link to stations on the ground.

The audio/video devices that the AVDS must control include various numbers of the following:

1. Camera Assembly. Each camera assembly consists of a television camera integrated with various video lens assemblies, which may be commanded to zoom, and mounted on a Pan and Tilt Assembly (PATA), which may be commanded to point the camera in a specific direction.

2. Video Tape Recorder (VTR). The VTR can be commanded to record, rewind, play (etc.) audio and video signals. Because commercial VTRs are not designed to interface directly to fiber optic cables, a special VTR Interface (VTRI) device is provided with each VTR to connect it to the fiber optics of the signal distribution system.

3. Special Effects Processor (SEP). The SEP provides two special capabilities for the displayed video. It can capture individual frames of video for freeze frame display, and it can provide a split-screen display of two independent input signals.

4. Video Monitors. The Freedom video monitors are typical CRT-type monitors with an adaptor to accept fiber optic input data.

Each habitat module will arrive on-orbit with an installed Audio/Video Switch Module (AVSM). The AVSM is based on a 16-input by 16-output cross-bar switch (as illustrated in Figure B.2). The input and output audio/video signals are carried by high-speed fiber optic cables. The optical input signal is received at the AVSM by a Fiber Optic Receiver (FOR) and converted to an electrical signal for routing within the AVSM. Each AVSM output is converted again to an optical signal by a Fiber Optic Transmitter (FOT) and transmitted on a fiber optic cable. The switch internal to the AVSM is commanded via a separate control bus to connect an input port audio/video signal to one or more output ports. The electrical input signal can be switched individually to any or all output electrical lines. Once the corresponding switch settings have been made, the audio and video signals received at the input port are passed transparently to the connected output port(s). The AVSMs will be interconnected also to allow the relay of signals among all the habitat modules.

The AVDS responds to commands from an operator at an on-board workstation or, alternatively, from a ground terminal via the communications up-link. These commands specify an audio/video source device and one or more destination devices. For example, a camera to be used to monitor an experiment in one module may have its images broadcast to several workstation monitors throughout the station and to monitors at mission control on the ground. Simultaneously, the audio and video signals from the camera can be routed to a VTR and recorded for later playback and analysis. In some cases, the signals from two cameras may be passed through a SEP and viewed with a split-screen display at the monitor. Figure B.3 shows the interconnection of the various devices in the AVDS.

In addition to controlling the routing of the audio/video signals, the crew must be able to command the various operating modes and specify operational parameters for the video equipment. For example, the scientist responsible for an experiment will need to point the camera and control the zoom setting while viewing the image on the display monitor. Other controls include VTR play/rewind/record commands and selection of operating modes of the SEP.

Commanding the Camera Assembly presents some special problems. Because the cameras are not on the Control Bus, the control commands to the camera lens and PATA must be sent over the fiber optic audio/video channel. With no direct fiber optic interface to the Standard Data Processor (SDP) on which the AVDS must execute, one input port of the AVSM is interfaced to the Control Bus instead of to a FOR. The AVDS can thereby send Camera Assembly control commands over the Control Bus to the AVSM. That AVSM input channel can be switched to

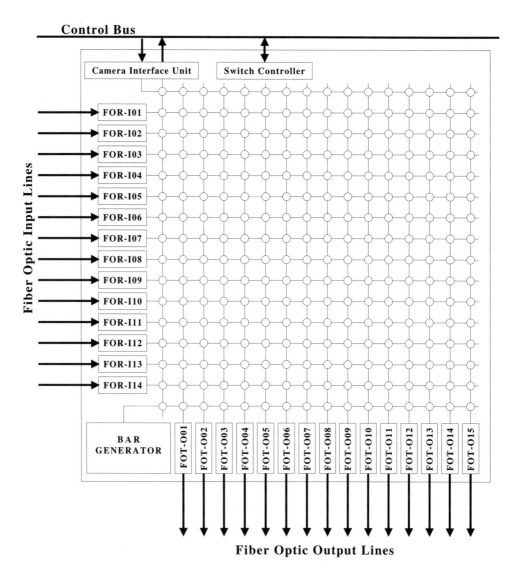

Figure B.2.   The Audio/Video Switch Module (AVSM) structure.

send its output to the Camera Assembly and thereby have the control commands transmitted to the cameras by a FOT. Similarly, status data from the cameras, in video format, must be captured by the Camera Interface Unit and transmitted back to the AVDS via the Control Bus.

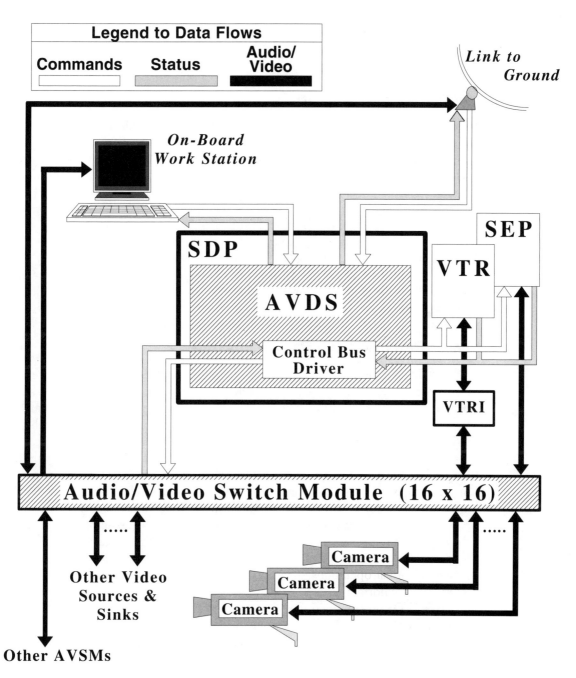

Figure B.3. The AVDS software ties to the Freedom's audio/video equipment.

The AVDS also must be able, on command, to set up a "privacy" mode for specific links. This mode could be used while monitoring classified experiments or to offer crew members private visits with friends and family on the ground.

OPERATING ENVIRONMENT

The AVDS must execute on a reprogrammable Standard Data Processor (SDP). The SDP is designed to be reprogrammed to support a variety of mission requirements. The AVDS software may be moved among any of the SDPs in the Freedom, so it cannot have any special-purpose hardware to support the communications mission. The SDP includes a distributed Object-Oriented Operating System (O^3S) to provide common access to the workstation's man/machine interface and the station-wide control bus. The AVDS must run "over" the O^3S.

Elements in the operating environment are each represented by an "object" in O^3S. Communication to and between these objects is provided invisibly by O^3S, so that an application never needs to know the physical characteristics of the end object. The O^3S is actually distributed, including O^3S elements running in the workstations.

FAULT DETECTION AND RECONFIGURATION

The AVDS must monitor all devices, including the AVSMs, to detect device failures. The software must isolate the faults to a single device, wherever possible. Without manual intervention, the AVDS must automatically reconfigure switches to maintain uninterrupted (or minimally interrupted) operational links when a switch fault is detected and alternate paths are available.

Each audio/video device must incorporate a Built-In-Test (BIT) capability. Device BIT includes two types: passive and obtrusive. Passive BIT runs continually in the background to detect many types of operational faults and failures. AVDS must poll each device once each minute for health and status data detected by its passive BIT. However, operation of most devices precludes exhaustive tests while the device is in normal use. To test a device completely, the operator must be able to command execution of more comprehensive BIT, which will be permitted to interrupt normal operations. This commanded BIT is called obtrusive because it interferes with normal system operation.

The AVDS, in conjunction with device BIT, must be able to detect 98% of all faults and isolate those faults to a single device or module for 95% of the detected faults. No more than 5% of the detected faults may be false indications (i.e., "false alarms").

REQUIREMENTS SUMMARY

The requirements for the AVDS may be summarized as follows:

1. When the operator commands connecting an audio/video source to one or more audio/video output devices, the AVDS must select a signal route through AVSM(s) to establish the needed path.

2. If the requested path is designated "private," the AVDS must disconnect any residual output devices from the path. Any devices disconnected from the private path must be connected to a test pattern generator. The AVDS must prevent any future connections from compromising the security of the private path.

3. The operator must be able to control the camera assembly's lens zoom setting and the pan-and-tilt parameters via the AVDS.

4. The operator must be able to control operation of the VTR via the AVDS.

5. The operator must be able to select the special effects available from the SEP.

6. The operator must be able to command any of the system devices to execute their comprehensive BIT.

7. The AVDS must detect and isolate faults with any system components.

8. If an AVSM fails, the AVDS must attempt to reroute any active paths through alternate routing, if available.

Case Study: A Doppler Navigator

This appendix provides the general specifications for a hypothetical *Low Cost Doppler Navigation System* (LoCoDoNS) to be installed in a hypothetical new-generation light attack helicopter, the LAH-33 *Python* (Figure C.1). The LoCoDoNS Computer Software Configuration Item (CSCI) refers to the software features that enable the *Python* to determine its current position and to provide guidance data to an Automated Flight Control System (AFCS) in order to follow a predetermined flight plan.

Doppler radar navigation has been used by the military services of the United States and other NATO countries since about 1955 and by international airlines for transoceanic navigation since about 1962, so the technology is not new. Modern Doppler radar units are lightweight (under 50 pounds), use little power (under 100 watts), and are relatively inexpensive.

Although almost everyone has some instinctive notion of what navigation is

Figure C.1.   Our hypothetical LAH-33 *Python* helicopter.

and what a navigation system should provide, these notions diverge in even the most basic definitions. To avoid specification ambiguities arising from the readers' diverse experiences and to introduce the vocabulary of this problem domain, I have included the definitions of key navigation terms used in specifying this system.

The LoCoDoNS CSCI specified in this document employs elements of *dead reckoning* navigation, integrated with *position updating by flyover*. Dead reckoning uses velocity data from either the Doppler Velocity Sensor (DVS) or the Air Data System (ADS) and heading data from the Directional Gyroscope (DG)/ Gyrocompass.

In addition, the LoCoDoNS must maintain a data base of information necessary to fly predetermined flight plans and correctly drive the pilot's instruments and displays.

BASIC NAVIGATION TERMINOLOGY

Figure C.2 graphically depicts many of the terms used throughout this appendix. Following are definitions of important terms used:

> **Dead Reckoning:** consists of extrapolating a "known" position to some future time. This requires accurate measurement of direction of motion and distance traveled.

The concept of dead reckoning is very straightforward. If you know your starting point and the direction and speed of travel, you can mathematically determine where you will be at some future time. If the intervals between new position computations are kept sufficiently short to track changes of direction accurately, then the system will be able to identify your current position accurately at any time. Limitations on dead reckoning navigation are based on the accuracy of directional measurement (equipment limitations and natural phenomena), the accuracy of speed measurement (relative to the ground at various attitudes and over a variety of terrains), the frequency at which update computations are performed (including round-off/truncation errors, etc.), and the accuracy with which the initial position is specified.

The LoCoDoNS shall provide dead reckoning navigation based on velocity data from either a Doppler Velocity Sensor (DVS) or the Air Data System (ADS) and heading data from the Directional Gyroscope (DG)/Gyrocompass.

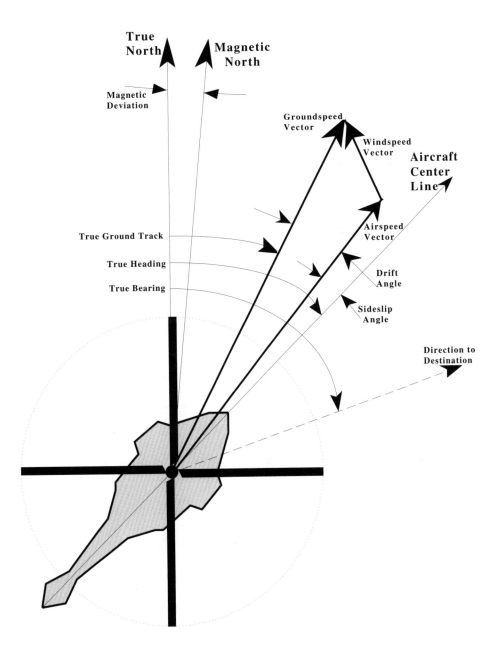

Figure C.2. Navigation terminology illustrated.

Position Updating: the determination of the position of the craft without reference to any former position.

There are several ways to accomplish position updating. The most common use individual measurements to establish "lines of position." For example, one type of radio navigator transmits signals at precisely known times that aircraft-mounted receivers precisely "time-in." Knowing the difference between when the signal was transmitted and when it was received, and the propagation time for radio waves, the on-board navigator can determine the aircraft's distance from the transmitter. That is, the aircraft is known to be somewhere on a circle at the computed distance from the transmitter. The common intersection of two or more nonparallel lines of position (such as two circles based on the time differences from two transmitters) constitutes the updated aircraft position.

Lines of position may be determined by observing the angle of celestial bodies, measuring the direction and distance to a recognized landmark at a known location, passing over an identifiable line such as a river or a highway, or by data from numerous radio navigation aids.

Pinpointing: a special case of position updating involving the observation of an identifiable landmark of known location directly under the aircraft.

The LoCoDoNS shall use flyover pinpointing to perform its *position updating* function.

The inverse of the *update* function, which corrects the aircraft position based on being at a known location, is called *location fixing*:

Location Fixing: assigning geodetic coordinates to a point on the ground, assuming the computed aircraft position is accurate.

Location fixing is important for missions such as search and rescue, identifying potential targets for future sorties, and providing navigation reference points for return route planning or future flights. The LoCoDoNS shall support *location fixing* by flyover. When the aircraft is directly over a point of interest, a signal from the crew will cause the LoCoDoNS to capture the current aircraft position and assign it a crew-provided label.

Dead reckoning and position updating complement one another. When position updates are intermittent, with relatively long periods (e.g., up to several hours) between updates (as with LoCoDoNS), the dead reckoning mechanization is considered the *primary navigation method*. It is a common characteristic of dead reckoning systems that the position error (i.e., the difference between the actual position and the estimated position) will accumulate over time. This means that the longer the aircraft goes between updates, the greater the error will be.

The LoCoDoNS must be able not only to determine the aircraft's position, but also to determine the relative error of that position from a predetermined flight path. This introduces the second key function of LoCoDoNS:

> **Guidance:** the comparison of navigation outputs to a previously planned flight path with the differences fed into an autopilot without the pilot's intervention.

Note the distinction between navigation, which is concerned with determining the aircraft's position, and guidance, which is concerned with automatically correcting errors in position relative to a desired flight path. LoCoDoNS shall provide the AFCS with two parameters needed to support a guidance element:

> **Cross Track Error:** the orthogonal (shortest) distance between the computed aircraft position and the desired flight path.

> **Track Angle Error:** the difference between the aircraft's current ground track and the ground track the aircraft would have if it were properly following the desired flight path.

Figure C.3 illustrates these guidance terms. With these two parameters, the AFCS can algorithmically determine the amount and direction of turn needed to intercept the desired flight path without causing the aircraft to make violent maneuvers.

Although numerous other terms are commonly used to describe navigation systems, these (and a few others introduced in the following descriptions of the sensors available to LoCoDoNS) will be sufficient for this case study.

THE PRIMARY NAVIGATION SENSORS

The LoCoDoNS requires several sensors to have sufficient data to satisfy its computational requirements. The following summarizes the key sensor subsystems.

Doppler Velocity Sensor (DVS)

The primary velocity measurements for LoCoDoNS will be provided by a Doppler Velocity Sensor (DVS) system. Operation of the DVS is based on a Doppler radar, defined as follows:

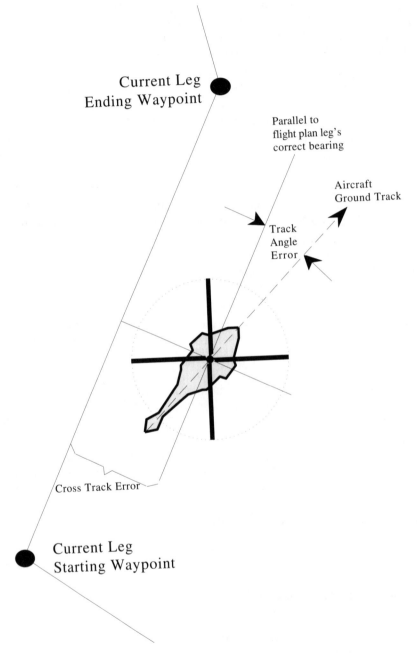

Figure C.3.   Guidance function terminology.

Doppler Radar: a radar transmitter-receiver that radiates electromagnetic energy from the aircraft downward to the earth's surface with several beams. Some of the energy is backscattered by the surface and received again by the radar receiver. The difference in the frequencies between the transmitted beam and the received reflected energy, known as the Doppler shift, correlates with the velocity of the aircraft relative to the earth's surface (i.e., the aircraft's groundspeed). In a typical microwave Doppler radar, the value of the Doppler shift is on the order of 20 to 30 Hz per knot of speed.

The principle of Doppler radar is familiar to all motorists. It is the same principle by which law enforcement officers measure the speed of automobiles with their "radar guns." Then, we can define the DVS as follows:

Doppler Velocity Sensor (DVS): an aircraft mechanism incorporating a multiple-beam Doppler radar and associated electronics to provide groundspeed velocity components.

Because each Doppler radar beam measures only a single component of the aircraft's velocity, a minimum of three beams are required to measure the three needed velocity components. These may be arranged in a variety of configurations. Any beam configuration that has both forward- and rearward-looking beams is called a *Janus configuration* after the Roman god who could look both forward and backward at the same time. The beam configuration for the LoCoDoNS is called a *4 Beam Janus X* and is illustrated in Figure C.4. In this configuration, the Doppler shift obtained with the right forward beam can be subtracted from that obtained from the right rearward beam to determine the velocity component along the aircraft's heading axis. Similar computations provide the lateral and vertical velocity components.

Each beam signal is transmitted and its return received individually. It therefore requires four separate samplings, one per beam, before a full set of velocity components can be determined by the DVS. If the LoCoDoNS Doppler radar can sample 30 beams per second, then a fresh set of velocity components will be available for processing at 7.5 times per second. This becomes important when determining the processing rates for the Doppler velocities with other sensors' data.

Thus, the Doppler radar measures the aircraft velocity with respect to the aircraft's coordinate system. That is, the velocity components are along the aircraft's longitudinal axis (the *heading velocity*, with forward positive), lateral axis (the *drift velocity*, with positive out toward the right wing), and vertical axis (the *vertical velocity*, with upward positive). To be useful, these aircraft relative velocity compo-

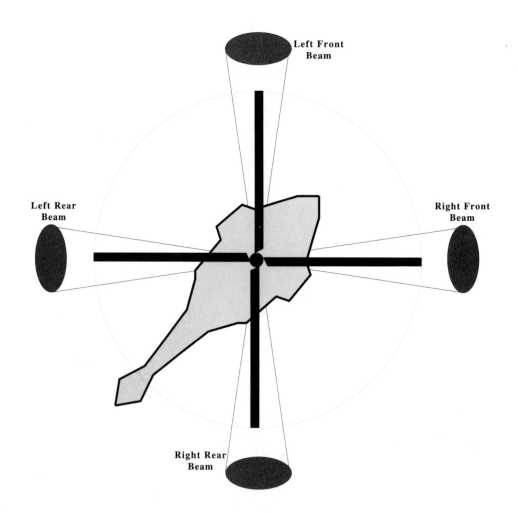

Figure C.4.   LoCoDoNS's Janus X Beam Pattern.

nents must be projected onto an earth relative coordinate system by a relatively simple coordinate transformation and then resolved into components along north/south (north positive) and east/west (east positive) axes. The coordinate transformation requires information about the aircraft attitude: *pitch* (how much the aircraft's nose is pointed above or below level flight, nose up positive) and *roll* (how much the aircraft is rotated from a "wings level" attitude, right wing down positive). The DVS selected for LoCoDoNS performs the required coordinate transformation if it is provided with the corresponding aircraft attitude data.

LoCoDoNS must therefore read aircraft pitch and roll attitudes from a Vertical Gyroscope (VG) device and relay them to the DVS. Resolving the earth relative velocity components into north and east components requires knowing the aircraft heading (the direction of the projected heading velocity component relative to north). For LoCoDoNS, the aircraft *heading* will be provided by a Directional Gyroscope (DG)/Gyrocompass.

The DVS provides the following data to LoCoDoNS:

1. Status

   a. Doppler data valid/not valid

   b. Self-test on/off

   c. Land mode/sea mode

2. Earth relative heading velocity

3. Earth relative drift velocity

4. Earth relative vertical velocity

5. Self-test Status

   a. Malfunction code

   b. Test inhibited code

LoCoDoNS must provide the DVS with the following data:

1. Mode select: land mode/sea mode

2. Self-test initiate command

3. Doppler sensor reset command

4. Attitude data

   a. Sine of the pitch angle

   b. Cosine of the pitch angle

   c. Sine of the roll angle

   d. Cosine of the roll angle

Air Data System (ADS)

The DVS can only measure velocity reliably when all radar beams are reflected. There are many aircraft attitudes wherein the bottom of the aircraft (containing the Doppler radar antennas) is not pointed toward the ground. Owing to the nature of helicopters, the number of maneuvers that result in the loss of signal reflection is considerably fewer than in fighter aircraft.

The Air Data System (ADS) is an alternate source of velocity data with which dead reckoning navigation may be performed. An ADS consists of sensors that measure the characteristics of the air surrounding the aircraft and convert them into digital data that the ADS computer uses to calculate such flight parameters as true airspeed, static air pressure, Outside Air Temperature (OAT), and Mach number (speed relative to the speed of sound).

The following definitions are important in understanding the operation of the ADS:

Static Pressure: the absolute pressure of the still air surrounding the aircraft.

Static Defect: the deviation from the static pressure at various locations on the aircraft skin due to the effects of the air moving past the aircraft.

All objects that move through the air cause deflections in the air resulting in increases and decreases in the pressure on the surface of the object. The science of aerodynamics attempts to control these changes in pressure by shaping the object to achieve a desired effect. An aircraft wing (or a helicopter main rotor) is an example where the reduced pressure above the wing and increased pressure below the wing cause the wing to have *lift*.

The static defect at a particular location on the aircraft depends on such factors as aircraft speed and attitude. To obtain a static air sample for a moving aircraft, often a series of holes are drilled into a tubular probe called the *pitot tube*, mounted to extend ahead of the aircraft and somewhat in the free flow of the air. In this position, the pitot pressure tends not to be as sensitive to mounting location as sensors mounted on the surface of the aircraft body or wing. The pitot tube probe is open at the front, closed at the rear, and aimed directly into the airflow ahead of the aircraft. From the probe, tubes carry the pitot pressure to transducers that convert the pressure to digital values for use by the ADS computer. Designing a pitot tube for a helicopter is particularly difficult because of the aircraft's ability to move sideways and backward. A fixed pitot tube, reading correctly for only forward flight, is usually used.

One of the primary outputs of the ADS is its Mach number (speed relative to the speed of sound). The Mach number is computed by the ADS as a function of the pitot pressure, the static pressure, and the specific heat ratio of air. Because the Mach number is the ratio of the aircraft's airspeed to the local speed of sound, derivation of *true* airspeed is relatively straightforward, needing additionally only the measured air temperature.

The velocity data from the ADS may be used to fill in during the brief intervals of the Doppler radar's intermittent loss of signals, such as during specific flight maneuvers. However, the ADS provides the velocity of the aircraft relative to the air mass in which it is moving and not to the ground. The difference is the velocity of the air itself, commonly called the *wind*.

To account for the effects of the wind, LoCoDoNS must estimate the current wind vector (i.e., the magnitude of its north and east components) whenever both the DVS and the ADS are working. The relationship between the groundspeed (from the DVS), the airspeed (from the ADS), and the wind vector was depicted in Figure C.2. The computation of the wind vector at any given moment is simply the vector difference between the aircraft groundspeed and its airspeed. Unfortunately, the wind is not a steady flow but varies significantly, even over a relatively short period. LoCoDoNS must therefore *filter* the computed wind components to remove the short-term variations in the estimated wind vector.

When the DVS loses its signal, the most recent estimate of the wind vector is added to the ADS-provided airspeed vector to determine an estimated groundspeed vector.

As the Doppler radar provides the DVS with velocity estimates in the aircraft-referenced coordinate system, so does the ADS provide airspeed estimates. Although the DVS, provided with data on the aircraft attitude, automatically transforms the groundspeed components into an earth-relative coordinate system, LoCoDoNS must transform the ADS airspeed components (there is little uniformity in sensor interfaces!). Then, as with the DVS groundspeed, the velocity must resolved into north and east components for navigation computations.

The ADS computer provides updated airspeed values at 30 times per second. For two reasons, LoCoDoNS will not use the airspeed at this rate. First, instantaneous readings of airspeed contain considerable variablility. Second, the airspeed vector will be used in computations with the groundspeed vector, which has a complete update at only 7.5 times per second. Therefore, LoCoDoNS actually needs airspeed data no faster than the rate of the DVS data update. A smoothing of the "noisy" effects of the airspeed may be achieved by averaging the individual samples over the interval for which data are actually needed. If navigation processing were to be done at 7.5 times per second (the fastest rate at which the DVS can contribute new data), then four successive samples of airspeed data should be averaged to arrive at the values to be used for computations. Such considerations of processing rates and the validity of the data used in computations are essential to good real-time system analysis and specification.

Another output of the ADS is a reading of the Outside Air Temperature (OAT). Because a thermometer mounted outside the aircraft would have its readings affected by the frictional heating of the airflow and compression on the sensor, the ADS provides a thermometer element in a probe similar to the pitot tube. This tube compresses the impacting airspeed to zero. This is helpful in reducing undesirable effects, but prevents the air at the element from refreshing to recognize changes in temperature. A small *leakage hole* is therefore provided at the rear of the probe to reduce the probe's lagtime when the temperature changes by allowing the air in the probe to change. From the data provided by the thermometer element, the ADS derives the OAT.

The ADS also can calibrate the free-stream static pressure (corrected for static defects) to provide the *pressure altitude*, based on a standard temperature/altitude profile of the air. All aircraft altimeters are built to allow the aircrew to set local sea level barometric pressure in flight to correct for local barometric fluctuations. The ADS can then convert the pressure altitude (in mBars) to a usable altitude in feet. Note that this altitude is referenced to sea level and does not provide any direct indication of clearance above the ground. The ground clearance altitude is provided by the Radar Altimeter, described below.

The ADS provides the following data to LoCoDoNS:

1. Status

   a. ADS good/failed

   b. Self-test on/off

2. Aircraft relative heading airspeed

3. Aircraft relative drift airspeed

4. Aircraft relative vertical airspeed

5. Self-test status

   a. ADS computer pass/fail

   b. Pitot tube sensor pass/fail

   c. Temperature element pass/fail

LoCoDoNS must provide the ADS with the following data:

1. Local sea level barometric pressure

2. Self-test initiate command

3. ADS sensor reset command

Directional Gyroscope (DG)/Gyrocompass

The Directional Gyroscope (DG)/Gyrocompass provides a constant source of magnetic heading. It is necessary to filter the high-frequency components (small "noisy" variations in readings) from the raw magnetic heading read from the DG. This filtering allows the navigation computations to sample at lower rates without loss of information. The magnetic heading from the DG is subject to two common sources of error for which compensation must be provided.

First, at most points on the earth's surface, there is a difference between the direction of True North (along the local meridian) and that of Magnetic North (the bearing to the magnetic pole, located in the Hudson Bay area of Canada). This angular difference is the local *magnetic deviation* (Figure C.2). Navigation systems normally work relative to True North and therefore must remove the local magnetic deviation. Down through the American Midwest, there is little difference between Magnetic North and True North. However, elsewhere in the world there is a significant angular difference between the direction of the Magnetic and True North Poles. To navigate relative to True North, the system must know of the *magnetic deviation* for the current position (typically computed algorithmically or derived from a table).

The second effect that introduces an error in the heading reading is the result of the magnetic field that drives the compass "bending" as it passes through the aircraft body. These deflections vary based on the aircraft heading because of the differences in the body in various directions. This type of error is called *magnetic variation*. Normally the compass must be calibrated to a specific aircraft by measuring the deflections at regular intervals around the compass. These values are fed to the computer so it can compensate for the magnetic variations in real time.

For LoCoDoNS, assume that the heading needed for navigation and guidance computations must be relative to True North. Therefore, LoCoDoNS must compute the corrections for both the local magnetic deviation and magnetic variations.

The DG provides the following data to LoCoDoNS:

1. Aircraft heading relative to Magnetic North

Vertical Gyroscope (VG)

The Vertical Gyroscope (VG) is a device that measures deviations from vertical in two planes: rotation about an axis that extends through the wings, measuring the deviation of the aircraft nose from horizontal (called the pitch attitude), and rotation about the longitudinal axis of the aircraft (called the roll attitude). For LoCoDoNS, a simple VG has been found that provides the required attitude values without needing any inputs from the LoCoDoNS computer.

The VG provides the following data to LoCoDoNS:

1. Aircraft pitch attitude

2. Aircraft roll attitude

Radar Altimeter (RAlt)

Certain aircraft computations require knowledge of the distance the aircraft is above the ground. The pressure altitude provided by the ADS would have to be compared to data from a terrain elevation data base to determine this value. However, a simple radar-based transmitter-receiver unit can provide such data directly. The *radar altimeter* (RAlt) transmitter radiates a signal directly down to the earth's surface and measures the time for the reflected signal to return. If the time for the round trip and the propagation speed of radio waves is known, the distance to the ground can be easily computed.

The RAlt provides the following data to LoCoDoNS:

1. Radar altitude (aircraft distance above the ground)

2. Data reliability signal from the RAlt transmitter/receiver

3. Self-test results

LoCoDoNS must provide the RAlt with the following data:

1. Self-test initiate command

FLIGHT GUIDANCE DATA BASE

For there to be a guidance function, there must be a data base containing the coordinates of the points along the desired "flight plan." The following terms describe the required navigation data bases.

Waypoint: a geographically referenced location that may be used as the source or destination point for a desired flight path. It takes two waypoints to describe a straight path from one to the other. Each waypoint is defined minimally by such parameters as its geodetic coordinates (latitude and longitude), a short text label, a code indicating the type of landmark (if any) at that location, and (optionally) its elevation (above sea level). Waypoints may be used for a variety of functions. For example, they could be used for navigation references, such as passage points or turn points. Or they could be used as mission reference points, such as a firing points, landing zones, forward area rearm/refuel points (FARP), and so forth.

Leg: a straight line desired flight path between two waypoints.

Flight Plan: an ordered sequence of legs, defined by the associated waypoints, that provide the overall desired flight path between two arbitrary points.

Typically, there will be two individual navigation data bases. The first, the Waypoint Data Base, is a collection of all predefined waypoints in a particular area. The second, the Flight Plan Data Base, defines the set of flight plans available to the crew. Each flight plan typically contains a set of pointers to the waypoints in the Waypoint Data Base. For a selected flight plan from the Flight Plan Data Base, the guidance function will be expected to fly to its successive waypoints, in order. For LoCoDoNS, these data bases should be considered as part of the *system* definition.

LoCoDoNS requires several interfaces with these data bases. For example, the location-fixing function can be used to add new waypoints to its data base. Additionally, the crew must be permitted to alter either data base manually (although most systems would not permit the crew to change the flight plan that is currently being followed).

When the crew activates the guidance function, it is reasonable to expect that a specific flight plan has been selected from the Flight Plan Data Base and (optionally) a specific leg of that flight plan chosen as the initial leg (if entry is to be made at other than the first listed waypoint in the plan).

The degree of authority given to the navigation guidance function varies from system to system. In some cases, the automated navigator is permitted to recognize when it approaches the termination of a leg and automatically transition to the next leg. Other systems will notify the crew that a waypoint is being approached and wait for the crew member to authorize continuing to the next leg. Assume that LoCoDoNS will automatically transition between flight plan legs.

REQUIREMENTS SUMMARY

To gather the requirements for a complex system, such as an aircraft navigator, the analyst must often collect data from several sources. Some information is interesting but does not contribute directly to the requirements for the system. The analyst must sift through the provided data, disregarding some data, and fill in other areas with good engineering judgments. This is usually a painstaking iterative process requiring frequent coordination with the system's ultimate users.

To assist in sifting through some of the data provided in this "specification," the following summarizes the requirements allocated to the LoCoDoNS:

1. Whenever the DVS is providing good velocity data, LoCoDoNS must:

   a. Use the DVS velocities to update the current estimated aircraft position.

   b. Update the estimated wind velocity vector, using airspeed data from the ADS (if available).

2. Whenever the DVS is not providing good velocity data, but the ADS is providing good airspeed data:

   a. Use the ADS airspeed data and the most recent wind vector estimate to estimate the current groundspeed.

   b. Use the estimated groundspeed vector to update the current estimated aircraft position.

3. When neither the DVS nor the ADS is providing good velocity data, inhibit the guidance function.

4. Recognize failures of the DVS and ADS in order to select the proper position update choice in 1–3 above.

5. Provide the AFCS with the computed guidance parameters and a data validity indicator.

6. Provide crew interaction for such functions as:

   a. Selecting or deselecting the guidance function.

b. Signaling pinpointing updates. A special case of pinpointing involves entering an initial navigation position, typically entered at a known point on the home base runway.

c. Executing the location fixing function.

d. Adding, modifying, or deleting waypoints in the Waypoint Data Base.

e. Adding, modifying, or deleting flight plans in the Flight Plan Data Base.

f. Selecting the desired flight plan for the guidance function from the Flight Plan Data Base.

g. Commanding modes and operations of the DVS and ADS.

h. Entering the local sea level barometric altitude for transfer to the ADS.

Appendix **D**

RTOOSA and
DOD-STD-2167A

This appendix suggests how the various products of RTOOSA can be used to fulfill the documentation requirements specified for projects developed in accordance with DOD-STD-2167A.

Development documentation is an important element of any software development project. Over the years, many companies and most Government agencies (such as NASA, FAA, etc.) have adopted variations of the Department of Defense standard as their model for software development. It should therefore be no surprise that most standards specify developmental documents that are very similar.

Three primary specification documents can use the products developed during application of RTOOSA to fulfill much of the content requirements. These are:

1. The System/Segment Specification (SSS)

2. The System/Segment Design Document (SSDD)

3. The Software Requirements Specification (SRS)

DOD-STD-2167A specifies the contents and formats of these documents in corresponding Data Item Descriptions (DIDs). Sections 1 (Introduction) and 2 (List of Applicable or Referenced Documents) are similar for all of these DIDs. Document specific contents begin in Section 3.

Figures D.1 through D.3 summarize the format and contents for the SSS, SSDD, and SRS, respectively. In each of these outlines, the places where products from RTOOSA apply have been identified. Refer to the respective DIDs for more details on document format/content requirements.

It is important to recognize that the contents of the various DIDs are open to interpretation and the customer on each job is the final authority regarding interpretation for that job. I have been involved in projects where we submitted documents to our customer, who found them satisfactory. Later, when the same basic documents were submitted to another customer for a system that was largely reused from the first, the second customer found those same documents unsatisfactory.

Several years ago I gave a briefing to an Air Force colonel on "lessons learned" from recent real-time software systems developments. When I finished, the colonel asked me what the Government could do to help reduce the cost to software development contractors. I told the colonel that when I was a young lieutenant in the Air Force twenty-five years earlier, I was given copies of the military standard and put into a position to evaluate contractor documents without any training as to how to interpret the standards. The colonel confirmed my suspicions that nothing had changed. I suggested that the Government establish training for all officers responsible for reviewing contractor documentation to provide a more uniform interpretation of the documentation requirements. Then, when all Government evaluators agreed what was required, please let the contractors know. Document recycling can be a significant cost driver for a software development program.

So, regardless of what I provide in this book, you may find customers who find the proposed content unacceptable. However, in many cases, customers are willing to discuss differences of opinion and work with the developer to try to keep costs down. The suggested inclusion of RTOOSA products into these documents, as shown in Figures D.1 through D.3, is a reasonable interpretation from which to begin customer negotiations.

3 SYSTEM REQUIREMENTS.

3.1 Definition.
[Brief description of the system, with a system diagram.]

> Insert the top-level system OFD, in which each of the
> objects represents a "segment."

3.2 Characteristics.

3.2.1 Performance Characteristics.
[Specifies system's capabilities in the context of the states in which
the system can exist and the modes of operation within each state.]

> Insert a top-level State Transition Diagram (STD) that
> identifies each of the system states.

3.2.1.X (State Name of 1st State).
[Identify and describe state in which the system can exist.]

> Insert a 2nd-level State Transition Diagram (STD) that
> identifies each of the modes in this state, if applicable.

3.2.1.X.Y (Mode Name and PUI).
[Describe a mode of operation within the system state identified
above.]

3.2.1.X.Y.Z (Capability Name and PUI).
[Describe purpose of capability; identify parameters associated with
capability, expressed in measurable terms.]

Figure D.1. System/Segment Specification (DI-CMAN-80008A).   *(continued)*

3.2.2 System Capability Relationships.
[Summarize relationships between system capabilities and states/modes of the system. Perhaps a matrix.]

3.2.3 External Interface Requirements.
[Describes requirements for interfaces with other systems. Details may be referenced in ICD(s).]

> Insert the system EID, which shows each of the interfaces to the "external objects".

3.2.3.X (System Name) External Interface Description.
[Identify an external interface to which the system interfaces; identify purpose of interface and describe the relationship between the interface and the states/modes of the system.]

3.2.4 Physical Characteristics.
3.2.4.1 Protective Coatings.
3.2.5 System Quality Factors.
3.2.5.1 Reliability.
3.2.5.2 Maintainability.
3.2.5.3 Availability.
3.2.5.4 Additional Quality Factors.
3.2.6 Environmental Conditions.
3.2.7 Transportability.
3.2.8 Flexibility and Expansion.
3.2.9 Portability.
3.3 Design and Construction.
3.3.1 Materials.
3.3.1.1 Toxic Products and Formulations.
3.3.2 Electromagnetic Radiation.
3.3.3 Nameplates and Product Marking.
3.3.4 Workmanship.

3.3.5 Interchangeability.
3.3.6 Safety.
3.3.7 Human Engineering.
3.3.8 Nuclear Control.
3.3.9 System Security.
3.3.10 Government Furnished Property Usage.
3.3.11 Computer Resource Reserve Capacity.

3.4 Documentation.

3.5 Logistics.

3.6 Personnel and Training.
3.6.1 Personnel.
3.6.2 Training.
3.7 Characteristics of Subordinate Elements.
3.7.X (Segment Name and PUI).
[States purpose of segment, describes the segment, identifies the system capabilities of the segment.]

> Insert the OT of the segment, including the OTs for the lower level objects of the segment.

3.8 Precedence.
3.9 Qualification.
3.10 Standard Sample.
3.11 Preproduction Sample, Periodic Production Sample, Pilot, or Pilot Lot.

4 QUALITY ASSURANCE PROVISIONS.

5 PREPARATION FOR DELIVERY.

6 NOTES.

3 OPERATIONAL CONCEPTS.
3.1 Mission.
3.1.1 User Needs.
3.1.2 Primary Mission(s).
3.1.3 Secondary Mission(s).
3.2 Operational Environment.
3.3 Support Environment.
3.3.1 Support Concept.
3.3.2 Support Facilities.
3.3.3 Supply.
3.3.4 Government Agencies.

3.4 System Architecture.
[Describes the internal structure of the system. Identifies and summarizes the purpose of the segments, HWCIs, and CSCIs. Describes the relationship among the segments, HWCIs, and CSCIs. Identifies and states the purpose of each external interface to the system. Must provide a system architecture diagram.]

> Insert the EID and OFDs through the level where all HWCIs and CSCIs appear as objects. Use a matrix to map CIs to segments. Use EID as basis of external interface definition.

3.5 Operational Scenarios.

4 SYSTEM DESIGN.
[Identifies each HWCI, CSCI, & manual operation of the system. Identifies which HWCIs are prime items and critical items. Describes relationship of HWCIs, CSCIs, and manual operations within the system. Provide a spec tree diagram(s).]

4.1 HWCI Identification.

Figure D.2.   System/Segment Design Document (DI-CMAN-80534).

4.1.X (HWCI Name and PUI).
[Gives purpose of HWCI; identifies each SSS requirement (by name and PUI) allocated to the HWCI, and each capability addressed by the HWCI. Identify each system external interface addressed by the HWCI. Identify any design constraints on the HWCI.]

> Insert the OTs for the HWCI object, and OTs of lower level objects, if applicable.

4.2 CSCI Identificaiton.
4.2.X (CSCI Name and PUI).
[Gives purpose of CSCI; identifies each SSS requirement (by name and PUI) allocated to the CSCI, and each capability addressed by the CSCI. Identify each system external interface addressed by the CSCI. Identify any design constraints on the CSCI.]

> Insert the OTs for the CSCI object, and OTs of lower level objects, if applicable.

4.3 Manual Operations Identification.
4.3.X (Manual Operation Name and PUI).
[Gives purpose of manual operation; identifies each SSS capability (by name and PUI) satisfied by the manual operation. Identify any constraints on the manual operation.]

4.4 Internal Interfaces
4.4.1 (HWCI-to-HWCI Interface Name and PUI).
[Identifies all HWCI-to-HWCI interfaces; identifies each signal transmitted between HWCIs, etc.]

> Interfaces identified on OFDs and supported by DDE definitions of "flows" between HWCIs.

(continued)

4.4.2 (HWCI-to-CSCI Interface Name and PUI).
[Identifies all HWCI-to-CSCI interfaces; identifies each signal transmitted between HWCI/CSCIs.]

> Interfaces identified on OFDs and supported by DDE
> definitions of "flows" between HWCIs and CSCIs.

4.4.3 (CSCI-to-CSCI Interface Name and PUI).
[Identifies all CSCI-to-CSCI interfaces; identifies each signal transmitted between CSCIs, etc.]

> Interfaces identified on OFDs and supported by DDE
> definitions of "flows" between CSCIs.

5 PROCESSING RESOURCES.
5.X (Processing Resources Name and PUI).
[Defines characteristics of the processors on which a CSCI executes.]

6 QUALITY FACTOR COMPLIANCE.

7 REQUIREMENTS TRACEABILITY.

8 NOTES.

3 ENGINEERING REQUIREMENTS

3.1 CSCI External Interface Requirements.
[Identifies each CSCI external interfaces by name and PUI. Describes each interface and references ICD or IRS for additional information.]

> Insert the CSCI EID, which shows each of the interfaces to the "external objects".

3.1 CSCI Capability Requirements.
[Correlate system states/modes to CSCI capabilities.]

> Insert the CSCI EERL to summarize the CSCI required capabilities...use to introduce the subparagraphs that follow.

3.2 CSCI Capability Requirements.
[Correlate system states/modes to CSCI capabilities.

> Insert the CSCI EERL to summarize the CSCI required capabilities . . . use to introduce the subparagraphs that follow.

3.2.X (Capability Name and PUI).
[States purpose and performance of capability. Identifies inputs and outputs. Identifies the allocated and derived requirements that the capability satisfies/partly satisfies.]

Figure D.3. Software Requirements Specification (DI-MCCR-80025A). *(continued)*

> Base "capability" on event/response pair, or a group of
> event/response pairs. Describe the "thread"through
> OFD(s) that "implement" the corresponding event/re-
> sponse pair(s). Optionally show the elements of the
> OFD(s) that address the event/response pair(s).

3.3 CSCI Internal Interfaces.
[Identify the interfaces between the capabilities of 3.2. Interface diagrams may be used to show data/control flows.]

> Reference the OFD network, included as an appendix.

3.4 CSCI Data Element Requirements.
[Specifies data elements, including PUI, description, units of measure, limit/range, accuracy, precision/resolution, etc.]

> Reference the Data Dictionary, which is included as an
> appendix. DDE attributes should include all required
> information on the data elements.

3.5 Adaptation Requirements.
3.5.1 Installation-Dependent Data.
3.5.2 Operational Parameters.

3.6 Sizing and Timing Requirements.
[Specifies required memory and the CPU processing requirements
for the CSCI.]

> DDE provides memory requirements for data elements. Sizing can be done for "processes" associated with all objects. Timing/loading can be based on "threads of execution" from the EERL.

3.7 Safety Requirements.

3.8 Security Requirements.

3.9 Design Constraints.

3.10 Software Quality Factors.

3.11 Human Performance/Human Engineering Requirements.

3.12 Requirements Traceability.

4 QUALIFICATION REQUIREMENTS.

4.1 Qualification Methods.

4.2 Special Qualification Requirements.

5 PREPARATION FOR DELIVERY.

6 NOTES.

Inu mo arukeba boo ni ataru.
[A dog that walks around will find a stick.]
— Old Japanese Saying

Appendix **E**

Forms for Use with RTOOSA

This appendix provides blank forms to be used when developing the graphics-based products of the RTOOSA Requirements Model. You are free to make copies of these forms for use on your project. Good luck!

This Appendix E has been identified as Appendix G on the diskette.

External Interface Diagram

Page___ of___

Project _____ Engineer _____ Date _____

KEY
(name) **System**   [name] **External Object**   ——name—▶ *Event Flow*   ——name—▶ *Discrete Data Flow*   ——name—▶▶ *Continuous Data Flow*

External Events/Response List

Project _____ Engineer _____ Date _____

No.	Event	Response	Perc.	Drives	Driven by	Event Group

Object Relationship Diagram

Page___ of___

Project _____ Engineer _____ Date _____

KEY		
name	⟨name⟩	≫ ◇ •
Object	*Relationship*	*Direction of Relationship*

Object Flow Diagram

Project _____ Engineer _____ Date _____

Page___ of___

KEY

(name)obj **Object**

(name) **Data Process**

(name) **Control Process**

name **Data Store**

name **Event Store**

≫ name **Object/Object Message**

name **Event Flow**

name **Discrete Data Flow**

name **Continuous Data Flow**

MILESTONE SCHEDULE

PROJECT(S) : _____

ORG : _____

DATE : _____   PREPARED BY : _____

PROJ No. _____   APPROVED BY : _____

ID.	Activity Description	Year	Month	Proj. Mon	1	2	3	4	5	6	7	8	9	10	11	12	13	14	15	16	17	18	19	20	21	22	23	24	25

KEY   Start: ◁ SCHEDULED EVENT   ◇ ANTICIPATED SLIP   ◀ COMPLETED EVENT   ◆ ACTUAL SLIP   ⊘ CRITICAL MILESTONE   ▷ TIME SPAN SCHEDULE

Compl: ▷

Bibliography

This bibliography contains a list of books, articles, and speeches that support or otherwise address the information presented in this book.

BORLAND INTERNATIONAL, INC., DOCUMENTS

Turbo Pascal 6.0 Library Reference, Borland International, Inc., 1990.

Turbo Pascal 6.0 Programmer's Guide, Borland International, Inc., 1990.

Turbo Pascal 6.0 User's Guide, Borland International, Inc. 1990.

GENERAL

The American Heritage Dictionary, Based on the New Second College Edition, New York: Dell Publishing, 1989.

Barry W. Boehm, "Software and Its Impact: A Quantitative Assessment," *Datamation*, Vol. 19, No. 5, May 1973.

Barry W. Boehm, "A Spiral Model of Software Development," *ACM Software Engineering Notes*, August 1986.

Fred Brooks, "No Silver Bullet: Essence and Accidents of Software Engineering," *IEEE Computer*, April 1987.

"The Business Issues Associated with Software Reuse," a report of a study conducted by the National Security Industrial Association, DRAFT, September 13, 1990.

John R. Garman, "The 'Bug' Heard 'Round the World," *ACM Software Engineering Notes*, Vol. 6, No. 5, October 1981.

Hassan Gomaa, *ADARTS — An Ada Based Design Approach for Real Time Systems*, SPC-TR-88-021, Version 1.0, August 1988.

Thom Hogan, *The PC Programmer's PC Sourcebook*, Redmond, WA: Microsoft Press, 1988.

Intel Microsystem 80 iAPX86 and iAPX88 Product Description, 1980.

Randall W. Jensen and Charles C. Tonies, *Software Engineering*, Englewood Cliffs, NJ: Prentice-Hall, 1979.

Ed Joyce, "Software Bugs: A Matter of Life and Liability," *Datamation*, May 15, 1987.

Steven Levy, *Hackers — Heroes of the Computer Revolution*, New York: Dell Publishing, 1985.

James Martin, *Design of Real-Time Computer Systems*, Englewood Cliffs, NJ: Prentice-Hall, 1967.

George A. Miller, "The Magical Number Seven, Plus or Minus Two: Some Limits on Our Capacity for Processing Information," *Psychological Review*, March 1956.

Congressman John Murtha, from the keynote address at the Tri-Ada '89 conference in Pittsburgh, PA, October 23–26, 1989.

General Bernard P. Randolph, "Software, Ada, and the Air Force," a speech at the Tri-Ada '89 conference in Pittsburgh, PA, October 23–26, 1989.

GOVERNMENT DOCUMENTS

AFSCP 800-14, *Air Force Systems Command Software Quality Indicators*, U. S. Air Force Systems Command, January 20, 1987.

DOD-STD-2167, *Military Standard — Defense System Software Development*, U. S. Department of Defense, June 4, 1985.

DOD-STD-2167A, *Military Standard — Defense System Software Development*,

U. S. Department of Defense, February 29, 1988.

Defense Management Journal, October 1975.

MIL-STD-1521B, *Military Standard — Technical Reviews and Audits for Systems, Equipments, and Computer Software*, U. S. Department of Defense, June 4, 1985.

INFORMATION MODELING

Peter Chen, "The Entity-Relationship Model — Toward a Unified View of Data," *ACM Transactions on Database Systems*, March 1976.

Peter Chen, "Principles of Database Design," *Database Design Based on Entity and Relationship* (edited by S. Bing Yao; in Chapter 5), Englewood Cliffs, NJ: Prentice-Hall, 1985.

Matt Flavin, *Fundamental Concepts of Information Modeling*, New York: Yordon Press, 1981.

OBJECT-ORIENTED SOFTWARE DEVELOPMENT

Grady Booch, *Object Oriented Design with Applications*, Redwood City, CA: Benjamin/Cummings, 1991.

Grady Booch, from his keynote address at the Harris Corporation OBJECTive.92 seminar, June 8, 1992.

Peter Coad and Edward Yourdon, *Object-Oriented Analysis*, Englewood Cliffs, NJ: Yourdon Press, 1991.

Patrick H. Loy, "A Comparison of Object-Oriented and Structured Development Methods," *ACM SigSoft Software Engineering Notes*, January 1990.

James Rumbaugh, Michael Blaha, William Premerlani, Frederick Eddy, and William Lorensen, *Object-Oriented Modeling and Design*, Englewood Cliffs, NJ: Prentice-Hall, 1991.

Sally Shlaer and Stephen J. Mellor, *Object-Oriented Systems Analysis: Modeling the World in Data*, Englewood Cliffs, NJ; Yourdon Press, 1988.

Sally Shlaer, Stephen J. Mellor, and Wayne Hywari, "OODLE: A Language-Independent Notation for Object-Oriented Design," Project Technology, 2560 Ninth St., Suite 214, Berkeley, CA 94710, 1990.

Paul Ward, "How to Integrate Object Orientation with Structured Analysis and Design," *IEEE Software*, March 1989.

Anthony I. Wasserman, Peter A. Pircher, and Robert J. Muller, "The Object-Oriented Structured Design Notation for Software Design Representation," *IEEE Computer*, March 1990.

REAL-TIME STRUCTURED ANALYSIS

Hassan Gomma, "Software Development of Real-Time Systems," *Communications of the ACM*, July 1986.

Derek Hatley, "The Use of Structured Methods in the Development of Large Software-Based Avionics Systems," from the *Proceedings of the AIAA/IEEE 6th Digital Avionics Systems Conference*, Baltimore, MD, December 1984.

Derek Hatley and Imtiaz Pirbhai, *Strategies for Real Time Specification*, New York: Dorset House, 1988.

Paul Ward and Stephen Mellor, *Structured Development for Real-Time Systems* (3 volumes), Englewood Cliffs, NJ: Yourdon Press, 1985.

Paul Ward, "The Transformation Schema: An Extension of the Data Flow Diagram to Represent Control and Timing," *IEEE Transactions on Software Engineering*, February 1986.

RELATING TO CASE STUDIES

Jack S. Ballard, *The United States Air Force in Southeast Asia — Development and Employment of Fixed-Wing Gunships, 1962–1972*, Washington, D.C.: U. S. Government Printing Office, 1982.

Larry Davis, *Gunships, A Pictorial History of Spooky*, Carrollton, TX: Squadron/Signal Publications, 1982

Miron Kayton and Walter R. Fried, *Avionics Navigation Systems*, New York: John Wiley & Sons, 1969.

STRUCTURED ANALYSIS

Tom DeMarco, *Structured Analysis and System Specification*, New York: Yourdon Press, 1978.

Chris Gane and Trish Sarson, *Structured Systems Analysis: Tools and Techniques*, Englewood Cliffs, NJ: Prentice-Hall, 1979.

M. Jones, "Using HIPO to Develop Functional Specifications," *Datamation*, Vol. 22, No. 3, March 1976.

Clement L. McGowan and John R. Kelly, *Top-Down Structured Programming Techniques*, New York: Petrocelli/Charter Publishers, 1975.

Meilir Page-Jones, *The Practical Guide to Structured Systems Design*, New York: Yourdon Press, 1980.

David Parnas, "On the Criteria for Decomposing Programs into Modules," *Communications of the ACM*, Vol. 15, No. 12, December 1972.

Gloria Harrington Swann, *Top-Down Structured Design Techniques*, New York: Petrocelli Books, 1978.

J. D. Warnier, *Logical Construction of Programs*, New York: Van Nostrand Reinhold Co., 1976.

Edward Yourdon, *How to Manage Structured Programming*, New York: Van Nostrand Reinhold Co., 1974.

Index

NO POSTAGE
NECESSARY
IF MAILED
IN THE
UNITED STATES

BUSINESS REPLY MAIL
FIRST CLASS PERMIT NO. 5475 NEW YORK, NY

POSTAGE WILL BE PAID BY ADDRESSEE

588 Broadway, Suite 604
New York, NY 10012-9741

NO POSTAGE
NECESSARY
IF MAILED
IN THE
UNITED STATES

BUSINESS REPLY MAIL
FIRST CLASS PERMIT NO. 5475 NEW YORK, NY

POSTAGE WILL BE PAID BY ADDRESSEE

OBJECT magazine

588 Broadway, Suite 604
New York, NY 10012-9741

NO POSTAGE
NECESSARY
IF MAILED
IN THE
UNITED STATES

BUSINESS REPLY MAIL
FIRST CLASS PERMIT NO. 5475 NEW YORK, NY

POSTAGE WILL BE PAID BY ADDRESSEE

THE SMALLTALK REPORT
588 Broadway, Suite 604
New York, NY 10012-9741

NO POSTAGE
NECESSARY
IF MAILED
IN THE
UNITED STATES

BUSINESS REPLY MAIL
FIRST CLASS PERMIT NO. 5475 NEW YORK, NY

POSTAGE WILL BE PAID BY ADDRESSEE

JOURNAL OF
OBJECT-ORIENTED *programming*
588 Broadway, Suite 604
New York, NY 10012-9741